TACTICS OF THE
CRESCENT MOON

TACTICS OF THE CRESCENT MOON

MILITANT MUSLIM COMBAT METHODS
ILLUSTRATED

H. JOHN POOLE
FOREWORD BY
MAJ.GEN. RAY L. SMITH USMC (RET.)

POSTERITY
PRESS

Published by Posterity Press
P.O. Box 5360, Emerald Isle, NC 28594
(www.posteritypress.org)

Cataloging-in-Publication Data
Poole, H. John, 1943-
Tactics of the Crescent Moon.
    Includes bibliography and index.
    1. Infantry drill and tactics.
    2. Military art and science.
    3. Military history.
I. Title.   ISBN 0-9638695-7-4   2004   355'.42
Library of Congress Control Number: 2004095824

Cover art © 2004 by Michael Leahy
Edited by Dr. Mary Beth Poole
Proofread by William E. Harris

Second printing, United States of America, February 2005

To the 241 U.S. Marines who died in the Beirut bombing.
May their sacrifice for regional peace be finally rewarded.

Contents

Illustrations

Foreword

Once again, John Poole proves himself to be on the leading edge of military writers and researchers with this book. As this book goes to press, the Department of Defense is beginning the process of seminars and study groups to look at Irregular Warfare and try to determine how the U.S. military needs to change its education and training processes to combat the "Tactics of the Crescent Moon". This effort is underway even as U. S. soldiers and Marines are engaged in deadly conflict with Muslim irregulars in both Iraq and Afghanistan.

Recent experience in Iraq reinforces the truism that the nature of war is changing. Fanatics and fundamentalists in the Middle East, using the flexible training techniques described in this book, have adapted and adopted a method of war that seeks to offset America's technical superiority with a tactics that use guile, subterfuge and terror mixed with patience and a willingness to die. This approach allows the weaker to take on the stronger and has proven effective against western-style armies.

It is critical that we recognize what has happened in the Middle East in the last 50 years. Since the Israeli war of independence, Islamic armies are 0 and 7 when fighting western style and 5 and 0 (or 5-0-1, if the current conflict is included) when fighting unconventionally against the more modern and powerful military forces of Israel, the Soviet Union, and now, the United States. The efforts underway within the Department of Defense are focused on the strategic level: how to better educate and prepare military leaders to deal with irregular warfare, how to adapt our intelligence agencies to deal with the low-tech and no-tech human element, etc. They appear to be looking for some future solution, perhaps even new methods and technology to deal with this "new" threat.

Poole's book makes the point that this threat is not new at all. More importantly, it addresses methods, tactics and techniques to deal with these irregulars in a far better way than we have in the past and to deal with them now, not in some undefined future 'transformation' of the U. S. military. He also makes the point—a point that seems obvious to me, even though it doesn't appear to be obvious to our current Defense leadership—that these irregulars are light-infantry forces and that what we most need to deal with them are highly trained light-infantry forces of our own.

As a great admirer of, and proponent for, light-infantry forces, I couldn't agree with him more—we absolutely need more, and better, light-infantry forces in the U. S. establishment. Precision weapons, even as precise as they have become, are not precise enough. Often the bursting radius is greater than the allowable clear area, so even when they hit the exact target that we want, they still do an unacceptable amount of collateral damage. I fear that the precision strikes that we see in the contested cities of Iraq create as many terrorists as they kill. We need good light-infantrymen to go into those cities and kill the terrorists without creating new ones with their 'collateral damage'.

Much like his previous efforts, there are things in this book that will make some American warriors mad. I dislike the idea of flattering terrorists by referring to them as good light-infantrymen, but Poole's main point—that these irregulars have flexible and adaptable training techniques and tactical methods—cannot be denied. This book should be on the shelf of every infantryman, from fire team leader through division commander. It would also be a good primer for those in Washington who send those young warriors into the fight.

MAJ.GEN. RAY L. SMITH USMC (RET.)

Preface

Again at war in the Middle East are Judeo-Christian and Islamic factions. More is at stake this time. The conflict could easily spread. Most dangerous is the belief that a worldwide clash of cultures is inevitable. Without extensive travel, one could easily come to that conclusion. *Jihad* is an integral part of Islam, and America has been trying to free the world. But to a Muslim, *jihad* has many definitions. Literally, it means "struggle." It can have a violent or nonviolent, and external or internal, connotation. To many Muslims, *jihad* simply means striving to live a better life.[1]

> It is said that when Mohammed returned from battle he told his followers, "We return from the lesser jihad to the greater jihad." The greater jihad is the more difficult and more important struggle against one's ego, selfishness, greed, and evil.[2]
> — John Esposito, well-respected U.S. Islamic scholar

A number of factors have contributed to this new conflict. To blame any one of the core religions is overly simplistic. While the Koran does take the most aggressive approach to conversion, its more militaristic passages are generally considered to be historically symbolic. If they were strictly followed by all Muslims, the world would have been continually at war since the Crusades. In Christianity, those who literally interpret the Old Testament are called "fundamentalists." Largely to blame for the recent turmoil within Muslim society are its radical fundamentalists. While good at rabble rousing, they constitute only a tiny fraction of the whole. Their viewpoints are not shared by its mainstream moral authorities.[3]

> Islam provides clear rules and ethical norms that forbid the killing of noncombatants, as well as women, children, and

the elderly, and also forbids the pursuit of the enemy in defeat, the execution of those who surrender, the infliction of harm on prisoners of war, and the destruction of property that is not being used in the hostilities (*Al-Hayat,* 5 November 2001).[3]
— Islamic Research Council, al-Azhar University

Christianity, Judaism, and Islam spring from the same Abrahamic roots.[5] All three reject terrorism.[6] This is a war in which both sides have—at one time or another—violated their own ethics. Neither side has so tempered its use of force as to justify calling the other evil. Whether they can reconcile will depend on how hard they try.

The United States has its fair share of churchgoing ultraconservatives as well. Some go so far as to openly boast about being "violently anticultural." They have apparently forgotten that America was founded by foreigners and revitalized by immigrants. On 11 September 2001, this country experienced evil beyond imagination. Yet, the Christian American who favors retaliation has ignored his/her Blessed Savior's central precept.

Vengeance is mine, I will repay, sayeth the Lord.[7]
— *New Testament,* Romans 12: 19-20

So that U.S. units might accomplish their missions with less force, this book reveals (but does not condone) opposition tactics. In attempting to revisit history objectively, the book may also touch upon a few things that Western Christians might prefer to forget. On the northern plains of Israel lies a place called Magiddo. Unimpressive by today's military standards, its ancient fortifications remain the prophetic site of the final struggle between good and evil. To keep the current conflict from spreading to Magiddo, Western forces must fully ascertain and then defeat the tactics of the crescent moon.

H. JOHN POOLE

Acknowledgments

This book would not have been possible without the learning ethos and media feedback of a free society. To that society and its divine mentor belongs most of the credit. That God still loves America should be abundantly clear to everyone in the world. His continued protection of the United States may have more to do with its varied ethnicity than foreign policy. At great expense (and now mortal risk), it has continued to provide refuge to the world's downtrodden. It gives them something they can't find at home—hope.

To all deployed U.S. service personnel also goes a vote of thanks. They have worked hard, shown great courage, and made considerable sacrifice overseas. For several years, they have had to endure an unrealistic operational tempo. America's success at promoting world peace will now depend on whether its technology-reliant infantrymen can tactically defeat their Eastern counterparts. In a world where unconventional warfare has become the state of the art, firepower no longer ensures victory. By alienating the local population, it provides a growing base of support to the guerrilla, terrorist, or "4th-generation" warrior. More productive in modern battle is the surprise that can only be generated through small-unit maneuver.

Finally, one must not forget those few individuals who have never stopped trying to get the U.S. infantry to improve its short-range, small-unit technique. Of late, their efforts have been particularly thankless. To evolve tactically in 1917, the German Army needed the specter of defeat. The U.S. Army and Marine Corps have another option. Within their active-duty, reserve, and retired ranks, they have the wisdom of every culture. Their traditional, "top-down" way of training and operating is of French and British origin. With the help of a few Asian or German Americans, they could easily shift over to the more productive "bottom-up" approach. Then, U.S. service personnel could accomplish more with less firepower. They might even come to see their foes as precious in the eyes of God. In turn, the world's half billion Moslems might start to see America as their friend. Violence begets violence. To restore order to Iraq and Afghanistan, U.S. soldiers and Marines must project less force. *Semper fidelis.*

Introduction

A Daunting Challenge

Several years ago during an evening stroll in Varanasi, India, the author and his wife were startled to see a bright star next to a crescent moon. Trouble had been brewing between the Hindus and Muslims, and the holiday firecrackers had everyone on edge. Just to India's west lies a region that is among the world's most volatile and convoluted. One does not solve any problem there without fully appreciating its history. If that problem happens to be military, the solution must necessarily incorporate cultural, religious, and political nuances.

Many Moslem nations have a star and crescent on their flags. They also have a growing number of young men who consider it their religious duty to expel foreign invaders from any Islamic country. While traditionally underestimated by the West, these "holy warriors" have recently scored major victories against "high-tech" armies. The *al-Quedu*-supported *mujahideen* drove a well-supported Soviet army out of Afghanistan in 1988. *Hezbollah*-led Shiites and Palestinians forced an end to the Israeli occupation of Southern Lebanon in 2000.[1]

Now that U.S. forces are facing these same two movements in Afghanistan and Iraq,[2] it's time for American commanders to entertain some potentially embarrassing questions. How could Muslim guerrillas with hand-held weaponry have defeated Soviet and Israeli regulars with "state-of-the-art" aircraft, artillery, and tanks? Did those guerrillas enjoy a tactical advantage at short range? If so, will American troops fare any better against them in close terrain? To find out, one must travel back into history—being careful not to blame Islam or any of its mainstream sects for the actions of a few members. In every religion, there will be those who misinterpret the will of God.

Islam's Earliest Days

In Arabia at the outset of the 7th Century, Islam was founded from Abrahamic roots by Mohammed.[3] "After his death in 632 A.D., Muslim armies quickly conquered (everything) . . . from Spain to the Indus Valley."[4] (See Map I.1.) Abu Bakr was installed as the Prophet's immediate successor, but Ali (Mohammed's son-in-law and cousin) thought himself the personal choice (imam). Ali eventually became the fourth caliph (successor) and was subsequently assassinated at Kufa. The formal schism between Shiite and Sunni came when Hasan—Ali's son and fifth caliph—was forced to abdicate.[5] When another of Ali's sons (Husain) was killed leading 72 men against 4000 at Karbala, the breakaway sect gained momentum.[6] From that point forward, Shiites thought that Mohammed had designated Ali, whereas Sunnis believed that the Prophet had authorized the selection of any peer.[7]

By the time the Muslim empire broke up, it had generated many converts. Today, their half billion descendents are roughly 90% Sunni and 10% Shiite.[8] Sunnis constitute the majority in Turkey, Jordan, Saudi Arabia, Pakistan, and Afghanistan.[9] Shiites enjoy the numerical edge in Bahrain, Iran, Iraq, and North Yemen. They also have large populations in Pakistan and India.[10] Most Shiites are Imamis (the state religion of Iran). Many of the rest are Ismailis.[11] Deep within Ismaili history lies the martyrdom tradition that has so confounded Western armies.

A Fledgling Sect Resorts to a Strange Method

Since the 11th Century, the Ismaili movement has had two main branches: the Mustalians and the Nizaris. To challenge the Seljuk Turks (who were Sunni),[12] Hasan bin Sabbah founded a "Nizari" state in Persia around 1090 A.D. Having just come from Egypt and Syria, he "managed through careful theological argument . . . to create a powerful sectarian sense of community based on the traditional secrecy and conspiratorial [revolutionary] nature of Ismailism."[13] Initially, Hasan bin Sabbah was only worried about security.

An armed unit of the fidai [faithful] warriors . . . adopted an upheaval method of guerilla [sic] warfare for defensive pur-

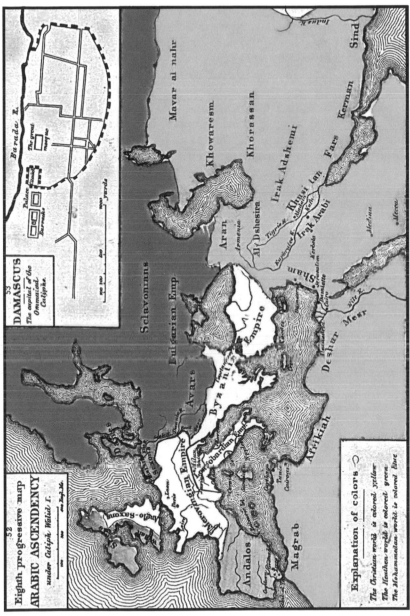

Map I.1: The Ancient Moslem Empire

(Source: Courtesy of General Libraries, University of Texas at Austin, from their website for map designator "arabic_ascendency 1884.jpg")

pose. Some scholars regard the Ismaili struggle a revolt, but it was positively a struggle for survival. It was a technique of the limited warriors to force the gigantic and colossal military machine to turn back by spreading awful milieu in their camps.[14]
— Ismaili Heritage Society website

Then to consolidate and expand this Nizari state, Hasan bin Sabbah resorted to more than just spies and missionaries. Later dubbed the "Old Man of the Mountain" by Marco Polo, he substituted political assassination for open warfare.[15] He created a school for assassins in the Alborz mountains just north of Tehran.[16] There, in a verdant valley below the fortress of Alamut, he may have given his teenage trainees a distorted glimpse of the afterlife and thus encouraged their martyrdom.[17] According to legend, they were lightly drugged and then carried to a garden simulating the Koran's description of paradise. After experiencing various sensual delights, they were redrugged and removed. When they awoke, they were told they had dreamed of heaven and could only go there by doing the Prophet's will (as interpreted by Hasan).[18] They subsequently lost their fear of death.

The chief [Hasan] thereupon addressing them, said: "We have the assurances of our prophet that he who defends his lord shall inherit Paradise, and if you show yourselves devoted to the obedience of my orders, that happy lot awaits you." . . .
. . . The consequence of this system was, that when any of the neighboring princes, or others, gave umbrage to this chief, they were put to death by these, his disciplined assassins; none of whom felt terror at the risk of losing their own lives, which they held in little estimation, provided they could execute their master's will.[19]
— Marco Polo

Hasan's graduates called themselves the *fidais* or "ones ready to sacrifice their lives for a cause."[20] The term can variously be translated as "devoted ones" and has several variants: *fedavi, fedawis, fida'is, fedais,* and *fedayeens.*[21] Hasan's operatives specialized in terrorizing local populations, bypassing sentries, and assassinating opposition leaders.[22] With a dagger as their weapon of choice, they could not have accomplished such feats without being fully sober. The *fidais* ("faithful") were subjected to an almost monastic discipline. Their food was plain, and their regimen austere. Hasan had banished all drinking from the castle.[23] To better focus on the here-and-now, the *fidais* were systematically trained to ignore preconceived notions and societal parameters.[24] As such, they behaved quite strangely and soon gained the unflattering nickname of *Hashishins* or "ones who use hashish."[25] While Marco Polo's garden trip may have been pure fantasy, the lone *Hashishin* was probably under some sort of mind control during his dangerous foray. To allay fear and pain, he may have used self-hypnotism—an East Asian *ninjutsu* technique.[26] (For how mind control is achieved through *ninpo*, see *The Tiger's Way*.) The *fidais* also shared the *ninja's* love for disguise. He was highly trained in foreign languages/beliefs and given a long time to stalk his prey.[27] As such, he probably lacked the short-range infiltration skill of a *ninja*.

The *Hashisins* Expand into the Levant

Soon the Nizari Ismaili state—dotted with mountain fortresses—extended from Eastern Persia (Iran) into Western Syria. Hasan had spent three years in Syria in 1081 and had no trouble bringing old acquaintances into the fold.[28] At this time, the Seljuk Turks also controlled the Holy Land.[29] In 1096, European Christians launched the first Crusade to take it back.[30] Upon capturing Jerusalem in 1099, the Crusaders slaughtered everyone inside (to include an estimated 40,000 Muslims, hundreds of Jews, and dozens of Eastern Orthodox Christians).[31] When Saladin recaptured it in 1187, he not only spared its non-Moslem inhabitants, but also forbade the desecration of the Christian holy sites.[32] All the while, Hasan's *Hashishins*—who would hire out to the highest bidder—had been fighting both Crusaders and Turks. *Fidais* killed the Christian king of Jerusalem around 1150 and made two attempts on Saladin's life.[33]

The most celebrated *Hashishin* chief in Syria was Sinan bin Salman bin Muhammad. He took over a cliff-hanging castle at Kahf in 1162 and was called the "Old Man of the Mountain" by the Crusaders. Sinan operated almost independently of Alamut. So strong and celebrated did he become that maps of the Middle East during the Crusades included a large, roughly triangular area in the moun-

(Source: *Corel Gallery Clipart*—Man, Totem, #28V005; Plant, Corel, #35A002))

tains behind the Syrian coast marked "Country of the Assassins."[34] While subsequent Crusades had limited success,[35] there were events in China that would greatly affect the eastern part of the Nizari State.

The Mongol Influence

In 1227, Genghis Khan captured Beijing and established what would become the Yuan Dynasty.[36] By the middle of the 13th Century, his Golden Horde had overrun much of the Middle East. For over 200 years, his Mongol Empire encompassed what would become eastern Turkey, northeastern Syria, eastern Iraq, Iran, Afghanistan, northeastern Pakistan, Kashmir India, and the southern Soviet Union.[37] During that extended period, the indigenous peoples of those regions got a good look at the Chinese way of war, and thus the teachings of Sun Tzu indirectly. To complete the lesson, most of their occupiers converted to Islam and stayed on to become part of the indigenous population.[38]

When the *Hashishins* lost their headquarters at Alamut to Hulagu's Mongols around 1265,[39] they scattered. Many moved to the Levant (Palestine, Lebanon, and western Syria).[40] Others went to Afghanistan.[41] They could do so because the Samanid dynasty state had stretched all the way to India until 1005.[42] There had been a sizable Ismaili presence in Sind (Pakistani Punjab) since 958. Sometime during the 13th Century, that presence embraced the Nizari ideology.[43] Its beliefs also took root in western India— with the Khojas. When displaced *Hashishins* joined the Indian *thuggee* gangs, they already had night-fighting skills—to include stealth and sentry removal.[44]

Bin Sabbah's Method Survives into the 20th Century

A vestige of Hasan's state may have survived well into the 20th Century. As late as 1929, the "uncivilized" area north of Tripoli, Lebanon, was reportedly "infested with" *Hashishins*.[45] "Historian Abul Fida (d. 732/1331[A.D.]) writes that Masiyaf, a town that was the headquarters of the Syrian [Nizari] Ismailis, is situated on a mountain, called Jabal Assikkin (Jabal al-Sikkin)."[46] The ancient fortress of Kahf was 30 miles east of Baniyas and 28 miles west of Hamah.[47] One can still visit a fort of that name near a town called Masyaf. Both are 30 miles inland from the Mediterranean and 30 miles north of the Lebanese border.[48]

Of late, warriors of the same name and method have been reported in Iran and "Occupied Palestine."

From 1943 to 1955, the "Fidais of Islam," a political/religious terrorist group, carried out a number of political assassinations in Iran. . . . [Then] the term [*fidais* or one of its variants] was revived by the militant wing of the Palestinian Liberation Organization [PLO]. From the 1960's onward, it designated the terrorist activists of that organization.[49]

In fact, "all modern Islamic terrorist groups trace themselves back to [identify with] this cult of killers."[50] But that's where the similarity ends. Whereas early *fidais* only assassinated political leaders, their modern namesakes are not as selective. Early *fidais* were fully prepared to die, but they did so at the hands of their enemies and were not therefore suicidal. No longer embraced by Nizari Ismailis, the original *Hashishin* method has all but disappeared from the region. It is an unholy mutation that has spawned the "suicide bomber."

Another Way of Fighting

Since the Crusades, Westerners have noticed how differently those who live east of Constantinople fight. Their Eastern adversaries routinely avoid set-piece battles and can win while appearing to flee.[51] After a large British force had occupied Afghanistan in 1839, only one of its 4,500 members survived the retreat.[52] That Muslim fighters do well at short range was once again proven at Gallipoli in 1915.

While Western soldiers were evolving technologically, Eastern soldiers may have been compensating tactically. Tactics are what happens where opposing infantrymen meet—something that countries with standoff weaponry seldom worry about. Not lost to the Third World is how the superpowers fared in Korea, Vietnam, and Afghanistan.

"In April 1978, a leftist group of Soviet-trained officers seized control of the [Afghan] government and founded the Democratic Republic of Afghanistan, a client state of the Soviet Union."[53] The Marxist regime soon encountered armed resistance, and the Afghan religious leaders announced a holy war or *jihad* against their atheistic oppressors. In December 1979, the Soviet army invaded Afghanistan to bolster the puppet government. Soon thereafter, "Afghanistan's neighbors, Pakistan and Iran . . . began providing training and material support to the Mujahideen."[54] Not until near the end of the Russian occupation would *al-Qaeda* appear on the scene. Its role would be to recruit and train foreign fighters.[55]

Then in 1982, Israel invaded Lebanon to corral the Palestinian guerrillas who had been expelled from Jordan in 1970.[56] Iran dispatched a contingent of Revolutionary Guards or *Sepah*. Founded by anti-Shah guerrillas,[57] the *Sepah* was no stranger to counterintelligence and psychological warfare. It had, in effect, sapped the Iranian army's will to fight.[58] Because its initial job in Iran had been to recruit and train militia or *Baseej* for the war with Iraq,[59] it had little trouble recruiting/training Lebanese Shiites and Palestinians to confront the Israelis.

At the same time Lebanon received the Iranian contingent, its *Hezbollah* or "Party of God" exploded in size. It had both the *Hashishin* and *Sepah* experience from which to draw tactical inspiration.

Iran has also intervened [directly] in Lebanon. Its presence began in 1982 when it sent a contingent of Iranian Revolutionary Guards to join the fight during the Israeli invasion. The Syrians never allowed the Iranians near the front, so they settled in the Bekaa Valley, where they now [as of 1988] train Shiite radicals. Further Iranian intervention also is evidenced by the extensive support provided to Hezbollah in its effort to establish an Islamic republic in Lebanon.[60]
— *Warfare in Lebanon,* Nat. Defense Univ.

Researching the Current Military Dilemma

U.S. forces are now experiencing in Iraq what the Israelis endured in Lebanon for 18 years. They are also meeting more opposition in Afghanistan. While *Hezbollah* and *al-Qaeda* may be ultimately responsible, their mutual lack of organizational structure makes it difficult to pin down their tactical and training methods. To arrive at those methods, one must study the battlefield exploits of their subsidiary guerrilla movements: the Palestinians, Iraqis, Chechens, and Afghans. Then, any trends in technique would help to define their infantry maneuvers. Those maneuvers would almost certainly have collateral psychological and media value. They would inflict enough casualties to erode the foe's popular support, while being safe enough to bolster friendly morale. They would involve thorough planning, a quick strike with limited objectives, and a rapid pullback. To keep from playing into the guerrillas' hands, the U.S. will have to carefully measure each military response and then use a nonmilitary means to remove the root causes of the discontent.

xxvii

This book attempts to make some sense of the thousands of recent media glimpses into Muslim combat. While the U.S. government may have access to more intelligence, it seldom tries to assess that intelligence from a tactical standpoint. It is generally more interested in the foe's technological profile. Many of its analysts are not even aware that the Eastern thought process differs from their own. As most Orientals, the people of Asia Minor will only show a Western opponent what they want him to see. Thus, the news from Iraq and Afghanistan must be carefully analyzed to determine enemy method—the book's ultimate goal.

Of course, this work cannot hope to completely unravel the political complexities of the Middle East. To gain media attention and protect each other, major terrorist groups may routinely take credit for things they didn't do. Many of the "militias" are actually amalgamations of factions. Still, the ruses and maneuvers of loosely confederated factions will naturally converge upon those that work best. That those factions are constantly seeking new ways to defeat the Western Goliath creates a thread of continuity. *Tactics of the Crescent Moon* covers—in considerable detail—how those militias fight. If their techniques are converging, U.S. troops deserve to know it. For by simply knowing what to expect, America's best could double their chances of survival.

When you are ignorant of the enemy but know yourself, your chances of winning and losing are equal.[61]
— Sun Tzu

Part One

A Heritage of Unconventional Warfare

Marco Polo warned of a "daytime darkness" (or dry mist) being conjured up by the caravan-raiding *Karaunas* of upper Persia.

(Source: *The Travels of Marco Polo,* ed. Manuel Komroff [New York: Modern Library, 1953], pp. 44, 45)

Gallipoli's
Underreported Tactics

● *Why were the Allies so soundly beaten?*

● *How sophisticated were the Turkish infantry techniques?*

BRITISH "LIFE GUARDS" TROOPER, 1914

(Source: Courtesy of Orion Books, from *Army Uniforms of World War I*, © 1977 by Blandford Press Ltd., Plate 106)

They Fight Differently Over There

As America struggles to bring democracy to Iraq and Afghanistan, it must remember that this region has hosted cultures much older than its own. From 618 to 906 A.D., the Chinese T'ang Dynasty ruled everything from northern India to Turkestan.[1] Thus available throughout Asia Minor for over a millennium have been "Sun Tzu"-like military precepts. As early as the 10th Century A.D., its westernmost fighters displayed a decided preference for small, highly mobile bands. Those bands did not operate like the armies of Europe.

3

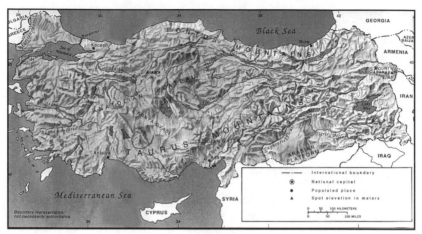

Map 1.1: Relief Map of Turkey
(Source: *DA Pam 550-80* (1995), Figure 7)

The Turks . . . [liked] ambushes and stratagems of every sort. . . . [I]n battle they advanced not in one mass, but in small scattered bands, which swept along the enemy's front and around his flanks, pouring in flights of arrows, and executing partial charges if they saw a good opportunity.[2]

In the first Crusade from 1095 to 1099 A.D., the Turks demonstrated that they could withdraw as expertly as their Mongol in-laws.

Their tactics skillfully blended surprise, mobility and firepower. . . .
The Turk was a master of feigned retreat. On occasion, he led Frankish horse [cavalry on] a chase lasting days, on other occasions, he lured them into prepared ambush. When attacking marching columns, he concentrated on separating the components, usually striking the rear. And, just as disconcerting, if things went wrong for the attackers, they did not hesitate in breaking off action and disappearing.[3]

This was no fluke. At the turn of the first millennium, even the East-Roman (Byzantine) occupants of Constantinople (Istanbul) followed a decidedly Asian military philosophy.

4

The generals of the East considered a campaign brought to a successful issue without a great battle as the cheapest and most satisfactory consummation in war. They considered it absurd to expend stores, money, and the valuable lives of veteran soldiers in achieving by force an end that could equally well be obtained by skill. . . . They had a strong predilection for stratagems, ambushes, and simulated retreats. For the officer who fought without having first secured all the advantages for his own side, they had the greatest contempt (Oman, *A History of War in the Middle Ages,* 1924, 1).[4]

In short, the fighters of this region have long preferred simulated retreats to set-piece battles. That way, they could more easily choose when and where to fight. When their adversary's formation and supply lines were sufficiently stretched, they would reappear at his rear. It is then that their zeal for close combat would become apparent. Having initially misjudged the reason for the backward motion, the Westerner was often surprised by the tightening noose. Anyone who fights in this region should be aware of its unconventional military tradition.

Expanding the Standard Image of Gallipoli

When thinking of Gallipoli, one imagines successive waves of British, Australian, and New Zealand infantrymen assaulting uphill against well-entrenched Turkish machineguns. While much of the battle did happen this way, there was another part that was less well reported. It occurred in the high brush and deep-ditches of the arid flatlands behind Suvla Bay. It is here that the legendary Sandringham company was last seen assaulting into a cloud of "etherial yellow mist."[5]

So strange an account could be easily discounted if it had not been the subject of a well-researched book and BBC/PBS documentary. Both bore the title "All the Kings Men."[6] To discover how much the WWI Turks knew about what the U.S. military now refers to as "unconventional" or "asymmetric" warfare, this is the battle to study. For that which boggled the Western mind 90 years ago, may still do so.

Geographic Orientation

The Gallipoli Peninsula juts into the Aegean Sea (an extension of the Mediterranean) from the European part of Turkey. (See Map 1.1.) Just to the east of the peninsula are the Dardanelles, a narrow body of water that runs northwesterly into the Sea of Marmara, Istanbul's Bosphorus Strait, and the Black Sea.

Suvla Bay is a third of the way up the western side of this peninsula. A few miles to its north is the Kiretch Tepe Ridge. Just to its east are a north-south string of hills that include Kavak Teppe and Tekke Tepe. Within those hills are the villages of Anafarta Sagir and Biyuk Anafarta. (See Map 1.2.) Just inboard of Suvla Bay is a one-mile-square salt lake. During the dry season, that lake may contain very little water.

The Vanishing of the Sandringham Company

Unfortunately, it was not just a British company that vanished at Suvla Bay, Turkey in 1915. It was the better part of an entire battalion—the 1/5th Norfolk. It and its sister battalion (1/4th Norfolk) were part of the 54th Division that had been landing at Suvla Bay since 5 August. The 1/5th Norfolk—along with the 1/5th Suffolk and 1/8th Hampshire ("8th Hants")—constituted the division's 163rd Infantry Brigade.[7] As the men of the 1/5th Norfolk came ashore on the afternoon of 10 August, they saw British 14-inch shells hitting the Anafarta villages in the low hills four miles inland. They soon encountered some captured Turkish trenches, decomposing bodies, and unexploded land mines. The weather was hot, and they were short of water. As a few officers reconnoitered the area, they stumbled upon a Lancashire company dug into a streambed. Its leaders warned that though the firing line was a half mile to the east, they had been "sniped at all day from a valley to their right."[8] That "valley" must have been the edge of the Salt Lake or mouth of its Azmak Deri tributary. (Look again at Map 1.2.)

Early on 11 August, the 163rd brigade (with 1/5th Norfolk on the right, 1/8th Hants in the center, and 1/5 Suffolk on the left) moved eastward.[9] Their formation was a line of platoons, each in double file.[10] Unfortunately, the terrain was a sniper's dream—full of thick scrub and tiny depressions. To make matters worse, the battalion was subjected to shell fire from their own ships.[11]

On the morning of 12 August, the 1/5th Norfolk sent a four-man reconnaissance patrol forward to see how far it could move uncontested. While there was intermittent shell fire throughout the area,

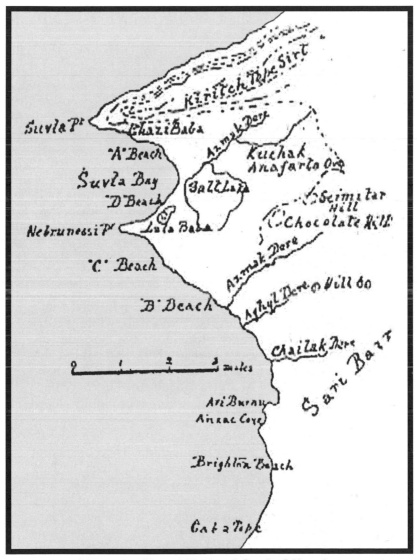

Map 1.2: Site of Ill-Fated Suvla Offensive

(Source: *The History of the Norfolk Regiment: 1685-1918*, Vol. II [Norwich, UK: Jarrold & Sons, Ltd., n.d.], © n.d.by F. Loraine Petre)

the patrol went a full 1200 yards before getting shot at with small arms.[12] At 4:00 P.M., the 163rd Infantry Brigade (with three battalions abreast) moved eastward toward Kuchak Anafarta Ova. Its mission was to clear the "valley to their front" of snipers.[13] That valley may have been the streambed that forked eastward from Azmak Deri. More probably it was the entire Kuchak Anafarta Ova basin. (Refer back to Map 1.2.)

The brigade was to join up with the 53rd Division on the right and the 10th on the left. It was then to dig in for the night in preparation for the next day's main attack (presumably against the string of hills and Anafarta villages).[14] Each battalion moved forward snake fashion in single file.[15] Suddenly, while still far from Turkish lines, the 1/5th was told in separate messages to turn half right, and then fix bayonets and advance at the double.[16] Soon shells were raining down on it from the Turkish positions atop Chocolate Hill.[17] Its lead elements found themselves among gnarled oaks with dense, widespread foliage and tiny fields surrounded by fences and deep ditches. As they pressed on through the dust of battle, they lost track of follow-on companies. Soon they were receiving heavy small-arms fire from the front, left, and rear![18] What happened next should serve as a warning to U.S. units in Southwest Asia. Here's the official version.

> Inside and immediately in front [of Suvla Bay] was a large, flat, sandy plain covered with scrub, while the dry salt lake showed dazzlingly white in the hot morning sun. Immediately beyond was Chocolate Hill, and behind this lay the village of Anafarta some four miles from the shore. As a background the Anafarta ridge ran from the village practically parallel with the sea, where it gradually sloped down to the coast.
>
> Beyond the plain a number of stunted oaks, gradually becoming more dense farther inland, formed excellent cover for the enemy's snipers, a mode of warfare at which the Turk was very adept. Officers and men were continually shot down, not only by rifle fire from advanced posts of the enemy, but by men, and even women, behind our own firing line, especially in the previous attacks. The particular kind of tree in this part, a stunted oak, lends itself to concealment, being short with dense foliage. Here the sniper would lurk, with face painted green, and so well hidden as to defy

detection. Others would crouch in the dense brushwood, where anyone passing could be shot with ease. When discovered, these snipers had in their possession enough food and water for a considerable period, as well as an ample supply of ammunition. . . .

The advance on August 12th did not commence till *[sic]* 4:45 P.M., the naval bombardment covering it having started at 4:00 P.M. The order of the three leading battalions was as given above, the 4th Norfolk following in support behind the 5th Suffolk on the left. Directly [after] the advance began, the 1/5th Norfolk received an order to change direction half right, which they did. This [same] order did not reach the 1/8th Hants, and consequently a gap was formed between the battalions, which continually increased as the advance proceeded.

As the brigade advanced, it at once encountered serious resistance, and came under heavy machinegun fire enfilading it from the left, and shrapnel on the right. The machinegun fire was the more effective in stopping the British advance, and the 5th Norfolk battalion on the right began to get forward quicker than the left. Touch had been partially lost in the close country, and companies and battalions were much mixed up.

What happened with the 5th Norfolk battalion is thus described in Sir Ian Hamilton's dispatch of December 11, 1915 describing what he calls "a very mysterious thing." "The 1/5th Norfolk were on the right of the line and found themselves for a moment less strongly opposed than the rest of the brigade. Against the yielding forces of the enemy Colonel Sir H. Beauchamp . . . eagerly pressed forward, followed by the best part of the battalion. The fighting grew hotter, and the ground became more wooded and broken. At this stage many men were wounded, or grew exhausted with thirst. These found their way back to camp during the night. But the Colonel, with sixteen officers and 250 men, still kept pushing on, driving the enemy before them. . . . Nothing more was ever seen or heard of any of them. They charged into the forest and were lost to sight or sound. Not one of them ever came back.". . .

It was not till four years later that any trace was discovered of the fate of this body. Writing on September 23,

1919 the officer commanding the Graves Registration Unit in Gallipoli says: "We have found the 5th Norfolks — there were 180 in all; 122 Norfolk and a few Hants and Suffolks with 2/4th Cheshires. We could only identify two—Privates Barnaby and Cotter. They were scattered over an area of about one square mile, at a distance of at least 800 yards behind the Turkish front line. Many of them had evidently been killed in a farm, as a local Turk, who owns the place, told us that when he came back he found the farm covered with the decomposing bodies of British soldiers which he threw into a small ravine. The whole thing quite bears out the original theory that they did not go very far on, but got mopped up one by one, all except the ones who got into the farm."

The total casualties of the 5th Norfolk battalion are stated in their War Diary to have been twenty-two officers and about 350 men.[19]

— *History of the Norfolk Regiment*

Reading between the Lines

There is some doubt as to who sent those two orders. Both were very strange. First, the 1/5th column was told to turn half right. Then, Brigadier Brusher (probably the 163rd Brigade commander) personally directed its soldiers to fix bayonets and double-time forward while still a mile and a half from Turkish lines.[20] The glint of raised bayonets made an inviting target in the afternoon sun. The increased speed hopelessly spread out the unit. The extra exertion caused its soldiers to be less vigilant.[21] Those soldiers soon came under heavy rifle and machinegun fire from the front, sides, and rear.[22] As the dust of shuffling feet and smoke of Turkish-lit brush fires grew thicker,[23] they began to notice well-concealed snipers in the trees around them. The other two battalions were nowhere to be seen. They had not turned half right and were being more strongly opposed.[24] So the 1/5th Norfolk made the mistake of exploiting its apparent success. The broken terrain caused its companies to become even more separated. Shortly before dusk, a brigade staff officer atop Kiretch Tepe Ridge spotted a British battalion advancing rapidly toward what he thought was Kavak Tepe. Then he saw a heretofore hidden concentration of Turks move out of a "gully southeast of Kidney Hill" and attack the British unit from its left flank and rear.[25] While the 1/5th Norfolks would have been heading toward Tekke Tepe, one must assume that they were the battalion spotted. When last seen, they were moving into a heavily wooded area.[26]

One thing is certain. The 1/5th Norfolk had not been abducted by aliens. It had simply fallen into a well-laid trap. That trap could have taken several forms. It may have been an "inverted U" ambush in which the opening shuts and one leg assaults.[27] At the forest edge, the battalion may have been allowed to pass through a well-camouflaged belt of Turkish positions.[28] Or it may have just entered a widely dispersed and below-ground unit formation. Whatever the scenario, the British troopers were summarily surrounded and all killed. Their bodies were later found on a small farm about two miles inland and two miles north of Chocolate Hill. (See Map 1.3.) On one thing every Westerner can agree—their opposition did not fight in a "conventional" manner. Yet, if that manner were routine, it would no longer qualify as "asymmetric."

One wonders how much of what happened was due to British bungling, and how much to Turkish genius. Since late 1917, U.S. ground forces have been organized like those of the French and British. What should be of concern to the contemporary American is that his British forefather fell victim to a style of fighting at Suvla Bay that was quite different from his own. He never realized that he had entered a kill zone, and he could do very little about the closing noose.

Telling Reports from the Reserve Battalion

Following in trace of the lead battalions that day was the 1/4th Norfolk. What its acting commander—Capt. Montgomerie—wrote in his journal reveals more about the Turkish method.

> "12th August. — . . . The advance started 4:00 P.M. My orders were to follow on the left flank, as that one was unprotected. The three battalions advanced rapidly and all seemed well until I came to the top of a hill which overlooked the valley on the other side of which were Turkish trenches. I could see that they (. . . the British) were under shrapnel fire and seemed to be in trouble. . . . An officer of

11

the 5th Suffolks [the leftmost lead battalion] came rushing back, asking for support and saying the enemy were surrounding him. He could not tell me anything definite. After he had cooled down a bit, he said that the enemy were getting round their right flank. . . . I, later, saw the brigade major, who told me they were having an awful time in front, and would probably have to retire, and that I must be prepared to help them back. All through the night men were coming in who had lost their units, and I think I had 200 men with me next morning. I gave them water, of which they were in great need.". . .

"13th. — Next morning we learnt [sic] that the first line of the brigade were holding their own in a clump of trees about 1,500 yards to our right front. I held part of the ridge overlooking the valley with three platoons; the enemy being on my left flank, from where he sniped us day and night, but luckily with very little effect. . . . The Essex brigade made an attack [from the left flank] towards the Anafarta wells, but it had no effect." . . .

All we could do was to keep down the fire of the snipers by shooting into the trees. Rumor has it that some of these snipers were tied to trees, with water and food within reach. Women snipers have been caught within our lines with their faces, arms, legs, and rides [tree perches] painted green.[29]
— *History of the Norfolk Regiment*

What Happened Here?

It would appear that Middle Easterners were using "maneuver warfare" at the individual and squad level some 65 years before Americans could do it at the regimental level. To lure an entire British battalion into a trap, the Turks had needed only bogus orders, brush fires, harassing fire, and deliberate withdrawal. While they initially employed some artillery, their ground force had performed the *coup de grace*. It consisted of female snipers, semi-independent six-man squads,[31] and a small maneuver element.[32] As the 1/5th Norfolk troopers advanced, some of the snipers moved just ahead of them as bait. Others hid in the trees or below ground and were bypassed. When they reemerged to stalk the flanks and rear of the British formation, they may have further enticed it to advance. By the time their quarry realized that it was alone and fragmented, it was too late. The battalion had unwittingly entered either a linear matrix, or circular nest, of tiny Turkish positions. From one to six people occupied each location. All were skilled at camouflage and marksmanship. Their positions may have been expertly prepared or relatively impromptu. The area was covered with scores of tiny stone farm houses.[33] Along each fenceline ran a trench-like ditch. The tiny patches of plowed ground and dry watercourses provided fields of fire. "The trees seemed alive with snipers, most of them painted green, including their rifles, and disguised with branches, twigs, and leaves tied around their bodies."[34] A six-man Turkish squad was found in a farm building.[35] Perhaps each squad was surrounded by a ring of snipers, with the resulting strongpoint forming a defensive-matrix building block. Or the snipers and squads may have randomly hidden throughout the area. Either way, these tiny elements were able to cooperate without any apparent direction or means of communication. "Working together" is not supposed to be the Middle Easterner's strongest suit. Either these elements or separate counterattack teams were able to swarm quickly in on the British from every direction. Such occurrences

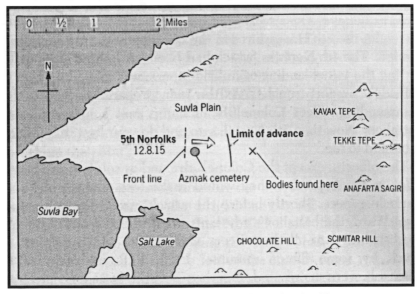

Map 1.3: Where the British Bought the Farm
(Source: *All the Kings Men* [London: Simon & Schuster UK Ltd., 1992], © 1992 by Nigel McCrery)

13

should still be of great concern to the Western tactician. For if the Turks could accomplish such a feat, so might the people of neighboring countries.

That the aforementioned treeline would later become the Turks' front line lends credence to the "strongpoint belt" theory. Here are the recollections of a member of F Company who saw the Sandringham company at the farm.

> Somehow we had moved beyond our objective and were inside enemy lines. . . .
> I saw the Sergeant of the Sandringham Company trying to rally his men around him. Many were already wounded or killed. . . . Others who were actually inside the Turkish defenses were outnumbered and overpowered.[36]
> — Pvt. Tom Williamson

However, the ambush theory is just as plausible. To destroy the British contingent, a Turkish unit may have used either the "closing U" or "cloud" battle array.[37] In the latter (ancient Chinese) formation, scores of well hidden, subordinate elements all converge toward the center on signal. The British would have found themselves instantly encircled and under attack from all sides. This would match the account of a medical officer from the Welch division fighting to the south of the lost battalion. At about 8:00 P.M. on 12 August 1915, some 18 soldiers of the 5th Norfolks came crawling into his dressing station with the most fearsome bayonet wounds he had ever seen. They said that while in a gully their unit had been jumped from all sides by no small number of Turkish soldiers.[38]

Whatever the details, the forward part of the 1/5th Norfolk was summarily wiped out. Here is the last known account of the final struggle.

> Despite the desperate casualties Colonel Beauchamp, with 250 officers and men, continued to advance through a wood towards the Turkish positions. The Colonel was last seen arm-in-arm with Capt. Ward inside a farm on the other side of the wood. His last known order was, "Now boys we've got the village. Let's hold it." This wood was then set alight [by the Turks] . . . . The remainder of the battalion was stopped from entering the wood.[39]

Still at issue is why those 250 British soldiers could not adequately defend themselves. As the Turks converged on each pocket of disoriented Brits, they may have employed another Oriental maneuver. While encircling the group, each may have randomly shot once while his intended quarry looked away. Then he may not have shot again until that quarry was again distracted. In that way, he and his comrades could have dispatched their adversaries without ever giving them the chance to return accurate fire. By taking good aim and staying behind cover, they could have avoided fratricide. As the Turkish noose tightened, some snipers climbed trees to get a better shot. Finally, what was left of the British battalion succumbed to the inevitable.

This way of annihilating a larger foe without much risk to oneself has been standard operating procedure throughout Asia for hundreds of years. It is what the companies of 1st Battalion, 9th Marines encountered near the "Marketplace" on Operation Buffalo in July 1968.[40]

The Turkish Army of 1915

By the fall of 1915, the Ottoman Army was well on its way to correcting many of the problems it had experienced in the Balkan Wars. For almost two years, a select group of German officers had been there to help.[41] Very possibly, those officers had shared their interest in Boer tactics. The Ottoman infantry platoon of the period was composed of six eight-man squads.[42] During the trench fighting, the Turks used secret approach tunnels on offense and covered communication trenches on defense.[43] Some were dug far below the surface.[44]

At Gallipoli, the Turks' "defense in depth" often consisted of several successive trenchlines.[45] To their front were frequently deployed squad-sized "static patrols."[46] Such outposts might have looked very much like the strongpoint defense with which the Germans replaced their trenches in 1917.[47] When hard pressed, the Turks saw less shame in falling back to avoid capture.[48]

After the initial, bloody counterattack at Gallipoli, the Ottoman Turks preferred to let their opposition do most of the attacking. Before mounting a cross-trench assault of their own, they would probe for weakness.[49] Those probes were conducted by lone squads.[50] The subsequent Turkish assaults were often not of the standup, "all-or-nothing" variety. In fact, the attackers sometimes carried sandbags to provide cover when the British started shooting.[51] Yet, to preserve the element of surprise, they still preferred not to discharge their own rifles. Instead, they depended on grappling hooks, demolition charges, grenades, and bayonets.[52] In preparation for such a foray, they regularly practiced skirmishing, bayonet fighting and grenade throwing.[53]

While burdened with bureaucratic process,[54] the Turks found ways around it. Platoon leaders held private discussions with battalion commanders.[55] To make a tactical decision, junior officers often relied on the consensus opinion of their noncommissioned officers (NCOs).[56] Still, most ranks showed very little initiative and preferred to do exactly what their immediate superior did.[57] Of note, the Turkish soldier could volunteer to become a regimental *"fedai."* That was a "self-sacrificing hero to conduct, or lead, a particularly dangerous but crucial mission."[58]

As other combatants from the Middle East have done since, the WWI Turks believed it their Islamic duty to seek revenge. A friend or acquaintance could assume that duty.[59] The Turks believed that the Western powers were trying to dismember the Ottoman Empire and their way of life in the process.[60] They fought in God's name.[61] They believed every dead comrade to be a martyr.[62] At Gallipoli, Allied naval bombardment may have created tens of thousands of martyrs.[63]

While German General Liman von Sanders was given command of the Turkish 5th Army to defend the peninsula, Mustafa Kemal Pasha was in charge of the Anafarta Sector facing Suvla Bay. To take back two positions lost to the British, he reportedly sent in one battalion of the "Fire Brigade Regiment."[64] Their accomplishments are not readily available.

Gallipoli Was No Fluke

Those who have come to believe that Western culture is superior in all things may consider Gallipoli an aberration—an ill-advised assault against impossible terrain. Unfortunately, the real reason for the disaster is much more complicated and controversial. It has to do with Eastern culture more easily producing light infantry.

According to the U.S. Department of the Army, a British expeditionary force marched on Baghdad that same year from a base established at Basra. That force was also soundly beaten by the Ottoman Army on terrain that perfectly suited the Western, attritionist style of war.[65]

Lessons from the Iran-Iraq War

2

- To what extent did the Iranians evolve tactically?
- Which techniques could guerrillas use?

IRANIAN INFANTRYMAN, 1978

(Source: Courtesy of Orion Books, from *World Army Uniforms since 1939*, © 1983 by Blandford Press Ltd., Part II, Plate 122; *FM-21-76* (1957), p. 89; *FM 90-3* (1977), p. 4-2)

Back When the United States Supported Saddam Hussein

In September 1980, Iraq attacked Iran to start what would become the 20th Century's longest conventional war.[1] (See Map 2.1.) Eight years and a million lives later, that war ended with neither side having much to show for it. Iran had achieved more tactically, but then Iraq had turned the tide with its chemical weapons. It's not completely clear why Iran enjoyed the tactical advantage. Its government had gone through a revolutionary change in 1979, and its armed forces had been subsequently de-Westernized.

Iranian forces did manage to expel the Iraqis and move on Basra,

19

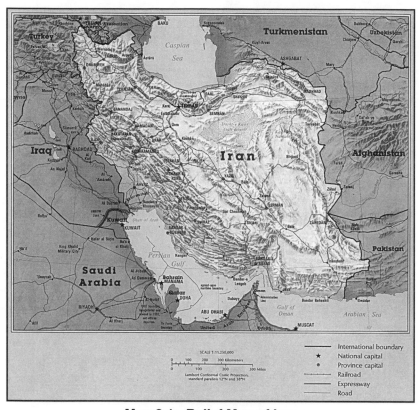

Map 2.1: Relief Map of Iran

(Source: Courtesy of General Libraries, University of Texas at Austin, from their website for map designator "Iran.jpg")

but they could not hold the bridgehead. Meanwhile, a small contingent of their "revolutionary element" succeeded in checking the Israeli invasion of Lebanon. With guerrilla roots and a dual, "quasi-political" mission, that element was about to change the power balance in the Middle East.

The Birth of a New Type of Organization

In 1979, Ayatollah Khomeini designated—as "guardians of the Revolution"—the *Pasdaran*.[2] (See Figure 2.1.) This unusual organization subsequently came to be known as the *Sepah* or Iranian Revolutionary Guard. Its role was to preserve the new Islamic State. "The *Sepah* was [at first] a diverse group of guerrillas who [had] initially fought against the Shah's regime but then joined . . . the successful insurrection of 11-12 February 1979."[3] Then its role expanded to include the following: (1) dislodging other guerrilla factions and restoring order to the cities, (2) suppressing ethnic uprisings in the countryside, (3) providing internal security to expand the Ayatollah's control, and (4) prosecuting the war with Iraq.[4] Inherently embedded in the first four missions was a fifth—the gathering of "human" intelligence.

To neutralize the anti-Khomeini underground forces, the *Sepah* needed meticulous intelligence and infiltration.[5] To keep an eye on (and counterbalance) the Iranian armed forces, it became an integral part of them.[6] The Shah's "top-down" military structure was to change into one where every member's allegiance was owed not to his commander, but to the Islamic State. This was called Islamization of the armed forces. In effect, the regular establishment was to be converted into a "people's army."[7] Far-Eastern "people's armies" depend more on light-infantry skills than firepower. So the whole focus of the Iranian military was about to change.

The *Sepah* was then tasked with training a 20-million-man-strong auxiliary or *Baseej*.[8] They were to be the frontline infantrymen. That just happened to be the exact head count of the Iranian "Party of God" or *Hezbollah*.[9] Obviously, they were one and the same—young men whose Islamic beliefs would be strengthened after enlistment and then brought into play on the battlefield. As the war with Iraq progressed, the *Sepah*-led *Baseej* would do most of the fighting. However, near its end, as many as 80% of the Guard's frontline troops may have been conscripts.[10]

The Guard's Multiple Mission Is Unique in the World

None of history's other revolutionary armies have been tasked with concurrently enforcing religious doctrine and maintaining political stability.

In rural regions . . . [Iranian] Guard bases [are] located in individual small towns. In more urbanized areas . . . a subordinate headquarters, which may even be a storefront

Figure 2.1: Ayatollah Ruhollah Khomeini
(Source: *Corel Gallery Clipart*—Man, One Mile Up, #28P006)

or large house, overseas further subdivisions of the city ("Duties, Aims, Policies of Guard," *Tehran Kayhan,* 14 February 1984, 167). The intention and result is that the Guard achieves maximum penetration of the civilian population, in contrast to the regular military, which only has internal security responsibilities in a crisis or emergency and is generally based in garrisons outside densely populated areas *(Defense and Foreign Affairs Handbook,* 1989, 514). . . .

. . . [T]he Guard's role in maintaining internal order and enforcing Islamic law distinguishes it from other revolutionary armed forces, especially those of Communist regimes. . . . In the Soviet Union and the People's Republic of China, the domestic intelligence function is not performed by the Red Army or the People's Liberation Army but by the KGB . . . and Ministry of State Security [respectively] (Richelson, *Foreign Intelligence Organizations,* 1988, 277).[11]

Many Communist countries station the bulk of their ground forces at the edge of heavily populated areas. The Revolutionary Guard didn't follow that model. It assigned a *Sepah* detachment to every Iranian town and neighborhood. From deep inside the society, it enforced Islamic law, collected intelligence, quelled antigovernment sentiment, and recruited/trained soldiers for a "people's army."

Control Was Decentralized throughout the Guard

In suppressing antigovernment sentiment, this local Revolutionary Guard contingent had full authority to take corrective action. It thus had the opportunity to experiment with various options and then pick the most effective. Unfortunately, some of that experimentation led to moral error.

> There is . . . no evidence that the Guard has ever had to await orders from the civilian leadership to disperse or arrest demonstrators, but rather the Guard appears to have assumed the authority to suppress demonstrations when they occur. . . .
> . . . The Guard . . . has never hesitated to use force against demonstrators, even when those demonstrators were clerics, apparently believing that any opposition to the regime constitutes treason against Islam.[12]

The various Guard contingents could also train their recruits as they saw fit. Many may have developed—through trial and error—some fairly sophisticated infantry techniques. Shiite Iran has a long tradition of small-unit action. As such, it encourages initiative at every echelon. In an ancient war with the Indian Army, Persian forces mounted small cannon atop camels. When ready to fire those cannon, they had the camels kneel. Soon, many of their heavily armed adversaries had fallen with their elephants. Two paintings commemorate this technique at the Sa'ad Abbad Military Museum in Tehran.[13] When asked about them, the government host for foreign visitors extolled the virtues of "ingenuity" in battle.[14] Against a mechanized adversary, decentralized control and ingenuity might make a lethal combination in mountains or cities.

23

Iranian Revolutionary Guard Tactics

At first, the Guard's tactics were much like those of the WWI Allies. Against prepared Iraqi positions, the *Sepah* sent thousands of recently recruited and hastily trained *Baseej* riflemen.

The Sepah preferred to rely upon close control infantry assault and, until 1985, human-wave tactics, whereas the armed forces favored selected strikes using the element of surprise and close air and artillery support.[15]

As the war progressed, the Guard began to use their human assets more wisely. Like the Chinese, they may have discovered that a human wave makes a good feint for a tiny penetration from a different direction.

The Guard Offense

From the very start of the war with Iraq, *Sepah* contingents showed more promise at commando-type operations than the regular army.

For example [in 1980], on November 7 *[Sepah]* commando units played a significant role . . . in an assault on Iraq oil export terminals at Mina al Bakr and Al Faw. . . . Iran [presumably *Sepah* commandos] also attacked the northern pipeline . . . and successfully closed Basra's access to the Persian Gulf.[16]
— U.S. Dept. of Army, "Iran Country Study"

In March 1982, a combined force of Iranian regular army and *Sepah* succeeded offensively, where regular Army armor alone had failed.[17] As the war progressed, surprise and infiltration helped to push the Iraqis across the border.[18] The Guard's subsequent "human-wave" attacks may have been prompted by the Tehran clergy's unwillingness to use supporting arms against predominantly Shiite Basra.[19] By 1987, the Islamic leadership had publicly opted for surprise attacks over those of the human-wave variety.[20] They had also adopted the Communist guerrilla policy of not fighting unless victory was virtually assured.[21] Near the end of the conflict with Iraq, the *Sepah* shifted back to the smaller-assault-element and occasional-infiltration tactics of its guerrilla beginnings.[22]

To this day, Tehran's Sa'ad Abbad Military Museum contains only one pictorial record of its eight-year-long war with Iraq.[23] That record is a small wall mural. It depicts a single Iranian infantry squad assaulting an Iraqi position through barren, broken terrain. Its elements are squad leader, sniper, a two-man RPG team, and three four-man fire teams. All are slightly separated and moving semi-independently around the five-foot-tall mounds of dirt. To the rear of the loosely defined formation is the squad leader. He is looking through binoculars to his direct front. The fire teams are roughly abreast, and one is moving forward. While the riflemen in each fire team are deployed shoulder to shoulder and on line, none are firing their AK-47's. There is no machinegun to provide cover fire.

Such a procedure is sufficiently complicated to require rehearsal. That makes it a technique. While far from "state of the art," it does contain advanced elements. Any sound during an assault erodes the element of surprise, but heavy small-arms fire completely forfeits it. Instead of a telltale machinegun, the Iranians are using a lone sniper to cover their forward movement. Rather than firing indiscriminately to keep defenders' heads down, their lead riflemen are waiting for well-defined targets. Like the sniper, the RPG team is stationed at the edge of the formation. His occasional shot might sound like a stray mortar or accidental mine to an Iraqi defender down the line and thus evoke no response. While probably completing a leapfrog, "fire-and-movement" approach, the various squad elements seem poised to come together in the final assault. All appear ready to follow the lead fire team (the only element moving) through its penetration in Iraqi lines. The Iranian squad leader seems more interested in spotting unforeseen trouble than following or giving orders. That implies "recon pull"—reconnoitering the enemy position while the attack is in progress. It was the marriage of rehearsed technique with "recon pull" that worked so well for the German Stormtrooper squads in the Spring Offensives of 1918.[24] When combined, they produce the accelerated facsimile of a deliberate attack—one that is more effective than a hasty attack. While this Iranian squad may not be the equal of its German or East Asian predecessor, it could still spearhead a maneuver force. That is something that its "command-push," noisy, and underrehearsed Western counterpart cannot do.

As *Sepah* was also the recruiter/trainer of espionage agents,[25] it may have developed some fairly sophisticated short-range infiltration techniques—like crawling through barbed wire, sneaking between holes, or stalking a sentry. Such methods would be useful to either mission.

The Guard's Defense

While stemming the initial Iraqi incursion, the relatively unstructured Guard may have discovered the lesson of Stalingrad—that tiny, loosely controlled teams of infantrymen can hold back a whole army in built-up terrain. It was the newly formed *Sepah* that fought the heavily supported Iraqis to a standstill at Abadan and Khorramshahr. Such a feat requires significant ability. The *Sepah*-led soldiers must have had sufficient individual and small-unit movement and hiding skills to counteract a severe deficit in firepower.

> The last major Iraqi territorial gain took place in early November 1980. On November 3, Iraqi forces reached Abadan but were repulsed by a Pasdaran [Iranian *Sepah]* unit. Even though they surrounded Abadan on three sides and occupied a portion of the city, the Iraqis could not overcome the stiff resistance; sections of the city still under Iranian control were resupplied by boat at night. On November 10, Iraq captured Khorramshahr after a bloody house-to-house fight. The price of this victory was high for both sides, approximately 6,000 casualties for Iraq and even more for Iran. . . .
>
> Soon after capturing Khorramshahr, the Iraqi troops lost their initiative and began to dig in along their line of advance.[26]
>
> — U.S. Dept. of Army, "Iran Country Study"

> [At Khorramshahr] the Iraqi forces enjoyed an advantage in numbers. This ranged from 3 - 4 to 1 for infantry strength and [was] 2.5 to 1 for tanks (McLaurin, "Military Operations in the Gulf War," 1982, 21). . . .
>
> As the fighting moved toward the city core, armor operations were reduced to a supporting role only. . . .

The duration of the Battle for Khorramshahr was 25 days. . . . The attacking Iraqi casualties have been estimated as high as 9,000. . . . Estimates for casualties among the Iranian forces *[Baseej* Militias] . . . range from 2,000-3,000 (Ibid.) . . .

. . . In Khorramshahr, the Iranian defenders were able to launch successful counterattacks disrupting the Iraqi attack.[27]

— *Marine Corps Gazette,* April 1999

For rural defense, the Guard's tactical progress is less certain. East of Basra in 1988, it lost in nine hours what it had taken two months to capture the year before.[28] At fault may have been its inability to absorb a chemical attack.

The Guard's *Piece de Resistance*

Through its counterinsurgency role, the *Sepah* has developed a formidable community watch apparatus in Iran. To counter civil disturbance at Tehran University on 3 June 2004 (the anniversary of Ayatollah Khomeini's death), the Guard deployed limited manpower wisely. They positioned a mobile, platoon-sized reaction force and command center at the University's main gate and a single uniformed *Sepah* on every street corner for several blocks in every direction. Any threat would have been immediately relayed (probably by cell phone) to the command center. Every gate in the University fence was locked. Outside each were two uniformed, billy-club-toting *Sepah* who gestured to the infrequent passerby to stay out of arm's reach. Just inside was an additional squad-sized reaction force.[29] Such an apparatus would be more difficult to infiltrate.

Israel's Expulsion from Southern Lebanon

- Who was mainly responsible for the Israelis' departure?
- What was their tactical method?

ISRAELI PARATROOP SERGEANT, 1983

(Source: Courtesy of Orion Books, from *Uniforms of the Elite Forces*, ©1982 by Blandford Press Ltd., Plate 24, No. 70; *FM 21-76* (1957), p. 194)

Lebanon's Unusual Structure and Recent History

Lebanon is a not a normal country. While it has a president and a parliament, it also has a foreign occupier on the streets of its capital and an armed "movement" in control of its southern buffer zone. (See Maps 3.1 and 3.2.) To fully appreciate Lebanon's inverted power structure, one must review its recent history.

During the "Black September" fighting of 1970, the Jordanian government expelled all armed Palestinians from its territory. Most settled in Southern Lebanon.[1] This, in turn, made Israel uneasy. When it launched a punitive invasion in 1982, Iran got involved.

International boundary
★ National capital
● Governorate capital
———— Railroad
———— Expressway
———— Road
▭ Urban area

SCALE 1:970,000

Lambert Conformal Conic Projection,
standard parallels 30°N and 36°N

Map 3.1: Relief Map of Lebanon
(Source: Courtesy of General Libraries, University of Texas at Austin, from their website for map designator "lebanon.jpg")

The Iranian Intervention

Ayatollah Khomeini was more of an expansionist than a *jihadist*. He was quick to see how the Israeli invasion could be exploited. His bloc of Islamic States would need Mediterranean ports.

In the early 1980's, Khomeini's "Party of God" *(Hezbollah)* had 20 million members inside Iran and adherents in Lebanon.[2] Those 20 million Iranians were soon mobilized by the Iranian Revolutionary Guard *(Pasdaran* or *Sepah).*[3] The *Sepah's* job was to transform the "unorganized forces or 20 million members of *Hezbollah"* into the people's militia *(Baseej)* for the war with Iraq.[4] Soon, Lebanon's fledgling "Party of God" would be greatly expanded after Iran dispatched a contingent of Iranian Revolutionary Guards to counter the Israeli invasion.[5] That contingent's mission was not personally to fight the Israelis but rather to prepare the locals (most notably the Palestinians) to do it.[6] From then on, the term *"Hezbollah"* has been commonly applied to their Lebanese creation. *Sepah's* ultimate goal was, of course, to create a sister Islamic State.

The Iranian logistical base in the Bekaa Valley is capable of providing adequate support to the estimated 4,000 Hezbollah militia fighters now under arms [as of 1988]. Hezbollah has been effective in undercutting the [Syrian-supported] Amal and is likely to continue such efforts, rallying support under the banner of an Islamic Republic of Lebanon.[7]
— *Warfare in Lebanon,* Nat. Defense Univ.

Lebanon Has Its Own Tradition of Martyrdom

The transplaced *Hashishins* had their headquarters just north of the Lebanese border at Masyaf, Syria. As late as 1929, people of the same name "infested the uncivilized region north of Tripoli, Lebanon."[8] Like the *Hashishin fidavi* ("daggerman"),[9] today's Muslim suicide bomber believes himself destined for paradise. One wonders to what extent his mental conditioning may have been like that of the *Hashishin.*

Martyrdom is also stressed in Lebanese *Hezbollah's* indoctrination of new fighters.[10] This may increase their willingness to engage in close combat.

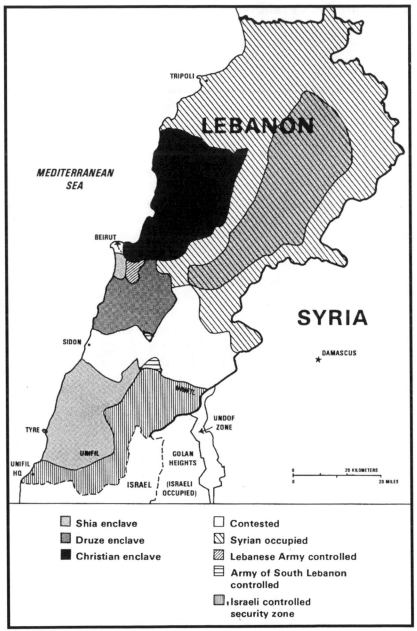

Figure 3.2: Areas of Control in 1985

(Source: *Warfare in Lebanon*, ed.Kenneth J. Alnwick and Thomas A. Fabyanic [Washington, D.C.: National Defense Univ., 1988], p. 6)

Lebanese *Hezbollah's* Goal

While Shiite *Amal* only sought security for southern Lebanon, *Hezbollah* wished to project the war with Israel across its borders.[11] *Amal* desired no armed Palestinian presence in Lebanon and a greater role for Shiites in a secular government. *Hezbollah* wanted help from armed Palestinians in expelling the Israelis from an Islamic Republic.[12] As the two organizations vied for power,[13] Lebanese *Hezbollah* had the edge. Its founders had already done the following for three years in Iran: (1) dislodge other guerrilla factions, (2) suppress ethnic uprisings, (3) provide internal security, and (4) prosecute open warfare.[14]

The Lebanese Trump Card

In Islamic *jihad,* there is no room for collaboration. Through religious edicts, *Hezbollah* was able to capture the loyalty of the Lebanese population.

The Grand Shiite cleric Mahdy Shams-al-Din announced that cooperation with the IDF is heresy and that armed resistance is the obligation every Shiite in Southern Lebanon (Zayed Center, U.A.E.; *Tahreer Janoub Libnaan,* 2002, 24-25).[15]
— *Marine Corps Gazette,* June 2003

Hezbollah also provided social services to the poorest elements of Lebanese society, thereby creating a quasi-state in the midst of chaos. In Southern Lebanon, it provided education, loans, grants, health care, and security.[16]

A New Twist on an Old Method

Instead of going after the opposition leader like the *Hashishins* had, Lebanese *Hezbollah* went after the opposition leader's whole staff. Twice, in 1982 and again in 1983, it succeeded in blowing up the Israeli Defense Force's (IDF's) headquarters in Southern Lebanon.[17] Both attacks were conducted by suicide car bombers. Sadly, the U.S. Marine barracks in Beirut was hit about the same time.

Capitalizing on the *Intifada's* Strength

Prior to the Israeli invasion of 1982, the Palestine Liberation Organization (PLO) had most of its military forces, unit headquarters, and training facilities in Lebanon. When the PLO began fighting with Syrian forces in 1983, independent Palestinians were forced out of eastern and northern Lebanon. The pro-Arafat fighters in the Beirut and Sidon refugee camps became more worried about Syrian-backed Shiites than Israelis.[18] In 1985, it was *Hezbollah* that forced the Israeli invaders to retreat from the suburbs of Beirut into the nine-mile-wide southern buffer zone. It did so through attrition spearheaded by suicide bombers.[19]

[T]he invasion misfired, exposing the IDF to effective guerrilla warfare for the first time and revealing the limits of its power. The spectacle of the mighty IDF with its thousands of tanks and vehicles reeling from Lebanon was not lost on the Palestinians.[20]

After the first Palestinian *intifada* began in Israel in 1987,[21] *Hezbollah* created the impression that the uprising had spread to southern Lebanon. Such an impression would prove as effective as ground maneuver. "Here numerical strength and technical superiority in weapons . . . conferred no considerable advantage."[22]

The more [the] activists were killed or arrested or incarcerated and deported, the more the ranks of the *[intifada]* uprising were replenished from below; indeed, very often relatives of those killed or imprisoned took action against their tormentors.

From the first, Israeli military authorities were at a loss in dealing with an uprising that had no central leadership and in which the "enemy" usually consisted of unarmed civilians. . . . [I]n this struggle, 95 percent of the firepower it had often deployed against regular Arab armies was irrelevant; neither the fighter-bombers nor the tanks nor the heavy artillery . . . were of any use when it came to controlling crowds or chasing small parties of teenagers over the limestone hills of Judea or down the alleys of the Gaza Strip refugee camps.[23]

Fighting this way had a fringe benefit—it demoralized the fire-power-dependent adversary. His infantrymen lacked the movement skills to accomplish their mission any other way.

In 1995, according to one survey that was leaked to the press, 72 percent of the [Israeli] troops interviewed felt that serving in the Occupied Territories was "very demoralizing"; no fewer than 46 percent had witnessed "inappropriate behavior" toward Palestinian civilians.[24]

[I]t was made worse by Rabin's policy of deliberately passing as many ground units through the Occupied Territories as possible, often on short notice and with little or no specialized training (Gal, *The Seventh War,* 1990, 143).[25]

Hezbollah's Penchant for Deception

There were many "friendly fire" clashes between Israeli units in Southern Lebanon.[26] Very possibly, they were triggered by someone in the middle.

Central to the Eastern way of war is luring one's foe into a trap. Within every one of this chapter's vignettes is some manner of entrapment.

The Eastern Guerrilla Method

Hezbollah was able to destabilize Southern Lebanon while concurrently destroying the opposition's strategic assets. Israeli supply columns were attacked en route to their bases in the buffer zone.[27] Those attacks were often by suicide car bomb.[28]

Of particular note was *Hezbollah's* expertise at "human" intelligence gathering. With good enough intelligence, one does not need state-of-the-art tactics.

Intelligence Gathering

After October 1995, Israel noticed an increase in *Hezbollah's* ability to determine the whereabouts of high-ranking personnel and

35

commandos.[29] While leaks in the Southern Lebanese Army (SLA) may have been part of the problem, a vast "neighborhood watch" had also been set up. *Hezbollah* depended mostly for real-time intelligence on the local population and long-range observation.[30]

Moshe Rudovsky, whose son was killed in an Israeli naval commando raid into southern Lebanon on 5 September 1997, says he learned from highly credible sources that the force had been detected by enemy radar.[31] Once ashore, the commandos were tracked by nonelectronic means. This can only be reliably accomplished by skilled stalkers.

> Rudovsky claims, however, that following the Hezbollah discovery of the "Israeli" force, the enemy declared a "radio silence," refraining from using any communications equipment that might disclose its presence, all the while tracking the IDF fighters.[32]
> — *Hare'etz* (Tel Aviv), 13 August 1998

According to *Christian Science Monitor*, the local inhabitants had been alerted to the impending raid by the increase in Israeli aircraft and boat activity.[33]

A Mine with Eyes

Hezbollah had become quite proficient with autonomous and remotely controlled mines.[34] After 12 of 16 members of the above-mentioned commando unit were killed by a single blast,[35] one wonders just how proficient. One of the following must have happened: (1) the Israeli's precise route was leaked, (2) their explosives were accidentally detonated, (3) a huge charge was tossed into their midst, (4) a preregistered artillery or mortar round got them, or (5) a mine was command-detonated nearby. While a map or aerial-photograph overlay could not have shown the route in enough detail to guarantee the success of a mine, the Israeli high command prefers the first two explanations. Both, albeit implausible, infer that the commandos were under surveillance. If they were also being tailed, they may have encountered one of the other possibilities during (or right after) a rest stop. This much night-fighting ability only seems impossible to a technology-oriented Westerner. While admittedly difficult, it would be well within the capabilities of a skilled tracker who knew the neighborhood. Luckily there exists a detailed account of what happened.

For 10 days, . . . the MK drone—a pilotless reconnaissance plane—had flown over the fields and orange groves at the northern end of Insariyeh. Ghalib Farhat had seen the drones clearly from his one-story house on the edge of the village. Their presence had puzzled him. Insariyeh was far from "Israel's" occupation zone and there was little that could interest the "Israelis" in the village.

The naval commandos silently emerged from the water onto a rocky beach. . . . The team had to sneak across the road and pass through a gate in a 3-meter high concrete wall running along the east side of the highway to reach the cover of banana plantations and orange groves before continuing up the hill to Insariyeh. . . . Under the cover of a banana plantation, the team began the hard uphill march to the cliff-top village. . . .

. . . Ghalib was . . . bothered. Hezbollah fighters were operating in the area. They had arrived in the village about the same time that the drones had appeared 10 days earlier. Each night at about 10:00 P.M., a car with its lights switched off drove slowly along the lane past his home toward the village of Loubieh, 1 kilometer to the north. Four or five people would climb out of the car and disappear into the orange groves. They were there again that evening.

Kurakin and his 15 [Israeli] soldiers were struggling up the hill, fighting through dense undergrowth. He paused and beckoned to the radio operator. Kurakin wanted to take a short cut. There was a track running westward between an orange grove and a windbreak of pine trees which would allow his team to move faster and bring him out midway along the lane between Insariyeh and Loubieh. His superior authorized the move and Kurakin led his team in the new direction. . . .

The "Israeli" team approached the lane between Insariyeh and Loubieh cautiously. Kurakin, the radio operator and one other soldier led the rest of the team by a few meters. As they reached the gate near the lane, Kurakin motioned them to halt. He and his two companions darted across the road and crouched beside a pile of garbage. Kurakin turned to order the other commandos forward. As he did so, a massive explosion engulfed the commandos, killing several of them instantly. Barely having time to recover from the shock of the blast, the team was hit by a second bomb which exploded in a huge bubble of orange flames with hundreds of steel ball bearings ripping through the "Israeli" unit. Kurakin raced back across the road to help the survivors. Then the machineguns opened up from the orange grove to the north. A bullet struck Kurakin in the head, killing him instantly. . . .

. . . Ghalib noticed through the window the flash of a third explosion among the orange trees to the north.

The third blast was caused by a bullet striking explosives carried by Sergeant Itamar Ilya, the unit's sapper. . . .

An "Israeli" Army commission of inquiry concluded that the commandos were the victims of a chance guerrilla ambush. Two more army inquiries were subsequently held over the next 18 months as well as a separate parliamentary probe. All were inconclusive. Hezbollah has maintained silence over the affair—a ploy to keep the "Israelis" guessing. Three years after the raid and three months after the "Israelis" left south Lebanon, Hezbollah's southern commander, Sheikh Nabil Qaouk, is still reluctant to reveal the truth behind the battle. "It's still too early to tell the secrets of Insariyeh. The "Israelis" know that Hezbollah was aware of the operation but they don't know how. But I will say that our presence there was not a coincidence," Qaouk told The Daily Star. . . .

Despite, Hezbollah's reticence, perhaps the clue to the heavy presence of resistance fighters in the area stems from an earlier "Israeli" commando operation. On the night of Aug. 4, a team of helicopter-borne commandos from the Golani Brigade landed on the outskirts of Kfour village, 16 kilometers east of Insariyeh. Spotted by local Hezbollah fighters, the two sides fought for two hours before the "Israelis" withdrew.

Shortly after dawn while on a sweep through the village, five Hezbollah fighters, including two senior commanders, were killed in a triple roadside bomb blast. The bombs had been planted by the commandos and detonated by a drone flying overhead.

Despite Hezbollah's subsequent air of secrecy, Sayyed Hassan Nasrallah, the party's secretary-general, perhaps gave the most accurate account of the circumstances surrounding the Insariyeh battle during a press conference the same day. He said groups of fighters armed with roadside bombs had deployed throughout the South following the Kfour operation in anticipation of further commando raids.

"The nightwatchers are in most towns and villages, and are waiting for them using booby traps, rifles and mortar fire," Nasrallah said. . . .

. . . [N]ear the gate leading into the orange grove, beside a pair of iron water pipes, there are two small holes in the ground, marking the spot where the bombs exploded. Seared onto the iron pipes in front of each hole are the flattened remains of dozens of steel ball bearings—the shrapnel in the bombs.[36]

— *The Daily Star* (Lebanon), 9 June 2000

A high-level probe later determined that there had been no intelligence leak.[37] The commandos almost certainly picked up a "tail" at the hole in the wall near the beach. After they entered the track running westward between orange grove and pine tree windbreak, their stalker somehow signalled this information to a roving claymore ambush team. The loss of these commandos severely shook the Israelis' confidence in their armed forces.

The Sniping Incident

More often than not, *Hezbollah* guerrillas would take IDF units under fire with small arms or antitank missiles from a populated area. They did so to draw enough return fire to alienate the local population. To evoke a full Israeli response, the Islamic guerrillas would lob a few Katyusyha rockets into their border settlements.[38] In essence, the guerrillas had learned to turn their foe's mindset against him.

"Israel" notes that Hezbollah carried out 104 operations in

July [1997], more than any other single month for years, according to Jane's Intelligence Review in London. But "only four were close-quarter ambushes, with the rest being [safer] long-range missile or mortar attacks," the Review says.[39]
— *Christian Science Monitor,* 20 October 1997

The Ambushing of Foot Patrols

It is not known if *Hezbollah* has ever done to an Israeli foot patrol what it did to those naval commandos in Southern Lebanon. There too, the technique would be highly effective.

"On several occasions, well-placed Hezbollah ambushes [have] managed to surprise Israeli patrols, normally those returning over routine tracks from night ambushes."[40] Israeli foot patrols have also been ambushed as they emerged from their compounds while under long-range observation.[41] In the heavily vegetated terrain of southern Lebanon, IDF troops seldom saw their enemy before he opened up on them with concentrated fire.[42] At short range, the weapon of choice was the command-detonated claymore.

The Convoy Ambush

Hezbollah may have also heard of the *haichi-shiki* ambush. It has been used effectively against U.S. forces by the Japanese, Chinese, North Koreans, and North Vietnamese.[43] It involves the following steps: (1) luring a quarry into an inverted U-shaped ambush, (2) closing the back door, and then (3) attacking him from all sides with a combination of ruses, long-range fire, and assaults.

[T]he Hezbollah . . . [was] attacking Israeli convoys with a variety of explosive charges, combined with ambushes, once their traveling troops dismounted from their protected vehicles.[44]

In Southern Lebanon, roadside bombs could be positioned to kill or just pave the way for a ground assault. The guerrilla often depends upon what he can steal or later barter for. On more than one occasion, hostages were taken during an ambush in the "Occupied Territories."[45]

Tank Killing

Unfortunately for Israeli armor, *Hezbollah* has also applied its mine-making skill to this endeavor. Wherever tanks are canalized, they become vulnerable. It was just a matter of time before Islamic village residents discovered how to kill them. First, the tanks must be summoned. While the following attack occurred inside Israel, its method was perfected in Southern Lebanon.

> In a coordinated attack, Palestinians unleashed gunfire and a roadside bomb on an armored bus traveling in a convoy through the Gaza Strip.
> No one was hurt. But when a tank arrived on a service road a short while later, a mine packed with at least 100 pounds (45 kilos) of explosives blew up directly underneath it. The blast blew the tank's turret off, detonated the tank's shells, and instantly killed three soldiers inside.
> Israelis were shocked by the sophistication of the attack, which many said was reminiscent of operations conducted by the Lebanese Islamic Party of God, known as Hezbollah, during Israel's 18 year occupation of southern Lebanon.[46]

— *International Herald Tribune*, 16 February 2002

Attack on a Fortified Position

Hezbollah likes its foes to establish fortified camps, because it knows that barbed wire promotes passive behavior.[47] This may be why it has not yet discovered the "stormtrooper technique" for secretly penetrating a prepared enemy position. While it has incorporated artillery and mortar fire into its infantry assaults since 1983,[48] it has not simulated that fire with concussion grenades.

> Hezbollah has turned lately to . . . combined assaults on Israeli and SLA fortifications, using platoon or even company-sized forces with artillery support. Some of these attacks have been mounted with considerable skill involving simultaneous attacks on several outposts over a wide area. But in most of these cases, the attack could be beaten off by

firepower and air support. There were only a few occasions when Hezbollah fighters were able to reach and capture an outpost, in all cases manned by SLA troops. . . .
    The forts . . . became focal points for the Hezbollah surprise attacks from which so many casualties resulted.[49]
    — *Marine Corps Gazette,* July 1997

Of *Hezbollah's* 104 attacks in July 1997, only four were from close quarters.[50] The others were from standoff range with mortars or rockets.

Israel berated the Lebanese Army for taking part in the Insarieh battle when the "Israeli" commando raid went wrong, and within a few days—for the first time—"Israel" directly fired upon a Lebanese armored vehicle, killing six soldiers. . . .
    Shortly after the Lebanese soldiers were killed, Hezbollah "dedicated" a wide-ranging revenge attack to their memory: the occupation zone erupted from end to end at 7:00 A.M. one morning with 17 simultaneous attacks on "Israeli" positions, among 25 launched that day.[51]
    — *Christian Science Monitor,* 20 October 1997

Within Lebanon, *Hezbollah* preferred to attack in the daytime. Its fighters did, however, conduct many of their approach marches before sunrise.

Short-Range Infiltration

A few *Hezbollah* members may be more talented than others. Separate newspapers confirmed the exploits of a single fighter.[52] He was able to secretly enter one of the most heavily fortified bases in southern Lebanon, stroll around, raise a flag, punch a soldier, and then get away.

An embarrassed "Israeli" army has launched an investigation to find out how a Hezbollah guerrilla was able to enter the formidable Sojod position on Sunday and wander around at will before escaping from a squad of elite paratroopers.

The incident occurred during heavy fighting on Sunday night between Hezbollah guerrillas and "Israeli" troops near Sojod in the Iqleem al-Tuffah.

The guerrilla, armed with two grenades and an M-16 assault rifle, apparently scrambled over the compound's fortifications and strolled around the interior of the hilltop bunker undetected.

According to one account in yesterday's "Israeli" press, the fighter raised a Hezbollah flag in the base and may have stolen classified communications equipment.[53]

— *The Daily Star* (Lebanon), 12 August 1998

That this happened at all means *Hezbollah* could conduct a short-range-infiltration attack on a fortified position. A few infiltrators can do considerable damage to command bunkers, ammunition stores, aircraft, fuel dumps, or other strategic assets. To hide their sabotage, they would only have to make timed explosions look like lucky incoming.

A Sophisticated Strongpoint Defense

Southern Lebanon is liberally sprinkled with hilltop villages. An IDF officer has likened the *Hezbollah* defense of this region to the Viet Cong (VC) equivalent.[54] As in Vietnam, it consists of a series of fortified villages that are only occasionally defended. And, as in Vietnam,[55] its local militias may continually move between 10 or so of these villages to keep from getting targeted.

[T]he guerrillas normally operate in small units that are hidden inside civilian villages and are difficult to locate.[56]

It's possible that *Hezbollah* has given each of these hilltop villages just north of the Israeli border a "disappear underground" capability.

As early as 1981, there was an "extensive system of underground bunkers that honeycombed the [Lebanese] refugee camps."[57]

If so, those villages would closely resemble the Vietnamese border

43

hamlets into which 17 fully supported Chinese divisions could only penetrate 30 miles in 1979.[58] Those hamlets were being manned by local militiamen too,[59] as all the Vietnamese regulars were off fighting the Khymer Rouge in Cambodia.[60] If those Lebanese villages had also been linked by tunnel, they would constitute a "soft, underground strongpoint defense"—the state of the art in rural defense. Any intruder risks surprise fire from every direction.

Inside the zone itself, the IDF is often pinned down in fixed positions, and no amount of air superiority can compensate for this weakness on the ground.[61]
— *London Financial Times,* 1997

Facts That Do Not Bode Well for the Future

"Throughout 1987 . . . incidents in which Palestinians clashed with Israeli troops . . . increased by leaps and bounds."[62] When Israeli forces finally withdrew from the Lebanese buffer zone in 2000, the *Hezbollah* victory was complete.[63] The Palestinians had witnessed the whole process and could now pursue it within Israel itself.

Hezbollah did not defeat the best equipped army in the region without some sophisticated weaponry of its own. Against the Israeli Merkava tanks, it used TOW missiles that Iran may have gotten through the U.S. "arms-for-hostages" trade.[64] However, the deciding factor—over 18 long years of war—was *Hezbollah's* improving light-infantry capability.[65]

In 1995, five Lebanese guerrillas were being killed for every Israeli soldier that died. By the late nineties, that ratio was approaching one-to-one.[66]

Until the Israeli withdrawal from southern Lebanon, Hezbollah fought the SLA and IDF. Both the IDF and Hezbollah developed commandos that specialized in warfare appropriate for the terrain of southern Lebanon. Hezbollah claimed to have modeled their Unit 13 after the IDF Navy Commandos, and claim a 1997 failed attack by IDF SEAL unit was ambushed by Unit 13.

Hezbollah ambushes of IDF troops sometimes occurred less than 100 meters from Israel's border. [With] difficulties in providing reinforcements and resupply by land . . . , the IDF took to the air and began using helicopters to resupply its troops in Lebanon.

Hezbollah AA units "Saladin's Falcons" equipped with SA-7, SA-14, SA-18 and Stinger missiles caused IDF helicopters to switch tactics and fly high and use flares in order to avoid heat-seeking missiles. . . .

Special actions of the Hezbollah Abu Ruhm Special Forces Unit against . . . South Lebanese Army forces resulted in assassinations of SLA intelligence services.[67]

Thus, Iran's strange blend of *Hashishin* and Mongol heritage had produced a new way of confronting a more powerful adversary. While sneaky and immoral, it was nevertheless very effective. After 20 years of refinement in Lebanon, it had become a unique blend of Shiite martyrdom, high explosives, and guerrilla tactics. Because it spilled over into politics, media, religion, and psychology, it qualified as "4th-generation" warfare. Concurrently being developed (in large part by Sunnis) in Afghanistan and Chechnya was a similar approach. Both would surface and then begin to share methods in contemporary Iraq. As such, their battlefield techniques deserve a closer look.

Part Two

Islamic Guerrilla Tactics

"The overall military strategy . . . to drive the Soviets out
[of Afghanistan] was . . . death by a thousand cuts."
— Gen. Akhtar Rehman, Pakistani ISI Head

Palestinian Fighters

- Which militant Palestinian faction is the oldest?
- What tactics does it now use inside Israel?

SYRIAN INFANTRY CORPORAL, 1973

(Source: Courtesy of Orion Books, from *World Army Uniforms since 1939*, © 1975, 1980, 1981, 1983 by Blandford Press Ltd., Part II, Plate 119; *FM 90-3* (1977), p. 4-2)

A More Detailed History of the Palestinian Movement

The Palestine Liberation Organization (PLO) "grew out of the Alexandria Summit Conference of 15 September 1963 and was financed by the Arab League."[1]

In spring 1964, about 400 Palestinians met in Jerusalem to form the Palestine National Congress and King Hussein of Jordan, who opened the meeting, resolved to establish a Palestine Liberation Organization and to open camps to train guerrillas.[2]

The Popular Front for the Liberation of Palestine (PFLP) arrived on the scene in 1968.[3] Because the PLO occasionally trained foreign militants, it was suspected of being at the center of international terrorism. By 1979, nearly 2000 foreign nationals had received instruction at nine Palestinian camps in Syria, Lebanon, Libya, Iraq, and South Yemen. Of those 2000, 580 were Iranians.[4]

When the Palestinian fighters were expelled from Jordan in September 1970, they moved to Lebanon.[5] To confront Yasser Arafat's PLO at its source, the Israelis invaded that country in 1982. (See Figure 4.1.) Iran sent in about 2000 *Sepah* to check their advance. When the firepower-heavy Israeli forces reached the suburbs of Beirut, U.S. Marines landed to preclude a blood bath. After the PLO fighters had been assured in writing (through the U.S. State

Figure 4.1: Israeli Corporal, 1967
(Source: Courtesy of Orion Books, from *World Army Uniforms since 1939*, © 1975, 1980, 1981, 1983 by Blandford Press Ltd., Part II, Plate 107)

Department's Habib Document) that their families would be safe, they withdrew by ship under U.N. auspices.[6] Eight days after the Marines re-embarked for Naples, Christian Phalangist militiamen (Israel's allies) struck at the Sabra and Shatilla refugee camps, massacring about 800 unarmed civilians.[7] (See Figure 4.2.)

The rest is all-too-familiar history. The Marines returned, took up defensive positions around Beirut airport, and came under almost immediate attack. When their barracks was bombed in October 1983, all U.S. forces pulled out of Lebanon. Shortly thereafter, the Israelis withdrew to its southern buffer zone, and the Syrians occupied the rest. Inside that zone (and Israel itself), the PLO—a coalition of groups that included *Hamas* and Yasser Arafat's *Fatah*—resumed their armed push for autonomy.

Figure 4.2: Christian Militiaman, 1983

(Source: Courtesy of Orion Books, from *World Army Uniforms since 1939*, © 1975, 1980, 1981, 1983 by Blandford Press Ltd., Part II, Plate 114)

Before the Israeli invasion, the Shiites of Southern Lebanon had endured heavy-handed PLO rule.[8] Once the hard-core PLO fighters had been evacuated from Beirut, Syrian-backed *Amal* and Iranian-backed *Hezbollah* emerged as the two competing powers. The more militant of the two came out on top. In Southern Lebanon, they would let the Palestinians do much of the fighting against the Israelis.

Hamas Is *Hezbollah's* Instrument in Palestine

Established in late 1987 for the first *intifada* against the Israeli occupation, *Hamas* (an offshoot of the Palestinian Muslim Brotherhood) bears a considerable resemblance to *Hezbollah*. Like *Hezbollah's* military wing, *Hamas* fighters refer to themselves as the "Islamic Resistance Movement."[9] *Hamas* differs from the other mainstream PLO groups in that it wants to form an Islamic state. The others would gladly settle for a secular state.[10]

Various *Hamas* elements have used both political and violent means, including terrorism, to pursue the goal of establishing an Islamic Palestinian state in place of Israel. Loosely structured, with some elements working clandestinely and others working openly through mosques and social service institutions to recruit members, raise money, organize activities, and distribute propaganda.[11]
— U.S. State Dept., *Patterns for Global Terrorism*

In 1989, the IDF sent 400 *Hamas* leaders into the "no-man's land" between Israel and Lebanon. *Hezbollah* took those leaders in and gave them three to four years of training. When they were returned to Israel in 1993, her military fortunes in the West Bank and Gaza began to worsen. (See Map 4.1.) The Palestinian militants were now well versed in *Hezbollah* tactical technique.[12]

[T]he Palestinian militant groups Hamas and Islamic Jihad have increasingly forged a common front against Israel, and there are signs they are also being guided by Lebanese Hezbollah guerrillas.[13]
— Associated Press, 28 October 2003

In 1992, the Qassem Brigade, a specialized military wing of *Hamas* became fully operational and "engaged in well-planned guerrilla warfare against Israeli military and police."[14] Since 1994, when

Map 4.1: Palestinian-Controlled Areas within Israel
(Source: Courtesy of General Libraries, University of Texas at Austin, from their website for map designator "occupied_map.jpg")

53

a Jewish settler entered a mosque and gunned down 29 worshippers, *Hamas* has shifted almost entirely to suicide bombings and assassination.[15] Israeli buses have been heavily targeted.

Hamas has now grown stronger. It has conducted the majority of attacks and also gained the majority of popular support.

> "While the U.S. is stressing security for Israel, Palestinian daily life is deteriorating—and this is empowering Hamas and marginalizing the moderates," says Said Ghazali, a Palestinian journalist and analyst. . . .
> A December [2003] poll . . . showed that Hamas has overtaken Fatah as the most popular political grouping in the Gaza Strip. . . .
> . . . [T]he movement is advancing not only because it is at the forefront of "armed resistance" . . . but also because it strives to serve the public's daily needs.[16]
> — *Christian Science Monitor,* 3 March 2004

Hamas's principal tactic has been placing suicide bombers aboard buses. Some 21 buses have been destroyed by suicide attacks over the last three and half years worldwide.[17] While a few bus bombings have occurred in Sri Lanka, most have happened in Israel. In true *Hezbollah* fashion, *Hamas* has now enlisted the cooperation of the al-Aqsa Martyrs' Brigade of Yasser Arafat's *Fatah* movement.[18] (See Figure 4.3.)

Other *Hezbollah* Proxies

Islamic Jihad (the Lebanese version) is nothing more than a front for *Hezbollah*. A separate affiliate is the Popular Front for the Liberation of Palestine–General Command (PFLP-GC). It split away from its parent organization (and the PLO) in 1968, claiming to want more fighting and less politics. It carried out dozens of attacks in Europe and the Middle East during the 1970's and 1980's. It is known for cross-border terrorist attacks into Israel using unusual means, such as hot-air balloons and motorized hang gliders. It focuses on small-scale attacks at the Israeli border, West Bank, and Gaza Strip. While it receives logistic and military support from Syria, it trains with *Hezbollah* and receives financial support from Iran.[19]

Figure 4.3: Yasser Arafat
(Source: *Corel Gallery Clipart*, Portraits, Corel, #01F007)

Why They Do It and Who's behind It

While hatred and hypnosis are powerful, they cannot get some-one to commit suicide.[20] The Palestinians are the most repressed population in the Middle East. They probably also provide the ma-jority of suicide bombers.

[T]he Palestinian response [to Israeli firepower] has been in the face of enormously oppressive conditions, . . . leaving them in a state of near collective desperation, a social and psychological condition that is very apt to breed suicide at-tacks.[21]
— Fr. Patrick Gaffney, authority on the Middle East

More often than not, the suicide bombers are young, idealistic, and impressionable. Wishing to support their communities and fami-

55

lies, they are easily lured by fame and fortune. Once the young bombers have agreed to become martyrs, mind control experts help them to follow through.

Lebanese guerrillas financing Palestinian suicide bombings have paid bonuses . . . for each Israeli killed, the chairman of the Israeli parliament's security committee said Tuesday.

Palestinian militants confirmed having received large sums from the [Lebanese] Hezbollah group, including single payments of up to $50,000, and said deadly attacks were rewarded, but denied there was a fixed pay scale.

The most recent bombing on Sunday . . . was claimed by the al-Aqsa Martyrs' Brigade, which has ties to Yasser Arafat's Fatah movement. Al-Aqsa has been one the main recipients of Hezbollah money.

Palestinian security officials said Tuesday they have evidence that Hezbollah funded Sunday's attack, as well as a bus bombing in Jerusalem on Jan. 29. . . .

The officials . . . said the Hamas and Islamic Jihad groups were also involved in the last two bombings.[22]
— Associated Press, 25 February 2004

The mind control procedures are less apparent. First, the volunteer is videotaped signing a contract so that he or she can't back out. Then the volunteer may be introduced to self-hypnosis. To induce a mental state free of fear, critical thought, or moral qualms, he or she may be given Sufi mantras to rehearse.[23]

A Telling Change in the Recruitment Base

As a repressed society loses hope, it offers less and less opposition to suicide-bomber recruiting. From the Palestinian community comes most of the region's bombers. With the help of *Hamas* or *Islamic Jihad,* disconsolation for any reason within the Gaza Strip or West Bank can lead to a young Palestinian's martyrdom. (See Map 4.2.)

Sixteen-year-old Iyad Masri started to withdraw from

everyone. He read loudly from the Koran after midnight, and blasted tapes of Koranic verses from behind his bedroom door.

His parents knew he was distraught over his younger

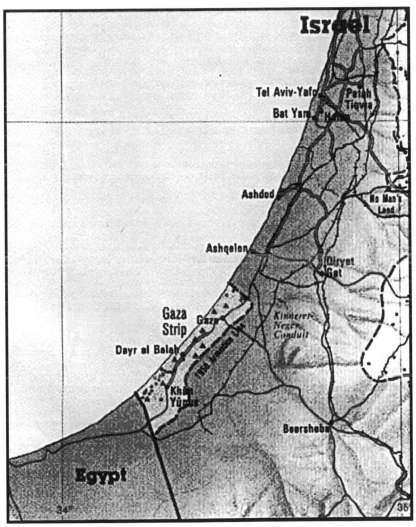

Map 4.2: The Gaza Strip Refugee Camps

(Source: Courtesy of General Libraries, University of Texas at Austin, from their website for map designator "occupied_map.jpg")

brother's death two months ago. But they never imagined that Iyad would consider strapping a belt of explosives around his waist. In early January, he met with members of Islamic Jihad. . . . Iyad died days later when the belt went off accidentally, killing only himself. . . .

Children here have increasingly grown to idolize suicide bombers and others who have sacrificed their lives for the Palestinian cause, says Dr. Eyad Seraj, a psychiatrist in the Gaza Strip. . . . In a poll last summer, 36 percent of 12-year-old boys in Gaza said they believed that the best thing in life was to die as a martyr.[24]
— *Christian Science Monitor,* 5 March 2004

On 24 March 2004, another 16-year-old was stopped just outside an Israeli checkpoint at Nablus on the West Bank. Here, the al-Aqsa Martyrs' Brigade takes responsibility for most of the attacks. The boy's story makes one wonder how farfetched the more risque versions the *Hashishin* conditioning process really are. Something strange is happening to these children. U.S. forces need to find out what it is.

"[H]e has the intelligence of a 12 year old," said his brother, Hosni. . . . "He told us he didn't want to die. He didn't want to blow up," [Israeli Lt.] Milrad said. . . . Abdo's family said the teenager was not affiliated with any militant group, [but was] going to rallies for all of them and identifying with whichever one carried out the latest attack on Israelis. They said he acted strangely Tuesday, giving candy to his family and neighbors and refusing to explain why. He got his hair cut in the style his mother, Tamam, likes and told her he would do anything she wants, she said. "You never are like this," she said. "What happened?" "I just want you to be happy with me," he responded.[25]
— Associated Press, 25 March 2004

[The young boy] was offered $22 for his mother and a trip to heaven. . . . He said, "I will sit in heaven and have fun."[26]
— ABC's Nightly News, 26 March 2004

The *"Intifada* Scrapbook" is the newest fad among Palestinian youngsters. In it, they can attach stickers depicting the various acts of martyrdom so far.[27] This is a war in which psychological manipulation has replaced technological delivery systems. There have also been "paradise" summer camps.

Weekend BBC television footage showed an Islamic Jihad-run summer camp in which young Palestinian boys are given military training and shown pictures of suicide bombers.

"We are teaching the children that suicide bombing is the only thing that make[s] the Israeli people very frightened. Furthermore, we are teaching them that we have the right to do it," said camp counselor, Mohammed el Hattab.

"We are teaching them that after the suicide attacks, the man who makes it goes to the highest state in paradise," he said. In paradise, they are taught, they will be greeted by 70 virgins.

Fourteen-year-old Mohammed was filmed drawing a picture of himself with explosives girded about his body. He said he wanted to become a suicide bomber "to liberate Palestine and be part of the revolution." . . .

. . . [A]ccording to a source who works in the PA [Palestinian Authority] controlled areas and who spoke on condition of anonymity, hundreds of children aged 11-15 are being trained in paramilitary camps in the Gaza Strip and West Bank. The camps are run, not only by Islamic Jihad and Hamas, but also by PLO Chairman Yasser Arafat's Fatah faction.[28]

— Cybercast Service News, 23 July 2001

The Guerrillas' Overall Strategy

The Palestinians are trying to intimidate the Israeli population while strangling their economy. They have already shut down one of Israel's most lucrative industries—its tourist trade.

To what extent this strategy is based on sheer desperation is not totally clear. What is clear is that the Palestinians have managed to capitalize politically on almost every Israeli military excess.

Targets of Strategic Value

The Palestinians have not limited their attacks to restaurants and markets. They have also gone after things of more strategic value to Israel. By bombing buses, they have interrupted its way of mobilizing and transporting reservists.

A couple of years ago, somebody tried to sneak an explosive-laden truck into one of Israel's biggest fuel farms. Luckily, it exploded prematurely. On 13 March 2004, two Palestinian suicide bombers blew themselves up near chemical stores in the well-guarded port of Ashdod.[29]

Ambushing Convoys

Over the years, there have been many attacks upon Israeli convoys. Of late, only the most sensational are reported. However, road minings and RPG attacks still occur.

> An Israeli helicopter strike killed three Hamas militants riding in a car Wednesday [in the Gaza Strip], the second such targeted attack in five days. . . .
> The Israeli military said one of those killed, 24-year-old Tarad Jamal, was behind several roadside bombings and rocket attacks on Israelis.[30]
> — Associated Press, 4 March 2004

Also targeted have been convoys carrying VIP's. For the second time in four months, U.S. diplomatic vehicles were attacked in the Gaza Strip in October 2003.[31]

Tank Killing

One month after a high-tech Merkava "MK III" tank was destroyed in the Gaza Strip, another met its demise within 100 meters of the first.[32]

> [Y]esterday's ambush was much more worrisome than the one on February 14. It showed the Palestinians were not just lucky in the first strike . . .

It appears that the attackers used the same kind of bomb they did last month, when they stuffed nearly 80 kilograms of explosives into an empty water heater and detonated it under the tank. . . .

Officials think the terrorists hid behind a mosque near the roadside and detonated the mine by remote control. . . .

While there are similarities between yesterday's attack and last month's, Brig.Gen. Tzvika Fogel, Southern Command's chief of staff, told reporters at the Karni crossing there were also differences. "More than 240 bombs have been planted in the area recently, and we discovered most of them," he said.[33]

— *Jerusalem Post* (Israel), 15 March 2002

On 10 May 2004, an Israeli "armored vehicle" was blown up by a large explosive buried in a city street at the western end of the Gaza Strip.[34] The very next day in the same location, another bomb in the road destroyed an armored personnel carrier full of troops.[35] According to a former armored division commander, the only defense to this devastating Palestinian technique is varying both route and time.

"In these kinds of wars, one of the most efficient moves is to change the routine and not always drive on the same road, and move at different hours," [Brig.Gen.] Yitzhaki said.[36]

— *Jerusalem Post* (Israel), 15 March 2002

Sniping

Many of the attacks at Israeli checkpoints were the doing of suicide bombers, but not all. In March 2002, a Palestinian sniper killed seven Israeli soldiers and three Israeli civilians at a checkpoint near Ramallah.[37] It is a wonder that these types of attacks do not occur more often. The urban sniper is very difficult to defend against.

In July 2004, from inside Lebanon, snipers killed two Israeli soldiers who were attempting to fix the radio antenna at their border outpost. *Hezbollah's* goal was to keep the Israelis from patrolling.

61

Defensive Tactics

Through trial and error, the Palestinian militants may have discovered some of the finer points in urban defense. During their two-week-long defense of Jenin on the West Bank in April 2002, they lost only 30 fighters to the Israelis' 23. That the Israeli assault also killed 22 civilians bolstered popular support for the rebels.[38] It was a loosely controlled "urban swarm" that halted the German offensive short of the Volga River at Stalingrad.[39] That swarm had tiny, semi-independent elements that attacked any intruder from every direction.

Several regiments of the North Vietnamese Army (NVA) were using a Maoist mobile defense inside the Hue City Citadel in 1968.[40] It consisted of a series of fallback positions on alternating streets. Most were connected by covered trenches. Hundreds of tunnels have now been discovered in Gaza.[41] Some are for smuggling ordnance from Egypt,[42] but others are for local resupply and reinforcement. When strings of fortified buildings or blocks are connected by tunnel, they form a "soft, underground strongpoint defense." This is the state of the art apparatus both self-protection and spoiling attack.[43]

Since the start of the *intifada,* Palestinian militants have dug hundreds of tunnels and used them to smuggle arms and bomb-making materials from Egypt into Gaza.[44]
— *Newsweek,* 5 April 2004

The Second *Intifada's* Successes So Far

As a result of assorted counterterrorist initiatives, the Israeli wall, and local cease-fires, the violence seems to have temporarily slackened. Still, the prevailing view is that this is just the lull before the storm.

The intensity of the strife subsided in 2003. The Israeli government says the conflict killed 213 Israelis in 2003, down from 451 dead the previous year. Palestinians continue to die in larger numbers than Israelis, but also at a reduced rate. The Israeli human rights group B'tselem says

579 Palestinians died in the occupied territories as a result of the conflict in 2002, down from 1,003 a year earlier.[45]
— *Christian Science Monitor,* 11 January 2004

Israel's Strategic Failure

Israel has been attempting a military solution to a societal problem. As a result, it has lost ground in the all-important battle for hearts and minds. *Hamas* and *Islamic Jihad* may have more Palestinian community service projects going than the Israelis.

Historically, Israel used undercover operations to maintain order in the Occupied Territories (Gaza and the West Bank). Of late, it has shifted more toward the American expeditionary model of standoff precision firepower, with little regard for "unintended victims."[46] Between 29 September 2000 and 12 July 2004, the Israeli Air Force extrajudicially executed 90 Palestinians in Gaza and the West Bank.[47] Of course, many around them also died. This "assassination" of resistance leaders has helped little to restore order. It has incensed Palestinians and Israelis alike.

[A] group of 27 Israeli reserve air force pilots signed a petition stating that they would no longer agree to carry out air strikes against Palestinians, calling the attacks illegal and immoral. . . .
Dozens of reserve soldiers in ground forces have opted to go to prison rather than serve in the West Bank and Gaza, reflecting growing Israeli unease with the protracted conflict.[48]
— Associated Press, 25 September 2003

On 22 March 2004, a rocket fired from an Israeli helicopter killed wheelchair-bound *Hamas* founder, Sheik Ahmed Yassin, outside his place of worship.[49] When the U.N. Security Council voted to condemn the attack, 11 countries agreed, three abstained, and one vetoed. That veto came from the United States.[50]

While knocking down homes to widen the buffer zone between the Rafah refugee camp and Egyptian border, Israeli tanks and helicopter gunships fired several shells/missiles into a crowd of protesters on 19 May 2004. By a 14-0 vote (with the U.S. abstaining), the U.N. Security Council condemned the act.[51]

63

Israel's Intended Pullout from Gaza and the West Bank

Israel Prime Minister Ariel Sharon wants to withdraw all 17 Jewish settlements from Gaza and more from the West Bank.[52] This could be viewed as a victory by *Hamas* and *Islamic Jihad* just as Israel's pullout from Southern Lebanon was by *Hezbollah.* Instead of defusing the conflict, it could actually fuel it. After Israeli armor was destroyed at the west end of the Gaza Strip on 11 and 12 May 2004, the Israelis finally acknowledged that they were facing "systematic guerrilla warfare."[53] They have yet to realize that its urban variant is almost impossible to defeat militarily. To defeat Jewish resisters during WWII, the Germans had to flood and completely raze the Warsaw Ghetto.

An Unsettling Tactical Development

As U.S. forces acquire more lethal weaponry, they will be attacked from below ground.[54] Enemy assault forces will hide beneath places about to be occupied or bypass obstacles and sentries through tunnels. During the Lebanese civil war, the Palestinians dug a labyrinth of huge tunnels beneath Beirut. What is now to stop them from doing the same thing in Gaza and the West Bank?

On 27 June 2004, the Palestinians successfully attacked an Israeli outpost at the Gush Katif junction, near Gaza's largest block of Israeli settlements. They did so by digging a 1000 foot tunnel and filling it with 3,300 pounds of explosive. The blast was timed to coincide with a shift change. *Fatah's* al-Aqsa and *Hamas* took the credit.[55]

About the same time, al-Aqsa founder Nayef Abu Sharkh and six of his men were killed in an underground tunnel complex in Nabulus in the West Bank.[56] As the militants continue to expand their tunnel networks, they will eventually discover that they can safely attack and then easily elude any surface opponent. Much of the strategic damage to U.S. forces in Vietnam was done through tunnels.

The Obscure Instigator

While the Israeli Palestinians have many complaints, it is Lebanese *Hezbollah* that is stirring up much of the armed confrontation. When *Hamas* leader Ahmad Yassin was killed in March, *Hezbollah* gunners from within Lebanon shelled the Israeli border posts.[57]

Generally accepted is *Hamas's* affiliation with *Hezbollah* and orchestration of the Gaza resistance. Israel estimates that Hezbollah also controls—through funding and guidance—between 70 and 80 percent of all militant Palestinian cells in the West Bank.[58]

Chechen
Rebels

- Who is now winning in Chechnya?
- Why have the Russians failed to put down the rebellion?

SOVIET JUNIOR TANK LIEUTENANT, 1972

(Source: Courtesy of Orion Books, from *World Army Uniforms since 1939*, © 1975, 1980, 1981, 1983 by Blandford Press Ltd., Part II, Plate 8; *FM 21-76* (1957), p. 88)

The Russians' First Chechen Disaster

The Soviet armored brigade that entered Grozny on 31 December 1994 lost 4800 of 6000 personnel, 20 of 26 tanks, and 102 of 120 armored vehicles within 72 hours.[1] (See Map 5.1.)

The Chechens waited until the armored columns were deep into the confines of the urban sprawl before initiating their ambush with a hail of hit-and-run rocket-propelled-grenade (RPG) attacks.[2]
— *Marine Corps Gazette,* October 2001

Map 5.1: Relief Map of Chechnya
(Source: Courtesy of General Libraries, University of Texas at Austin, from their website for map designator "chechnya_rel01.jpg")

The Chechens had formed tiny, antitank hunter-killer teams—
each with its own machinegunner and sniper to suppress enemy
infantry. Several such teams would pick a place where buildings

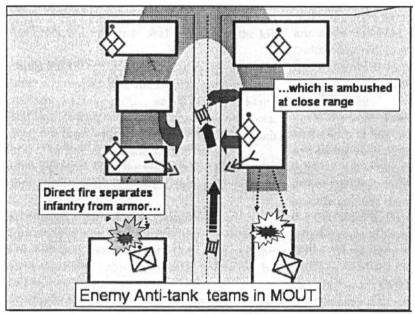

Figure 5.1: The Chechen Ambush of an Armored Column
(Source: U.S. Army, *Infantry Magazine*, January-February 2004, p. 41.)

canalized and restricted the movement of armor. To seal the vehicles in the kill zone, they would deploy in an inverted "U" formation. (See Figure 5.1.) They engaged the Soviet air-defense guns first. Then five or six teams fired—simultaneously—at the Russian tanks from basements, ground level, and upper-story positions on both sides of the street. Well aware of where those tanks had reactive armor, they would aim elsewhere from the top, flanks, and rear.[3] When a second armored thrust was likewise ambushed, the Soviets fired up to 4000 artillery rounds an hour for 20 days just to extract their survivors.[4] After a three-month bombardment, the Russians finally captured the city on 26 February 1995.[5]

In August 1996, the insurgents counterattacked in much the same way the NVA had at Hue City.

[T]he Chechen rebels infiltrated Grozny along three axes and attacked at dawn on 6 August 1996. The Chechens had conducted detailed reconnaissance of Russian garrisons and posts. . . . They used this information as they besieged every Russian position (manned by 12,000 Russian troops) and captured the city in a single day! . . .

The Chechens conducted both tactical and operational maneuver consistent with Maoist revolutionary war strategy. The decisive aspect of this asymmetric approach was their extensive reliance on urban areas to "level the playing field." The Chechens recognized that employing a fixed defense based on urban strongpoints would allow the Russians to bring their firepower to bear, so instead, they used a mobile area defense strategy.[6]

— *Marine Corps Gazette,* October 2001

After losing Grozny in August 1996, the Russians settled for a cease fire and departed the country.[7] Their military campaign for Chechnya had been an operational failure.[8] In 1999, they found a reason to come back.

The Russians' Second Chechen Campaign

In August 1999, a series of unfortunate events dashed the hopes of the Chechen separatists, and the Russians re-invaded with a vengeance. The British Royal Military Academy at Sandhurst has chronicled the effort.[9]

[I]n the morning of 2 August small groups of fighters from Chechnya crossed over the Snegovyy Pass into Dagestan, entered the village of Agvali in [the] Tsumadinskiy rayon [region] and attempted to establish control and Islamic order there. . . . On 7 and 8 August 1999, it became clear that this was no ordinary raid, but an "invasion," a large-scale penetration into Dagestani territory to secure a bridgehead as part of a wider operation. Chechen *bandformirovaniya* (bandit formations) and Islamic extremists numbering up to 2,000 men led by Shamil Basayev and the Saudi Arabian field commander Khattab seized a number of villages in Botlikhskiy and Tsumadinskiy rayony [regions] of Avaristan causing a degree of panic in the Dagestani capital Makhachkala. . . . From 26 August, having 'pacified'

Tsumadinskiy and Botlikhskiy rayony, military action continued with a Federal assault on the Wahhabi villages of Kadar, Karamakhi and Chabanmakhi in Buynaksk rayon with the aim of disarming fighters and destroying the Wahhabi complex which had been a thorn in the side of the Dagestani authorities for over a year.[10]
— Sandhurst Study

By mid-September they [the Russians] had largely concluded their operation in Dagestan. In September 1999, explosions destroyed an apartment block for officers in Buynaksk in Dagestan and apartment blocks in Moscow and the southern Russian town of Volgodonsk. Chechens were blamed by the Kremlin for these bombings. . . .
. . . On 1 October [Russian] federal forces entered Chechnya to set up a security zone. . . . However, . . . their objective appears to have been to crush Chechnya's de facto independence, that had been secured by the Khasavyurt accords of August 1996 and the Russo-Chechen treaty of May 1997.[11]

The second invasion of Chechnya involved 93,000 Russian troops.[12] It was very similar to the U.S. move into Iraq.

Any Chechen positions that were discovered in the course of the advance were quickly engaged by the artillery and aviation available to the company or battalion commander in whose zone of responsibility they were located. Once an area had been occupied bases were occupied and fortified, with platoon-sized strongpoints and smaller checkpoints in key positions. The Russians would then begin to reconnoiter their next advance, using fixed wing aircraft, helicopters, drones, ground patrols, radar and radio intercept, before beginning the process of fire destruction and advance again.[13]
— Sandhurst Study

The Russian Army was then committed to fight in Chechnya itself, and slowly advanced across Chechnya's plains, preceded by conventional artillery fire. When the advance finally reached Grozny and the mountains, the advance stalled. Conventional artillery could not force out the Chechens and the Russian Army looked for other ways to move them. Two methods were apparently proposed—chemical weapons and thermobaric weapons. The Russian political leadership apparently vetoed the use of chemical weapons, but allowed the use of ground-delivered thermobaric weapons.[14]

The Chechen Rural Defense

Despite the "shock and awe" of the Russian bombardment, the rebels fought back. At various places across their flatlands, they excavated an in-depth, strongpoint defense.

Preparations not only included weapons and ammunition caches but also the excavation, digging and fitting out of trenches and strongpoints. When the Federal authorities assaulted the villages of Karamakhi, Chabanmakhi and Kadar they were amazed by the sophistication and echeloning of the defenses.[15]

— Sandhurst Study

The Russians Again Try to Take Grozny

In January 2000 with more "human intelligence," troops, and preparatory fire, the Russians attempted to retake Grozny. This time, their tanks stayed on its periphery.[16]

Tanks and artillery ringed the city while dismounted infantry and special forces personnel, accompanied by artillery forward observers and snipers, slowly crept into the city searching for Chechen strong points. When they found them, artillery and long-range tank fire was directed to eliminate the strong point and crush the building. Large segments of the city were flattened before ground forces moved into the city. The damage to Grozny was much more severe during the second campaign.[17]

— Sandhurst Study

As the battle raged for the city, the Russians showed the rural population what would happen to anyone who tried to lend assistance.

The Observer reported last week that, on Feb. 4, Russian forces killed 363 civilians in the village of Katyr-Yurt using "vacuum" bombs, fuel-air explosives banned by the 1980 Geneva Convention. A similar reprisal attack was reported earlier on another village, Gekhi-Chu, where land-based, TOS-1 fuel multiple-launch [thermobaric] missiles, not fuel-air bombs, were used.[18]
— *Moscow Times,* 9 March 2000

A Change in the Rebels' Urban Tactics

The insurgents fought fiercely against overwhelming odds in Grozny, but fell victim to a cruel paradox of war. Their greater degree of organization made impossible the "urban swarm" they had used in 1995. Still, they showed some initiative. Their use of snipers to alter the attacker's direction has only been noted in one other war—Vietnam.[19]

Chechen tactics remained versatile and flexible. They boarded up first floor windows to slow Russian access to buildings, continued to "hug" Russian forces . . . and operated in a very centrally controlled fashion instead of in the "defenseless defense" or "let the situation do the organizing" mode of 1995. This was an obvious adjustment because the Russians refused to enter the city exposed and in mass formations. The Chechens used trenches more than in the first battle in order to move between buildings. They also positioned snipers in a "misdirection" tactic. . . . They constructed escape routes from their firing positions, and interconnected these positions.[20]
— *Marine Corps Gazette,* April 2000

When the rebels were displaced at night, they counterattacked during the day. When they withdrew along the avenues of least resistance, they often stumbled into Russian minefields.[21] Having endured laser-guided bombs and shoulder-fired thermobaric weapons for almost a month, the main force left the city on 8 February 1999.[22] They left behind a reminder of their growing tactical sophistication.

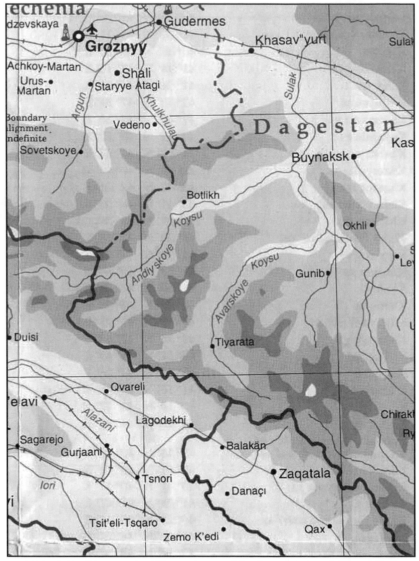

Map 5.2: Mountain "Base Areas" in Georgia and Dagestan

(Source: Courtesy of General Libraries, University of Texas at Austin, from their website for map designator "caucasus_region_1994.jpg")

On 2 March 1999 (almost a month after the city had been declared secure), 300 rebels rose out of the rubble and sewers. They then ambushed a motorized column of elite *OMON* Interior Ministry troops in the same way they had defeated the armored thrust of 31 December 1994.[23]

An estimated 200-300 rebels are still in the Chechen capital of Grozny, even after more than a month of Russian occupation, according to Valery Manilov, deputy head of the armed forces General Staff.[24]
— Cable News Network, 11 March 2000

A top Russian commander said Friday that nearly 37 troops from an elite police unit died in a guerrilla attack Thursday in the Chechen capital Grozny, a city that the Russian military had claimed was completely under its control. . . .
. . . In Thursday's attack, the rebels ambushed a column of riot police traveling in nine trucks to a guard post in the Staropromyslovsky district of the Chechen capital. One eyewitness said the first and last trucks of the column were hit by incendiary rockets and a four-hour battle between Russian forces and rebels using machineguns and grenades ensued.[25]
— Cable News Network, 3 March 2000

A Rearguard Action outside the City

The main rebel force headed south toward the Argun Gorge and their safe areas in the Caucasus Mountains. (See Map 5.2.) Those fighting the first rearguard action were forced by necessity to disperse and defend by "urban swarm." Those tiny Muslim contingents held out for almost a week and then most probably exfiltrated the Russian encirclement.

For the fifth day in a row, crack [Russian] troops have been attacking the village of Komsomolskoye, which was seized by a group of rebels who broke through the Russian lines south of Grozny.

75

The village "is completely blockaded," and Russian troops are now occupying the northern part of it, General Manilov said.[26]
— BBC News, 10 March 2000

Rebels who seized Komsomolskoye on Sunday have reportedly broken into small formations under a relentless Russian assault that has left the village in ruins.
But despite repeated statements that Komsomolskoye was about to fall, the small rebel groups have stalled the Russians with fierce resistance.[27]
— Cable News Network, 11 March 2000

The next rebel stronghold to the south was Shatoi (renamed Sovetskoye).[28] As the town had been bombed continually since November 1999, the retreating rebels didn't stay there long. Ten kilometers farther into the Argun valley—at a place called Ulus Kert— they would repay their tormentors.

A Russian Airborne Company Gets in the Way

Then the Russians decided to block the rebel retreat with an airborne battalion—in the classic hammer-and-anvil maneuver. From 29 February to 3 March 2000, the two forces fought. Though extremely courageous, the commanders of the blocking force lacked the tactical ability—and their troops the individual and small-unit skills—to get the job done. One Russian company was wiped out.

The [6th] company commander established a linear defense in the saddle between the hills, fronted by a minefield facing west toward the gorge. The defense focused on the Chechen forces' expected direction of escape. . . .
At 1230, a 6th Company reconnaissance patrol encountered approximately 20 fighters just outside company defensive positions. That the Chechens could approach that close without detection shows that the Russians had conducted no deep reconnaissance of the approaches to the saddle.
The Chechens, armed with automatic weapons, grenade launchers and mortars, reacted quickly, seizing the initia-

tive. The small force was probably followed by a combat element, which would have been consistent with Soviet-style reconnaissance doctrine that places great value on immediately seizing the initiative in any engagement by having a strong combat element close behind the advance reconnaissance element. Chechen reconnaissance elements also worked their way around the Russian position in the saddle and attacked from the rear [of the terrain] where there were no defenses (TV RTV, 14 March 2000; Sokirko, "Airborne Troops . . . ," *Moskovskiy Komsomolets,* 14 March 2000). With Chechens in the rear and no escape routes through their own minefield, 6th Company pulled back and dug in on Hill 776. . . .

Early in the morning on Hill 1410, a reinforcement group of two VDV SPETSNAZ platoons, one Vympel SPETSNAZ group and two airborne companies departed on foot for the saddle. The group encountered several ambushes while traversing terrain as steep as 70 degrees. At approximately 0330, one VDV SPETSNAZ platoon broke through to Hill 787 but was forced to dig in because of stiff Chechen opposition.

The 1st Company was also sent to reinforce 6th Company. While attempting to cross the Abazolgul River northeast of Ulus-Kert, the unit encountered a Chechen ambush force of up to 60 men. Despite repeated attempts to fight through the Chechen ambush, the 1st Company was forced to dig in on the river's bank. At 0300, during a brief lull, 2d Airborne Battalion deputy commander Major Aleksandr Dostovalov, with 4th Company's third platoon, broke through to the encircled company. While relief forces were being held back by ambushes, waves of Chechen fighters continued to assault 6th Company on Hill 776 (Prokopenko, "To the Death," *Krasnaya Zvezda,* 11 March 2000). When Romanov's legs were blown off by a mortar round, the battalion commander took over. . . .

. . . In his report to defense minister Igor Sergeyev, Shpak states that 2d Airborne Battalion "was supported by a self-propelled artillery battalion of the 104th Parachute Regiment and by army aviation" (Prokopenko, "Eighty-Four Airborne Troops . . . ," *Krasnaya Zvezda,* 11 March 2000). The presence of an artillery forward team with 6th Company, which included a battery commander, indicates that artillery support was at least adequate. . . . Only one Russian helicopter in the Chechen theater had night capability. This supports Shpak's statement that 6th Company received no aviation support at night. Helicopter support was further limited by foggy conditions during the fighting (Kondrashov, "Military Industrial Complex . . . ," *Argumenty i Fakty,* 4 April 2000; Williams, "Russian Admits . . . ," *Washington Post,* 11 March 2000).

The Chechens continued heavy attacks on Hill 776 from all directions throughout the early morning. . . .

At approximately 0500, the Chechens breached 6th Company defenses. . . . The already wounded battalion commander took over the radio from the wounded Romanov and [personally] called in artillery fire on his own position (Falichev, "They Strode Into Immortality," *Krasnaya Zevzda,* 16 March 2000). . . .

. . . The Chechens had been throwing themselves at Hill 776 to keep open a path for the rest of their force. This movement was interrupted by the arrival of the relief force from Hill 1410. Major Andrey Lobanov, commanding a 45th VDV Reconnaissance Regiment SPETSNAZ group, was with this force. He noted that hundreds of pack animals [the rear of the train] had already passed by. The Russians moved into the saddle and found 6th Company's abandoned positions and soon encountered a large Chechen group. The Russians retreated to Hill 787 from which they could cover the saddle. . . .

. . . With the remnants of 6th Company still holding out on Hill 776 and new Russian forces on neighboring Hill 787, the Chechen escape route was dangerously constricted. . . .

Late in the morning [2 March], the 1st Company broke through Chechen forces and reached the battle area. However, it could not relieve 6th Company, which was still under close attack.

The struggle for control of Hills 776 and 787 ended on the fourth day [3 March] of the fighting. The last 11 [Russian] paratroopers on Hill 776 were killed (Wines, "Russian City . . . ," *New York Times,* 15 March 2000; Interfax, 10 March 2000). . . . The surviving Chechens, who had not been able to escape over the saddle before the relief's arrival, slipped back down into the gorge pursued by paratroopers and hunted by helicopters. . . .

. . . The [Russian] force showed a glaring loss of basic tactical skills at the company level during the encounters.[29]
— *Military Review,* U.S. Army, July - August 2001

A Tenuous Calm after Heavy Fighting

The Russians claim their cordon held at Ulus Kert. Yet, the U.S. Army research infers that most of the insurgents got away. Unfortunately, 1,000 of them were "mercenaries" from Arab countries, Afghanistan, Ukraine, Bosnia and the Baltics.[30] As training cadre, such thoroughly seasoned fighters could prove invaluable to *al-Qaeda.*

Rebel commanders claimed that about 2,500 of their fighters had escaped east from the Argun Gorge into the Vedeno Gorge early Friday.[31]
— Cable News Network, 3 March 2000

The rebels were heading for their rest and resupply areas, much as their Afghan counterparts had done. While the base areas for the *mujahideen* had been in remote parts of Iran and Pakistan, those for the Chechens were in the Pankisi (Pankiyskiy) Gorge area of Georgia and Dagestan.[32] This has also been the longtime lair of *al-Qaeda.*[33] To reach it overland from Pakistan, one must traverse Iran.

The Argun gorge provided a lifeline for the Chechens to the south, via Itum Kale to Shatili in Georgia, hence the importance to the Federal Command of controlling this passage. Indicative of Federal difficulties here were the loss of a whole company of airborne troops at Ulus-Kert in March, and in April Chechen ambushes and raids on Federal troop groupings at Staraya Sunzha, Mesker-Yurt and Dzhaney-Vedeno.[34]
— Sandhurst Study

After the Argun Gorge embarrassment, the Russians proceeded to outpost the entire region. Their intention was to curtail rebel activity through long-range observation and supporting-arms fire. However, they only managed to forfeit the initiative. With most of the Russians behind barbed wire, tiny contingents of revolt-oriented civilians could more freely roam the countryside.

After several bloody excursions into these regions, the Russian Army has established a series of garrisons in the cities and towns and a string of outposts to guard the roads. The present Russian plan (May 2000) appears to be to deny the Chechen resistance access to the towns and roads while making sporadic raids into the mountains and forests.[35]

The Rebel Edge at Close Range

The Russians have yet to acknowledge that their mushrooming interest in firepower and technology has all but sapped their ability to win a short-range firefight. In Afghanistan, this political oversight spelled their doom.

During the First Chechen Campaign, Russian losses were particularly heavy in close combat—out to 300 meters. Within that space, Chechen forces "hugged" Russian forces to avoid Russian supporting artillery fire and air strikes while Chechen small arms and RPG fire exacted a blood tax on those same Russian forces. Reluctant Russian conscripts were frequently engaged by older, seasoned Chechens in uneven close fighting. . . . As the Russian military planners prepared for the next campaign, they realized that, whenever possible, it was to the Russian Army's advantage to keep the Chechens at least 300 meters away from the conscript Russian ground force. Three hundred meters is the maximum effective range of the Kalashnikov assault rifle and the RPG-7 antitank grenade launcher when fired against a stationary target.[36]
— Sandhurst Study

The Guerrillas' Anti-Air Defense

The Chechens have learned something of air defense. They also realize the strategic/psychological/media value of downing an opposition aircraft. In August 2002, they succeeded in bringing down a fully loaded Russian helicopter that was flying at an elevation of 600 feet. They did so with rockets and machineguns as that helicopter slowed to land at a Russian base. That helicopter fell into a minefield. Of the 132 troops on board, only 32 survived. Six other Russian helicopters have come down (for whatever reason) since February 2000.[37]

> Chechen air defenses . . . were based on the twin 23mm antiaircraft gun, heavy machine guns, small arms and even an occasional RPG-7 antitank grenade launcher. Some man-portable surface-to-air missiles, such as the U.S. Stinger, the British Javelin, and the Russian SA-7 and SA-14 were available. Chechen air defenders camouflaged their positions carefully and changed them often. Their favorite shot was made at the rear of an aircraft as it was turning, to prevent the pilot from observing where the fire was coming from. Anti-aircraft fire was conducted in short bursts to avoid detection. Tracer ammunition was usually not used.[38]
> — Sandhurst Study

Guerrilla Knowledge of Short-Range-Infiltration Tactics

Few Chechen sapper attacks have been reported, but they may still be occurring. Chechnya is, after all, a part of Asian Minor. Asian forces routinely demonstrate with a big unit while attacking with a tiny, covert element.[39] If that element is skilled enough (as in Vietnam), it leaves little trace of its sabotage. Russia believes it is fighting foreign mercenaries as well as local rebels.[40] If any of those mercenaries are aware of East Asian technique, the Russians are in trouble. That the American and Russian armies now fight very much alike should serve as a warning.

> It is clear to us that both in Dagestan and in Moscow we are dealing not with independent fighters, but with well-trained international saboteurs. They are not self-taught men, but specialists in subversive operations and demolition work.[41]
> — Vladimir Putin, 14 September 1999

81

The New Chechen Strategy

The guerrillas' strategy is to undermine the government's infrastructure while isolating its forces. Most heavily targeted in the first category are fuel sources and travel means.

The criminals are out to destabilize [the] situation in Grozny, Argun, and Gudermes. The document [on a captured commander] gives a detailed description of how Russian helicopters should be brought down, which locals and Chechen policemen should be murdered, and where ambushes on the roads should be set. The criminals are out to prove their worth to their foreign masters. . . .

. . . A joint special operation is under way currently. The federal troops and the Chechen police are trying to restore order in oil production. . . . We destroyed almost 300 mini-refineries in the last four days. . . . Rosneft [the] president and I once met and calculated what oil thefts in Chechnya cost Russia at least $50 million a year! [42]
— Col.Gen. V. Moltenskoy, 28 September 2002
United Federal Group Commander

A Growing *al-Qaeda* Presence

From the very start, the Chechens rebels had a smattering of foreign *jihadists*. Then *al-Qaeda's* true level of commitment became apparent.

Russian intelligence officials have recently been saying that Chechen fighters have been trained and assisted by Osama bin Laden and his al-Qaeda organization.[43]
— BBC News, 19 August 2002

Because some of the Chechen units now have *al-Qaeda* leaders, one wonders about their overall ethnicity. The Russians confirm an increase in foreign fighters but claim that rebel commander Abu Walid was killed in April 2004.[44]

Saudi-born Abu Walid is believed to have taken the lead role in Chechnya's rebel movement, according to U.S. and

Russian intelligence sources. . . . He also trained in Afghanistan, specializing in explosives.[45]
— *Christian Science Monitor,* 13 February 2004

How the Guerrillas Are Currently Fighting

As the Russians have progressively tightened their grip, the Chechen rebels have further decentralized. By so doing, they can more easily flow in and out of the civilian population that provides their sustenance.

[T]he criminals operate in small groups now, 3 - 5 men strong, and always have official papers on them. That's what enables them to set mines, open fire, and disappear in the crowd afterwards. . . . [G]unmen work in shifts nowadays. Take Grozny for example. There are few gunmen in the city center which is full of the troops and policemen. All terrorists stick to the outskirts. As a rule, they operate in groups that come for a week or so. They set a mine or two and disappear again. . . . [G]unmen do not keep weapons at home. Weapons are hidden somewhere nearby for fear of checks.[46]
— Col.Gen. V. Moltenskoy, 28 September 2002
United Federal Group Commander

Mesken-Yurt is a criminal den. A gang at least 50 men strong operated there. Federal convoys were regularly ambushed and fired at in the vicinity of the settlement. . . . The criminals with support of some locals also specialized in abductions by force and assassinations. . . . [A] great deal of weapons were stored there, and illegal oil business bloomed. . . . [W]e found, the local cemetery alone contained a whole arsenal. . . . The documents we found indicate that there was a sniper training school in the village. . . .
. . . A week ago we arrested a major of the local corrupt police, mining the road. Still, it is rather an exception, not a rule. That is why our priority nowadays is to prevent criminal infiltration of the local power structures and local police. We do not want them to commit acts of sabotage and

destroy what we are building in Chechnya with all these
difficulties.[47]
— Col.Gen. Vladimir Moltenskoy, 11 June 2002
United Federal Group Commander

Though tiny, the Muslim elements are still effective. The goal
in war is to destroy the opponent's strategic assets. Three-man
groups can more easily approach those assets. The Chechen rebels
have had RPO-A thermobaric weapons and FAE-tipped RPG-7
rounds for years.[48]

The Russians Are Losing Again

The Russians may now control what's left of Grozny, but they
don't control the countryside. As in Afghanistan, they have assumed
a defensive posture to create the impression of security. As early as
June 2000, their situation was tenuous.

Although the rebels may not be able to repeat their
counteroffensive of August 1966 [1996] in the near future
they retain the ability to hit Russian positions or ambush
convoys several times a day. Russian official casualty figures suggest that they are losing at least 20 men a week
and often about 50. This has been going on for some months
and there is no sign that the Russian forces can reduce this
drain on their manpower.[49]
— Sandhurst Study

Now, the Chechen rebels and their unnamed sponsors are fighting across the entire psychological, political, and media spectrum.
They have also carried the fight beyond their borders.

Chechen rebels continue to kill about a dozen Russian troops
weekly in Chechnya, and are thought to be behind a wave
of suicide bombings this summer. . . . In the latest incident,
a powerful truck bomb exploded on Monday outside the headquarters of the Russian FSB security service [now running
the Chechen war] in Magas, the capital of Ingushetia, next
door to Chechnya.[50]
— *Christian Science Monitor,* 17 September 2003

"Suicide bombings blamed on Chechen separatists have killed more than 275 people in and around Chechnya and in Moscow in the past year [2003]. Russian troops in Chechnya suffer daily losses in rebel attacks and land-mine explosions."[51] The Russians have once again achieved a tactical stalemate, and their morale has begun to suffer.

"Permanent bases in Chechnya are even worse than prisons. They are surrounded by three rows of barbed wire, trenches and a minefield, and the soldiers have nowhere to go. They are surrounded by enemy territory," said Ida Kuklina of the Committee of Soldiers' Mothers.[52]
— *Moscow Times*, 17 March 2004

As in Afghanistan,[53] the Russians still lack the "leg" or light infantry they need to win the war.[54]

Latest Developments from the Battlefield

To look good back home (take fewer casualties), the Russians have now turned much of the fighting over to puppet regime paramilitary police. They have declared Chechnya a secure area and reclassified its guerrilla activity as criminal behavior.

Still the fighting continues near the southern foothills where the rebels are believed to be concentrated. On 13 April 2004, a Russian convoy was shelled near Shali, a vehicle drove over a land mine, and several Russian soldiers were killed when their positions came under fire.[55] The rebels have a mind game of their own. It's called "let the occupier think he is winning, while he actually controls less and less of the countryside." Chechnya's infrastructure is in shambles. As of 17 May 2004, Grozny's Severny airport had still not opened.[56]

When the pro-Putin Chechen president—Akhmad Kadyrov— was assassinated on 9 May 2004, the Russian people may have realized how inept their armed forces really were. Meanwhile, the opposition was getting smarter. To kill the president, they had hidden a command-detonated bomb in the fresh concrete of his reviewing stand.[57]

About 23 June 2004, up to 1000 fighters suddenly appeared in Ingueshetia,[58] a Russian province next to Chechnya. They assaulted

20 police, security, and administrative offices in Nazran, its main city. Chechen separatist leader Aslan Maskhadov took responsibility for the operation and promised a shift in tactics from sabotage to large-scale attacks.[59]

As the election of a new president drew near on 29 August 2004, the rebels tried indirectly to seize control of more Chechen towns. They launched attacks against police stations throughout the region.[60]

Afghan Mujahideen

- *With which tactics did the mujahideen expel the Soviets?*
- *How instrumental was al-Qaeda in that defeat?*

MUJAHIDEEN ANTI-AIRCRAFT GUNNER, 1981

(Source: *DA Pam 550-65* (1986), p. 285)

The Historical Cost of Occupying Afghanistan

Over the centuries, Afghanistan has been invaded by Greeks, Persians, Mongols, British, and Russians. (See Map 6.1.) For those without the sense to keep going, it became a graveyard. In 327 B.C., Alexander the Great only briefly added it to his empire.[1] Though having conquered everything to Punjab in the 4th Century A.D., the Persian Sassanids had little control over Afghanistan.[2] In the 16th Century A.D., Babur—a descendent of Tamerlane—pushed into the area. He preferred Kabul to Delhi, and it became his final resting place.[3] The British entered Afghanistan on three separate

87

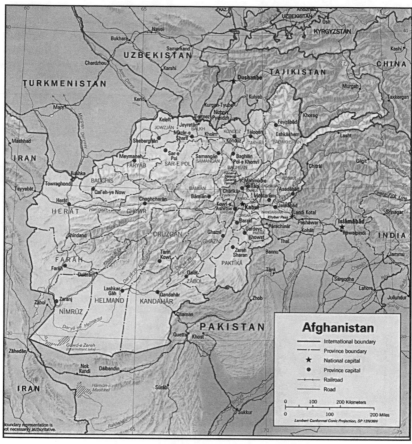

Map 6.1: Relief Map of Afghanistan
(Source: Courtesy of General Libraries, University of Texas at Austin, from their website for map designator "afghanistan.jpg")

occasions: 1839, 1878, and 1897. In the first invasion, only one man survived the retreat.[4] During the last, some 40,000 soldiers got no farther than the Khyber Pass.[5]

The Afghans have learned well how to repel powerful invaders. They do so not by conventional defense, but by discouraging occupation.[6]

Afghanistan's *Hashishin* Tradition

The population is only 15% Shiite.[7] Ismailis are in the minority, but all are Nizaris.[8] "Afghan Ismailis, in the words of Canfield, 'follow the contours of the Hindu Kush Mountain range from its southern extremity in Besud northeastward into the Pamirs, even into Russian Central Asia and Northern Pakistan.'"[9] There is also a large Nizari Ismaili presence just across the Pakistani border in the autonomous northwest territories.[10] To what extent they embrace the *Hashishin* tradition is unclear.

The *Mujahideen*

Afghanistan is a rugged land of Muslim tribal peoples with varying ethnicity and language. Those who declared a holy war or *jihad* against their putsch-installed Communist regime in 1978 became *mujahideen* or holy warriors.[11] When the atheistic Soviets invaded to bolster that regime in December 1979, many foreign nationals arrived, believing it their Muslim duty. They were funneled into a disjointed alliance of tribes. Much of the *mujahideen's* tactical success was due to its lack of organization. A Soviet agent would have found nothing to infiltrate, no irreplaceable head to cut off, and no standardized method to expect.[12]

The mujahideen who warred against the Soviets were really a motley collection of seven Pakistan-based resistance groups, divided by region, clan, politics, and religious ideology. Worse, the resistance commanders inside Afghanistan had only the loosest of links to the seven groups. For them, party affiliation was merely a matter of access to weaponry— the groups were awash in guns and money, provided by the CIA through Pakistan's Inter-Services Intelligence [ISI].[13]

To expel the Soviets, the *mujahideen* received support from several outside sources. "Worried by Soviet expansionism, Pakistan, Iran and then the U.S.A. (especially), China and some European and Arab states began to supply money and arms to the mujahideen."[14]

While the Afghan uprising may have been somewhat impromptu initially, it didn't stay that way for long. By tradition, Afghans like

89

to pile onto a powerful interloper from every direction, fall back, and then repeat the process. That is the essence of a Maoist mobile defense. That every attacker shares the same objective takes the place of orders from above.

Whenever there was any fighting, all the mujahideen would move to the area to help out. All large mujahideen operations were combined and were coordinated by the Mujahideen Council.[15]

The *mujahideen's* first "coordinating agency" was the Mujahideen Council.[16] It probably operated out of Peshawar, Pakistan, as that is where the *mujahideen's* captives were sent.[17]

Then we moved him [the Soviet captive in 1980] to Tezin, near Jalalabad, for a few more days. Finally, we took him across the border to Peshawar, Pakistan, where we turned him over to one of the factions. I do not know what happened to him.[18]
— Shahabuddin, a *mujahideen* commander

At that time [1984] a few Soviet prisoners were kept by the Parties in their unofficial jails on the outskirts of Peshawar. On this occasion Rabbani had thirty-five such captives, together with several suspect KHAD [puppet regime secret police] agents, locked up near his warehouse.[19]
— Brigadier Yousaf, Afghan Service Bureau Chief

Then Pakistan's Inter-Services Intelligence (ISI) got involved. It funneled supplies to the *mujahideen,* provided them with military training,[20] and "struggled to coordinate the actions of the various factions into some comprehensive plan."[21] To do so, it relied on an ingenious method.

Commanders, being Afghans, seldom missed the chance of enhancing their own prestige by fair means or foul. We exploited this by offering training and weapons to those who undertook specific operations in their area; if they succeeded they got more training and bigger and better weapons, thus boosting their status as Commanders. Our policy was as simple as that, as we were never able to issue orders direct to our forces in the field, this manipulating of the supply of arms, and training in their use, was the only effective way of getting an operational strategy implemented.

It was fundamental to our system that training should be mission-orientated.[22]
— Brigadier Yousaf, Afghan Service Bureau Chief

For whatever reason, guerrilla leader Gulbuddin Hekmatyar—a "fundamentalist internationalist"—may have received a lion's share of the aid.

Hekmatyar's [Islamic] party [HIH] received more outside aid from Pakistan, the United States, and Saudi Arabia than any other party.[23]

The Degree of Iranian Involvement

Shiite Iran may have funneled some of its aid through Sunni Pakistan and also operated its own distribution network. Despite ethnic and religious differences, the two countries have always been closely allied. To this day, the Pakistani embassy in Washington, D.C., handles all of Iran's consular affairs.

During the Soviet-Afghan War, much of the Iranian assistance went to the tribes in the predominantly Shiite north around Mazar-e Sharif. The Afghan bands operating along the Iranian border were also given Iranian arms. Among them was the Islamic Revolutionary Movement (IRMA) of Mohammad Nabi Mohammadi.[24] When the Soviets got too close, these bands simply moved their base, staging, and rest areas back into Iran.[25]

There is also evidence of a deeper Iranian involvement at the center of the country. In the Khakrez mountains just northwest of Kandahar was the moderate Harakat-i-Islami (HI), or Islamic Revolutionary Forces. Mostly Shiite, HI had been founded in Iran by Ayatollah Asef Muhsini.[26] It cooperated easily with the fundamentalist Sunni factions around Kandahar.[27]

Al-Qaeda

Al-Qaeda did not appear on the scene until near the end of the

Soviet occupation and will be discussed more in later chapters. Around 1987, it assumed responsibility from the Pakistan-based "Afghan Service Bureau" for recruiting and instructing foreign volunteers.[28] These foreigners traveled to Afghanistan not to defeat the Soviets per se, but rather to fulfill their *jihadic* duty.

The *Mujahideen's* Strategic Objectives

The Afghan *mujahideen* wanted to discredit the puppet regime and segment/isolate its forces. To do so, they attacked infrastructure and sidestepped response. While under assault, they moved backwards. When their opponent retreated, they were close on his heels.[29] They succeeded for many of the same reasons that Stalingrad's defenders had in 1942. Operating in tiny, semi-autonomous groups, they could easily adapt to a fluid situation. All they needed was a little strategic guidance from above.

Attempting to guide the Mujahideen Council was the Afghan Service Bureau of Pakistan's Inter-Services Intelligence (ISI). Its primary objective was Kabul itself.

I had to fight a guerrilla war of a thousand cuts. I knew my enemy's sensitive spots—Salang Highway, aircraft on the ground, the power supply, the dams, the bridges, the pipelines, the isolated posts or convoys and, at the center of them all, Kabul. . . .

Our strategy had three features. First, there was a concerted effort on my part to coordinate attacks aimed at cutting off Kabul from supplies or facilities coming from outside the city. This involved ambushes on convoys on roads leading to Kabul, the mining of dams that provided its water, or cutting its power lines. Next was sabotage and assassination from within. I always emphasized that our targets were Soviets, KHAD agents, government officials and their facilities in Kabul. . . . These attacks could range from a knife between the shoulder blades of a Soviet soldier shopping in the bazaar to the placing of a briefcase bomb in a senior official's office.

The third way of hitting Kabul was by standoff long-range rocket attacks.[30]

— Brigadier Yousaf, Afghan Service Bureau Chief

Like the enemy in Vietnam, the ISI wanted to create the impression that there was no security. By doing so, it could make its opponent assume a defensive posture.

These tactics had the effect of creating a deep sense of insecurity in the minds of the Soviets and Afghans. They reacted by deploying more and more troops in static guard duties, thus reducing their ability to mount offensive operations.[31]
— Brigadier Yousaf, Afghan Service Bureau Chief

Damaging the Opposition's Public Utilities

The Afghan rebels targeted hydroelectric dams and transmission lines. For the dams, they often only had enough explosives to damage control rooms, flumes, and flood gates.[32] Kabul would be most affected by the loss of electricity.

We instructed the mujahideen to throw large stones underneath [the electrical pylons] to set off any mines before laying the charges — a simple, but effective method.[33]
— Brigadier Yousaf, Afghan Service Bureau Chief

Interrupting the Adversary's Lines of Communication

There are fewer means of access to a mountainous region. The *mujahideen* went after the bridges and roads near bases. They marched all night, rigged plastique with copper wire and acid-release pencils, and then beat a hasty retreat.[34] They also went after helicopters. (See Figure 6.1.)

The mujahideen launched never-ending attacks on the Soviets' long, vulnerable lines of communication, both back to the U.S.S.R. and within Afghanistan. Security of the open, western LoC [operational zone] required only three battalions, but the difficult eastern part needed 26 battalions manning 199 outposts and constantly patrolling or escorting convoys. Generally, at any given time, over three quarters of the [Soviet's] Limited Contingent was tied down in

essential security missions of various sorts, drastically reducing the numbers available for offensive action.[35]
— Sandhurst Research

The *mujahideen* also raided the Kandahar Communications
Center,[36] Radio Afghanistan building,[37] and Kabul Metropolitan Bus
Transportation Authority.[38] Kabul airfield came under mortar and
rocket attack continually.[39]

Destroying the Foe's Wartime Supplies

Ammunition and fuel were favorite targets of the *mujahideen*.
They watched for such trucks in convoys, and they attacked their
respective storage facilities.

Figure 6.1: Narrow Valleys Make Helicopters Vulnerable
(Source: *DA Pam 550-65* (1986), p. 209)

To get at the ammunition dump inside the Soviet base at Qarga in August 1986, Abdul Haq's men advanced through wind, rain, and a barrage of butterfly mines.[40] Then four 107mm rockets did the rest.[41] Of note, the planning for this attack took three weeks. Afghan army contacts provided information about where the dump was inside the base. Then the distance from the perimeter to the launch site was measured by pace count. Finally, diversionary attacks on outposts provided enough confusion to carry the rockets to their launch sites. One of those rockets caused a fire that later ignited the ammunition.[42]

The *Mujahideen* Resupply Effort

There are many similarities between how the *mujahideen* and Viet Cong were resupplied. What they couldn't capture from their oversupplied foe, they brought in by carefully hidden resupply routes.

The mujahideen were forced to bring in food and medical supplies, mainly from Pakistan, as well as the weapons and ammunition being provided in increasing quantities from abroad. These had to be stockpiled in a series of dispersed base depots, sited in inaccessible areas. Such bases were also needed for training and rest and the treatment of wounded. Still valuable, but less critical because they were smaller, were forward supply points established to support current operations. The latter could be moved relatively quickly and frequently to avoid attack. The former, on the other hand, required defending. In defense, the guerrillas exploited rugged or otherwise difficult terrain and their detailed knowledge of it. They also put immense efforts into preparing their bases for defense, as for instance in the Zhawar cave and tunnel complex in Paktia province or the green zone of Baraki Barak district between Kabul and Gardez.[43]
— Sandhurst Research

Actually, there were six major resupply conduits into Afghanistan from Pakistan. (See Map 6.2.) One Pakistani route originated in Baluchistan and transited eastern Iran.

There were six main routes leading into Afghanistan (see Map 9 [6.2]). Starting in the north, from Chitral a high route led to the Panjsher valley, Faizabad and the northern provinces. This was the shortest, cheapest and safest passage to these regions, but it was closed by the snow for up to eight months every year. We could only use it from June to October. Next came the busiest route. From Parachinar (the Parrot's Beak) via Ali Khel into Logar Province was the gateway to the Jihad, through which some 40 per cent of our supplies passed. This was the shortest route to Kabul, only a week's journey away. We also used it for journeys north over the mountains to the plains around Mazar-i-Sharif, although this could take a month or more. The disadvantage lay in the strong enemy opposition that tried to bar the way. When the Soviets wanted to decrease pressure on Kabul it was in the eastern provinces that they launched their largest search and destroy missions.

A little further [sic] south, the third route started around Miram Shah via Zhawar, again into Logar Province. Supply trains could either swing south near Gardez or Ghazni, or north to join the second route over the mountains. This was another busy route, but enemy interference was relatively light.

The fourth route started in Quetta, crossed the frontier at Chaman, before leading towards Kandahar and nearby provinces. There was much open country which meant vehicles were required to shift the bulk of the supplies quickly. We aimed to get trucks to their destination in one day's or night's fast driving. Suspicious vehicles were subjected to enemy ground or air attacks.

Over 400 kilometers further west, on the southern border of Helmund Province, was the smaller and unpopular base at Girzi-Jungle. It was used to replenish Helmund, Nimroz, Farah, and Herat Provinces. It was unpopular as vehicles were so vulnerable to attack. Seldom did we send in a convoy without incident. It was an arid, open area, sparsely populated, with little possibility of early warning of attack. Trucks travelling north were easily spotted from the air and were often shot up by gunships or ambushed by heliborne troops propositioned ahead of them. To reach Herat by vehicle took a week.

Finally, the sixth route was via Iran. A glance at Map 9 [6.2] will show that to get supplies quickly and safely to Farah and Herat Provinces a long drive west along the Baluchistan border to Iran, then another 600 kilometers north from Zahedan in Iran to the Iran-Afghanistan frontier opposite Herat, a three-day journey, was the answer— in theory. In practice it was very different. Although we did use this route it took up to six months for the Iranians to grant a special permit, then only small arms could be carried, while every convoy was checked, inspected and escorted by Revolutionary Guards. It was the same when our empty vehicles reentered Iran.[44]

      — Brigadier Yousaf, Afghan Service Bureau Chief

There's no telling how many U.S. "Stinger" missiles were issued to the rebels and never used. It is known that the Passadars (Iranian Border Scouts) absconded with several in 1987.[45] The *mujahideen* may have also gotten a sophisticated piece of barrier-breaching equipment.

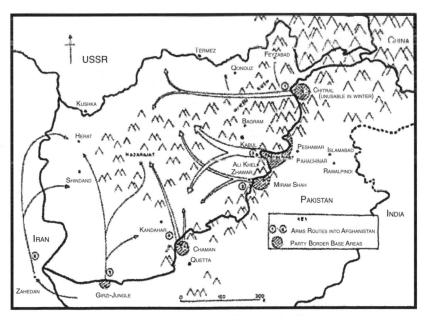

Map 6.2: *Mujahideen* **Resupply Routes**
(Source: *Bear Trap*, by Brigadier Mohammad Yousaf and Maj. Mark Adkin, © n.d. by Leo Cooper)

97

In the same week in April 1988 that the Soviet Union signed an agreement in Geneva to withdraw its troops, terrorists blew up an ammunition depot outside the Pakistani capital of Islamabad. . . . The equipment destroyed at the depot was destined for the mujahideen. It included a large shipment of primacord, a rocket-fired cable that explodes two feet above the ground.[46]

Whatever else the rebels needed they stole from opposition convoys and outposts. Unfortunately, the Soviets combat-tested several of their thermobaric systems in Afghanistan.[47] From Soviet convoys, the rebels may have captured early prototypes of the shoulder-fired "Shmel."

Some [Soviet] platoons were being equipped with a highly demoralizing incendiary weapon. It resembled a bazooka [unlike the "Tanin" RPG system] and fired a shell up to 200 meters which exploded into a fireball on hitting the target.[48]
— Brigadier Yousaf, Afghan Service Bureau Chief

Another veteran of Afghanistan, the RPO-A [Shmel "Bumblebee"] flamethrower is a shoulder-fired, single-shot, disposable weapon. . . . It weighs 11 kilograms (24.25 pounds). The Shmel's zone of destruction is 50 meters in the open and 80 meters inside a structure (Human Rights Watch).[49]
— Sandhurst Study

Mujahideen Tactics

The Afghan guerrillas attacked often. Among their favorite targets were opposition headquarters and convoys. Every time they ambushed a convoy, they severed their foe's lifeline and resupplied themselves. The *mujahideen* would only defend when backed into a corner. With little firepower, they relied on surprise during both offense and defense.

While not nearly as tactically sophisticated as an East Asian guerrilla, the individual Afghan fighter had the field skills, initiative, and courage to make him a natural infiltrator.

Ambushing Motorized Columns

The *mujahideen* made the attack of a convoy into an art form. As previously ambushed stretches of road were seldom reconnoitered by dismounted Soviet infantry, "the guerrillas used favorable sites (and field works) time and again."[50] The Afghan rebels learned to take out command vehicles early because they knew that "junior Russian leaders were often unable to take over effectively."[51]

To maximize surprise, the *mujahideen* would often attack a whole convoy at once. Sometimes that meant spreading tiny teams over a distance of 5-7 kilometers.[52] As they routinely formed six-man teams,[53] they may have also discovered a particularly lethal variation. Picture RPG teams digging spider holes beside a road at the same interval that trucks doctrinally maintain. By all popping up at once, those two-man teams could have done some real damage.

After firing their RPGs, the rebels would normally withdraw. If after the convoy's cargo, they would instead dig positions that could withstand bombardment for up to an hour.[54] Then, they pulled out along covered avenues of egress—e.g., stands of trees.[55]

The Afghan rebels would move to these ambush sites before dawn.[56] Then, they split up into several squad-sized groups. Some of these groups were tasked with security or support; others with blocking or assault. To cover the assault group, the heavy-weapons support group was often placed on dominant terrain behind it. By immediately opening fire, it could mask the assault group's location. If in search of supplies, the *mujahideen* had a logistics support and spoils removal group as well. After the ambush, any flank security elements would move to cover the withdrawal.[57] When several groups took part in the assault, they opened fire with RPGs simultaneously. If they had taken turns like the enemy in Vietnam, they could have precluded accurate return fire.

Each ambush formation was uniquely tailored to the terrain. To hold enough vehicles to make the ambush worthwhile, the kill zone was seldom less than 1-2 kilometers in length.[58] Whether the assault groups attacked from one or both sides of the road depended on the availability of cover. It was from one side when a roadside streambed obstructed vehicular counterattack and aided friendly withdrawal.[59] Mostly it was from both sides. Then, the assault groups would sit across from each other only when both were above the road.[60] Highly reminiscent of the East Asian *haichi-shiki* was the *mujahideen* "U-shaped" ambush. It occurred where the road entered a side valley.[61] The quarry took fire from three sides.

Often the *mujahideen* placed heavy machineguns, recoilless rifles, or mortars on the high ground to the direct front or rear of a straight stretch of road.[62] From there, they could more easily adjust their fire.[63] Only in constricted terrain would they mine or otherwise disable the convoy's forward security element. They did so to preclude a "drive-through" by the main body.[64] Occasionally, they planted antitank mines along the road at places where the enemy's armor might deploy after an ambush.[65]

To limit the armored response, the *mujahideen* would sometimes attack when half the column had crossed a bridge.[66] For psychological effect and added protection,[67] their first targets were fuel or ammunition trucks at the middle or rear of the convoy.[68] Often a convoy commander would not take the time to send back enough combat power to deal with such a threat.[69] Normally, the *mujahideen* shot quickly and left before the helicopter gunships arrived.[70] Only occasionally would they close with the convoy to systematically destroy its vehicles.[71] Late afternoon was their favorite time to appear. This limited the Soviet response.[72] Sometimes the ambushers would let a convoy through their site unmolested and then hit it on the return trip.[73] They required only visual signals, as most of their control had been preestablished through rehearsal.[74]

Once—like a Maoist mobile defense—the *mujahideen* set up several antivehicle and antipersonnel ambushes in the same place.[75] Soon, the *mujahideen* were enjoying so much success with their roadside ambushes that they began to bait Soviet armored columns. Abdul Haq pioneered the concept of using dummy *mujahideen* convoys to lure them in.[76] As more and more positions were dug at the best ambush sites, the *mujahideen* would reuse those sites over and over (only shifting between holes).[77] They took few precautions with exposed flanks, because the Russians had shown little interest in enemy pattern or ground pursuit.[78]

The Role of the Remotely Controlled Bomb

The improvised explosive device (IED) is not a recent addition to war. Most *mujahideen* mines were of the pressure-release variety, but not all.

The mujahideen were also enthusiastic proponents of mine warfare (during the war, the Soviets lost 1,191 vehicles and 1,995 men to mines). They mostly employed antivehicle mines (often piling three on top of each other for a catastrophic kill) and delighted in improvising huge homemade mines. Mines, sometime command detonated, were usually covered by fire and dug up for reuse if not set off by enemy vehicles.[79]
— Sandhurst Research

In October 1982, I was a *[mujahideen]* combatant. . . . We expected a [Soviet] convoy from Darulaman to Kabul the next day. We all moved to the area at night and surrounded the area. Our mining teams emplaced seven remote-controlled (shartaki) mines. Then they camouflaged them. After positioning two observation posts and designating a detonation team, the mujahideen withdrew. . . .
. . . He [the commander] told the observer to take off his turban and wave it when the first two vehicles had passed the mined stretch of the road. He would do this since we could not see the mined stretch from the detonation position.[80]
— Mohammad Humayun Shahin

Raids

The *mujahideen* also raided Democratic Republic of Afghanistan [DRA] outposts to obtain weapons and ammunition.[81] Only their approach march was like that of the North Vietnamese. Several bands would come together at night along separate routes.[82] They would assemble, hide, and rest for a day. Then, they would subdivide into 20-man assault, support, containment, and supply/evacuation teams. By attacking an objective from three or four directions at once, they could create their own diversion.[83] While one or more assault teams closed in on the objective, support teams covered sister positions by fire, and containment teams ambushed counterattack routes. That way the quarry heard firing on all four sides and didn't know which side of his position to reinforce. The assault teams tried to enter their objective by stealth (or with the help of an inside accomplice). However, they would easily settle for taking it under RPG and machinegun fire from beyond its minefield. To cross such a minefield, the *mujahideen* would sometimes heave huge rocks.[84] During withdrawal, the support team stayed briefly behind.

The location of the outpost made a big difference. Soviet airstrikes and artillery were ineffective in narrow canyons.[85] On one occasion in June 1982, the Afghan rebels closed with a Soviet position by hiding in a flock of sheep.[86] As the sheep drifted away, they hid in the microterrain. When most of the defenders went to dinner, they attacked. To limit air response, the *mujahideen* often hit after 4:00 P.M.[87] They also raided at night because the Soviets were reluctant to leave their garrisons after dark.[88] On one occasion in July 1980, the insurgents had an inside man drug the defenders' evening meal.[89] The *mujahideen* became accomplished raiders, as surviving quarries can attest. Their various ruses and techniques are only now coming to light.

Raids served several purposes. Such high profile attacks as those on the Soviet embassy and the DRA and KHAD (secret police) headquarters and MoD [Ministry of Defense] in Kabul, and on district HQs demonstrated the ability of the mujahideen to strike anywhere, with consequent effects on the morale of both sides. They were used to destroy enemy facilities and/or to draw government or Soviet troops into ambush. Raids on security outposts undermined enemy morale. Above all they were a primary source of arms and ammunition for the guerrillas. Like ambushes, raids depended for success on good intelligence (often coming from within DRA/militia ranks), careful recce [reconnaissance], covert deployment and concentration, flank and rear security, surprise and careful coordination. Fire suppression of supporting posts, quick execution and withdrawal were usually important to negate enemy reactions. The mujahideen generally preferred quite large raiding parties, from scores to a few hundreds of fighters, rather than the dozen or so used by special forces. In part, this was due to the need for manpower to carry off spoils and casualties. Late afternoon and, more commonly, night were the times of choice for raids as darkness generally inhibited enemy reactions and rendered artillery and air support ineffectual. Two major problems beset raiders. Protective minefields were effective

against fighters lacking mine detection and clearance means more effective than a nearby flock of sheep to drive into the obstacle or the use of boulders as stepping-stones.[90]
— Sandhurst Research

The *mujahideen* didn't deploy a base of fire during these raids, but rather posted however many security elements they would need to prevent enemy reinforcement and facilitate their own withdrawal.[91]

Precluding Enemy Reinforcement

During a big firefight in Afghanistan, Soviet or DRA forces could not automatically expect overland reinforcement. The precipitous terrain canalized it, and the guerrillas knew how to take advantage of this fact.

There were occasions when the mujahideen established road blocks at river crossings or in mountain passes which were intended to hold for days or even weeks. This was done in support of other operations, to deny access to mujahideen bases, to prove a point or, on occasion, simply because an ambush developed into a prolonged battle. . . . Indeed, towards the border with Pakistan, where the ground was as favorable to the guerrillas as it was vital, some roads were blocked for months, even years. . . . The town of Khost, for instance, was permanently sealed off from the rest of the country and besieged, and the DRA garrison had to be supplied by air.[92]
— Sandhurst Research

Counterambushing

When deep in friendly country, the *mujahideen* columns took few, if any, precautions. As the conflict dragged on, they got smarter.

More savvy mujahideen commanders took tedious, time-consuming precautions before moving supplies or combat forces. They would check with local guerrillas for intelligence and

to arrange coordination, prove the route and establish security posts on dominant terrain and likely ambush sites. They would vary the routes they used and times of travel. Columns would move well spread-out and in groups with an hour or so between each (not least through fear of air attack); forward, flank and rear security patrols would be formed. Anti-ambush drills would be established and rehearsed: if the ambushers were outnumbered, efforts would be made to roll them up from a flank; if the ambush was too strong . . . , an attempt would be made to bypass and head for the nearest cover.[93]
— Sandhurst Research

As Abdul Haq traveled through the mountains around Kabul, he sent out lateral—as well as forward and backward—patrols to make sure he was never ambushed.[94] Like the East Asians before them, the *mujahideen* travelled in small groups that were widely separated on the same track. To the front and sides of this disjointed snake (within voice range) were often separate reconnaissance patrols.[95]

Breaking Out of a Trap

There are many ways to escape an encirclement. One is hide underground until the tightening noose passes overhead. Another is to make a loud demonstration at one point of the cordon and quietly exit another. A third is to exfiltrate the encirclement.

When cut off by tanks one night in June 1984, 30 *mujahideen* were told to "exfiltrate individually through the intervals between the tanks." "Using masking terrain," they managed to do just that.[96]

Attacking a Strongpoint

The Afghan rebels took their time attacking a strongpoint. In one attack on a hydroelectric dam, they were satisfied to advance 10 meters per night by manually probing through the protective minefield.[97]

In September 1982, 1,000 *mujahideen* surrounded and shelled the well-fortified town of Panjwayee, 25 kilometers southwest of

Kandahar. The shelling had little effect on the well-bunkered roof-top defenders, and the *mujahideen* could not directly assault them. After three days, their commander led a group of 25 men to the edge of town. They quietly dug through the adobe walls of adjoining houses until they reached the town's center. When they popped out, the town's defenders assumed it had already been captured and fled.[98] "Tactically, a 25-man detachment accomplished what a 1,000 man force could not."[99] Attacking a built-up area from the inside out is state-of-the-art. It is like the North Vietnamese "blooming lotus" maneuver.[100]

The attack on a strongpoint was often launched from several sides,[101] as containment groups kept sister strongpoints under fire.[102] While assaulting an outpost for Kabul's Balahessar Fortress in the fall of 1983, the *mujahideen* left tiny security elements to watch their escape route and nearby outposts. The squad-sized assault force fired no small arms in the initial penetration, but relied instead on explosives. This mortar attack ruse was pioneered by the German stormtroopers late in WWI.

> We crept up to the outpost, climbed the wall, got up on the roof of the outpost and then attacked it. I led the assault group. We hit the sentry with a RPG and he vaporized. We blew open the doors with RPG rockets.[103]
> — Shahabuddin, a *mujahideen* commander

Urban Operations

Afghan guerrilla tactics in the city differed from those in the country.

Urban guerrilla groups were usually small, not least through fear of KHAD informers. They lacked the same level of organization, command and control, equipment, training and cohesiveness as their rural counterparts. For these reasons, actions tended to be small-scale and of short duration. They sought political and psychological rather than military impact. Ambushes and raids (for example on the Soviet embassy and the DRA's MoD) were practiced. The favorite tactic, however, was the [nonsuicide] bomb attack. The aim

was usually the elimination of selected individuals or targets and the consequent inculcation of fear amongst government servants and supporters.[104]
— Sandhurst Research

Guerrilla leader Abdul Haq had hundreds of safe houses in
Kabul. Their occupants hid infiltrators, distributed pamphlets,[105]
and occasionally guided raiding parties. Once, a journalist was
transported into Kabul in a secret compartment of a car trunk. First,
the car fell in behind a Soviet convoy. Then, at the last checkpoint,
a DRA friend of the driver conducted a cursory search. Once inside
the city, a uniformed officer drove the journalist to a safe house in a
government sedan.[106] Instead of openly attacking cities and risking
a drop in popular support, the *mujahideen* leaders simply discred-
ited their foe's ability to govern.

He [the guerrilla leader] figured that . . . the best way to
take Kabul was not to take it at all: better to let it implode
through the cumulative weight of Khalq-Parcham infighting, well-timed rocket attacks and defections, and the pick-
ing off of all the government posts circling the city, blockad-
ing it step by step. Lack of food and electricity was something the population would not like but would understand.
Indiscriminate rocket attacks, however, they would not understand. And mass support for the mujahideen was crucial if the Communist power structure was to cave in.[107]

While fully capable of political assassination and prisoner abuse,
the *mujahideen* never singled out groups of Soviet or Afghan citizens for destruction.[108] The code of conduct for *jihad* disallows the
killing of noncombatants unless they directly supported combatants.[109] They preferred to embarrass the government. One night, a
group of Hekmatyar's fighters made it to the center of Kabul undetected, fired mortars and recoilless rifles at the Afghan Defense Ministry, and then fled the city.[110] In a subsequent raid into Kabul, they
dropped off two men on each street corner to cover their withdrawal.[111]

In the city, a *mujahideen* raiding party would sometimes post
100 members along their prospective escape route.[112] They liked to
send one man at a time across streets,[113] travel along rooftops, enter walled compounds through buildings,[114] and clear structures from

the top down.[115] Among their many attack options was burning down their objective.[116] They frequently had inside help. Here's what happened during a weapons raid on the DRA 15th Infantry Division garrison at Kandahar in the fall of 1987.

We crept to the building and saw that our contacts had placed a ladder against the wall for us. Some 50 of our group took up positions outside the compound while our raiding group of 50 climbed the ladder up onto the roof of the building. Then we climbed down from the roof inside the compound walls.[117]

— Akhtarjhan, *mujahideen* commander

Infiltration Tactics

Inside "sympathizers" normally planted the bombs in government locations. Once, rebels became trusted vendors at a bus stop to attack it more effectively. When the vendor's cart blew up, everyone at the stop, an arriving bus, and its passengers were destroyed. Most explosives were detonated by timing pencil.[118]

The *mujahideen* may have also discovered an East Asian trick for destroying enemy aircraft on the ground. As has already been mentioned, the field skills, initiative, and courage of the individual rebel made him a natural infiltrator. Once, a single 107mm rocket purportedly set off a chain of explosions that destroyed eight Soviet planes.[119] A lucky string of mortar rounds was also rumored to have destroyed seven helicopters at Marble Mountain in Vietnam. As Marble Mountain was later discovered to be hollow, there is little doubt as to what really happened. To covertly operate, VC sappers would rig their explosives to detonate during a subsequent indirect-fire barrage. Japanese infiltrators did the same thing at Henderson Field on Guadalcanal. Unfortunately, whoever uses this technique normally has enough ability to easily penetrate a Western-style defense.

Inside the city military and communist government targets were selected for rocket attacks, while acts of sabotage or assassination were undertaken against installations and individuals.[120]

— Brigadier Yousaf, Afghan Service Bureau Chief

107

The *Mujahideen* Defense

As the Soviet-Afghan War progressed, the rebel defense was refined to the point that it could defeat a cordon-type operation.

In the early days, the mujahideen were vulnerable to search and destroy operations. However, they quickly learned through experience to prepare their heartland areas for defense. Capitalizing on their intimate knowledge of the terrain, they created large numbers of well-camouflaged field fortifications with deep, artillery-proof shelters and communications trenches; redundancy was an important feature as the intention was to conduct an active, area, maneuver defense which exploited interior lines. Their forces would be organized in small groups for maneuver between fortifications and the launching of small counterattacks from many directions. A central reserve was kept to reinforce critical sectors at critical times. The search force would precede its sweep with heavy artillery and air attack, usually of minimal effectiveness. When it advanced, however, it would find that the mujahideen defense and local counterattacks slowed and fragmented its efforts and that the intermingling of forces and the poor nature of the targets provided by the guerrillas reduced the effectiveness of supporting artillery and aviation. The problem of fighting through was further compounded by generally poor [Soviet] tank infantry cooperation. . . . The typical two-man fighting position was a 2x3m pit with a log roof topped with 1.5m of earth and rocks. . . . Neither the DRA nor Soviet forces tried to break cordoned areas down into more manageable subsectors, clearing each systematically and thoroughly in turn. Rather, if the offensive made progress at all, the sweep tended to be perfunctory, missing many guerrilla groups. Moreover, large cordons, even when established on favorable ground, tended to be porous and large numbers of mujahideen (expert in the role) would exfiltrate at night as individuals or in small groups.[121]
— Sandhurst Research

In the relatively inaccessible areas that had not been attacked lately, the Afghan defense had flaws. Unfortunately, they were largely based a lack of respect for the now Westernized Soviet tactics.

[M]ujahideen security tended to be lax in areas they controlled or where the enemy had not visited for some time. Security posts were frequently placed too near the target to give adequate notice of an enemy approach so that the guerrillas could not deploy or withdraw in time; and sentries were often inattentive. The problem could be compounded by the lack of fighting positions, plans (preferably rehearsed) for reaction to attack and standard drills to cope with emergencies.[122]
— Sandhurst Research

Tank Killing

Like the North Vietnamese had at Hue City, the *mujahideen* massed their antitank fire at close range from several different directions.[123] This confused the tank's crew and made its accurate return fire almost impossible. Often the Soviet tanks were not engaged until they were 20-30 meters away.[124]

Air Defense

The Afghan rebels liked to bait traps in narrow valleys for Soviet aircraft.[125] As the Russian planes swooped in, they received plunging anti-aircraft or heavy machinegun fire from both sides of the gorge.

When the United States made "Stinger" anti-aircraft missiles available to the *mujahideen* in 1987, the Soviets could no longer resupply the outposts that had already been cut off from ground reinforcement. (See Figure 6.2). They had little choice but to leave the country.

The Individual Skills of the *Mujahideen*

The Afghan rebel was fearless and relished close combat. He

expected to be cut off and outnumbered, and prepared accordingly. He spent much of this time outdoors and could easily blend in with his surroundings.

He had two conflicting traits: hospitality and vengeance. He felt protective of foreign asylum seekers and obligated to take revenge for any killing of his family or tribe.[126]

Signalling

In a world of electronic eavesdropping, the guerrilla has only to revert to the nonelectronic means of communication. The *mujahideen* used runners.[127] During an attack on a government installation, they would sometimes use a flashlight to signal to their inside man to open a gate or lean a ladder.[128] The remote controller of a vehicular ambush could be signalled by waving a turban.[129]

Sniping

A single sniper can cause a large Western force to delay or change direction. Among the Afghan *mujahideen's* favorite tactics were sniping and ambush.[130] With those two tactics, they could disrupt the invader's momentum.

The Specter of Mao

General Akhtar Rehman—Head of the Pakistani ISI—had wanted to turn Afghanistan into a Vietnam for the Soviets.[131] His intent alone implies interest in the Maoist method. China does, after all, abut both Afghanistan and Pakistan. Some of the guerrilla leaders were Maoist.[132] One would expect similarities between autonomous tribes and infantry elements that can shift at will between mobile, positional, and guerrilla warfare.[133] Both are loosely controlled and thus heavily reliant on the frontline fighter's initiative. And both have had to contend with the Western Goliath. While big and powerful, that Goliath telegraphs his every intention (through aerial surveillance or preparatory fire), lacks light infantry, attacks only in the daytime, slows when engaged, and gets confused by multidirectional return fire. To U.S. veterans of the inane

Figure 6.2: U.S. "Stinger" Downs Soviet "HIND"
(Source: *Corel Gallery Clipart—Weapon, One Mile Up, #45A117*)

Vietnam-era "sweeps," the *mujahideen* recollections in *Afghan Guerrilla Warfare* will seem like a cruel out-of-body experience. The similarities between Afghan and Vietnamese guerrilla tactics are startling. (That the North Vietnamese and Viet Cong based their methods on the teachings of Mao has been amply proven in *Phantom Soldier* and *The Tiger's Way.)*

Indicative of a Maoist mobile defense is wide dispersion, close combat, and rearward movement. A powerful intruder is allowed to enter the position and is then attacked at close range from every direction at once. He cannot employ his supporting arms for fear of hitting his own people. By the time he gets his bearings, he is facing only a rearguard. The tiny *mujahideen* factions lived in the separate villages at the periphery of their assigned defensive sectors.[134] As the Japanese, Chinese, and Vietnamese had done before them, they constructed artillery/bomb-proof shelters near their fighting holes.[135] These fighting holes were redundant so that the loss of a few would not compromise the formation.[136] Having more emplacements than necessary also reduced the effect of aerial bombardment. What resulted in Afghanistan's "green zone" was a strongpoint defense that was highly reminiscent of the flatland VC. As in Vietnam, the Afghan rebels placed mines to the front of their positions to slow down opposition sweeps.[137]

The mujahideen build elaborate camouflaged defensive shel-

111

ters and fighting positions connected with interlocking fields of fire, communications trenches, and redundant firing positions.[138]

The mujahideen would emerge from their bunkers, occupy fighting positions and wait for the approaching [Soviet or DRA] infantry. We were hard to see since we had excellent fighting positions and wore garlands of grapevines as camouflage. We let the enemy get closer than 10 meters before opening fire.[139]

— Akhtarjhan, *mujahideen* commander

Our SOP [standard operating procedure] for defense against an attack was to spread the forces over a large area at strongpoints in some 20 villages. . . . We fought the enemy in the green zone by confronting him with multiple pockets of resistance anchored in fortified fighting positions. When the enemy tried to concentrate against one pocket, mujahideen from the other pockets would take him in the flanks and rear. The enemy could not fragment his force to deal with all the threats, but had to stay together for security. We would let the enemy chase us from strongpoint to strongpoint and attack him whenever we could. Eventually, the enemy force would become exhausted. . . .
. . . We had covered [bomb] shelters and covered fighting positions in each village. The enemy was very stylized and never did anything different. We knew from where they would come, how they would act and how long they could stay. Our defensive positions were connected with communications trenches while the [Soviet and DRA] enemy was always in the open. . . . We had two kinds of maneuver. One was the dispersal maneuver [like the Chinese cloud array] forcing the enemy to chase all over to find us. The second was internal maneuver within a strongpoint where we could shift between positions without being observed. We had these positions in the villages and throughout the area. . . .
. . . The enemy infantry was the weakest part of their armies—DRA and Soviet.[140]

— Mawlawi Mohayddin Baloch, *mujahideen* leader

The *mujahideen* also kept a mobile reserve of 150-200 men resting within each sector. "Every evening [night], the relief group would move forward, carrying rations and relieve the force that would go back and rest for two days."[141] If the defense became untenable, that reserve probably acted as decoy/rearguard while the others broke contact.[142] As the attacker entered the village complex, the *mujahideen* fell back along carefully reconnoitered routes to backup positions.[143] From there, they continued to engage him, allowing their brethren to move out of his line of fire. Before they left the area altogether, they would bury their ammunition.[144] As in Vietnam, the sweeps were so cursory that the individual guerrilla had only to hide below ground to escape it.[145] To give the majority of defenders time to escape an encirclement, the factions nearest the intruder's avenues of advance would block them.[146] This included both roads and LZs (landing zones). During a single helicopter assault in April 1986, the *mujahideen* captured 530 DRA commandos by quickly overrunning an active LZ.[147]

> They learned to mine likely LZs, [to] employ massed RPG fire against hovering or landing helicopters, and to . . . overrun a[n] LZ before the air assault forces had an opportunity to get organized.[148]

Where the terrain was precipitous, the *mujahideen* placed machineguns along both edges of narrow canyons.[149] From there, they could use plunging fire to defend against helicopter assault. When those machineguns were additionally recessed in caves, they became virtually immune to aerial bombardment.[150] The *mujahideen* also dug caves near their fighting holes to give them protection from bombardment.[151] When Soviet smart munitions blocked (and then unblocked) their tunnels in April 1986, they began to make connecting tunnels between caves.[152]

Prominently displayed on the Pakistani ISI map are the "Party Border Base Areas." (Look again at Map 6.2.) In Maoist jargon, a "base area" is a place where guerrillas can rest and refit.[153] To confound the Western mind, Mao also called each guerrilla contingent's temporary encampment a "base area."[154] Almost every one of the 95 *mujahideen* interviewed in Lester Grau's book talks of his "bases." The impoverished Afghans didn't have Western-style "bases." That the *mujahideen* so freely used the term again infers that Mao's miniature "base area" concept (in which each encampment routinely moves) was in general practice. In Vietnam, the guerrilla bands continually rotated between the "underground hide facilities" of the 10 or so hamlets in each commune.[155] The hamlet temporarily serving as hideout was carefully ringed with boobytraps. Perhaps the most compelling evidence of this maneuver in Afghanistan came from the commander of a group of guerrillas in March 1983. "At that time, we did not have a permanent base but moved from village to village in the Dara-i-Nur Valley." Later, another *mujahideen* commander admitted to moving between four different village/suburb bases.[156]

To transit a suburb on the way to an urban objective, the *mujahideen* would enlist the help of local guerrillas.[157] Using local inhabitants as guides is also the way North Vietnamese maneuver elements avoided both U.S. ambushes and Viet Cong boobytraps 30 years ago.

Also as the Viet Cong had done, the *mujahideen* took ordnance from an overstocked opponent and food from a supportive population. Whatever else the Afghan guerrilla parties needed, they brought from Iran and Pakistan along well-established supply conduits.[158] From the ISI's Ojhiri Camp in Rawalpindi, the supplies went to forward ISI depots in Peshawar and Quetta, and then into party warehouses for transhipment along the various routes.[159] (Refer back to Map 6.2.) One supply route originated at Miram Shah, Pakistan.[160] Its waystations just inside Afghanistan were elaborate and below ground.[161] Due to the region's scarcity of vegetation, most of the conduits probably followed narrow gorges or irrigation ditches/tunnels whenever possible.[162] They then branched out into thousands of feeder routes, each leading to its own terminal cache.[163] These caches were often hidden below ground, just outside of the towns and villages.[164]

While the 2001 publication *Phantom Soldier* discussed Communist tactics in Korea and Vietnam, the U.S. Special Forces community claims it accurately predicted how the Afghan opposition would fight in 2002. All guerrillas depend upon the common sense of the bottom-echelon fighter and thus dabble in the methods mentioned above. But not all make collective common sense into standard operating procedure. Mao is the recognized authority on guerrilla warfare. A "bottom-up" Asian culture more easily assimilates his concepts or their homegrown equivalent. To be doing Mao-like things, the Pakistanis and their Afghan affiliates need not have Chinese manuals or advisors.

A Summary of the *Mujahideen's* Tactical Shortcomings

As the *mujahideen* became less afraid of their largely predictable and increasingly besieged adversary, they developed two bad habits: (1) neglecting to provide local security while deep within their own territory, and (2) using the same ambush sites over and over.[165]

The Soviets' expeditionary force depended almost entirely on artillery and air support and seldom went after their opposition on the ground. As a result, that opposition got used to a particular way of fighting. A more responsive occupier could have capitalized on that pattern.

While the Afghans instinctively sought to damage or capture Soviet supplies, they had trouble seeing why it should be done secretly (to limit the response and protect the method). For this reason, they had difficulty embracing tactical innovation.

In fact what was wrong with my method was that it lacked noise and excitement. It was not their [the *mujahideen's*] way to fight, with no firing, no chance of inflicting casualties, no opportunity for personal glory and no booty. Their method was to bombard the posts with heavy weapons by night at long range, move closer to fire mortars, get 30-40 men to surround them, and at short range open up with machineguns, RPGs and RLs (rocket launchers). If the garrison withdrew, the posts were captured and the mujahideen secured their loot in the form of rations, arms and ammunition, all of which could be used or sold. Then, only then, was the charge laid on the fuel pipeline. If the garrison stuck it out, the pipeline remained untouched.

It often took a serious setback, with quite severe casualties, to force a *[mujahideen]* Commander to review his methods. Like most soldiers the Mujahid hated digging. He was decidedly unhappy in a static defensive role; it was alien to his temperament; it restricted his freedom to move, and he could seldom be convinced of the need to construct overhead cover. Similarly, his fieldcraft was often poor as he was disinclined to crawl, even when close to an enemy position. The hard stony ground, or the possibility of mines, may have had something to do with it, but I had the im-

pression that it was a bit beneath his dignity. Walk, or crouch perhaps, but crawling was seldom acceptable.[166]
— Brigadier Yousaf, Afghan Service Bureau Chief

7 More Recent Afghan Resistance

● *Where did the Taliban come from and go?*
● *How is the U.S. occupation being contested?*

TALIBAN SUPPORTERS, 1994

(Source: *DA PAM 550-65* (1986), cover)

The Rise of the Taliban

Early in 1994, disillusioned *mujahideen* under Mullah Mohammad Omar and *madrasa* students from the Pakistani refugee camps coalesced to form the Taliban ("students"). They attacked local warlords and soon acquired a reputation for military prowess. By October 1994, their movement had attracted the support of Pakistan. Taliban forces took control of Herat and then Kabul. Soon, they would be providing refuge to *al-Qaeda.*[1]

In February 1998, *al-Qaeda* chieftain Osama bin Laden declared war on the United States. At the same time, he issued a *fatwah*

117

(religious degree) authorizing the killing of American civilians.[2] When *al-Qaeda* then bombed two U.S. embassies in Africa, the U.S. launched cruise missiles against its camps in Afghanistan. After the 11 September 2001 tragedy, U.S. forces invaded Afghanistan to drive the Taliban out of Kabul and *al-Qaeda* out of sight.

Afghanistan has since fallen back into its historical pattern of factional strife. The U.S.-sponsored regime controls little of the countryside.

Afghanistan remains a land controlled by private armies, militias, and armed gangs, each with its own ethnic power base and ambition to get a piece of the national pie.[3]
— *Christian Science Monitor,* 14 October 2003

Where Did *al-Qaeda* and the Taliban Go?

At Pakistan's border with Afghanistan are its North-West Frontier Province (NWFP) and four federally administered tribal areas. These semi-autonomous areas were never conquered by the Persians, Mongols, or British.[4] They have largely escaped government interference since then.[5] During the Soviet-Afghan War, the *mujahideen* could easily rest and refit within the refugee camps that sprang up all along this tribal belt. They received intelligence, strategy, and other "headquarters-like" support at the camps outside Peshawar, the capital of NWFP.

The mujahideen safe-havens in Pakistan and Iran were absolutely essential for the survival of their force. Pakistan was particularly important since most of the external aid came through Pakistan. These safe havens allowed the mujahideen a place to shelter their families, resupply, treat their wounded, train, sell war booty to support their families, rest and exchange tactical information and intelligence.[6]

From this remote region, the Pakistani ISI orchestrated the war. Its leader—Gen. Akhtar Abdul Rehman—favored the creation of an Islamic State but tried to distribute arms based on each party's strategic contribution. "In practice some 70 percent of logistic support was given to the fundamentalist parties," according to his Afghan Service Bureau chief.[7] His bureau also provided training contact teams and tactical advisors to the mujahideen until 1987.[8] Ahmed Shah Massoud—the North Alliance's legendary leader— claimed the Taliban were using Pakistani advisors as late as mid-1999.[9] The Taliban still operate out of Pakistan's border region,[10] as they share ethnicity with its Pashtun tribesmen. While that border is long and its terrain precipitous, the Taliban have at their disposal a preestablished network of infiltration routes and waystations.

Recently getting more involved in Afghanistan is a paramilitary affiliate of the same Pakistani party that ran the Taliban-producing *madrasas*. Previously, it fought mostly in Kashmir. "Closely linked with Osama bin Laden's al-Qaeda group . . . [is] the Harakat ul-Mujahidin *[(HUM)* that] operates terrorist training camps in Afghanistan in conjunction with al-Qaeda."[11]

The HUM is an Islamic militant group based in Pakistan that . . . is politically aligned with the radical political party, Jamiat-i-Ulema-i-Islam['s] Fazlur Rehman faction (JUI-F).

[It is] based in Muzaffarabad, Rawalpindi, and several other towns in Pakistan, but members conduct insurgent and terrorist activities primarily in Kashmir. The HUM trained its militants in Afghanistan and Pakistan.[12]
— U.S. State Dept., "Patterns for Global Terrorism"

Al-Qaeda's Headquarters

While bin Laden is believed to spend much of his time in Afghanistan's inaccessible Kunar province,[13] he has other headquarters. One is near Wana in South Waziristan. Pakistani troops combed the area for months in early 2004.[14] Here, there are concentric circles of walled compounds that could provide early warning of ground assault.[15] In January 2004, Pakistani troops raided three such compounds in the village of Kosha. After returning fire, all 15-20 foreign occupants escaped.[16] This may mean that most compounds have escape tunnels or "hide-below-ground facilities" like the hamlets along Vietnam's northern border.[17] In March 2004, thousands of Pakistani troops cordoned off a 25-square-mile area southwest of Wana. Inside this cordon, they encountered fierce resistance from Arab, Uzbek, Chechen, Uighur (Muslim Chinese), and

119

Yargul Keil (local clan) fighters.[18] The Yargul Keil are a subgroup of the Zali Khel clan of the Ahmed Zai Wazir tribe that fought the Soviets and "is believed to be leading the resistance to the Pakistani military onslaught."[19] The villages encircled are Shin Warzak, Daza Gundai, Kallu Shah, Ghaw Khawa, and Khari Kot.[20]

Pakistani officials say some 400-500 al-Qaeda militants are engaged in the fighting. Local tribal sources say the foreign militants also have been recruiting and training some 2,500 tribesmen, which locals call the Men of al-Qaeda.[21]
— *Christian Science Monitor,* 23 March 2004

The walled compounds were square and arrayed in concentric circles around a headquarters complex. That complex was, in turn, surrounded by cleared fields. (See Figure 7.1). On 22 March 2004, another group of encircled militants escaped. Below their position were tunnels, one two kilometers long.[22] While the compounds along each concentric circle may have been connected below ground, it is more probable that those along each radial were. At least, that was the case in the Vietnamese hamlet array. (See Figure 7.2.) The long Pakistani tunnel led beneath the town of Kaloosha (Kallu Shah) to the mountains.[23]

Forces first found a tunnel connecting the heavily fortified compounds of two tribal elders. . . .
From that passage, they found the mile-long tunnel running under the town of Kaloosh, about nine miles from the Afghan border, to a dry steam bed on the edge of the . . . mountains that straddle the frontier.[24]
— Associated Press, 23 March 2004

Because of the frequency of tribal clashes, there are well-armed, fortress-like compounds throughout the Pakistani tribal belt.[25] When in the area, bin Laden almost certainly shifts between ten or so villages, just as the Maoist groups did in Vietnam. "Taliban operatives also say that wherever bin Laden stops these days, he tells his followers to plant mines and pockets of high explosives around his clandestine bivouac."[26] This again is how the VC bands protected their currently occupied headquarters.
During the sweep of March 2004, Pakistani troops met "[some] 'fierce resistance' from . . . fighters entrenched in fortress-like build-

ings" and had to pound with artillery and helicopter gunships several "fortress-like, mud-walled compounds."[27] As at Iwo Jima, each compound was probably protected by the interlocking machinegun fire from the two behind it.[28]

> Hundreds of Pakistani troops have moved into three South Waziristan towns—Azam Warsak, Shin Warsak and Kaloosha—against entrenched positions. . . .
> About a dozen helicopters buzzed over Wana, the main town in South Waziristan, early Thursday, flying toward the operation zone about six miles to the west. . . .
> The raid has sparked outrage in the tribal region, which fiercely covets its autonomy and has resisted outside intervention for centuries.
> In another part of the tribal region, North Waziristan, attackers launched a rocket and fired gunshots at a Paki-

Figure 7.1: *Al-Qaeda's* Flatland "Strongpoint" Defense
(Source: Courtesy Associated Press, captioned "Al-Qaeda Cornered," from "U.S. Assists Pakistan in Battle," by Riaz Khan, 20 March 2004,© 2004)

stan army post before dawn Thursday. . . . The official also said assailants threw a hand grenade at an army truck heading to Miram Shah, North Waziristan's main town [and old arms route entrance].[29]
— Associated Press, 18 March 2004

A Sophisticated Defense

The Pakistanis were "badly mauled" in their attack on *al-Qaeda's* refuge, according to ABC's Nightly News.[30] They had sent in 10,000 military and paramilitary troops, backed by artillery and helicopter gunships, against 400-500 *al-Qaeda* fighters.[31] Of the 100 killed, most were Pakistani soldiers, and only a "handful" were foreign fighters.[32] The rest of the rebels escaped the cordon, with none being captured.[33] This is what a soft, underground strongpoint defense can do for an undergunned defender.

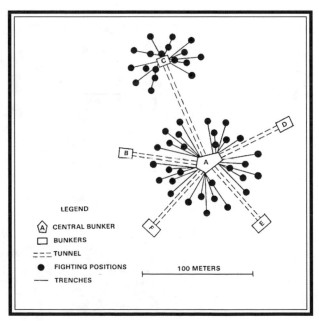

Figure 7.2: East Asian Strongpoint Pattern
(Source: *Counterguerrilla Operations*, FM 90-8 (1986), p. A-6)

Unfortunately, one of bin Laden's suspected hideouts near Kandahar is also a "mud-walled complex" with "drainage tunnel!"[34] "Concentric circles of walled compounds" are characteristic of Pashtun villages through Kandahar and Helmand provinces.[35] Perhaps others constitute, or have been converted into, below-ground strongpoint clusters. As in Vietnam, they could function as flatland "base areas." The first paramilitary unit into the Wana complex encountered fire from all sides. It had many of its own men killed and captured.[36]

The Pakistani Border Remains Porous

As was the case during the Soviet-Afghan War, the Pakistani ISI may have its own private agenda. If it doesn't, *Jamaat-i-Islami* or *Jamiat-i-Ulema-i-Islam* does. This will make the closing of *al-Qaeda's* safe haven virtually impossible. During the massive Pakistani sweep of March 2004, the border remained open.

> An hour's drive from where Pakistani troops are waging their biggest assault ever against al-Qaeda, men of fighting age stream back and forth across the border unhindered by lounging Pakistani guards. . . .
> Flags of Pakistan's ultraconservative Jamaat-i-Islami religious party hung among the buildings on the Pakistan side of the border. . . .
> Afghan officials in Paktika province, across the border from South Waziristan, also voiced skepticism about the raid. They said it was a show put on by Pakistan for the Americans—repeating the common charge by many Afghanis that Pakistan, a one-time patron of the Taliban, continues to support the hard-line militia privately while publicly aiding the United States.[37]
> — Associated Press, 21 March 2004

After sweeping South Waziristan, the Pakistani Army released 50 of the local "Men of *al-Qaeda*" and granted amnesty to five more, in return for their promises to not aid foreign fighters. It did so in an attempt to remove the tribal support for *al-Qaeda*.[38] While the Pakistani government also offered amnesty to foreign fighters, none had registered by the 30 April 2004 deadline.[39] Meanwhile, "frequent attacks continued on the American forces just across the border."[40]

What Goes On Just inside Afghanistan

Right across from Wana lies the Afghan province of Paktika. From firebases Shkin and Orgun, motorized U.S. troops patrol the border.[41] As the Russians before them, they have been repeatedly ambushed at various chokepoints in the road. These chokepoints are often situated in ravines close to tree cover. "The ousted militia has staged several ambushes and frequently fires rockets at U.S. bases in the area, with fighters retreating across the border into Pakistan afterward."[42] After one such encounter, the U.S. reaction platoon narrowly avoided ambush by paralleling (instead of following) clearly defined footprints in a gully. According to the 10th Mountain Division troops, the enemy was inflicting casualties to get a shot at a medical-evacuation helicopter.[43]

There is ample evidence of cross-country infiltration routes, but they have yet to be exploited. As in Vietnam, U.S. units may have failed to use enemy sightings to establish each approximate trace and mantrackers to pinpoint its trail. While the CIA is using a few mantrackers in the region, most guerrillas in transit have probably eluded the U.S. interdiction effort. U.S. forces cannot enter Pakistan without undermining the political position of its friendly President Musharraf.[44]

[W]hat draws U.S. forces to this unexplored part of Paktika . . . is an anomaly of sorts: a sparsely inhabited district with well-tended roads—roads leading to border crossings such as Khan pass that have for centuries served as conduits for Afghan trade, and that today are known to be frequented by al-Qaeda and Taliban fighters. . . .

Suddenly, around 7:00 A.M. [on 25 October 2003], an intense barrage of fire from heavy machine guns, AK-47's, and rocket propelled grenades (RPGs) bombard the [U.S.] convoy from several positions on the high ground to either side of the road. . . .

. . . "The enemy had a wedge formation. They were prepared and experienced fighters," says Hamid. . . .

The problem is rooted in a clever, virtually invisible enemy. . . .

. . . [A]sk any 10th Mountain infantryman on his second tour here, and he'll rattle off a list of what the enemy has learned. . . .

Guerrillas in Paktika have a "robust early warning system alerting them to U.S. troop movements, according to a military intelligence officer. They communicate using radios and wireless phones. . . .

Along a likely escape route, 1st Lt. Richard Steinbacher's platoon . . . found a bunkhouse built for eight to 10 men with food and other winter supplies, military sleeping bags, and rooms with hidden entrances.[45]

— *Christian Science Monitor,* 14 January 2004

Afghanistan's New Self-Defense Force

Defense Minister Mohammed Fahim controls the fledgling army. He is Tajik and from the Northern Alliance whereas Karzai is Pashtun.[46] One wonders how long their liaison will last.

What made the DRA so ineffectual was the ease with which their members could be persuaded to change sides. With a turncoat ready to open the gate, one no longer needs advanced assault techniques.

Recent Developments in the U.S. War Effort

Afghanistan has long been a place that is easier to enter than to leave. As did the Russians in their second invasion of Chechnya, U.S. forces have already resorted to thermobaric bombs. In the initial fighting, not all were launched against tunnel entrances.[47] Unfortunately, such weapons violate the Geneva Conventions, and the guerrilla phase of the Afghan-American War is just getting started.

The fighting in Afghanistan may have slipped below the radar for most of the world, but for the soldiers on the ground things appear to be getting worse. Attacks on the Americans and their Afghan allies are increasing. The enemy is becoming better organized and better armed. Despite the presence of 8,500 U.S. troops in Afghanistan, the influence of al-Qaeda and the Taliban is spreading. A new U.N. security report reckons that one-third of the country is too dangerous for aid distribution. . . .

. . . "During the jihad against the Soviets, the fighters were crossing over in threes and fours," says a European diplomat in Kabul. . . . Now, says the diplomat, who has access to intelligence reports, "they are coming across in hundreds." The U.N. Security Council met in closed consultation late last week to discuss the situation in Afghanistan. "It is really very bad, much worse than Iraq," says a senior ambassador who took part.[48]

— *Time Magazine,* 3 November 2003

The Afghan war, code-named Operation Enduring Freedom, is getting nastier. In the last six months—the bloodiest period since the Taliban's fall in late 2001—hundreds of people have been killed, many of them civilians, including two foreign relief officials and nearly a dozen Afghans working for international agencies. Last week the United Nations announced that it was suspending its refugee-repatriation program and pulling all foreign workers out of southeastern Afghanistan. "We're going to have to refight Enduring Freedom because we didn't finish the job," predicts retired Marine Gen. Anthony Zinni, former head of U.S. Central Command.[49]

— *Newsweek,* 1 December 2003

Insurgents of the former ruling Taliban regime and al-Qaeda have launched repeated attacks in the lawless south and east of the country in the past year, despite the efforts of 11,000 U.S.-led coalition forces to hunt them down.[50]

— Associated Press, 24 February 2004

In a bold daylight attack on 18 January 2004, Afghan guerrillas fired machineguns and RPGs at the American outpost near Deh Rawood [this may be the same location as the July 2003 wedding tragedy]. In response to the attack, a U.S. warplane mistakenly killed 11 civilians. More than

140 people have been killed and injured since the Jan. 4 ratification of a new Afghan constitution, most of them civilians.[51]

Al-Qaeda is suspected of making two recent attempts to kill Pervez Musharraf, the pro-Western president of Pakistan.[52] One wonders who else might benefit from that country's destabilization. After many months of occupation, the U.S.-backed administration of Afghan President Hamid Karzai still holds little sway outside the capital.

> Kabul . . . is patrolled by [a] 5,900-strong NATO-led peacekeeping force. Another 11,000 mostly U.S. forces are fighting the Taliban and hunting for terror suspects, including Osama bin Laden. . . .
> Deteriorating security, particularly in the south and east, has raised serious doubts about whether the [election] polls will go ahead on schedule.
> Moreover, militias in several of the most troubled areas are . . . suffering many of the casualties in clashes with insurgents.[53]
> — Associated Press, 8 February 2004

As 70,000 Pakistani troops combed South Waziristan for bin Laden in March of 2004, U.S. forces came increasingly under attack at their outposts along the border. At one such outpost, a large-caliber rocket attack was apparently used to draw out a motorized patrol. That patrol was subsequently ambushed by IED.[54] At another outpost, RPG and heavy machinegun fire rained in on the U.S. defenders.[55]

Afghan government positions have also come under attack. On 13 March 2004, "about 60 Taliban fighters armed with rockets and heavy machineguns raided a district chief's office in Southern Kandahar province, near the border with Pakistan."[56] To the north on 5 March 2004, Afghan National Army (ANA) forces came under attack by forces with heavy machineguns, RPGs, and mortars at the village of Sesandeh in Paktika province. In that incident, some of the attackers were Pakistani.[57]

> Out of 22 districts [in Paktika province], 14 are no longer reliably under government control, according to a recent UN

internal report. One of these, Barmal district, fell to Taliban forces nearly a year ago. . . . In the 13 remaining districts, local government provides few benefits and little effective control.[58]

— *Christian Science Monitor,* 15 March 2004

Ominous Precedents

On 27 January 2004, a man with artillery and mortar rounds strapped to his chest blew himself up next to a NATO convoy. According to Associated Press, this is "a tactic previously unknown to Afghanistan."[59] Later, at the funeral of the Canadian killed in the first attack, a taxi bomb killed a British soldier.[60]

On 30 January 2004, a guerrilla weapons cache exploded killing seven U.S. soldiers.[61] Command detonating or boobytrapping weapons caches is also unique to this region. The literature contains few examples of East Asian guerrillas destroying their own limited supplies of ordnance. Whenever there are tactical precedents in an area, one suspects a new guerrilla presence—perhaps that of *Hezbollah.* Radio Free Europe has warned of the Iranian Revolutionary Guard's involvement for years.

Mohammad Yusef Pashtun, an aide to Kandahar Province Governor Gul Agha Shirazi, claimed that senior Iranian military officers have been operating in Farah, Nimruz, and Helmand provinces. He said that Iranian generals using the names "Baqbani" and "Dehqan" were offering cash and other incentives in an effort to lure local warlords from their commitments to the administration in Kabul, according to reports in the 24 January issues of "The New York Times" and "The Los Angeles Times."

Iran has sent about 20 trucks filled with money for Ismail Khan [Herat governor] to pay his troops, "The Guardian" reported from Herat on 24 January. Some of Ismail Khan's commanders say that the approximately 12 trucks a day that come from Iran carry weapons, uniforms, and other war materiel. Indeed, the troops in Herat are better outfitted than those in Kabul. And on 21 January, Kandahar intelligence chief Haji Gulali said that Ismail Khan was working with the Islamic Revolution Guards Corps (IRGC) and allies of Gulbuddin Hekmatyar, the mujahideen commander who has been based in Iran for the last few years, to arm and fund opponents of the interim administration. Meanwhile, there is increasing concern about possible Iranian involvement with the creation of a national Afghan army. Defense Minister Mohammad Fahim was in Tehran in mid-January, at which time he met with the heads of the IRGC and the Ministry of Defense and Armed Forces Logistics.[62]

— Radio Free Europe, January 2002

On 6 May 2004, legendary Gulbuddin Hekmatyar, leader of the largest anti-Soviet *mujahideen* clan, joined remnants of the Taliban regime and promised to drive out the foreign troops and unseat Karzai.[63] In July 2004, Karzai wisely bypassed Fahim for vice president.[64]

The Foe Is Discouraging All Outside Interference

Even humanitarian groups are now targeted. As of 17 November 2003, a U.N. relief worker had been killed, a U.N. car blasted by IED, and U.N. headquarters car-bombed.[65] As of 9 January 2004, "suspected Taliban attackers possibly helped by *al-Qaeda* have struck almost daily in the south and east of the country, targeting U.N. workers, government troops and installations, and, increasingly, civilians."[66] Very probably, those civilians were thought to be collaborators.

On 22 February 2004, a lone gunman sprayed a civilian helicopter that was setting up medical clinics 40 miles southwest of Kandahar.[67]

Deja Vu in Tactics

During Operation Anaconda in early 2002, a company from the U.S. 10th Mountain Division encountered opposition on all three sides of a feeder draw into Shah-e-Kot Valley.[68] This style of defense was used on Iwo Jima—strongpoints so positioned as to create firesacks in the low ground between them.

In this new uprising, the rebels do not appear to be fighting

129

much differently than they did 20 years ago. The contemporary *mujahideen* are avoiding set-piece battles. They are shooting just enough to get U.S. forces to retaliate with supporting arms. They are disrupting security just enough to force U.S. troops into a defensive posture. During the Pakistani cordon operation of March 2004, two Chechen fighters died while trying to exfiltrate the encirclement.[69]

Disturbingly, those trying to take the pressure off the *al-Qaeda* encircled at Wana were operating as hit-and-run, two-or-three-man RPG teams in built-up areas.[70] This is reminiscent of the "urban-swarm tactics" with which the Soviets held on to several tiny enclaves along the west bank of the Volga River at Stalingrad.[71]

An Unwanted Glimpse of the Future

As of 25 June 2004, the South Waziristan tribes' pledge to rid their area of foreign militants had not been fulfilled. Resentful of Pakistani Army meddling, most honored a Pashtun tradition that forbids handing over a guest. "Al-Qaeda maintains support in the tribal belt through a mixture of ideology, shared history fighting the Soviets, and money."[72]

Inside Afghanistan, things have continued to heat up in the Southeast—an area predominantly Pashtun. On 27 June 2004, the Taliban killed 16 men simply because they had registered to vote.[73]

While not heavily reported, there has been an increase in guerrilla activity all across the country. As of 10 August 2004, the United States had 18,000 troops in Afghanistan, and NATO was soon to have 10,000.[74] Soon, the warlords were vying for the city closest to Iran—Herat.[75] On 16 September, a rocket just missed President Karzai's helicopter as it was about to land. The very next day—with two hours notice—a full battalion of the 82nd Airborne was rushed from Fort Bragg, North Carolina, to Afghanistan.[76]

130

The Iraqi
Opposition

- *Which foreign movements are the most active in Iraq?*
- *Why are their battlefield tactics now converging?*

MUSLIM IRREGULAR, 1982

(Source: Courtesy of Orion Books, from *World Army Uniforms since 1939*, © 1975, 1980, 1981, 1983 by Blandford Press Ltd., Part II, Plate 115; *FM 90-3* (1977), p. 4-2)

A "Delayed Defense" of Iraq

After quickly capturing Baghdad in April 2003, Coalition forces encountered more and more guerrilla activity. (See Map 8.1.) Five local groups were involved: (1) the Return Party of Baathists; (2) Muhammed's Army of former intelligence and security personnel; (3) Saddam's *Fedayeen* of prewar irregular militia; (4) the *Muntada al-Wilaya* of Shiite extremists; and (5) *Ansar al-Islam* of Sunni extremists.[1] While operating independently, all shared the same goal—expelling the occupier. Then foreign *jihadists* began to appear. They had sponsors.

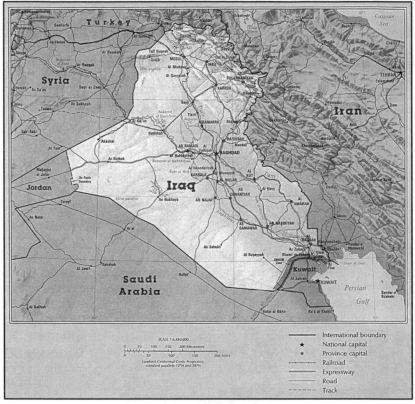

Map 8.1: Relief Map of Iraq
(Source: Courtesy of General Libraries, University of Texas at Austin, from their website for map designator "iraq.jpg")

The Return Party

With all former government officials out of work in Iraq, the Return Party would have no shortage of members. To achieve another Sunni-dominated state, they may actively oppose the Shiite majority.

Muhammed's Army

Among the most dangerous of the homegrown insurgents are the former intelligence and security officials. With international intrigue and covert activity their stock in trade, they have planned an unconventional defense of the homeland from the outset. In a compound once occupied by the Special Operations Directorate of the Iraqi Intelligence Service was found evidence of their post-occupation mission—the making of improvised explosive devices (IEDs).[2] During the invasion, U.S. forces also discovered hundreds of pre-assembled suicide-bomber vests and belts. According to the U.S. Deputy Secretary of Defense, the explosives section of the M-14 Branch of the former Iraqi Intelligence Service produced them.[3] On 29 April 2004, he said that M-14 may have designed a resistance that decentralized control so that no one cell leader could compromise the others.[4] Those cells would need very little strategic guidance to mount a concerted effort.

Fedayeen

Videotaped during a prewar parade were Saddam Hussein's *Fedayeen*. (See Figure 8.1.) They were much more than just loyal "militia." Clothed in black tunics, sashes, and headdresses, they carried no rifles. The newscaster said they were skilled with knives and unafraid of death.[5] One wonders to what extent they were emulating the Persian *Hashishins*. At ceremonies, the *Hashishins* wore white tunics with red sashes—the colors of innocence and blood.[6] In the modern Islamic world, a white burial shroud over one's shoulders symbolizes a willingness to die as a martyr.[7] While wearing the wrong color, Iraqi *Fedayeen* may have nevertheless been groomed for lone heroics. The original *Hashishin fidais* or "devoted ones" have variously been called *fedavi, fedawis, fida'is, fedais,* and *fedayeens*.[8] During the post-invasion de-Baathification period, Saddam's *Fedayeen* were reportedly drawn toward Wahhabi fundamentalism (the religion of *al-Qaeda's* founders).[9]

An al-Jazeera/Associated Press (AP) photograph of 2 May 2004 shows an Iraqi fighter running alongside a burning U.S. fuel convoy.[10] In a white tunic and headdress, he is carrying only a stick. The caption identifies the place as Al'Amarah (near the Iranian border) and the ambushers as Shiite.[11]

Figure 8.1: Saddam Hussein
(Source: *Corel Gallery Clipart*—Man, One Mile Up, #28Q004)

Ansar al-Islam

Helping *al-Qaeda* fighters to enter Iraq through other countries is *Ansar al Islam*—a Sunni group of ethnic Kurds from northern Iraq.[12] Its former members describe many links to *al-Qaeda,* to include using their videotapes during training.[13] *Ansar al-Islam* is the prime suspect in the U.N. headquarters bombing of October 2003 and the pamphlets that announced it.[14]

While the U.S. administration was slow to admit that *al-Qaeda* had expanded its *jihad* to Iraq,[15] Iraqi border police claim that *al-Qaeda* fighters have joined the thousands of Shiite pilgrims "being smuggled" across the Iranian border.[16] As of mid-November 2003, American intelligence estimated that "several hundred to several thousand" militant Sunnis had entered so far.[17] In January 2004, hundreds of Sunni operatives from Yemen, Pakistan and other Muslim states also entered Iraq through Saudi Arabia disguised as Shiite pilgrims.[18]

The Saudi border is as porous as the Iranian. By August 2003, Saudi security authorities suspected that 3000 of its young men had already entered Iraq to fight the Coalition forces.[19] In an attack on a terrorist training camp west of Baghdad in July of 2003, U.S. forces killed fighters from Yemen, Saudi Arabia, Afghanistan, and Sudan.[20] While disenchanted with Saddam, bin Laden has urged cooperation with the remaining Baathists.[21]

Muntada al-Wilaya

Hosting *Hezbollah* fighters from Lebanon is *Muntada al-Wilaya*—an extremist Shiite group from Baghdad and southern Iraq.[22] Most of the Lebanese have been entering Iraq through Syria.[23] Wherever Lebanese *Hezbollah* goes may also go their founder—the Iranian Revolutionary Guard.

Muntada al-Wilaya may also be welcoming "Party of God" fighters directly from Iran. In the far south of Iraq, they would have the help of a local *Hizbullah*.

A subset of the rural Shiites is the so-called marsh Arabs, said to be about 500,000 strong. They once dwelled in the swamps of southern Iraq, working as fishermen, hunters, farmers and smugglers. In the 1990s, the swamps were used by Iran-based paramilitary organizations of Iraqi expatriates to infiltrate into Iraq and strike at Baath targets, and the marsh Arabs themselves often resisted Baath rule. They were organized politically and militarily by the Iraqi Hizbullah, a radical group that fought a guerrilla war against the Iraqi state. The Baath found it difficult to operate in the marshes and therefore drained them. The marsh Arabs were forced to settle in poor southern towns such as Majar al-Kabir, or to go to small cities like Al'Amarah, where they largely subsisted in poverty, having lost their livelihoods. In the aftermath of the second Gulf War, 'Abd al-Karim Mahmud al-Muhammadawi, a marsh Arab who had fought guerrilla actions against the Baath under the nom de guerre of Abu Hatim, emerged as an important civic leader in Al'Amarah. He provided security with the help of his tribal militia (presumably Hizbullah).[24]

— *Middle East Journal,* Autumn 2003

Lebanese *Hezbollah's* Involvement

As *Hezbollah* had often done in southern Lebanon, Iraqi insurgents passed out pamphlets forecasting the shootdown of a U.S. helicopter on 1 November 2003.[25] By that same date, according to the U.S. Secretary of Defense, most of the 400 foreign fighters captured in Iraq were from Lebanon and Syria.[26]

Contrary to popular opinion, the suicide vest did not originate with *al-Qaeda*. It was the brainchild of Lebanese *Hezbollah*.[27] Palestinian groups such as *Hamas* and *Islamic Jihad* have since made it an integral part of their second *intifada*.[28] In early December 2003 at the Syrian border, U.S. troops stopped a truck carrying four foreigners and two suicide vests.[29] As of February 2004, that border remained extremely porous.[30]

Additionally, the suicide-vehicle wasn't used against Russians in Afghanistan,[31] it was used against Americans in Beirut. "Shia Islam has a particularly powerful martyrdom tradition."[32] On 27 October 2003, three Baghdad police stations were car-bombed, and a fourth nearly ruined by a driver carrying a Syrian passport.[33] On 13 December 2003, a suicide car bomb (driven by a Palestinian from Lebanon) blew up at the Khaldiyeh police station killing 23 of its occupants.[34]

Hezbollah is further implicated by the sheer number of suicide bombings in Iraq. It is the *Hezbollah*-affiliated Palestinian organizations that have adopted the suicide attack as their favorite tactic. From September 2000 to March 2004 in Israel, there were 112 suicide bombings. During the first year of Iraqi occupation, there were 24 suicide bombings, of which six were by suicide vest.[35]

The most convincing proof of a significant *Hezbollah* presence came on 14 February 2004. During a daring daylight raid on a Fallujah police station, there were far too many coincidences.

> The audacious assault . . . by some 35 well-organized insurgents killed 22 policemen . . . and freed more than 70 prisoners. . . .
> A senior Iraqi civil defense officer . . . . says . . . a two-pronged assault. . . .
> "They blocked off the street and controlled the corners around both buildings and the two groups of attackers were in radio communication with each other."[36]
> — *Christian Science Monitor,* 17 February 2004

Before the attack, the gunmen set up checkpoints and blocked the road leading to the police station, but residents did not notify police. . . . Nearby store owners were warned not to open Saturday morning. . . .

One wounded policeman, Qais Jamell, said he heard the attackers speaking a foreign language that he speculated was Farsi [Iranian]. Rumors were circulating that a Shiite Muslim militia with ties to Iran, the Badr Brigade, was behind the attack. . . .

In Saturday's attack, about 25 gunmen . . . stormed the police station, witnesses said.

At the same time, two dozen more attackers pinned down forces at a nearby compound of the Iraqi Civil Defense Corps [ICDC] with a barrage of RPGs and gunfire. . . .

ICDC officer, Daeed Hamed, said the assault could have been launched to free two Kuwaitis and a Lebanese captured earlier this week on suspicion of being insurgent fighters. . . .

The same [ICDC] compound came under attack only two days earlier by gunmen who opened fire from rooftops with RPGs and automatic weapons as Gen. John Abizaid . . . was visiting. . . .

Police said two of the slain gunmen had Lebanese identification papers.[37]
— *Associated Press,* 15 February 2004

Lebanese *Hezbollah's* Iraqi Objectives

Hezbollah wants to accomplish in Iraq what it did in Lebanon— i.e., to create a Shiite state by showing the populace how to evict their occupier. No one knows to what extent Tehran supports this agenda. While *Hezbollah* primarily recruits, trains, and advises locals, it will occasionally launch an exemplary attack on its own. To escape attention or inspire action, *Hezbollah* might launch such an attack in a Sunni-dominated area. It is now working hand-in-hand with *al-Qaeda* and may not yet need to consolidate its power. In Lebanon, it waited several years before contesting Syrian-backed Shiite Amal.[38] For the time being, *Hezbollah* is cooperating with most of the other dissident factions within Iraq.

Hezbollah cannot create another Shiite state without Sunni help in ending the occupation. In this part of the world, power struggles are as common as sunrise. As long as mutual objectives are met, differences of opinion are set aside.

Iran's Hand in the Shiite Power Struggle

The power in East Baghdad belongs to the million-member Sadr Movement. Named after Muhammad Baqir al-Sadr (who theorized an Islamic state and was executed in 1980), it remains today a "militant and puritanical movement dedicated to the establishment of an Iran-style Islamic Republic in Iraq."[39] Its radical leader, Karbala-based Muqtada al-Sadr (the founder's grandson) has gone so far as to declare his own government.[40] To say the least, the al-Sadr movement is fertile ground for *Hezbollah* influence.[41] On 4 April 2004, al-Sadr's followers rioted in Najaf, Baghdad, Nasiriyah, and Al'Amarah (among other places).[42] Then more about his background surfaced.

In March 2003, days after the American invasion of Iraq, Tehran sent al-Sadr into the country, well-padded with Iranian weapons, intelligence, combatants, and cash, which are still on tap.[43]
— Israeli intelligence analysis bulletin, 5 April 2004

U.S. officials have long suggested that al-Sadr receives direct support from Iran's Revolutionary Guard and Lebanon's Hezbollah. One London-based Al-Sharq Al-Awsat newspaper quoted what it called a Revolutionary Guard source who described three military camps on the Iran-Iraq border for up to 1,200 Mahdi army recruits.[44]
— *Christian Science Monitor,* 19 April 2004

On 31 August 2003, ABC News reported that assassinated Shiite cleric Mohammed Baqir al-Hakim had 15,000 Iranian Revolutionary Guards in his service. More probably, he had 15,000 local recruits of that organization. According to *Newsweek,* his Badr Brigade has several thousand fighters who trained for nearly 20 years with Iran's Revolutionary Guards.[45] Still unclear is whose truck bomb killed Hakim. He had threatened to cut ties with Tehran after junior cleric Muqtada al-Sadr was feted during his visit to Iran in June 2003.[46] Al-Sadr is already suspected of killing the moderate Shiite leader Abdel Majid al-Khoei in April of 2003.[47]

The assassinated al-Hakim was the leader of the *al-Da'wa* Party. It was that party that spawned the Tehran-based Supreme Council for Islamic Revolution in Iraq (SCIRI).

> Iran's official media has confirmed the close links between SAIRI [SCIRI] and the Guard. In the last days of the Iran-Iraq war, the Guard publicly called for a mobilization of SAIRI volunteers (Iraqis who had defected to Iran) to the warfront with Iraq ("IRGC Announces SAIRI . . . ," Tehran Domestic Service, 14 July 1988).[48]

SCIRI maintained a paramilitary wing, the Badr Corps of about 10,000 trained men. After the fall of the Baath, its members began infiltrating back into Iraq.[49] As of 6 April 2004, SCIRI was one of Iraq's two biggest Shiite political parties and had a seat on the governing council.[50] During the subsequent "Sadr Rebellion," it encouraged U.S. forces to "negotiate with al-Sadr, rather than press the confrontation."[51]

The most influential of the Najaf clerics is Iranian born Grand Ayatollah al-Sistani.[52] Having rejected the U.S. plan for regional caucuses, he is demanding a general election.[53] During the Sadr Rebellion, al-Sistani had coyly condemned both the Coalition's methods of and the disruption to order.[54] Subsequent to al-Sadr taking refuge in Najaf, "al-Sistani issued a *fatwa* to the effect that any American troops to enter Karbala or Najaf would be crossing a 'red line.'"[55] Najaf's Imam Ali Shrine is the holiest site in Iraq.[56] Najaf is second only to Qom (in Iran) as the intellectual center of the Shiite world.[57]

Not unexpectedly, Iran broke off talks with the U.S. on how to resolve the fighting of April 2004. Its foreign minister claimed that "Washington's reliance on military forces was fueling violence in Iraq." Shortly thereafter, Iran's supreme religious leader Ayatollah Khamenei issued an inflammatory statement on state-run radio.[58] Where the export of Shiite fundamentalism is concerned, he controls much of the power. In March 2003, Baghdad's Baathist regime posed little short-term threat to its neighbors. It did, however, provide a natural buffer to Shiite expansionism. With its demise may come long-term problems.

Al-Qaeda's New Foothold in Iraq

While there was little *al-Qaeda* presence in Iraq before the U.S. invasion, there is plenty now. Osama bin Laden has made it a new arena in which to confront the West.

> During the Muslim holy month of Ramadan [November 2003], three senior Qaeda representatives allegedly held a secret meeting in Afghanistan with two top Taliban commanders. . . . At that meeting, according to Taliban sources, Osama bin Laden's men officially broke some bad news to emissaries from Mullah Mohammed Omar, the elusive leader of Afghanistan's ousted fundamentalist regime. Their message: Al-Qaeda would be diverting a large number of fighters from the anti-U.S. insurgency in Afghanistan to Iraq. Al-Qaeda also planned to reduce by half its $3 million monthly contribution to Afghan jihadi outfits. . . .
> Despite bin Laden's apparently fresh interest in Iraq, sources in the region say there remains scant evidence that he had links to Saddam before the war.[59]
> — *Newsweek,* 15 December 2003

While U.S. officials have now admitted more *al-Qaeda* involvement in Iraq, they have yet to fathom its portent. With Saddam Hussein's removal, they have let the *"jihadic"* genie out of the bottle. Not only has Iraq become the destination of choice for foreign *jihadists,* but also a fertile recruiting ground.

> "The capture of [Hassan] Ghul is pretty strong proof that al-Qaeda is trying to gain a foothold here to continue their murderous campaigns," [Lt.Gen. Ricardo] Sanchez said.
> Ghul was arrested by U.S.-allied Kurdish forces while trying to enter Iraq from Iran. Officials in Washington reported his arrest Saturday, describing him as a senior recruiter for al-Qaeda.[60]
> — Associated Press, 30 January 2004

U.S. officials say Mr. Ghul has ties to captured al-Qaeda leader Khalid Sheikh Mohammed, one of the organization's

top planners. General Sanchez said . . . al-Qaeda has been operating in Iraq for at least three months, and that Ghul was tied to a truck-bombing in Nasiriyah last November that killed 28 people, most of them Italian soldiers.[61]
— *Christian Science Monitor,* 2 February 2004

The highest ranking *al-Qaeda* operative in Iraq may have originally come there only for medical treatment.

In 2000, [Jordanian] Zarqawi traveled to Afghanistan, where according to U.S. intelligence he ran an al-Qaeda training camp that specialized in chemical and biological agents before being wounded in the leg by a U.S. bombing raid during the Afghan war in 2001. He then fled to Iran and thence to Iraq, where doctors reportedly amputated his leg and fitted him with a prosthetic limb.[62]
— *Christian Science Monitor,* 23 January 2004

Al-Qaeda's Objectives in Iraq

Al-Qaeda's long-term goals are to expel the Coalition and form an Islamic state. While it wants a Sunni state, it needs the help of Iraq's Shiite majority to end the occupation. If the terminal strategies of Soviet-Afghan War are any indicator, *al-Qaeda* wants a puppet regime that can be easily isolated. While it may be pushing for civil war to prevent a representative form of government, it is more probably exploiting the Coalition's lack of security.

When Mr. Ghul was captured near the Iranian border, he was carrying an electronic letter to the *al-Qaeda* leaders in Afghanistan. Purportedly written by al-Zarqawi, it suggested a civil war to forestall elections.[63] That might explain the attacks on Kurdish parties in Irbil and Shiite shrines in Najaf, Baghdad, and Karbala.[64] Al-Zarqawi has been named as prime suspect in the bombings of U.N. headquarters, all three mosques, and the Italian contingent.[65]

Hassan G[h]ul may have helped Zarqawi move terrorists and money around the country. . . . Zarqawi avoids capture by sometimes taking refuge in Iran.[66]
— *Newsweek,* 9 February 2004

141

On the other hand, the Kurds and Shiites may have been attacked by radical elements of their own (or Baathist) sects. Of the 15 people detained in Karbala after the Shiite attacks, five spoke Farsi (Iranian).[67] The most influential Shiite—Grand Ayatollah al-Sistani—blamed the Coalition for failing to provide security from extremists in general. "U.S. officials have disregarded the claim by 12 insurgent groups that al-Zarqawi was killed by American bombing last year."[68] *Al-Qaeda* needs only a figurehead to mobilize Iraq's Sunni population.

The Situation Was Worsening Strategically

America's 30-year-old nightmare was happening again. With no jungle for cover, foreign fighters were easily entering the country. They didn't have to sneak in, just profess to be Shiite pilgrims. For the Lebanese and Iranians, this wouldn't be hard.

> Unlike in Saddam's day, Shiite visitors are now allowed to come to Iraq's holy places by the tens of thousands from Iran, Afghanistan, and Lebanon, from Bahrain, and Kuwait and Saudi Arabia.[69]
> — *Newsweek,* 1 March 2004

As of 14 October 2003, insurgents were attacking U.S. occupation forces 22 times a day.[70] As of 12 November, the number of attacks had risen to 30-35 times a day.[71] While Saddam's capture in December 2003 brought a slight decrease in the number of attacks, it did not lessen their strategic impact. The very next month produced the second highest U.S. casualty total of the war.[72] As of 5 April 2004, unofficial tallies of attacks were ranging as high as 150 a day.[73] On 1 May 2004, they rose to 200 a day.[74]

Evidence of a Guerrilla Plan from the Outset

On 25 March 2003, the lead story in the *Christian Science Monitor* was "Guerrilla Tactics vs. U.S. War Plan."[75] On 27 March 2003, ABC News quoted Saddam Hussein as saying that U.S. troops would be confronted on every street in Baghdad and all along their tenuous resupply routes.[76]

Implied, of course, was an unconventional style of defense. On 28 March 2003, ABC News reported that "U.S. troops are coming under attack wherever they go from roving bands of militia."[77] On 30 March 2003, it reported Coalition forces fighting guerrillas in Basra.[78]

On 3 April 2003, National Public Radio (NPR) announced that every street corner in Baghdad was being manned by soldiers ready to wage guerrilla war.[79]

A Classic Guerrilla Strategy

With no polls to worry about, the Middle Eastern guerrilla has time on his side. He has a dual objective: (1) to make the average citizen's life so miserable he will join, and (2) to make the occupier's life so miserable he will leave. Both can often be accomplished at the same time. By killing a few Americans every week, the Iraqi rebels hope to get U.S. forces to use a heavier hand and thereby alienate the local population. By sabotaging Iraq's infrastructure, they hope to discourage Congress from indefinitely funding the occupation. So far, water mains and treatment facilities,[80] oil pipelines and storage tanks,[81] and electrical grids have been repeatedly attacked. All the means of transportation have also been targeted: (1) airplanes, (2) helicopters, (3) trains and train stations,[82] and (4) truck convoys. As in Vietnam, the enemy has even gone after highway bridges.[83] With such attacks, the rebels are telling the Iraqi people that their occupiers can provide neither security nor basic services.

> In a country the size of California, no number of soldiers can protect every hospital, hotel, bridge, electrical station, water and oil pipeline, especially from determined suicide attackers.[84]
> — Knight Ridder News Service, 24 August 2003

As was the case in Afghanistan, the Muslim militant's primary target in Iraq is fuel. On 24 April 2004 at Umm Qasr, the insurgents barely missed blowing up Iraq's offshore oil terminals with explosive-laden dhows. By destroying a pipeline north of Baghdad two days earlier, they cut the flow of refined petroleum into the city by half.[85]

Foreign Rebuilders of Infrastructure Have Been Targeted

Between 15-19 March 2004—in two separate attacks—gunmen killed two Europeans and four American missionaries working on water projects.[86] In a hotel bombing on 17 March 2004, the rebels killed foreign employees of the Coalition.[87] Another contractor hotel bombing occurred on 10 May 2004.[88]

After the Sadr Rebellion of April 2004 had cooled a bit, Osama bin Laden offered a truce to the European nations if they would pull their people out of Iraq.[89] Then foreign workers began to leave in large numbers, thereby putting the rebuilding of its infrastructure on hold. First to pull out was, of course, Russia.

A parade of 20 blue-and-white buses filled with Russian and Ukrainian oil workers lumbered out of Baghdad yesterday—the first exodus of 800 contractors Moscow ordered to leave. Thousands of foreign contractors are still working on electricity, pipelines, roads, and buildings in Iraq. But the pace of rebuilding is slowing and in some cases grinding to a halt.[90]
— *Christian Science Monitor,* 16 April 2004

Soon, any foreign national remotely involved with the infrastructure would become fair game for hostage taking and beheading. While *al-Qaeda* took the credit, the tactic evoked memories of Lebanon.

The Attack on Collaborators

The Iraqi resistance has been also doing all that it can to discourage internal cooperation with the Coalition. On 31 January 2004, two suicide bombers with explosives wired to their bodies killed scores of people at the two main Kurdish party headquarters. While some reports had the bombers masquerading as Muslim clerics,[91] others said they were disguised as media journalists.[92] The ancient *Hashishins* loved disguises.

As of 7 November 2003, legislators, judges, mayors, and police chiefs were considered collaborators.[93] City halls and police stations have been the most heavily targeted. Three police stations were car-bombed in Baghdad on 27 October 2003.[94] On 6 October

2003, a police station at Beiji—an oil-refining city just north of Tikrit—withstood a 75 minute barrage of mortar, RPG, and small-arms fire.[95] A car bomb blew up the Kaldiyeh police station on 13 December 2003.[96] On 27 December 2003, the Karbala City Hall was car-bombed.[97] On 13 January 2004, Fallujah city hall was hit with a barrage of RPG rounds.[98] On 30 January 2004, the Mosul police station was car-bombed.[99] On 10 February 2004, a car bomb blew up outside at police station at Iskandariyah killing would-be recruits waiting in line.[100] Then, there was the 14 February 2004 ground assault on the Fallujah police station. On 23 February 2004, the police station at Kirkuk was car-bombed.[101] On 23 March 2004, two policemen and nine police recruits were shot on Baghdad's out-skirts.[102] Then, the Sadr Rebellion targeted police stations and government facilities in several cities. In and around Basra on 21 April 2004, car bombs were simultaneously exploded outside three police stations and two police academies.[103] From the U.S. invasion in April 2003 to May 2004, 710 Iraqi policemen in all were killed. Unfortunately, the bloodshed has not stopped with the transition to Iraqi government. In July 2004, a truck bomb killed 70 people outside a police recruiting station in Baqubah.[104]

The war against "collaborators" reached a new low on 21 January 2004 and again on 17 May 2004. On both dates, several Iraqi women were slain simply because they worked for the Coalition.[105] On 29 January 2004, "shopkeepers in Ramadi . . . reported receiving leaflets warning Iraqis to stop working for or with Americans within 10 days or face death."[106] Similar pamphlets were a tool used to evict the Israelis from Lebanon and the Soviets from Afghanistan.

The Effort to Isolate U.S. Forces

The resistance undoubtedly realizes that the U.S. Congress will quit funding any war that lasts too long. As such, it is working hard to limit the internationalization of the occupation. The U.N.,[107] Jordanian,[108] Turkish,[109] Dutch,[110] and Red Cross headquarters (or embassies) have been attacked with car bombs. In the U.N. attack, over a ton of explosives were used to kill its envoy.[111] On 29 November 2003, seven Spanish intelligence personnel and two Japanese diplomats were killed.[112] On 27 December 2003, four Bulgarian and two Thai troops were slain.[113] Reminiscent of Beirut, the Italian barracks was truck-bombed on 13 November 2003.[114] On 18 February 2004, two suicide trucks exploded outside the Polish camp killing 26 Poles and some Hungarians, Bulgarians, and Filipinos.[115] After the Madrid train station bombing on 11 March 2004, Spain decided to remove its 1300 troops from Iraq.[116] A month later, Honduras and the Dominican Republic followed suit with contingents of roughly 300 each.[117] During the Sadr Rebellion of early April 2004, Japanese hostages were threatened with immolation if their country did not remove its 530-man humanitarian contingent.[118] Japan did not comply with the demand.

The opposition is particularly interested in keeping the United Nations out of Iraq. On 27 January 2004—on the eve of a U.N. visit to discuss free elections—an ambulance blew up outside a hotel for foreigners.[119]

The Effort to Demoralize the New Iraqi Army

On 11 February 2004, a car bomb exploded outside an Iraqi army recruiting station killing 47. Some 300 recruits had been forced to wait outside the fortified center.[120]

During the Sadr Rebellion of April 2004, many Iraqi policemen opted to change sides. A whole battalion of the new U.S. trained Iraqi security forces refused to fight at Fallujah.[121]

About one in every 10 members of Iraq's security forces "actually worked against" U.S. troops during the recent militia violence in Iraq, and an additional 40 percent walked off the job because of intimidation, the commander for the 1st Armored Division said Wednesday.[122]
— Associated Press, 22 April 2004

The Effort to Sway U.S. Popular Opinion

The foe may be smart enough to know that by creating political embarrassment, it can cause the U.S. military to further centralize control. In a guerrilla war, the side that shows the most initiative at the lowest echelons wins.

The U.S. headquarters in Baghdad has also been repeatedly

attacked.[123] A U.S. headquarters hotel was hit by rocket-firing donkey cart with the U.S. Assistant Secretary of Defense in residence.[124] This smacks of the security leaks that plagued Israeli forces in southern Lebanon. A huge truck bomb was detonated inside the U.S. controlled Green Zone at the Coalition headquarters gate on 17 January 2004. This occurred "on the eve of a meeting between U.S. administrator L. Paul Bremer and U.N. Secretary-General Kofi Annan to discuss Iraq's future, including whether Iraq is safe enough for the world body to return." It was no coincidence that scores of cued-up Iraqi workers were killed or wounded by the same blast.[125]

U.S. Strategic Assets Are Being Heavily Targeted

In battle, U.S. forces are among the best supplied in the world. For them, the loss of a truck here and a few supplies there doesn't qualify as much of a problem. But "state-of-the-art" gear is expensive. When multiplied thousands of times over (as it was in Vietnam), the replacement cost can significantly influence a war's outcome.

With Baghdad Airport and U.S. truck convoys under intermittent attack, U.S. resupply lines have been stretched thin. Even the rest compounds along Route 1 receive "mortar attacks with great regularity."[126] On 5 November 2003 alone, three separate convoys were attacked near the northern, and relatively safe, city of Mosul.[127] As the interchange of 110,000 U.S. troops with all of their equipment began, a convoy was hit on 24 January 2004,[128] and two more on 27 January 2004.[129] During the fight for Fallujah in April 2004, the roads around Baghdad became very dangerous. On 8 April 2004, somebody ambushed a U.S. fuel convoy west of the capital, killing 9 U.S. service personnel.[130] The next day, they attacked another fuel convoy in approximately the same place.[131] On 12 April 2004, a convoy was attacked just south of Baghdad.[132] Then humanitarian-aid convoys were blasted by IEDs on either side of Fallujah.[133] At that point, U.S. forces had little choice but to close large stretches of road to the north, west, and south of Baghdad.

Many logistics bases have also been shelled or rocketed.[134] With the Sadr Rebellion of April 2004, convoy ambush and logistic base mortaring became so prevalent as not to merit individual media coverage.

Only Peripherally like the Maoist Method

As there is still no hard evidence that sappers have been secretly sabotaging U.S. assets during indirect-fire attacks, one cannot refer to the Iraqi rebels' tactics as Maoist. Nor has any Iraqi guerrilla unit admitted shifting between underground hide facilities in the same general location. Still, that is the way Saddam Hussein eluded capture for so long and others are probably doing it as well. Of course, Saddam's last hiding place was very different from what an East Asian Communist would build. Though in a courtyard, its styrofoam plug was covered with a telltale rug, and its ventilation pipe was plainly visible above ground.[135]

Only time will tell how much *al-Qaeda* can learn from its Uighur Chinese. *Hezbollah*, on the other hand, receives support from a country that is closely allied with both China and North Korea.

The Remotely Controlled Bomb

While the foe in Vietnam had the technology, he seldom resorted to remotely detonated ordnance. He let his foe set it off with a tripwire or pressure device. While he had claymores, he did not fabricate an anti-vehicular equivalent. For tanks, he pulled an antitank mine on a string from a spiderhole. Thus, the IED is a Southwest Asian anomaly. East Asians prefer close combat.

Hezbollah and its Palestinian allies used IEDs to drive the Israelis out of South Lebanon. *Al-Qaeda* and the *mujahideen* also used them to evict the Russians from Afghanistan. Of the two most effective IED variants from those wars, one has already appeared in Iraq. That is where a tank is lured into a narrow road and destroyed by buried bomb. Hopefully, the other never will. With it, a patrol is tailed until it enters a line of drift (like a trail). The stalker calls ahead on his cell phone to shift a roving claymore ambush into the patrol's path.

At present, the Iraqi IEDs would be fairly obvious to a student of visual detail. They are often hidden in burlap bags or animal carcasses along roads.[136] As time goes by, their locations will become more obscure. Some resembling curbs have already been reported. Then the only hint will be metallic glint, wire segment, fresh dirt, wilted foliage, or color/texture irregularity. One may also spot straight or rounded lines. Behind the IED offensive may be "Muhammed's Army" of former intelligence and security personnel. In the Iraqi Intelligence Service compound was found evidence that mines and grenades would be hidden in dolls, stuffed animals, and food containers.[137]

> The Army has found bombs disguised as curbs. Others have been hidden in lamp posts, animal carcasses and the Army's ubiquitous brown plastic ration bags. "We've seen some pretty ingenious disguises," Sirois told AP last week. "You name it, they hide IEDs in just about anything—tires at the sides of roads, trash piles." . . . The rebels' bombs have grown smaller, less complex and less deadly, he said. At the height of their attacks—from late August to early November—rebels were able to interconnect 15 or more large artillery shells into a single bomb that may have been assembled and buried at the side of a highway over a period of several nights or a week, he said. Some bombs used plastic explosives as well as artillery or mortar shells. But for the past six weeks, most bombs have been smaller, sometimes a single, converted artillery or mortar round. . . . The military has also cleared the roadsides of brush, trees and trash, removing hiding places. Last week, U.S. soldiers could be seen bulldozing huge eucalyptus trees that line the main highway north of Camp Anaconda.[138]
> — *Herald Sun* (Australia), 6 January 2004

Iraqi insurgents have recently been spacing IEDs at the same interval trucks normally drive along a particular stretch of road.[139]

The Rebels' Growing Use of Deception

As the rebels have deployed more IEDs, they have devised ways to draw in or distract their quarry. Among them are a preliminary blast, misdirected small arms, or civil disturbance.[140]

During the Fallujah fighting of April 2004, Coalition forces discovered suicide vests and U.S. Army desert fatigues.[141] It may not be long before *Hashishin* devotees start masquerading as American soldiers.

149

Car- and Truck-Bombing Diversions

In Beirut, a yellow Mercedes truck simply plowed through the gate and into the Marine living quarters in 1983. In the 13 November bombing of the Italian barracks in Nasiriyah, the offending truck was accompanied by a "base of fire" vehicle and preceded by a decoy car going the other direction.[142]

When Red Cross headquarters and three police stations were car-bombed on 27 October 2003, two bombers used disguises. The Red Cross bomber drove an ambulance. One police station bomber was dressed as a policeman and drove a police car.[143] Three of these attacks also involved feints.

In at least three of the [four] attacks, witnesses said a vehicle was used to distract or confuse perimeter guards to allow the bomber's vehicle to slip through.[144]
— Associated Press, 1 November 2003

Tank-Killing Tactics

On 27 October 2003, Iraq insurgents destroyed a 68-ton American "Abrams" tank with a "land mine or makeshift bomb" north of Baghdad.[145] As noted in Chapters 3 and 4, this has happened in Southern Lebanon and Israel's West Bank to more than one Israeli "Merkava" tank.

A U.S. "Bradley" armored personnel carrier suffered the same fate 20 miles north of Baghdad on 17 January 2004. On that occasion, several U.S. 155mm artillery rounds were command detonated inside a culvert. As the Bradley's occupants had been searching for IEDs, there is a good chance that one had been used as bait.[146] Ominously, on 31 March 2004, "five [U.S.] troops died when a bomb exploded under their military vehicle west of Baghdad."[147] That "vehicle" was later determined to be an M-113 armored personnel carrier.[148]

During the fighting for Fallujah in April of 2004, insurgents fired RPG rounds—from every direction—at armored vehicles trying to resupply Marine outposts.[149] First observed in Hue City, this tactic was successfully used by Chechen separatists in Grozny in 1995.

In July 2004, U.S. armored patrols came under attacks similar

150

to those so successfully used in Grozny in 1995. From both sides of the road, the Bradleys withstood a barrage of IEDs, RPGs, and machinegun bullets.[150] As ground forays ensued, one automatically suspects the "closing door" formation.

Deja Vu in Ambushing

"Representatives for the 2nd Armored Cavalry said a patrol in the area [near Karbala] was lured into an ambush and had to fight its way out past a gauntlet of as many as 500 armed men."[151] This is highly reminiscent of the *haichi-shiki* or "closing-horseshoe" ambush of the Korean and Vietnamese Wars.[152] On a different occasion, a U.S. convoy experienced something similar near Samarra.

After barricading a road, the attackers began firing from rooftops and alleyways [on both sides] with small arms, mortars, and rocket-propelled grenades.[153]
— Associated Press, 1 December 2003

What makes this attack unique is that 12 of the 50 ambushers assaulted the convoy.[154] In a classic *haichi-shiki,* a mortar takes the quarry under fire from the front and then one whole side of the inverted "U" assaults. That the convoy was carrying a lot of Iraqi currency is also unsettling. East Asian guerrillas took much of what they needed from convoys.

While the assault portion of the *haichi-shiki* may be rare in Iraq, some of its other elements may have been refined. They include tandem mines, dual obstacles, microterrain utilization, and an old Japanese trick—climbing trees.

The move in went on schedule, the tanks, personnel carriers, and HMMWVs rolling along smoothly while the Kiowas who dropped to our company frequency, flew ahead observing anything unusual. . . . [T]he Kiowa pilots spotted nothing through the thick canopy of date palms, and no activity along the roadways on either side of the canal. We started our move back, the Kiowas with us the entire way.
The ambush was initiated by seven 152mm artillery rounds hidden in the weeds on the shoulder of the roadway that paralleled the canal. They were daisy-chained together.

The lead tank absorbed the bulk of the blast, shrapnel cutting through the main gun tube in several locations. The blast created a debris field of dust and asphalt, denser than any smoke screen I have seen. . . . Then the small-arms fire started. . . .

. . . [A]s abruptly as it had started, it stopped. The firefight lasted about 45 seconds. . . .

. . . My scout platoon found detonation wire and traced it back along a wall between two fields, out of sight from the road. . . .

On the left side of the road, the NCFs [noncompliant forces] used a cinderblock wall for cover, and the canal as an obstacle. From the right side of the road, they used climbing rigs (used for harvesting dates) to shimmy up palm trees and engage us with direct fire, using a wire fence and depression as an obstacle. Once return fire became too hot, they dropped from the trees and fled through the groves, which have a floor 8 to 10 feet lower than the roadbed. Our rounds passed harmlessly over their heads.[155]

— Capt. John P. Nalls, B Company, 67th Armor

Hampering the Movement of Coalition Foot Patrols

To beat guerrillas, one must run foot patrols. Vehicles are too easy to target. On 18 March 2004, a car bomb exploded in Basra as a British patrol passed by.[156] To discourage offensive action in Southern Lebanon, *Hezbollah* blew IEDs on Israel foot patrols as they left their bases.[157] Luckily, U.S. forces have never had to endure this tactic on a wide scale. In Vietnam, the boobytraps mostly protected places of strategic significance to the VC. There were exceptions, of course, like those on the return route from listening posts.

No Evidence Yet of Advanced Assault Technique

As in Vietnam, U.S. troops are now being routinely mortared and rocketed in Iraq.[158] To each explosion, they attach less significance and thus become more susceptible to the concussion grenade deception.

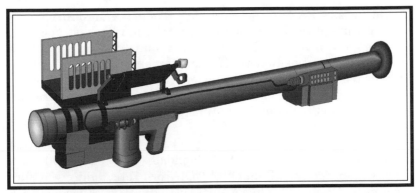

Figure 8.2: U.S. "Stinger" Shoulder-Fired Anti-Aircraft Missile
(Source: *Corel Gallery Clipart*—Weapon, One Mile Up, #45A118)

So far, there is no direct evidence of the insurgents running a "stormtrooper-style" (grenade-and-bayonet) assault after an indirect-fire barrage. However, the guerrillas will eventually discover that prepositioned explosives can be discreetly detonated during an indirect-fire attack.

The Air War

Somewhat shocking is the extent to which "high-tech" U.S. aircraft have been threatened by "low-tech" guerrilla weaponry. As of August 2003, 21 had drawn fire at Baghdad Airport alone.[159] As of 14 January 2004, nine U.S. helicopters had been shot down, and three U.S. fixed-wing transports damaged.[160] Of note, the last one was hit while shadowing a moving convoy.[161] On 25 February 2004, an eyewitness saw a missile bring down a U.S. helicopter west of Baghdad.[162] (See Figure 8.2.) While vintage Soviet SA-7 shoulder-fired missiles are suspected in most of the attacks, one more advanced Russian SA-16 was reported.[163] There are unconfirmed rumors of Russian FAE-tipped RPG rounds and at least one U.S. "Stinger" also being involved. The Russians dispatched RPO-A thermobaric weapons to both Afghanistan and Chechnya.[164] They have also sold them on the international market.[165] Chechen rebels have been seen with them.[166] As for the "Stingers," they were amply supplied to the *mujahideen* during the latter stages of the Soviet-Afghan War.

On 20 March 2004, unspecified hostile fire brought down an American helicopter just west of Baghdad. On 7 April 2004, another was shot down at Baqubah.[167] On April 10th, a third was shot down near Baghdad.[168] On 12 April 2004, an AH-64 Apache attack helicopter was brought down by shoulder-fired missile at Fallujah.[169] About the same time a CH-53 was forced down by hostile fire.[170] On 23 June 2004, a helicopter crash-landed during a firefight.[171] That brings the total count of helicopters shot down—as of 23 June 2004—to 16. As of 24 January 2004, there had been another six helicopters lost to "unidentifiable causes."[172] On 30 July 2004, a helicopter pilot was killed, but there was no report of a shootdown. During the Second Sadr Rebellion of early August 2004, three U.S. choppers were destroyed by enemy fire. By mid-September, two more had been forced down—one near the Syrian border.[173]

Down a Familiar Road

For most Americans, the Iraqi insurgency has few comparisons to Vietnam. In the Middle East, there are no jungles in which to hide. There is no sister country in search of unification. Yet, one thing hasn't changed—U.S. troops are still having trouble distinguishing friend from foe. Theirs is a firepower ethos. As they get injured by people of every sex, age, and description, they may come to distrust Iraqis and Muslims in general. Most have never been told that there is another, widely practiced style of warfare—one in which disguise and deception are the norm. They don't realize that "establishing firepower superiority" fuels the popular support on which the guerrilla so badly depends. Most have no other way to fight back. They lack the movement skills to close safely with an elusive enemy. America must now do one of two things: (1) stop getting embroiled in unconventional wars, or (2) give U.S. enlisted personnel better training.

The rules of engagement instruct U.S. soldiers to bring withering force to bear on positions they're attacked from, even when an insurgent ducks into a private house for cover.

One sergeant in northern Iraq puts it this way: "If someone runs into a house, we're going to light it up. If civilians get killed in there, that's a tragedy, but we're going to keep doing it and people are going to get the message that they should do whatever they can to keep these people out of their neighborhoods."[174]
— *Christian Science Monitor,* 21 January 2004

Despite the turnover of power, the U.S. military is planning to stay in Iraq. To bring stability, it must do something different than the Russians did in Afghanistan and Chechnya and Israelis did in Lebanon.

The Army will temporarily boost its forces by 30,000 during the next four years, Chief of Staff Gen. Peter Schoomaker told Congress. . . . Schoomaker told lawmakers the Army plans a larger troop presence in Iraq through 2006.[175]
— *Christian Science Monitor,* 30 January 2004

With the wholesale replacement of U.S. forces in early 2004 came a new "public relations" tactic. So as not to "help the enemy," those forces will no longer report how each member dies.[176] Needless to say, that enemy already knows which of its tactics are working. Prerequisite to beating a highly opportunistic foe is freely admitting one's errors. Otherwise, in a politically charged environment, there is no reason to change. One of the Communist's biggest advantages in Vietnam was his greater willingness to admit to a tactical defeat. This made him more aware of changing circumstances.

The Hint of Another Numbers Game

To appear better able to handle the deteriorating situation, the U.S. military has turned many of its security responsibilities (to include Baghdad airport) over to civilian contractors. There are well over 20,000 private contractors working for the U.S. government in some capacity.[177] "Peter Singer, national security fellow at the Brookings Institution in Washington . . . estimates that 20,000 people in Iraq now handle jobs that used to be held down by military personnel."[178] Unfortunately, the opposition has been targeting those contractors.[179] On 1 April 2004, the U.S. military admitted to not knowing how many of its 15,000 U.S. contract personnel had been killed.[180] One wonders how many Iraqi and foreign nationals may also be performing military missions.

No War Is Exactly the Same

The ongoing struggle in Iraq may not only reestablish the power of the urban guerrilla, but also set some precedents in technique. As every tactician knows, even a badly outgunned defender has a huge edge in a built-up area.

Baghdad is three times the size of 1945 Berlin. It covers a full 2,000 square miles. For a guerrilla, sprawling urban terrain provides better cover than a jungle. By mixing with the local population, he denies an attritionist opponent his only genuine capability—firepower. Then by converting/subverting local officials, he undermines that opponent's ability to govern. For intelligence gathering, assassination, or ground assault, he has inside help. He even uses the illusion of inside help as a weapon. Every time a government official appears to cave in, the guerrilla's cause is furthered. On 10 March 2004, two U.S. civilians from the occupation authority were gunned down at a checkpoint by rebels pretending to be policemen.[181]

The Sadr Rebellion of Spring 2004

While Fallujah may lie inside the Sunni Triangle, it was also where the *Hezbollah*-like assault took place on a police station on 14 February 2004. When four American contractors were subsequently killed and mutilated there in late March, the U.S. military had little choice but to move in. By so doing, they may have unwittingly played right into the opposition's hands.

Then a Marine position at the governor's palace in nearby Ramadi came under ground assault. This was no impromptu protest; the Marines lost 12 dead and 20 wounded.[182] Paradoxically, the assault force was once again Shiite.

> The Sunni Triangle Shiite force . . . was secretly trained and prepared over the past year by thousands of Iranian Republican Guards infiltrators in conjunction with the Iranian protege, Lebanese Hezbollah terror-master Imad Mughniyeh. This force numbers an estimated 5,000 combatants, who are better equipped, organized and trained than [al-Sadr's] Mahdi Army militiamen.[183]
> — Israeli intelligence analysis bulletin, 7 April 2004

It was therefore no coincidence when trouble broke out in several other cities as U.S. forces were preparing to go into Fallujah.[184] In East Baghdad, al-Sadr's followers took control of neighborhood police stations and government buildings. On 3 April 2004, 5000 of his self-styled militia—the "Mahdi Army"—marched unarmed in its streets while sharpshooters watched from the rooftops.[185] In and around Najaf, Shiite militants besieged the Spanish garrison and stole guns from a police compound.[186] They then captured the town of Diwaniyah 30 kilometers east of Najaf after repulsing repeated Spanish attempts (backed by U.S. helicopters) to regain control.[187] In Nasiriyah, other Shiites attacked something of more strategic value.

> In Tuesday's most protracted battle, Italian troops clashed with al-Sadr's supporters in Nasiriyah, about 200 miles southeast of Baghdad. The Iraqis tried to seize bridges over the Euphrates River and attacked the headquarters of the U.S.-led administration.[188]
> — *Washington Post,* 6 April 2004

It was probably *Hezbollah* fighters who attacked the U.S. contractors' tiny convoy in Fallujah, because they did so by ground assault. Then, they mutilated the bodies to generate a heavy-handed U.S. response. When that response came, al-Sadr Shiites launched attacks in East Baghdad and at least eight other major cities: Baqubah in the north; Muqdadiyah, Al Kut, Najaf, Kufah, Karbala, Nasiriyah, and Al'Amarah in the south.[189] In East Baghdad alone, they captured at least seven police stations—each with an estimated 80 AK-47 assault rifles.[190] In Baqubah, they again went after government/police facilities.[191] In Nasiriyah, al-Sadr's militia succeeded in seizing the strategic bridges over the Euphrates.[192] At the end of

8 April 2004, Al Kut, Kufah, Najaf, and Karbala were variously reported in rebel hands.[193] Polish and Bulgarian patrols had been attacked near the center of Karbala.[194] Ukrainian forces had been forced to abandon their base inside Al Kut, along with its many weapons. Unfortunately, al-Sadr then moved to Najaf.[195] A thousand U.S. troops backed by tanks quickly retook the police stations and government buildings in Al Kut.[196] Najaf and Karbala—two of the holiest cities in Islam—were wisely left alone during the al-Arbaeen pilgrimage weekend.[197] There had been trouble in Kirkuk as well, but it may have been from a different source.

After bombing and rocketing the rebel-occupied Abdel-Aziz al-Samarrai mosque in Fallujah,[198] U.S. forces instituted a cease-fire on 9 April 2004.[199] Soon, the rebels' full intent became apparent. In almost every city, their targets had been the same: (1) occupier bases or patrols, (2) police stations, and (3) government buildings. They had also attempted to sever the main roads into Baghdad: (1) the one to the west at Fallujah, (2) the one to the south at Muqdadiyah, and (3) the one to the north at Baqubah. The other main artery to the south crosses the Tigris River at Al Kut and the Euphrates River at Nasiriyah. Ominously, the main road to the Baghdad's west crosses the Euphrates at Fallujah.

At the same time, what were believed to be Sunni militants ambushed convoys and abducted foreign workers in West Baghdad.[200] They threatened to burn an American and three Japanese alive if occupation forces didn't leave Fallujah alone.[201] Throughout Iraq, some 50 hostages were taken in all, including a U.S. serviceman.[202] On 15 April 2004, an Italian hostage was killed. The Italian contingent is the third largest in the Coalition.[203]

On 13 April 2004, to avoid a U.S. assault on Iraq's holiest sites, al-Sadr supposedly removed his militia from government buildings in Najaf, Karbala, and Kufah.[204] However, his militia set up checkpoints and still controlled the streets of Najaf and next-door Kufah.[205] Then, they (or the pro-Iranian Badr Brigade) did likewise in Karbala.[206] On 6 May 2004, U.S. forces retook the governor's office in Najaf.[207] In subsequent days, they raided al-Sadr offices, police headquarters, and government buildings in Baghdad and the three holy cities.[208] In response, the Mahdi Army spread its revolt to Basra and Al'Amarah.[209] On 10 May 2004, al-Sadr called for a general uprising.[210] At the same time, in a direct reference to the Iranian/ *Hezbollah* way of fighting, a Mahdi militiaman said, "It has become the Iraqi people's war."[211]   Al-Sadr did, after all, threaten to use suicide vest bombers. And he does have his own courts, police, and detention centers.[212]

The Fight for Fallujah

In the initial attack on Fallujah, some 600 Iraqis were killed. The city hospital director claimed that most were women, children, and elderly, but the Marine commander said most were insurgents.[213] Throughout the cease-fire, the rebels fought with forward deployed Marine units. Repeatedly, the Marines called in their AC-130 gunships. While fairly accurate and quiet, that plane's 105mm howitzers, 40mm cannons, and Gatling guns show little mercy on the ground. On 16 April 2004, the Marines dropped a 2000 pound bomb inside the city (presumably laser-guided).[214] On the night of 26 April 2004, they reportedly dropped 30 more bombs (presumably laser-guided 500 pounders).[215] Shortly thereafter, they were replaced by the "Fallujah Protective Army."[216] Initially represented by two Baathist generals (sporting their old uniforms and flag),[217] this impromptu force consisted of former-regime soldiers from Fallujah, possibly to include a few resisters.[218] This valiant attempt at a "political" solution marked the end of de-Baathification.[219] Minimal force might also have worked, but only with the state-of-the-art "blooming lotus" maneuver and troops specially trained in urban infiltration and assault."[220]

The Enemy's Urban Combat Techniques

During the initial American assault on Fallujah in early April 2004, Muslim fighters appeared to withdraw through a series of hastily prepared positions. One Marine indicated on TV that his unit was being drawn into a series of ambushes.[221] Rebels could be seen vaulting from rooftop to rooftop.[222] They soon started employing some of the same sniper tactics that had been so destructive in Grozny, Seoul, Manila, Berlin, and Stalingrad.[223] As intended, those sniper rounds drew tank fire.[224]

Snipers fired repeatedly at patrols from rooftops and

windows, and others lobbed mortars and rockets at military convoys and bunkers dug around the perimeter of the city. . . .
. . . Many enemy fighters were dressed in black and had scarves wrapped around their faces.[225]
— *Washington Post,* 6 April 2004

Snipers began to turn up, with optical sights on rifles. Some would work in pairs. One would shoot and the other would wait for the Marines to move forward in response and try to shoot them in the back.[226]
— *Washington Times,* 12 April 2004

As the Marines waited to resume their attack on Fallujah in mid-April 2004, they saw Muslim gunmen moving into buildings and onto rooftops at the city's outskirts. They also believed them to be digging tunnels between the houses.[227] One night, several Marine positions came under simultaneous attack. To counter the Marines' night vision capability, one Islamic unit lit up its objective with flares and then "unleashed heavy, continuous gunfire."[228] More ominously, the rebels were operating in groups of two to four men with some carrying crew-served weapons.[229] This is highly reminiscent of the Russian killer teams in Stalingrad.

On 17 April 2004, just over a hundred rebels attacked a Marine battalion at Husaybah (near the Syrian border), fought for 24 hours, and inflicted a score of casualties.[230] While Marine intelligence said the fighters came from Ramadi and Fallujah, it didn't mention their sect or organization. Fighters this bold and skilled probably came from a *Hezbollah* unit in transit. What makes this "attack" unique is the deceptive manner in which it was fought. First, a roadside bomb was detonated at Baath Party headquarters as a decoy. Then, the responding unit was met with machinegun and RPG fire. Finally, U.S. reinforcements were mortared and taken under small-arms and RPG fire from both sides of the road. "All of the slain Marines were killed during the first 90 minutes when they went to clear a house and were ambushed by Iraqis hiding in the building."[231] The outdoor events perfectly mirror the Eastern (feigned-retreat) way of fighting. The indoor event is more disturbing. There are ways to turn a building into a deathtrap for hastily trained soldiers.[232] Hopefully, *Hezbollah* will never discover them. For obscure movement is not the U.S. infantry's longest suit. On 18 April 2004, an American platoon was photographed crossing a Husaybah vacant lot with every member fully exposed.[233]

On 26 April 2004, several U.S. soldiers were hurt or killed while investigating a report of chemical munitions in a Baghdad warehouse. When the whole front of the one-story structure exploded, four military vehicles were set ablaze.[234] Hopefully, the guerrillas haven't started to lure U.S. troops into boobytrapped buildings.

Evidence of a Tunnel War

During the initial battle for Fallujah, insurgents were seen entering a "cave."[295] As most cities do not have caves *per se,* one wonders about its origin. On 7 April 2003, *Newsweek* indicated that "Saddam has built an extensive underground tunnel system that could be used to ambush forces or as a quick getaway."[236] Even unprepared urban terrain offers subterranean access to strategic assets.

In the subsequent fight for Najaf, al-Sadr's forces took full advantage of underground parking and subterranean burial facilities. In all probability, they used the old city's sewers as well.

The Enemy's Successes So Far

While preventing the government from providing basic services, the Islamic militant isolates its forces. So far, the Iraqi resistance has accomplished both. It has created an environment so chaotic that most of the aid allocated for reconstruction has gone toward security. It has demoralized the new Iraqi police and military forces and relegated U.S. units to the countryside.

Last summer they [U.S. forces] were running about 2,400 patrols a day nationwide, according to official figures. In the latest reports, the figures had fallen to 1,400. Most American troops live huddled in a few sprawling encampments that have grown into small cities. Of 105,000 U.S. military personnel now stationed in Iraq, more than half are housed in just four megabases. There used to be 60 U.S. bases in Baghdad, but the last of those posts is to be

closed by the end of this month, and U.S. troops will have pulled back to eight big suburban enclaves. The only base within the city will be inside the Green Zone protecting the CPA [Coalition Provisional Authority]. Already it is possible to spend an entire day traveling around the capital's Iraqi sectors without seeing a single GI.[237]
— *Newsweek,* 12 April 2004

On 17 May 2004, Iraqi militants managed to kill—at the main gate to Baghdad's supersecure Green Zone—the president of Iraq's Governing Council.[238] A suicide car bomber pulled past the other vehicles in line and stopped next to the president's car.

The Foe's Miscalculation

On 11 May 2004, an *al-Qaeda*-linked website released a gruesome videotape. It showed someone claiming to be Abu al-Zarqawi beheading an American free-lance relief worker with a knife. The executioner first declared the act in retribution for U.S. excesses at Abu Ghraib Prison. Murder and suicide are not authorized by the Koran. By resorting to them in war, the Muslim militant will loose favor with his Creator.

Hopefully, the untimely death of 26-year-old Nicholas Berg of Philadelphia, Pennsylvania, will encourage U.S. soldiers and Marines to follow the Christian model.[239]

The Second Phase of the Sadr Rebellion

In May 2004, U.S. forces began to take back the government facilities held by the Mahdi Army in Baghdad, Karbala, and Najaf. Even in the holy cities, they made full use of their firepower.[240] In response, al-Sadr began to recruit additional fighters for Najaf and expanded the war into the south.[241] As tiny groups of militia carrying rifles, RPGs, and mortars attacked police stations and armored thrusts in Najaf,[242] al-Sadr's representatives were stirring up the populations of Basra and Al'Amarah.[243] In Samawah (possibly Samarra), al-Sadr supporters tried to seal off the streets in the downtown area.[244] Finally on 17 May 2004 in Nasiriyah, al-Sadr's fighters managed to drive the Italians out of their main base.[245] In response, U.S. forces continued to raid the three holy cities. Their limited use of laser-guided bombs, AC-130 gunships, and artillery triggered Shiite demonstrations in Beirut and Tehran. Then in late May 2004, the militants left the center of Karbala. Local leaders had brokered a deal between the Mahdi Army and Coalition forces.[246] The first would leave if the second did as well. Of course, the Badr Brigade was still there. Then al-Sadr started talking about pulling his fighters out of Najaf and Kufah under the same conditions, with only Iraqi police allowed back in.[247] In this kind of war, any chance at a cease fire must be explored. Unfortunately, as in Lebanon, not every promise will be kept. Particularly disturbing were reports of a new *Hamas* office in Nasiriyah and *Hezbollah* offices in Basra and Safwan.[248] According to the *New York Times,* al-Sadr had announced his intention as early as 2 April 2004 to open *Hamas* and *Hezbollah* chapters in Iraq.[249]

Then, in early June 2004, 10,000 Iranians signed up in Tehran for suicide attacks against Israel and U.S.-led forces in Iraq. They had been recruited by an organization calling itself the Commemoration of Martyrs of the Global Islamic Campaign.[250] Such activities don't happen in Iran without the expressed permission of the *Sepah.* Shortly thereafter, the Ukrainian contingent in Iraq picked up 40 armed Iranians crossing the border to join the anti-Coalition guerrillas.[251] The influx of fighters directly from Iran (instead of via Lebanon) had probably been sparked by Ayatollah Khamenei's remarks at the 3 June celebration of Ayatollah Khomeini's death. His assertion that the U.S. was intentionally humiliating the Iraqis had evoked chants of "death to America" from the crowd.[252]

The Pre-Turnover Offensive, 10-28 June 2004

With the scheduled turnover only weeks away, the level of violence in Iraq picked up. On 10 June 2004, al-Sadr's men broke their cease fire agreement. They seized a Najaf police station and then quickly withdrew.[253] Oil pipelines were blown up at Hamdamiyah, a village 25 kilometers from the Basra export terminal.[254]

On 24 June 2004, a week before the scheduled turnover of power, what were supposedly members of al-Zarqawi's "Tawhid and Jihad" Movement launched car bomb and rocket-propelled-grenade attacks across the northern half of Iraq. On the first day alone, 100 Iraqis

163

(mostly policemen) and three Americans were killed in Mosul, Baqubah, Ramadi, Fallujah, Baghdad, and Mahaweel. The targets in Mosul were police stations, a police academy, and a hospital.[255] In Ramadi, an estimated 40 gunmen stormed the police station.[256] While Ramadi is at the edge of the Sunni triangle, it is also on the road to Syria. A Marine sentry post had just been "ambushed" there.[257] *Hezbollah* is one of the few groups in the area with enough infiltration skill to accomplish such a feat. In Baqubah, guerrillas shot their way into a government complex, two police stations, and the police chief's home.[258] The day after the attack, they were still roaming the streets.[259] In response, the U.S. resumed dropping heavy, precision ordnance—to include eleven 500 pound bombs and a 2000 pounder. They were then able to reoccupy most of the affected areas.[260]

After three of the four Italian hostages were rescued,[261] other hostages were taken to pressure Coalition partners into withdrawing. First a Japanese man was beheaded.[262] Then, three Turkish contract workers were caught and released. Next, the long-held American soldier was shot. Finally a U.S. Marine interpreter was captured, with his abductors claiming to have infiltrated his compound.[263] Infiltration is every bit as plausible as unauthorized absence. On 28 June 2004, a contract truck driver reported security so lax at many camps that he was being cursorily waved through the entrance.[264] Perhaps insurgents dressed as Coalition soldiers grabbed the Marine. When the Marine, who was of Lebanese descent, later showed up at the U.S. Embassy in Beirut, the identity of his abductors became more apparent. Since April 2004, most kidnappings have occurred in the Sunni-dominated area west of Baghdad, but there have also been some in the Shiite holy city of Najaf. As was the case in Lebanon in the 1980's, free-lance kidnappers may be able to sell their captives.[265]

Fallujah Exemplifies the Problem

Soon U.S. forces began to realize that it did little good to have former Iraqi soldiers police the streets of Fallujah.[266] The soldiers and gunmen were cooperating.[267] The ensuing U.S. bombardment highlighted a far more sinister problem. The Pentagon's new "transformation" policy—of knowledge, precision, and speed—had taken on a life of its own. It seemed bent on asserting itself under every wartime circumstance. Unfortunately, it was never designed for a guerrilla war. Guerrilla groups routinely change location, and even valid "human" intelligence takes a while to process. Ergo the bombs hit the wrong people.

On 19 June 2004, the U.S. began a series of precision airstrikes against suspected al-Zarqawi safe houses in Fallujah after warning its citizens by pamphlet to give him up.[268] As of 5 July 2004, there had been six separate missile strikes within the city killing roughly 60 people.[269] There were many women and children among the dead, but no confirmed *al-Qaeda* combatants.[270] Then on 6 July 2004, U.S. planes dropped two tons of bombs—four 500 pounders and two 1000 pounders—on another purported militant safehouse in Fallujah. This time 10 people were killed.[271] On 18 July 2004, those planes struck again. While onlookers admitted that 25 Tawhid and Jihad fighters had recently been in the area, they also asserted that none of the 14 killed were combatants.[272] Either the U.S. style of war had been exploited by enemy media, or it had just revealed its own shortcomings. One wonders how long the citizens of Fallujah will have to endure the fruitless bombardment.

The Post-Turnover Period

As per U.N. Security Council resolution, "full sovereignty" was passed from the CPA to the new Iraqi regime on 28 June 2004. While al-Sadr announced support for the new government, his actions spoke otherwise. On 29 June, his forces captured and released (probably after extracting a promise) 25 policemen in Najaf.[273] Two days later, his forces were fighting the police in Al'Amarah.[274] On 4 July 2004, he declared the new government illegitimate and vowed to keep fighting. He also spoke of turning his movement into a political party.[275] On 15 July 2004, the *Christian Science Monitor* reported al-Sadr's forces were regrouping and rearming in Najaf with the help of 80 Iranian agents. They continued to kidnap local policemen, occupy government buildings, and arrest anyone they wanted. On 5 August 2004, they ran a night attack on a police station in Najaf and then shot down a U.S. helicopter.[276]

Meanwhile, hostage-taking continued with the seizure of a Filipino and execution of a Bulgarian. As a result, the Philippine government decided to withdraw its contingent. As of 27 July 2004, the remaining major contributors to the Coalition were Great Britain, Italy, Poland, Ukraine, Holland, Australia, Romania, South Korea, Japan, Denmark, Thailand, Bulgaria, El Salvador, and Hungary.[277]

On 4 July 2004, the oil pipelines at Musayyib, 50 miles south of Baghdad, were once again severed—halving the export total.[278] On 15 July 2004, the oil lines north of Baghdad were blown.[279] The "U.S. logistical hub" at the sprawling Balad Airbase has been mortared and rocketed almost daily.[280] The base is protected by "Predator" drones carrying "Hellfire" missiles. To confuse U.S. countermeasures, guerrillas have been using timers to unexpectedly fire their ordnance from multiple directions.[281] Airborne electronic gadgetry cannot yet see below ground. So much for trying to fight a guerrilla war without light infantry.

"The real lessons of Iraq are that the nature of conflict has changed and that our military doesn't perform very well in these new circumstances," says retired Navy Capt. Larry Seaquist. For example, says Captain Seaquist, the so-called information revolution did not furnish critical intelligence information.

"The huge investment in computer networks, drone aircraft, and the other high-tech gadgetry failed to provide situational awareness about the only thing that counted—which Iraqis favored and which opposed the occupation," says Seaquist. "That failure led to the need to snatch thousands of Iraqis for interrogation—a strategy that turned out not only to be ineffective but a strategic disaster for the entire enterprise."[282]

— *Christian Science Monitor,* 2 July 2004

The Real Force with Which to Be Reckoned

There was little, if any, hostage taking or suicide bombing during *al-Qaeda's* participation in the Soviet-Afghan and first Chechen Wars. Those are tactics from Lebanon. As the summer of 2004 dragged on, something became more apparent in Iraq. Repeatedly resisting the peace process was a faction with Lebanese ties—*al-Sadr's* Mahdi Army. On the 6th of August, it began fighting much harder for Najaf than it had in the spring. The unrest quickly spread to the predominantly Shiite areas of East Baghdad, Nasiriyah, Al'Amarah, and Basra.[283] Amid the news reports was evidence of a hidden sponsor.

> Al-Zurufi, the Najaf governor, . . . said 80 of the fighters at the cemetary *[sic]* were Iranian. "There is Iranian support to al-Sadr's group and this is no secret," he said.[284]
> — Associated Press, 7 August 2004

Those 80 men might be from an Iranian Revolutionary Guard contingent or somewhere else. For most Americans, Muqtada al-Sadr's repeated attacks, broken promises, and direct references to *Hezbollah* would be adequate proof of that organization's deployment to Iraq. Of course, the Iranian Revolutionary Guard is deeply involved as well.[285] One wonders why the U.S. administration has been slow to acknowledge these things. Like *Hezbollah* in Lebanon and *Hamas* in Israel, the Mahdi Army has set up a parallel government that aspires to Shiite statehood. That government has its own social programs, religious courts, police patrols, and town councils.[286] In fact, al-Sadr's every action hints of a Lebanese blueprint. Musa al-Sadr (no relation to Muqtada) was the Iranian-born leader of the Lebanese Shiites in 1979.[287] *Hezbollah's* command center near Beirut Airport is at the Imam "al-Mahdi" mosque.[288] That Muqtada's army bears the same name is no coincidence. "Islamic Response, the security wing of the National Islamic Resistance," claimed responsibility for the capture and subsequent release of the Lebanese-born Marine interpreter.[289] *Hezbollah's* military wing is also called the "Islamic Resistance Movement."[290] On 28 August 2004, Iraqi insurgents released a short video of two kidnapped Frenchmen. Boldly displayed behind the hostages was a drawing of *Hezbollah's* favorite logo—an upraised fist clutching an AK-47.[291]

The Second Sadr Rebellion

Under heavy attack at Najaf in early August of 2004, al-Sadr's forces went on the offensive elsewhere. On the 11th, they fired mortars or rockets at government facilities throughout Baghdad and mined the main street into Sadr City. At Basra, they threatened the oil pipeline.[292] On 12 August 2004, they went after police stations, city hall, Iraqi National Guard barracks, and a Tigris River bridge at Al Kut.[293] During renewed fighting in Al'Amarah, hundreds of Iraqi National Guardsmen vowed to join al-Sadr until U.S. forces left Najaf.[294] All the while, Mahdi Army recruiters/trainers were hard at work.[295]

When U.S. journalist Micah Garen and his translator were abducted from a Nasiriyah market on 13 August, the most probable instigator of the April kidnappings became more apparent.[296] This time it was Najaf that U.S. troops were supposed to leave. Taking credit for the seizure was the "Martyrs Brigade."[297] While this term normally refers to the al-Aqsa faction of *Fatah,* a variation has occasionally been used by *Hezbollah* itself. In this particular case, the hostage was released at al-Sadr's office after his personal request. Of course, there is a very good reason why the Muslim cleric had such quick communication and great influence with the kidnappers.

True to form, al-Sadr agreed to a peace plan on 18 August and then allowed his forces to keep fighting. While stalling for time in Najaf, they blew up oil pipelines near Al'Amarah on 20 August and Basra on the 21st.[298] Then, on 25 August, Grand Ayatollah al-Sistani brokered a peace deal and brought in pilgrims.[299] While emotionally soothing, his effort closely resembled a military delaying and replacement operation. On 26 August 2004, 20 oil pipelines were simultaneously attacked in southern Iraq, effectively shutting off the export of oil.[300] Four days later, Mahdi Army fighters bragged about having recruited 3,000 suicide bombers during the Najaf standoff.[301]

Things Were Not Going Well Overall

All the while, the size of the insurgency had been increasing. While 5,000 Iraqis were previously thought to be involved, that estimate was upped to 20,000 on 9 July 2004.[302] By the end of August, 100,000 Iraqis were participating in the Sunni portion of the rebellion,[303] and who knows how many in the Shiite portion. The mobilization efforts of *al-Qaeda* and *Hezbollah* were apparently working. Also hard to ignore was the impression that the two movements had been taking turns causing trouble—*al-Qaeda* in the Sunni Triangle and North, *Hezbollah* in East Baghdad and South. Even more disturbingly, both were now concentrating on the same targets:

police facilities, foreign hostages, and oil lines. In response, the new government cracked down on vagrants and prepared to take a more active role in the country's defense. By summer's end, U.S. forces were routinely bombing Fallujah.[304] On 7 September 2004, they had yet to resume patrolling that city.[305] Two days later came the admission that insurgents were "firmly in control" of Fallujah and several other cities. At the top of the list were Ramadi, Baqubah, Samarra, and Al Tafar (near the Syrian border).[306] For the previous month nationwide, the total of attacks against U.S. forces had risen to 646.[307] On 14 September 2004, the U.S. administration announced that it would take three more years to restore Iraq's basic services (water, electricity, sewage, etc.).[308]

Thus, peace seemed more distant than ever. U.S. forces were having trouble dealing with so devious an opponent. They would soon have to choose between established procedure and ultimate victory.

Part Three

Bringing Peace to the Region

A nation that continues to spend more money on military defense than on programs of social uplift is approaching spiritual death. — Martin Luther King

(Source: "The Martin Luther King Jr. America Has Ignored," *Christian Science Monitor,* 16 January 2004)

How Islamic Guerrillas _____ Are Trained

9

- Do the Muslims prepare mostly for short-range combat?
- Is their small-unit training superior to that of U.S. forces?

ALGERIAN NATIONAL LIBERATION ARMY MAN, 1960

(Source: Courtesy of Orion Books, from *World Army Uniforms since 1939*, © 1983 by Blandford Press Ltd., Part II, Plate 54; *FM 21-76* (1957), p. 56; *FM 90-3* (1977), p. 4-2)

How the Koran Says to Fight

The Islamic holy book—Koran—promises paradise to martyrs. It stresses close, hand-to-hand combat with knives. It says to fight though badly outnumbered. It disallows moving backwards except to a better position from which to attack. It implies that opposition forces should be surrounded while they attack and ambushed as they retreat.[1] Unfortunately, when literally interpreted, the Koran's militaristic guidelines match the central precepts of Maoist "mobile warfare" (and what has come to be known in the West as "maneuver warfare").

173

Early Palestinian Training Camps

No information could be found on the learning objectives and instructional methods at the early Palestinian training camps. At least nine such camps existed in Syria, Lebanon, Libya, Iraq, and South Yemen before 1979.[2] They were heavily attended by the future trainers of the Iranian Revolutionary Guard and Lebanese *Hezbollah*.

Iranian Revolutionary Guard Training

The Iranian Revolutionary Guards or *Sepah* came from two groups: (1) those who had fought against the Shah after some training at Palestinian or Lebanese camps,[3] and (2) those who had fought against the Shah without any previous training.[4] Not much is known about how the second group was prepared to fight the Iraqis.

In terms of training, the central *[Sepah]* command organized half a dozen "academies" throughout the country, where battle-tested commanders who had fought in the anti-insurgency campaigns in 1979 and a selective group of regular military officers would instruct the recruits in classical military training.[5]

Sepah was responsible for recruiting, training, and leading the mobilized citizen soldiers or *Baseej*. Just to train the *Baseej*, the second group must have been shown the composite steps to rudimentary tactical techniques. Then, unfettered by doctrine, they probably discovered—through teaching—how to refine those steps. Students make perfect subjects for ongoing tactical research.

> [T]he strides the Guard has made in developing its training programs are impressive. . . . [I]n 1982, the Guard inaugurated its first "high school," . . . which combined general education, military training, and the teaching of Islamic ideology ("IRC to Get Own High School . . . ," *Iran Press Digest,* 18 August 1982, 10). . . . Students at the school . . . spent part of the two and one half year program at Guard military camps. Over the next two years, the Guard estab-

lished branches of its high school in all of its administrative districts throughout Iran ("Khamenei Attends IRGC . . . ," *Tehran IRNA,* 7 March 1988). . . .

. . . For the Guard's ground forces, its basic training program consisted of a compulsory three months of instruction in Guard tactics and weapons use ("History and Present Status of IRGC," *Tehran Iran Press Digest,* 7 August 1984, 14). This basic training was conducted at Guard bases and garrisons throughout Iran and at the front. . . . To facilitate its increased use of special commando operations and elite units, the Guard also established a separate Infantry Center . . . in Tehran, which offered an intensive infantry training course ("IRGC Minister Addresses . . . ," *Tehran IRNA,* 28 February 1988).[6]

From the start, the Guard had to adapt to changing circumstances and improvise.[7] Light infantry must do the same thing. To win consistently, its frontline soldiers must be allowed to make many of their own decisions. In the 1980's, the Iranian Revolutionary Guard were running guerrilla training camps patterned after the *Hashishins'* Alamut in north Tehran's Manzariyeh Garden and just north of Qom.[8] It also had training facilities near Baalbek in the Bekaa Valley. (See Map 9.1.) Like the "Old Man of the Mountain," they had discovered how to defeat a powerful force with tiny elements.

How the *Baseej* Were Trained

The Guard did not send the *Baseej* to the regular army for training; it conducted its own. By some accounts, its instruction covered automatic rifles and hand grenades and lasted two weeks.[9] At many locations, however, it may have contained much more.

During the first few years of the war with Iraq, the *Baseej* training has been variously described as rudimentary,[10] intensive, and three months long.[11] Light-arms training could last as long as a month.[12] As the *Sepah* were generally considered assault and close-combat specialists,[13] they would have looked for ways to generate surprise. Their instruction almost certainly included night assaults.[14]

Hezbollah Training

"[T]he Lebanese Hezbollah has become a substantial military force that has demonstrated considerable skill . . . in guerrilla war-

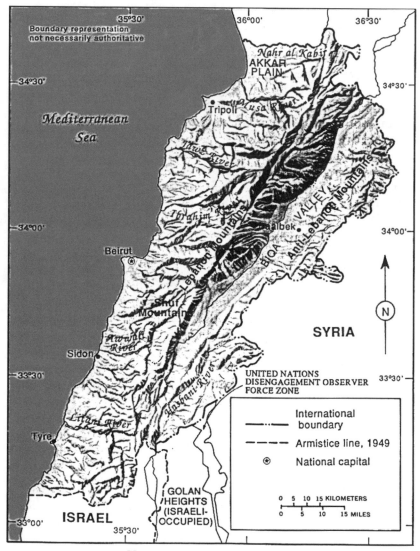

Map 9.1: The Bekaa Valley
(Source: *DA Pam 550-24* (1989), Figure 3)

fare in South Lebanon."[15] That skill was very probably in the area of short-range tactics, for that would have been the by-product of an experimental approach to individual and small-unit training.

> The combat units are trained by Iranian experts in a training facility at Sheikh Abdallah, near Baalbeck *[sic]* in the Bekaa Valley. . . . Individual training is also being performed abroad. In Iran, the Revolutionary Guards, or Pasdaran *[Sepah]*, are operating training camps at Imam Ali Camp in northern Tehran, where leadership courses are held for the El-Kuds fighters of Lebanon. On their return, graduates serve as instructors for operational cadres. Courses for urban combat are held at Isfahan. Near the town of Khoum, Imam Rada camp trainees undergo courses on sabotage and demolition. At Mashad, specialist courses are held for Hezbollah and other terrorist groups.[16]
> *Marine Corps Gazette,* July 1997

The Guard's relative freedom from political control may have given it better learning dynamics than most Western armies.[17]

Joint Ventures

In October 2003, a PFLP-GC leader admitted that his group, *Islamic Jihad, Hamas,* and *Hezbollah* all train together in Lebanon and Syria.[18] Such collaboration occurs routinely in the Bekaa Valley. It also occurs inside Syria.

> The Ayn Tzahab terrorist training camp in Syria is supported by Iran and is used for operational training for Palestinian terrorists including Hamas and Palestinian Islamic Jihad operatives.
> There is a wide variety of training in the camp, including sabotage, artillery training, guerilla *[sic]* warfare and even aeronautical training. Some of the terrorists . . . are operatives who come to receive advanced training and then return to Palestinian Authority territory in order to establish an operational terrorist infrastructure. . . .
> . . . [T]he Hamas headquarters in Damascus recruits and trains Palestinians in Hezbollah training camps. The

training includes manufacturing explosive devices and explosive belts, intelligence collection, training in kidnapping, and instruction in preparing and carrying out terrorist attacks against military and civilian targets.[19]
— Israel News Agency, 5 October 2003

Sudan does more than host Chinese, *Hezbollah,* and *al-Qaeda* visits. It may have become the preferred training ground for militant Palestinians.

We have seen the transcription of President Bashir's speech earlier this month in which he called for the establishment of camps [in Sudan] to train militants for the Palestinian intifada.[20]
— U.S. State Dept. Briefing, 23 April 2002

Afghan *Mujahideen* Training

The Afghan Service Bureau of the Pakistani ISI conducted the majority of the training of the local *mujahideen.*

From 1984, through to 1987, over 80,000 mujahideen went through our training camps. . . .
Each camp had a staff of 2-3 officers, 6-8 JCOs and 10-12 NCOs. . . . As the months passed our program expanded to cater for a wide variety of both weapon training and tactical subjects. We set up a two-week heavy weapons course for antitank and anti-aircraft guns, and 82mm mortars; there was a mine-laying and lifting course; demolition courses to cover the destruction of bridges, electricity pylons, gas or oil pipelines, and road cratering; urban warfare, which was designed to teach sabotage techniques for use in Kabul or other cities; long communication courses; instructor courses for mujahideen and junior leader courses. Most of these were held at the outdoor, tented camps.[21]
— Brigadier Yousaf, Afghan Service Bureau Chief

The ISI may still be training insurgents for a Taliban resurgence in Afghanistan.

The analysts of the Indian special services informed [that] there were 127 training camps working in Pakistan itself and on Kashmir's territory which is occupied by this country. There are 80-100 gunmen in each of those camps.[22]
— *Pravda* (Russia), 18 September 2001

Al-Qaeda

Al-Qaeda has trained between 25,000 and 50,000 fighters since its inception in 1987.[23] It is dangerous, not because it has the most sophisticated tactical techniques in the world, but because it has a training methodology that will eventually discover those techniques. *Al-Qaeda* must be beaten before it becomes as proficient as the VC.

These people are using extremely effective training methods![24]
— U.S. *"Al-Qaeda* Training Tape Assessment"

Like *Hezbollah* in 1982, *al-Qaeda* started out as a recruiting and training institution in 1987. To the casual observer, its training looks like a strange mixture of obstacle course, "live-fire" exercise, and aggressor role playing. In actuality, it is a realistic way to refine its growing portfolio of tactical techniques. Unfortunately, *al-Qaeda* widely distributes those refinements over the Al Battar and other internet sites. That gives every *al-Qaeda* cell and allied guerrilla group immediate access to the latest discovery. Here's how Iraqi surrogate—*Ansar al-Islam*—trains:

"It was unlike any training I had ever seen," says Mansour. "They put down ropes to cross an area, and put sacks of soil on their backs and climbed mountains while avoiding bullets. They used kung fu, and learned how to counterattack with a gun at your back."[25]

Al-Qaeda trainers follow a modified "battledrill" methodology that allows them to situationally tailor and constantly refine their techniques. A standard "battledrill" has attention gainer, lecture, demonstration, practical application, and practical-application testing. By using aggressors during the practical-application-test portion of each battledrill, *al-Qaeda* trainers can continually reassess the technique on which that battledrill is based. The tactical sophistication of a maneuver is inversely proportional its production of friendly casualties. By simulating casualties, measuring speed, recording stealth, and assessing deception, *al-Qaeda* trainers can determine each maneuver's degree of surprise. Thus, while U.S. instructors are forced by doctrine to stick to standardized procedure,[26] *al-Qaeda* trainers are constantly improving their techniques through experimentation. At *al-Qaeda* camps, students learn briefly about equipment but then spend most of their time running through combat scenarios. Those scenarios have realistic sound effects, life-size mockups, and casualty-counting role players. Because each student also gets feedback on when he was last "killed," he improves individual-movement skills on subsequent tries to survive similar circumstances.

> This [technique] was [practiced] on a number of scenarios that were shown first as a diagram and explanation, then progressing to dry fire walk through and finally to a live-fire exercise. . . . In one iteration . . . the security/overwatch element was exercised [by] firing on possible responding law enforcement officers.[27]
> — U.S. *"Al-Qaeda* Training Tape Assessment"

The Power of the Muslim Chants

One of the master *ninja's* favorite techniques is that of self-hypnosis.[28] It helps him to better concentrate on the job at hand.[29] Based on ancient Himalayan (Tantric) spiritual teachings,[30] *ninpo mykko* reveals the source of better focus to be meditation.[31] During spiritual refinement *(seishin teki kyoyo),*[32] the practitioner achieves a relaxed mental state,[33] and then he channels his energy through chants and finger weaving *(kuji-in).*[34]

Harnessing one's subconscious through self-hypnosis falls under the broad category of mind control *(saiminjitsu).*[35] It helps the user to gain inner strength through meditation,[36] to transcend fear or pain,[37] and to enhance his external awareness.[38] The latter is in turn accomplished several ways: (1) concentrating on sensory impressions,[39] (2) paying attention to detail,[40] (3) reading the thoughts of others,[41] (4) perceiving danger,[42] (5) making clutch decisions,[43] and (6) visualizing the task to be accomplished.[44] Hypnosis has long been recognized as a remedy for fear and pain.[45] It should therefore have battlefield application. U.S. veterans of the Pacific, Korea, and Vietnam have long talked of foes who appeared less than fully sober. Many of those foes were self-hypnotized.

Ninjutsu was carried to Japan and Southeast Asia around 900 A.D. by soldiers of the collapsing Chinese T'ang Dynasty.[46] Most *ninja*-like skills had probably spread along the trade routes to the Middle East by the 11th Century.

On 3 April 2004, seven suspects in the Madrid Railway Station bombing blew themselves up after loudly chanting in Arabic.[47] The "9/11" bombers had done some chanting as well. One left a "telltale" instruction sheet behind.

> [T]hey [the hijackers] may have been manipulated by sophisticated psychological methods involving repetitive readings of selective passages of the Koran along with mesmeric techniques of Islamic mysticism. . . .
>
> At first, it [the document] seemed an inscrutable list of practical and religious advice. . . .
>
> The letter was much more than a checklist, Cole [a researcher] concluded. It was a mechanism or tool for "autohypnosis" and "psychological manipulation." . . .
>
> To reinforce this [the reader's association with martyrdom], the document invokes an intricate prayer system apparently borrowed from Sufi mysticism, a narrow branch of Islam, Cole says. But while Sufi mystics used mantra-like repetition to achieve enlightenment, al-Qaeda adapted it for use with the hijackers to induce a mental state free of fear, critical thought, or moral qualms.[48]
> — *Christian Science Monitor,* 30 October 2003

A student of Asian mysticism and psychology confirms that mantras could be of great use to a soldier.

> Chants, from the Hindu through the Buddhist, and apparently the Sufis, have the intent of creating what the Buddhists call "Mindfulness"—as in walking meditation. . . . For example, the supreme mantra or chant of Buddhism is said to be this one: "Om gate (pronounced 'Got ee') gate,

paragate, parasam gate, Boddhi Svaha," which means "Gone, gone away, totally gone away, all is totally gone away." The intent of the mantra is to focus the devotee on the impermanence of this world, leaving . . . [him] empty (or motiveless). . . .

. . . Jihad, in its purest form . . . is not warfare against the infidel "out there" [e.g., Judeo/Christians] . . . , but rather against the infidel "in here," meaning within ourselves. More specifically, it is intended to address or "kill" . . . thoughts/ emotions that keep us . . . "addicted to the earthly desires." I believe it could be used by the soldier/combatant . . . to cleanse his/her own motives for . . . doing what . . . [he or she] is doing.[49]

— Dr. David H. Reinke, Eastern psychology docent

10 The Muslim Militants' Pattern

- *Do opposing sects share the same strategic objectives?*
- *How do their fighting styles differ?*

IRANIAN SPECIAL FORCES TROOPER, 1983

(Source: Courtesy of Orion Books from *Uniforms of the Elite Forces*, ©1982 by Blandford Press Ltd., Plate 26, No. 77; *FM 90-3* (1977), p. 4-2)

Principal Threats to the Coaltion

The Iranian Revolutionary Guard sent an expeditionary force to Lebanon in 1982 and may have deployed another to Iraq more recently. Or its headstrong creation—Lebanese *Hezbollah*—may have dispatched its own contingent. Either way, *jihadist* Arabs would emulate their tactics.

Of course, *al-Qaeda* is also present in both Iraq and Afghanistan. From its Sunni heritage and Soviet exposure, it has acquired a slightly different tactical heritage. That heritage now encompasses the Chechen experience.

183

The Iranian Revolutionary Guards

While *Islamic Jihad* took the credit,[1] it was Iranian Revolutionary Guards who planned the Marine barracks bombing of 23 October 1983 in Beirut, Lebanon.[2] The truck's 20-year-old driver was, after all, Iranian and a member of that country's "Party of God."[3]

It was also Iranian Revolutionary Guards who trained Lebanese *Hezbollah.*[4] When that creation kicked the "high-tech" Israel army out of Southern Lebanon in 2000, the world took notice.

One of *Sepah's* original missions was the export of Islamic revolution.[5] Its agents have since assassinated several of Tehran's opponents abroad.[6] That it has now ceased to chase Khomeini's dream of a bloc of Islamic States is doubtful. As an autonomous organization, it may have continued to do so without the total permission of the Tehran government.[7] *Sepah* now works more for "Supreme Leader" Ayatollah Khamenei than for Iranian President Khatami.[8] It has endeavored to spread the Islamic Revolution abroad.

> The [Revolutionary] Guard retains its extensive covert network abroad. . . . [I]n 1987 the FBI announced that members of the Guard had entered the United States as students ("Iran Guards in U.S. . . . ," *New York Times,* 9 March 1989). . . .
>
> . . . [T]he Guard may [now] give greater support to Shia rebels in . . . Iraq as well as . . . Algeria, Tunisia, Jordan, Egypt, . . . the former U.S.S.R., Afghanistan, and the West Bank and Gaza. . . . [It] is already establishing a significant presence (1000-2000 Guards) in . . . Sudan, setting up camps to train the Sudanese army and "Islamic fundamentalist militants from [other countries]" ("Iran Shifting Its Attention . . . ," *New York Times,* 13 December 1991, A7). In a late 1991 interview, [Guard Commander] Reza'i said . . . , "If there is unity between Iran, Pakistan, and Afghanistan, this will strengthen Muslim solidarity and enable the peoples of Soviet Central Asia and Kashmir to join in ("The JDW Interview," *Jane's Defense Weekly,* 16 November 1991, 980)."[9]

Sepah is more than just a military, police, and counterespionage force. It is at the very center of Iranian life.

A Summary of Iranian Revolutionary Guard Tactics

At first, the Guard attempted a "people's war" against the Iraqis.[10] While the concept was successfully applied by German *Volksgrenadier* battalions at the Bulge and Berlin,[11] its roots are with Mao Tse-Tung. Like the Chinese People's Liberation Army (PLA), the Guard didn't adopt military ranks until 1990.[12] Early in the war with Iraq, the *Sepah* sent *Baseej* volunteers on numerous human-wave assaults—with little or no fire support from the regular army.[13] As the Chinese in Korea,[14] the Guard may have discovered how to facilitate rearward infiltration by feigning frontal assault. It may have also avoided preparatory fire to keep from telegraphing intentions. As the war progressed, the Guard's tactics improved. "Surprise and infiltration helped to push the Iraqis across the border."[15] By 1987, the Islamic leadership had publicly opted for surprise over human waves.[16] They had also embraced the Communist guerrilla policy of not fighting unless victory was virtually assured.[17] Still, the Guard had tried to clear Iraqi minefields with a few "martyr-bent" *Baseej*. So its cultural predisposition toward tiny, highly risky forays may have survived.

The Iranian Guard is a revolutionary army. That puts it in the same category with the Chinese PLA and Soviet Red Army.[18] Most Eastern armies have been forced by their lack of wherewithal to tactically evolve more quickly than U.S. forces. Despite an early fling with antiquated tactics, the *Sepah* has the same chance. Chinese "mobile" warfare grew out of, and easily transitions back into, guerrilla warfare. There is no telling how much the Iranian Guard may have learned from its guerrilla victory over the Israelis in Lebanon. To make matters worse, a rare Guard psychological warfare publication contains repeated references to Sun Tzu and the Viet Cong.[19] With a little historical research and field experimentation, battle-seasoned Guard instructors could easily discover the state of the art for small-unit infantry tactics.

> [T]he Iranian Revolutionary Guards Corps and its commanders, free from over-centralized control and unaffected by traditional military staff college training—manifested much innovation and ingenuity in the midst of battle.[20]

Of note, the Iranian Guard was the recruiter/trainer of espionage agents as well as frontline soldiers.[21] As such, it may have developed some fairly sophisticated short-range infiltration techniques. Iran has subterranean aqueducts that date back to the time of Christ.[22] To confront a technologically superior foe, its ground forces would be quick to move below ground on both defense and offense.

Sepah differs from Chinese and Soviet armies in that it plays a greater role in the internal security of the nation, the collection of human intelligence, and the export of revolution. In China and the Soviet Union, other organizations perform those functions.[23]

The Guards are experts at psychological warfare. Their methods are as follows:

(1) deception [e.g., misinformation];
(2) stupefying [e.g., pushing the material over the spiritual];
(3) inciting [e.g., encouraging hatred];
(4) alluring [e.g., using incentives];
(5) enlightenment [e.g., highlighting enemy deficiencies];
(6) creating fear [e.g., exaggerating danger]; and
(7) indirect induction [e.g., talking in a roundabout way].[24]

Their economic objective is to increase the gap between societal expectations and an unstable economy. Their military objective is to further distrust, undermine discipline, discourage political/ideological awareness, and fan discrimination in the opposing force. Their political objectives are to exacerbate the instability, insecurity, and lack of supervision of a central government. Their social objectives are to create negative attitudes, preferential treatment, and ideological/religious expediency.[25]

Sepah handles counter-initiatives through several means: (1) pinpointing objectives, (2) attacking vulnerabilities, (3) destroying prestige, and (4) ridicule.[26] To do so, it works through the indigenous population. It encourages their faith/conviction and avoids factional/religious disputes.[27] It blames Western colonialists for the trouble between Sunnis and Shiites.[28] As a revolutionary organization, it works through the common man. It informs and intimidates him, and then it learns from him. The indigenous population provides its greatest source of real-time intelligence. *Sepah* operatives work and live among the Iranian people. The people tell them things.

Like the Holy Prophet of Islam, the Iranian Guards gather intelligence by sending out patrol-reconnaissance teams, deploying spies, and extracting information from POWs.[29] They use the psychological-warfare methods of their Islamic ancestors:

(1) inciting;
(2) terror;
(3) feigning power [e.g., downplaying own weaknesses];
(4) spreading rumors;
(5) giving sermons;
(6) displaying symbols [e.g., flags or special headdresses];
(7) chanting slogans [e.g., "Allah akbar (God is Great)" or heroic poems]; and
(8) generating deception.[30]

At the same time, *Sepah* has learned how to adapt to modern technology. It easily floods electronic eavesdropping equipment with too much information.[31] It readily sways public opinion through every form of media.

Hezbollah

Based in Lebanon, *Hezbollah* has many aliases: *"Hizballah," "Hizbullah," "Islamic Jihad,"* "Revolutionary Justice Organization," "Organization of the Oppressed on Earth," "Followers of God," "Islamic Resistance," "Organization of Right Against Wrong," and "Followers of the Prophet Muhammed."[32] While still closely affiliated with the Iranian Revolutionary Guard and Ayatollah Khamenei, *Hezbollah* has now assumed its own identity. While it does have a "secretary general" (currently Hassan Nasrallah), it is more of a movement than an organization. As such, it doesn't struggle with bureaucratic problems. Even its military wing calls itself the "Islamic Resistance Movement."

Hezbollah forms a nebulous umbrella over various Shiite groups. All follow a Khomeinistic ideology. Though *Hezbollah* never disarmed, it still maintains 11 seats on the Lebanese parliament. Its degree of control over Lebanon has been progressive. Many of the country's Marionite Christians are now rumored to be leaving. Unfortunately, *Hezbollah* has much more in mind than just recapturing Jerusalem and destroying Israel.

The Hezbollah organization views as an important goal the fight against "western imperialism."[33]
— Excerpt from *Hezbollah's* political platform

Like Iran and the Peoples' Republic of China, *Hezbollah* views ongoing revolution as necessary to progress. It has cells in Europe, Africa, South America, North America, and Asia. It also operates throughout the Middle East. Some 130 of its militants have been released from prison in Turkey alone.[34] There is mounting evidence that *Hezbollah* may have deployed a small expeditionary force to Iraq. The Naval Postgraduate School at Monterey admits only to a *"Hezbollah* presence."[35] Still, the circumstances in Iraq are identical to those on which two thousand *Sepah* capitalized in Lebanon 20 years ago. Lebanon's million Shiites would provide sufficient manpower to make such an undertaking possible. For the right price, many of its destitute Palestinians would gladly become suicide bombers. *Hezbollah* currently runs a much larger recruiting and training operation than it needs to defend Lebanon and attack Israel.

The organization maintains a training apparatus in Lebanon throughout the villages and their surroundings, as well as outside of Lebanon. Training is aimed at building a reliable manpower source for its military forces as well as for its terror arm.[36]
— Info. Div., Israeli Foreign Ministry, Jerusalem

Lebanese *Hezbollah* has as little organizational structure as its founder (the Iranian *Sepah).* Its rank-and-file members are more committed to Islam than to any parent nation or military superior. Its "cells" operate semi-independently, bound together only by the mutual goals of *jihad.* As such those cells can easily adapt to battlefield circumstances. Because of this decentralization of control, *Hezbollah* can also more easily evolve tactically than a "top-down" military bureaucracy.

It [Lebanese *Hezbollah]* has been an organization that is constantly evolving and innovating in the field of light infantry combat. . . . Readers will discover a dynamic organization that has earned the admiration of jihadist networks

like al-Qaeda and whose [infantry] techniques have been
imitated by . . . Hamas.[37]
— *Marine Corps Gazette,* June 2003

To enhance battlefield control, a Western army standardizes its
small-unit tactical procedures. It determines which to doctrinally
require of all units by "staffing" them. Unfortunately, staffing tends
to produce the lowest common denominator—that upon which every staffer can agree. As each staffer is thinking about a slightly
different set of combat circumstances, the result is often so simplistic as to no longer have any value as technique. In other words, any
small unit foolish enough to replicate it in combat would suffer unnecessary casualties or be defeated. Muslim guerrillas don't have
this problem. Instead of surprise-deficient procedures to obey,
Hezbollah disseminates battlefield-tested techniques to refine. It
does so through its TV network *al-Manar* ("the Lighthouse"), radio
station, *al-Nour* ("the light"), monthly paramilitary magazine *Qubth
Ut Allah* ("the Fist of God"), and several websites.[38]

A Recap of *Hezbollah* Tactics

As the newly formed Revolutionary Guard had done during the
Iranian rebellion of 1979, *Hezbollah* uses civil disturbance as a
weapon. It knows that Westernized, firepower-dependent armies
lack the skill and initiative at the squad level to exercise minimal
force. It counts on them overreacting to civil disobedience and thus
alienating the population as a whole. To create distrust between
the occupier and his local defense/police force, it corrupts the latter.
It also conducts military operations while dressed as one or the other.
In Israel, its proxies have gone so far as to sneak between the two to
provoke firefights. In Jerusalem's old walled city, those proxies routinely harass Israeli sentries with hand claps that sound just like
sniper rounds.

Hezbollah is the region's most accomplished guerrilla organization. While it has yet to perfect its ground assault technique, its
ambushing skills are on a par with the Viet Cong, and its early
warning apparatus is better.

It uses tall structures as observation posts and plainclothes sentries every few blocks. Then, through a combination of religious duty, financial incentive, and implicit threat, it enlists the help of the average citizen. That help can range from an intelligence tip to blocking the road. Through cell phones and the "call-for-prayer" loudspeaker system, *Hezbollah* can quickly transmit an alert.

One can quickly ascertain the effectiveness of this intelligence network by poking around Beirut's bookstores for information about the Israeli defeat. In most places, such activity would evoke little more than community pride. Unfortunately, many of Beirut's citizens apparently believe what they hear on *al-Manar* TV. They are also interested in claiming the cash bonus for phoning in information. To make matters worse, every block (at least at the strategically important coastline and city center) appears to have its own plainclothes *Hezbollah* representative. While looking for books in June 2004, the author first heard a shop owner say *"Hizballah"* during a phone call. Then he noticed the same customer in subsequent stores. Finally, he was universally told that no books were available on biggest event in recent Lebanese history.

During the Lebanese civil war, *Hezbollah* learned more about tunnel warfare and short-range infiltration. The Lebanese traditionally hid their rifles in the garden under a distinctive plant. Soon, beneath the city of Beirut, appeared a vast honeycomb of huge tunnels. Then Farsi speaking infiltrators started somehow slipping into army positions to kill soldiers in their sleep.[39] When Husain, the Prophet's grandson, fought 4000 men with 70 in 680 A.D., he established somewhat of a Shiite tradition. Unlike most Western armies, Shiite forces respect what tiny, loosely controlled contingents can accomplish collectively. Such contingents more easily escape detection and show more initiative.

Hezbollah is still on a wartime footing with Israel, according to Sheihk Naim Qassem (its deputy secretary general). With the Lebanese government's tacit permission, it still attacks the disputed border area of Shebaa Farms.[40] It also supports Palestinian attacks on Israel. As late as 9 June 2004, Israeli warplanes rocketed the entrance to a suspected PFLP underground base nine kilometers south of Beirut.[41] Lebanon is not an autonomous nation. Its government is little more than a facilitator of Syrian and Iranian influence. Syria still occupies much of the country, while *Hezbollah* has free rein along the Israeli border. Its military wing is openly supported by the Lebanese government.[42] As of early 2003, *Hezbollah's* political front held 12 seats in parliament.[43] To a retired U.S. Marine, Beirut

Airport felt like the "belly of the beast."[44] No divinely inspired movement would place strategic value on the recruiting of suicide bombers.

In recent speeches, Mr. Nasrallah [Lebanese *Hezbollah's* leader] has gloated that the most accomplished military minds have failed to develop a means to counter suicide attacks. "What will protect Jerusalem, its holy places, and get it and Palestine back, is the path of the Palestinian people, through martyrdom seekers who astonish the world each day and night," he said at the [Beirut] Jerusalem Day parade on Nov. 29.[45]
— *New York Times,* 24 December 2002

Hezbollah recruits and trains local fighters. It pays them well (and their families if they are martyred). It also pays for information and hostages. All the while, it creates infrastructure within the communities of its otherwise oppressed recruiting base. Its social programs include construction, agricultural outreach, medical services, and numerous charities.[46] It has schools, hospitals, and orphanages. It may also enforce the collection of church tithes. This "4th-generation" approach to war is now being used by Sunni *jihadists* as well.

Al-Qaeda

Al-Qaeda was first established in 1987 to recruit and train *jihadists* for the Soviet-Afghan War. Since then, it has changed its way of operating and widely expanded its sphere of influence. Now, *al-Qaeda* (literally, the Base) deploys *jihadist* cells throughout the world to wage guerrilla war on what it calls the "immoral" West.[47] It is sometimes referred to as the "Osama bin Laden Network" or "Islamic Army for the Liberation of the Holy Places." Under the banner of the "World Islamic Front for Jihad Against the Jews and Crusaders," it issued a statement in February 1998 that "it was the duty of all Muslims to kill US citizens—civilian or military—and their allies everywhere." *Al-Qaeda* condones the killing of any number of noncombatants once its opponent has set the precedent.[48]

Al-Qaeda merged with Egyptian *Islamic Jihad* in June 2001.[49]

As of October 2003, it had 1000 fighters in Chechnya alone.[50] As early as 2002, an *al-Qaeda* member promised a much wider conflict than Afghanistan.

> We the mujahideen are getting ready to begin . . . the phase of guerrilla warfare. We are now developing the fronts along all lines to make it a large-scale war—the war of ambushes, assassinations, and operations that take place in the most unexpected places for the enemy.[51]
> — Abu Laith al-Libi

Al-Qaeda's principal aim is the political and religious mobilization of the local populations.[52] Then, it does what a highly stratified and standardized military cannot. It constantly refines its tactics through experimentation, widely disseminates its findings through the media, and supports its semi-independent cells through traveling trainers.

> The structure and nature of al-Qaeda enables it to tap into the wealth of operational knowledge and expertise from around the world. The group is then able to transfer this knowledge through extensive training initiatives. Al-Qaeda has assembled more than 10,000 pages of written training material, more than a hundred hours of training videos and a global network of training camps. When needed, al-Qaeda is able to tap into this network to find the requisite skills for any kind of operation. Thus, specialized training can be provided to any operational cell.[53]

A Condensation of *al-Qaeda* Tactics

Al-Qaeda is most adept at guerrilla "hit and run" tactics. At present, it does much of its damage with explosives and indirect fire.

> In guerrilla warfare training, a heavy emphasis is placed on ambushes, rocket attacks, and roadside bombings.[54]

Through its veterans of the Soviet-Afghan and Chechen wars, *al-Qaeda* also has experience with certain types of conventional operations. Its strongest suits are ambush and defense. Its mobile variant of the latter brings the intruder under close contact from every direction. Its positional variant features an underground strongpoint array, complete with hidden escape tunnels. As *al-Qaeda* cells constantly change location, their guerrilla headquarters may also rotate through 10 or so underground sites (as the VC did in Vietnam).

It is extremely difficult to deal an effective preemptive strike against a highly mobile and agile organization that does not have fixed premises.[55]
— Excerpt from an *al-Qaeda* website

Through its Grozny veterans, *al-Qaeda* has learned how to conduct a state-of-the-art, "blooming-lotus" type of urban assault. It has also developed some fairly effective street-fighting techniques. During the forced entry of a building, it enhances surprise through the minimal use of small arms. Raids on enemy compounds are initiated by RPG. Guard shacks are taken out by grenade. Walls are breached by hand-placed explosives. Whereas Western soldiers prefer to enter a building or room at one location, *al-Qaeda* operatives make multiple entries. Each is preceded by a fuse-lit distraction device (concussion grenade). Then, the two men of the clearing team assume a back-to-back stance near the center of the room. Escape is often by truck or motorcycle with a security team prepositioned to impede pursuit.[56]

While *al-Qaeda* has not yet developed a "stormtrooper" type of rural assault, it may be close to doing so. Already, its assault elements withhold their small-arms fire whenever possible.[57] Their focus on attack preparation and lessons-learned dissemination may eventually produce state-of-the-art technique. Whereas a Viet Cong unit would reconnoiter and rehearse an attack for months, an *al-Qaeda* cell often does so for years. It can thus tailor its tactical techniques to every conceivable circumstance. It also exploits each attack across the full range of political, psychological, and media options.

To gain media attention, *al-Qaeda* operatives will often try harder to kill many people than to escape themselves. Still, they seek covert or surreptitious entry to their objectives. To date, this entry has been largely accomplished through disguise. However, targets have also been infiltrated through tunnels, storm drains, and sewers. After withdrawal, explosives have been detonated by clock timer or electronic command.

Tactical Trends among the Three

Hezbollah and *al-Qaeda* operate in much the same way as the Iranian Revolutionary Guard. They recruit, train, and advise local *jihadists*. The Guard and its Lebanese creation pioneered suicide attacks, but *al-Qaeda* may now be adopting the tactic. While unafraid of close combat, all three would rather blow things up from a distance than assault them. They compensate for their shortage of indirect-fire weapons with command-detonated explosives and shoulder-fired missiles. By repeatedly attacking their foe's infrastructure and strategic assets, they gradually isolate his forces.

To thwart Western intelligence, *Hezbollah* and *al-Qaeda* will often employ attack elements that are unaware of each other's identity and home base. One might function as the assault element, while the others conduct holding attacks.

Just as *Sepah* in the Iran-Iraq War, *Hezbollah* and *al-Qaeda* are fairly good at urban defense. True to Eastern tradition, they have learned how to win while moving backwards. They have also learned how to consolidate a neighborhood. Among their incentives for cooperation and intelligence are religious duty, monetary incentives, and collaborator punishment. Ground assaults on limited objectives like police stations generally follow the same pattern. Checkpoints and lookouts are posted for many blocks around to effectively isolate the target. Then any nearby source of reinforcement is taken under fire while the assault is in progress. The initial entry is facilitated by turncoat, disguise, or car bomb.

As all three organizations try to mobilize the local population, their method looks more and more like "people's war"—a concept generally associated with Asian Communists but also adopted by Germans late in the WWII.

As time passes, the Muslim guerrillas will get more proficient at what they do. They will combine decoys with new ways to detonate explosives from a distance. Most already have fuel-air-explosive tipped RPG-7's. They have been in guerrilla hands for some time in both Chechnya and Afghanistan.[58] They have also been sold on the international market for many years by the Vazov Machine-Building Works in Sopot, Bulgaria.[59] Then, there are the devastating shoulder-fired, thermobaric RPO-A "Shmels." Russian snipers have already seen them in Chechen hands.[60] They have also been for sale on the international market.[61] Of particular concern, any number of Islamic guerrillas may inherit U.S. "Stinger" anti-aircraft missiles from Afghanistan. If the *jihadists* are somehow able to combine this advanced weaponry with advanced tactics, American troops may be in for a long, costly conflict throughout the Muslim world.

All three organizations rely heavily on disguise. They have made IEDs to look like any number of things. They have donned military and police uniforms. They have arrived in police cars, ambulances, and military vehicles. They have shot rockets from donkey wagons and planted mines in food vending carts. Recently in Iraq, what were thought to be Chechen fighters approached a convoy in white SUVs—the trademark of the Coalition.[62] Elsewhere suicide bombers were using white, four-door passenger vehicles.

All Three Have Dabbled in the Maoist Method

While Iran is not Communist, its revolution is much like that in China. Like the East Asian Communist armies, *Hezbollah* and *al-Qaeda* are both loosely controlled. That may partially explain why their small-unit infantry tactics are so similar.

So far, the rebels in Iraq have fought back with RPGs, mortars, and mines. As U.S. troops hear more explosions, they worry less about ground assault. That's why the North Vietnamese and North Koreans preferred RPGs to small arms. On parade in early September 2003, a large North Korean unit was photographed carrying nothing but RPGs.[63]

If the Muslim militants ever find out the full particulars of the Maoist method, the Coalition is in for a long slog in both Iraq and Afghanistan. Just as each Viet Cong band did in Vietnam, Saddam Hussein moved through a series of "underground hide facilities."

> By all accounts, the [Iraqi] fighters are taking Mao Zedong's classic advice for guerrillas to move among the people like fish through water. They live in the civilian population, depending on its support and using it for protection.[64]
> — *Newsweek,* 18 August 2003

While U.S. forces now have a device that can detect changes in soil density for several feet below ground, that device had nothing to do with Saddam Hussein's capture. A low-ranking soldier noticed a surface abnormality and pursued a hunch. As is often the case in "top-down" organizations, he received little credit for his initiative.

> [A]t 8:26 P.M. [on 20 December 2003], a soldier noticed a crack in the earth under a lean-to adjoining a mud hut on a small sheep farm. . . . The crack revealed a hidden door. The soldiers carefully shoved aside some bricks and dirt and opened up a Styrofoam hatch covered with a rug.[65]
> — *Newsweek,* 22 December 2003

Of course, some of the higher-ranking militants still have a lot to learn about hiding. No self-respecting VC commander would enter a hole lacking a rear entrance.

They Know How to Capture Battlefield Momentum

If a Muslim force could somehow impede a Western-style offense, it would more easily seize the initiative. For decades, U.S. forces have depended more on firepower than surprise. Their foot infantry have been underutilized. They can no longer move unnoticed along the ground. Their tactics have become more defensive than offensive in nature. For them, being inserted by helicopter (with little surprise) and fighting in place (as in Operation Anaconda) constitutes an attack. The Islamic guerrilla has learned how to exploit this "defensive" approach to war. He does so through the remotely controlled bomb. Every time the Westerner ventures forth from his protected enclosure, he gets hurt. Every time he stays home, he suffers an imperceptible loss of strategic assets and offensive spirit. The assets are destroyed by indirect fire or sapper, and the spirit is destroyed through inactivity. Such defeats seem inconsequential to a rich and proud country. But—as was proven 30 years ago—they are cumulative and potentially devastating over the long term. The only difference between the Muslim and Maoist method is how the mine is detonated.

Whereas the Western unit more easily occupies successive pieces of rural terrain, its Muslim counterpart more easily consolidates a region. Through a combination of fear and religion, it "enlists" cooperation.

They Know How to Achieve Popular Support

All three organizations have determined how to combine communal resolve with battlefield tactics. From a defensive standpoint, this gives them an early warning system that is second to none. Its principal sources of information are government turncoats and neighborhood sympathizers. Both are ideologically motivated, and both know the price of collaboration.

From an offensive standpoint, their combining of tactics with politics/religion gives them easy access to government installations. Such access can come from manual laborers who preposition ladders, sentries who look the other way, and office workers who smuggle in time-fuzed bombs.

While all three combatants may still be using rudimentary tactics, those tactics have had a tremendous impact. That is what Israel and the Soviet Union have already found out the hard way.

They May Have a Mutual Parent

Over the years, *Hezbollah* and *al-Qaeda* have shared the same goal—more Islamic States in the region.[66] They have shared the same role—recruiting and training Islamic guerrillas. That they also follow the same battlefield strategies may mean a mutual parent. That parent need not be a nation. *Hezbollah* was blatantly created by Iran. *Al-Qaeda* has more obscure roots. A closer look at their respective births might reveal a suspect.

To What Extent Might the World Powers Be Involved?

While Muslims and Christians are now fighting at several locations around the world, both may have been subtly drawn into contention. A third party—with an expansionist history and deceptive nature—may be involved. It may be a prospective superpower that fears for its petroleum supply or needs a diversion to take back a breakaway province. While China is not the only country that fits this description, it is the modern world's most accomplished master of deception.

In a stunning revelation, London's Sunday Telegraph is reporting in today's editions [27 August 2000] that China has . . . many . . . troops in the Sudan and is preparing to enter that country's civil war [on the side of the government].

According to the British paper, for the past three years China has been bringing Chinese nationals into the Sudan by cargo jets and boats. Ostensibly, the Chinese were to serve as guards at oil fields and facilities controlled by the China National Petroleum Corporation.[67]

David Hale, an economist who specializes in Chinese affairs, said in a recent speech that China has deployed about 4,000 troops to southern Sudan. The troops are there to protect an oil pipeline, Mr. Hale said.

The Chinese presence was first disclosed by South African government officials who told Mr. Hale about the troops during a recent visit to South Africa. . . .

The reported Chinese troop presence in Sudan follows an Internet report several years ago that there were 700,000 Chinese troops in Sudan. That report proved to be false.[68]
— *Washington Times,* 5 March 2004

In March 2004, China signed a $20-billion liquefied natural gas deal with Iran. It already gets much of its oil from Iran.[69]

Which Middle Eastern Nation Is on the Move?

After Iran expelled most Iraqis from its territory in 1982, its expansionist leanings became more apparent.

[T]he War was no longer a war of self-defense, for territories lost to Iraq had been all but liberated. It was instead a revolutionary war to extend Shia fundamentalism to one neighboring country which contained the largest Shia community outside Iran.[70]

As Iran's overall strategy was now political, its military operations had to promote civic consolidation. Who better to provide that service than the Iranian Revolutionary Guards. Then Iran sent a detachment of *Sepah* to Lebanon. As early as 1980, Ayatollah Khomeini had expressed an interest in exporting his Shia revolution to other states in the region.[71] His successors may share the same dream. In Israel, *Hamas* is being funded not only by Saudi nationals, but also by the Iranian government.[72] Ahmad Chalabi—the Iraqi who so heavily influenced U.S. invasion policy—has since leaked secrets to, and taken refuge in, Iran.

Iran's Involvement with *Hezbollah* and *Hamas*

Palestinian *Hamas* has been associated with Lebanese *Hezbollah* for years. *Hamas* was founded in 1987, seven years after *Hezbollah*. That is about the same time *al-Qaeda* was appearing on the scene in Afghanistan. Over the years, all three organizations have received support from Iran.[73]

[T]he government of Iran contributes approximately 3 [three] million dollars per year for all Hamas activities. . . .
In October 1992, Abu Marzuq headed a Hamas delegation to Tehran for the purpose of concluding a number of political and military cooperation agreements with Iran.[74]

In early 2001, Iran hosted a conference for all those opposed to Israel's presence in the "Occupied Territories." Seated side-by-side at the conference were senior *Hamas, Hezbollah,* and Iranian officials.[75] What was once a loosely controlled "top-down" structure may have since metastasized into a many headed hydra.

Iran's Complicity in Iraq

After a bloody war with Sunni Saddam, Iran would certainly prefer a country run by Iraq's Shiite majority. The *Sepah's* Qods Force—Iranian Special Forces—have been linked to the Iraqi *Muntada al-Wilaya.*[76]

Recently, Iranian President Khatami recommended more dialogue than warfare between civilizations. Unfortunately, he holds little sway over Iran's religious hierarchy (Ayatollah Khamenei) and its semi-autonomous organizations (like *Sepah)*.

> Khatami's vision holds out hope that, as the West evolves and possibly declines, Islam will regain its position as the leading progressive world civilization.[77]
> — John Esposito, well-respected U.S. Islamic scholar

In Iraq, the "Sadr Rebellion" was far from spontaneous. As noted in Chapter 8, Iran helped to train and fund al-Sadr's militia.

> Indeed it [the rebellion] was prepared well in advance at the behest of Tehran—with the collaboration of Damascus and the Hezbollah—by the Shiite master terrorist Imad Mughniyeh. Its purpose: to trigger Iran's Spring Offensive against the Americans in Iraq.
> Sunday night, the young radical cleric al-Sadr told cheering followers in Kufa: "From now on we are the beating arm of the Hezbollah and Hamas in Iraq." The crowds, raising clenched fists, declared: "The occupation is over! Sadr is our ruler!"
> Our military analysts read this as a battle cry—not only to launch the young Shiite cleric's bid for power in the whole of Iraq—but also for spreading the unrest around the Middle East at large. The Lebanese Hezbollah, which controls the most effective military-terrorist force in the region and is heavily armed with an array of missiles and artillery, will not want to sit on the sidelines; likewise the Hamas and its Gaza-based "military arm," Izz e-Din al-Qassam. However, both must be guided in their next steps by the Iranian leadership topped by Ali Khamenei [only its religious leader] and the Syrian president Bashar Assad who have been holding separate emergency round the clock conferences in the last few hours.[78]
> — Israeli intelligence bulletin, 5 April 2004

Iran's More Obscure Involvement with *al-Qaeda*

Al-Qaeda was purportedly founded by Abdullah Yusuf Azzam.

Azzam was born in 1941 at the village of Seelet al-Hartiyeh, in the province of Jenin on the West Bank. After fighting in the Six Day War with Israel, he emigrated to Jordan and joined the *jihad* against the Israeli occupation.[79] "He was a Jordanian member of the Palestinian Muslim Brotherhood and one of the founders of *Hamas*."[80] Only later did he move to Saudi Arabia, link up with the fundamentalist Wahhabi Sunnis, meet Osama bin Laden, translocate to Pakistan, and join the Afghan *jihad*.

> He [Azzam] constructed the religious ideology for the war against the Soviets in Afghanistan, recruited Arab mujahideen to implement his vision, and built the international network that his disciple, Osama bin Laden, would turn into al-Qaeda. . . .
>
> Political Islam's Great Communicator and traveling salesman, Azzam trotted the globe during the 1980's to promote the Afghan jihad against the Soviets. . . .
>
> His Mujahideen Services Bureau in Peshawar, Pakistan, served as a way station and training ground for fresh recruits as they arrived. . . .
>
> Azzam, however, had always seen the Afghan war as a training ground for the ultimate war in Palestine. Now he hoped to transfer the mujahideen to his homeland and take the war directly to Israel.[81]

Headquartered in Peshawar, Pakistan,[82] Azzam's "Mujahideen Services Bureau" (the precursor to *al-Qaeda)* must have had the tacit approval (if not blatant blessing) of Pakistan's Inter-Services Intelligence Agency [ISI]) and Mujahideen Council.[83] It was also supported by *Jamaat-i-Islami*—the region's pioneer equivalent to the Muslim Brotherhood.[84] To put a stop to *mujahideen* feuding, Pakistani President Zia established a Seven-Party Alliance in 1983. Its fundamentalist parties were led by Hekmatyar, Khalis, Rabbani, and Sayyaf; its moderate parties by Nabi, Gailani and Mujaddadi.[85] Khalis and Rabbani had the closest ties to Iran.[86] It was Khalis' *(HIK)* guerrillas who reputedly let "four U.S. 'Stinger' launchers and sixteen missiles" fall into the possession of the Iranian Border Scouts in 1987.[87]

As Pakistan eventually sponsored the Taliban,[88] it should come as no surprise that the ISI's "Afghan Service Bureau" secretly directed the war against the Soviets.[89] That same bureau has been directly linked to *al-Qaeda's* birth.[90] So too has the more mysterious "Arab Service Bureau."[91] While its name suggests an ISI branch, there is no hard evidence of this and many other possibilities.

> For every US dollar that was supplied by the Americans to the CIA's arms buying fund, the Saudis equalled it. Hundreds of millions of dollars were given by Saudi Arabia, and her generous assistance is what keeps the mujahideen in the field today [in 1987] when American aid has been so severely curtailed. Other rich Arab individuals from all over the Middle East have also contributed very substantial sums to particular parties. Prince Turkie, the then head of the Saudi intelligence service, was a frequent visitor to Islamabad, and his relations with Akhtar [ISI Head] were excellent. Both believed fervently in the importance of an *Islamic brotherhood* which ignored territorial frontiers [italics added] .[92]
>
> — Brigadier Yousaf, Afghan Service Bureau Chief

It is known that Iran was one of the first countries to provide money and arms to the Afghan guerrillas.[93] As mentioned in Chapter 6, it directly supported the *IRMA* and *HI* guerrilla factions. If Iran had been willing to send people all the way to Lebanon to create an Islamic State, it would certainly have done so next door. Because Ayatollah Khomeini had called for an Islamic revolution by both Shiites and Sunnis, he would have applauded Azzam's efforts. "The [Iranian Revolutionary] Guard's first formal commander Abbas Zamani was posted to Pakistan in the early 80's."[94] As Zamani had received his guerrilla training in Lebanon and had PLO and Lebanese guerrilla ties dating back to 1970,[95] he was undoubtedly the architect of the Lebanese deployment. Why then was he sent to work with the Pakistani army, if not to help with a similar, more covert, effort inside Afghanistan?

> Iran's leaders generally supported the cause of the Afghan resistance. Iran provided financial and limited military assistance to those Afghan resistance forces *whose leaders had pledged loyalty to the Iranian vision of Islamic revolution* [italics added]. Iran also hosted about 2.3 million refugees who had fled Afghanistan.[96]
>
> —U.S. Dept. of Army, "Iran Country Study"

During the Soviet-Afghan War, one of the Afghan Service Bureau's six major supply routes started in Pakistan's Baluchistan region and ran through eastern Iran. It operated under the full auspices of the Iranian Revolutionary Guards.[97] As mentioned in Chapter 6, *mujahideen* units had base camps inside Iran. After the U.S. invasion, *al-Qaeda's* leaders found political asylum there.[98]

> According to European, Saudi, and U.S. government sources, several high-level members of al-Qaeda are either in Iran or moving freely across the Afghan-Iran[ian] border. Those include Osama bin Laden's No. 2, Ayman al-Zawahiri; Mr. bin Laden's son, Saad bin Laden; the No. 3 in charge of military operations, Said al-Adel; and Abu Gheith, al-Qaeda's spokesman. Up to a dozen "serious al-Qaeda members" are there, and a total of some 50 foot soldiers, as well as family members, swelling the total figure to about 300.[99]
> — *Christian Science Monitor,* 24 October 2003

Additionally, some of *al-Qaeda's* top operatives have been allowed to move at will across the Iran-Iraqi border. The one now getting the most attention has ties with *Hezbollah.*

> Mr. Zarqawi, a one-legged Jordanian Bedouin currently thought to be hiding in Iran, has emerged as central suspect in one al-Qaeda-related plot after another. . . .
> Though intelligence analysts differ over Zarqawi's exact relationship to Osama bin Laden, they agree . . . he has used his leadership of Al Tawhid, a Jordanian extremist group, to develop links not only with al-Qaeda but also with Ansar al-Islam, . . . Lebanese Hezbollah, and with North African cells in Europe. . . .
> American intelligence officials have said they tracked Zarqawi to a meeting in south Lebanon in August 2002 with Hezbollah leaders.[100]
> — *Christian Science Monitor,* 23 January 2004

In short, *Hezbollah* was created by Iranian elements; *al-Qaeda* has been helped for almost a decade by Iranian elements; and they all get together regularly to discuss things. Officially, Iran is opposed to *al-Qaeda.* But then so too is Pakistan. Still, neither Iran nor its religious hierarchy qualifies as mutual parent.

Another Look at the Birth of *Al-Qaeda*

Many intelligence analysts believe Osama bin Laden to be just a figurehead and that his top lieutenant Ayman al-Zawahiri is actually in charge.[101] Like Azzam, al-Zawahiri was a product of the Muslim Brotherhood.[102] The only difference is that his branch was Egyptian. By 1983, he had become a leader of the Egyptian *Islamic Jihad*. After the killing of Anwar Sadat, he moved to Saudi Arabia and visited Sudan. That's where he met bin Laden in 1985. They co-established a political party and went on to Afghanistan.[103] When the Soviets were defeated, al-Zawahiri returned to Egypt and then to Sudan with bin Laden.[104]

By 1987, the Iranian Revolutionary Guards had entered countries other than Lebanon. (In Sudan, they had thousands of fighters by 1991.) Within Pakistan, they may have supported the birth of *al-Qaeda*. While fundamentalist Shiites and Wahhabi Sunnis don't generally get along, reluctant "short-term" alliances are common to the region. So too is getting someone else to do one's fighting. "Sacrifice Minor Concerns for the Sake of the Overall Mission" and "Seize the Chance to Increase the Odds" are two of the famous 36 Stratagems. Without the Sunnis' help in evicting the Soviets, the Iranians would have had no chance to achieve their revolutionary goal.

How Deeply Involved Is the Muslim Brotherhood?

From the ranks of the "Muslim Brotherhood" came Azzam and al-Zawahiri—two of the three people most closely associated with the birth of *al-Qaeda*. Azzam was from its Palestinian branch and al-Zawahiri from the Egyptian nucleus.

The Muslim Brotherhood preaches the forceful rejection of Western influence. It has operated throughout Egypt, Sudan, Syria, Palestine, Lebanon, and North Africa since 1938.[105] Both Egyptian *Islamic Jihad* and *Hamas* were direct offshoots of the Muslim Brotherhood.[106] In fact, the Muslim Brotherhood has been called the grandfather of all Muslim resistance organizations.[107]

Before the Iranian Revolution ever occurred, nearly 2000 foreign nationals had been trained at nine Palestinian camps in Syria, Lebanon, Libya, Iraq, and South Yemen. Of those 2000, 580 were Iranians.[108] Many of the Iranian Revolutionary Guard's first instructors were graduates of those camps.[109] Abbas Zamani—the Guard's initial commander—had received his guerrilla training in Lebanon and planned the deployment. As such, he was instrumental in the militarization of Lebanese *Hezbollah*.

The Islamic Party, led by Muhsen Abdel Hamid, is the affiliate of the Muslim Brotherhood in contemporary Iraq.[110] Its role in the unrest is not completely clear.

Did the Taliban Really Go Away?

Founded in 1941 at Lahore by Sayyid Abul A'la Maududi, *Jamaat-i-Islami* is Pakistan's pioneer religious movement. In 1974, guerrilla chieftain Rabbani started an Afghan branch.[111] While initially helping refugees, it may have eventually done much more than that. In the war with the Soviets, it supported Hekmatyar's fundamentalist party/militia.[112] During the Pakistani cordon operation of March 2004, *Jamaat-i-Islami* flags were flying all along the Afghan border.

Jamaat-i-Islami may have supported Hekmatyar and endorsed *al-Qaeda's* inception, but it is an organization with similar name (and different roots) that bears watching. It not only helps the Taliban; it may be the Taliban. The extent of their interaction is considerable.

Late in 1994, Afghanistan witnessed the rise of an improbable militia that would go on to unite 90 percent of the country and declare the Islamic Republic of Afghanistan. After almost eighteen years of Soviet occupation followed by civil war, a seemingly endless cycle of carnage and chaos was abruptly reversed by the astonishing success of a new Islamic movement.

Late in 1994, as if out of nowhere, the predominantly Pashtun Taliban, a band of *madrasa* (seminary) students *(taliban)* who had been living as refugees in Pakistan suddenly appear. . . . Within two years they swept across the country, overwhelming the Northern Alliance of non-Pashtun minorities. . . .

. . . [B]y 1998 they had subdued 90 percent of the country. . . .

... [The Taliban's] political expression and ideology were transformed with Pakistan's Jamiat-i-Ulema-i-Islam (JUI), a religious party with a rigid, militant, anti-American, and anti-non-Muslim culture. Many of the Taliban were trained in hundreds of JUI madrasas. Often run by semiliterate mullahs, these schools were first set up for Afghan refugees in the Pashtun-dominated areas of Pakistan, along the border with Afghanistan. Many were supported by Saudi funding that brought with it the influence of an ultraconservative Wahhabi Islam. Students received free education, religious, ideological, and military training. . . .

When they came to power, the Taliban turned over many of their training camps to JUI factions, who in turn trained thousands of Pakistani and Arab militants as well as fighters from South and Central Asia . . . in their radical jihad ideology and tactics. Assisted by military support from Pakistan and financial support from the Wahhabi in Saudi Arabia, with JUI mentoring and influenced by Osama bin Laden's evolving radical jihadist political vision, the Taliban promoted their own brand of revolutionary Islam.[113]

As mentioned in Chapter 7, a paramilitary affiliate of *JUI* is now back in Afghanistan.

A Growing Bond between *Hezbollah* and *al-Qaeda*

During the Soviet occupation, civil war, and Taliban rule of Afghanistan, Iran lent most of its support to Shiite factions. The Northern Alliance was largely Shiite, and its legendary (now dead) commander—Ahmed Shah Massoud—had Iranian arms.[114] He was a member of Rabbani's fundamentalist party.[115] When the radical Wahhabi Sunni Taliban overran the areas around Mazar-e Sharif, they executed many Shiites. But the various religious and ethnic groups in this part of the world have been at each other's throats for centuries, and they don't seem to harbor irreconcilable grudges. To bolster their fleeting power, many are quick to cross ethnic and religious lines to make new alliances. By backing the Northern Alliance, the U.S. may have unwittingly helped Iran to pursue its revolutionary goals or another much larger neighbor to bog down the United States.

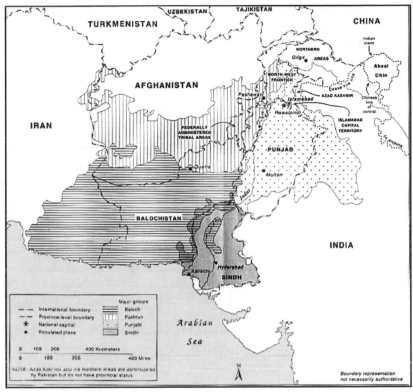

Map 10.1: *Al-Qaeda's* **Pashtun Corridor to Iran**
(Source: *DA Pam 550-48* (1996), Figure 7)

To defeat a mutual opponent, the Iranian Shiites and Wahhabi Sunnis may be temporarily willing to overlook their theological differences. During the Soviet-Afghan War, *HI* factions from Iran operated just west of Kandahar and fought alongside fundamentalist Sunni bands.[116] More recently, the Pashtuns have constituted the Taliban's power base. A Pashtun-controlled corridor extends all the way from Osama bin Laden's hideout in Northwest Pakistan to Iran. (See Map 10.1.) With Iran's permission, *al-Qaeda* operatives could easily deploy to the Iraqi theater. Iran radio regularly broadcasts

"Pashtun service" throughout the region.[117] While Iran might be a little leery of *al-Qaeda's* efforts in Iraq, it would still support them. For by fighting Americans, *al-Qaeda* takes the pressure off Lebanese *Hezbollah*. *Hezbollah* would be most supportive of a Shiite State.

There has been evidence of a working alliance between *Hezbollah* and *al-Qaeda* since the early 1990's. Bin Ladin has personally met—more than once—with Imad Mughniyeh, *Hezbollah's* director of operations. On 1 February 2002, *The* (British) *Times* reported that a senior *al-Qaeda* operative had just traveled to Lebanon to discuss relocation with *Hezbollah* leaders. The operative was identified as a Yemeni national traveling under the alias of Salah Hajir.[118] In July 2004, *Hezbollah* was reportedly supporting al-Zarqawi.[119]

The loudest allegations of a *"Hezbollah-*and-*al-Qaeda"* alliance came from the Israelis right after the tragic events of 11 September 2001.[120] According to the 9/11 Commission, *al-Qaeda* personnel were trained in the use of explosives at *Hezbollah's* Bekaa Valley camps in 1993.[121] The Commission additionally disclosed that Khalid Sheikh Mohammed—9/11 mastermind—had an "allegiance" with Abdul Rasul Sayyaf. Sayyaf's Sunni faction was part of the Northern Alliance.[122] That Alliance contained many Shiites and was heavily supported by Iran.

The Possibility of Global *Jihad*

The West should not forget what happened to the Crusaders. Over a number of years, they gradually withdrew into well-protected forts. Then—when Acre fell in 1291—they withdrew altogether.[123] Without more empathy for the Islamic way of life, Coalition forces may find themselves repeating history.

In 1979, Iran called for a global Islamic revolution by both Shiites and Sunnis.[124] *Al-Qaeda, Hezbollah,* and the Iranian Revolutionary Guard share the same goal—a confederation of Islamic States. All were established to recruit and instruct fighters. Their founders were graduates of PLO training camps. In their minds, they have already defeated one superpower and another regional giant. They know that the "bottom-up" way of training and operating is more situationally responsive than the "top-down" variety.

"Azzam's *jihad* was global in scope, aimed a recouping the glories and lands of Islam."[125] The ancient Islamic Empire stretched from southern Spain, across north Africa, throughout the Middle East, into the Balkans and southern portions of the old Soviet Empire, and to the borders of India and China. Since then, large Muslim societies have sprung up in Bangladesh, Malaysia, Indonesia, and the southern Philippines. One wonders how broad Azzam's dream really was. Could it have included Spain?

> This duty will not end with the duty in Afghanistan; jihad will remain an individual obligation until all other lands that were Muslim are returned to us so that Islam will reign again; before us lie Palestine, Bokhara [in central Asia], Lebanon, Chad, Eritrea, Somalia, the Philippines, Burma, Southern Yemen, Tashkent, and Andalusia (southern Spain).[126]
>
> — Azzam, the Jordanian founder of *al-Qaeda*

11 The Response Must Be Unconventional

- *Can all wars be won by force of arms?*
- *What else will be needed in Southwest Asia?*

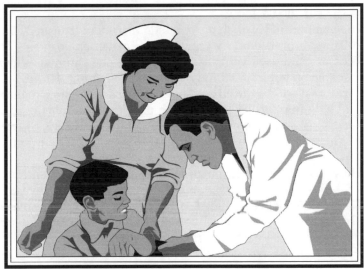

(Source: Corel Gallery Clipart, People, Miscellaneous, Corel #34C021)

Every Culture Has Its Strengths

Many a U.S. leader seems unaware that older cultures exist, much less excel at various things. He doesn't realize that the people at the bottom of an organization can often do more by working together than one man at the top could direct. So, he works diligently to remove opposition leaders. Unfortunately, an Eastern army accomplishes much of what it does from the bottom up. That means one cannot kill it by cutting off the head. Thus, the organizers of terror must be largely combatted through political and humanitarian means.

211

Within the Muslim culture, there are extremists who miscon-
strue the Koran. As the suicide bomber springs from a misinterpre-
tation of ideas, he or she can be stopped through a reinterpretation
of those same ideas.

A Startling Coincidence

There is one tactic from Lebanon and Israel that did not make
it into Iraq or Afghanistan until after Saddam Hussein's capture.
That's the suicide vest.

The bombers of Kurdish party headquarters in Iraq on 31 January 2004 set a precedent by carrying their own explosives. Their
predecessors had used vehicles.[1] Though no one claimed responsibility, suspicion fell immediately on *Ansar al-Islam.*[2] However, the
perpetrators were disguised as Muslim clerics or media journalists.

On 27 January 2004, a man with artillery and mortar rounds
strapped to his chest blew himself up next to a NATO convoy in
Kabul. According to Associated Press, this as "a tactic previously
unknown to Afghanistan."[3] His garb is not known.

These two distant but concurrent events may mean nothing. A
room full of suicide vests was found during the initial invasion of
Iraq. Yet, on 9 February 2004, a man wearing an explosive belt
blew himself up outside the Baghdad home of two tribal leaders
who had cooperated with American forces.[4] Over the years, many
separatist groups have occasionally resorted to wearing explosives.
However, the January 2004 precedent in both theaters raises questions. Why wasn't the suicide attack used during the Afghan-So-
viet War? Why has it only recently been introduced to the Chechen
War? One of two things is occurring: (1) either *Sepah / Hezbollah* is
getting more involved, or (2) *al-Qaeda* is copying their tactic.

The suicide attack makes no sense to the Western mind, but it
is very effective. Where a fleeting target is concerned, it provides a
delivery system for high explosives that is every bit as precise as
the latest technology. Anyone seriously interested in bringing peace
to the Middle East must discover how to stop it.

The Martyrdom Tactic

Many of the suicide bombers may be Palestinians from Lebanon. On 21 May 2004, thousands of Shiites marched in Beirut after *Hezbollah* leader Sheik Hassan Nasrallah accused the U.S. of desecrating holy shrines in Iraq. The marchers were wearing white shrouds to symbolize their willingness to die in defense of the holy cities of Najaf and Karbala. On the same day, similar demonstrations took place outside the British embassy in Tehran.[5]

Within every faith, there are those who misinterpret the Word of God. Many lack the religious and cultural tolerance to coexist with anyone else. Unfortunately for Islam, a fledgling branch—the Iranian Ismaili Nazaris—tried to combine mind control with self defense. While most present-day Muslims frown on *Hashishin*-like activity, their TVs still carry its images. In one 2002 television interview, a young Palestinian man thanked his brother for nominating him to carry a suicide bomb and looked forward to many virgins in paradise.[6] Some Muslims still think that heaven can be earned through suicide or the murder of enemy noncombatants. Luckily, orthodox (mainstream) Islamics disagree.[7] In fact, the Koran forbids suicide and the killing of noncombatants.[8]

On 14 January 2004, a young Palestinian mother of two—who was about to blow up herself and four Israeli soldiers at a Gaza checkpoint—was videotaped reading a statement. Throughout that statement, she looked down and occasionally smiled.[9] One would not expect such behavior. She was either quite insane or under some sort of external influence.

> In my understanding . . . , one will never do under hypnosis what one would not do otherwise. . . . That this [Palestinian] lady read from a script and giggled occasionally suggests . . . [an] inappropriate affect [mood] for the episode, so she may have been in a psychotic state—of her own [making], or induced chemically. It doesn't sound like the act was done of her own complete volition, so I would look for a controller. . . . She may have been sacrificing her life in the service of her family.[10]
> — Dr. David H. Reinke, practicing psychologist

America's Unhappy Experience with Such Things

In September 2003, a jury discounted the defense's claim that Lee Boyd Malvo—the younger of the D.C. snipers—had been brainwashed by his partner. "Lee was unable to distinguish between right and wrong and was unable to resist the 'impulse' to commit the killings," said Neil Blumberg [defense psychiatrist], who examined Malvo 20 times in jail.[11] Which impulse is that? Very troubling are the similarities between Malvo's background and Marco Polo's description of the *Hashishin* conditioning process just north of Tehran.

> The defense said Muhammad had "indoctrinated" Malvo with his beliefs . . . leaving the young man unable to tell right from wrong. . . .
> . . . Muhammad convinced Malvo that the killings were "designed to achieve a greater good of a fairer and [more] righteous society" . . .
> "Lee could no more separate himself from John Muhammad than you could separate from your shadow on a sunny day," defense attorney Michael Arif said in closing arguments. "He was not the idea man. He was a puppet molded like a piece of clay by John Muhammad."[12]
> — Associated Press, 19 September 2003

A "Witch Hunt" Is Not the Answer

Most contemporary Nizari Ismailis live in Pakistan or Iran.[13] Under the spiritual guidance of Prince Karim Aga Khan IV, they pursue mostly humanitarian goals. Yet, their legacy of radical fundamentalism and "mind control" still haunts the Muslim world. Secret militias march with hidden faces, misguided teenagers blow themselves up, and radical *madrasas* teach children to hate.

> The Nizari lsmailis, numbering several millions and accounting for the bulk of the Ismaili population of the world, are now scattered over more than 25 countries in Asia, Africa, Europe and North America.[14]

> To this day, the [Nizari] Ismailis (claimed to be 12 to 15 million in number) still take as their Imam the fourth (and present) Aga Khan, a handsome, benevolent, pin-striped Harvard man. . . .

The Assassins have long disappeared into history. Yet there is still abroad in many parts of the world the illusion that murder committed for religious or political purposes is an ennobling act.[15]
— *Smithsonian,* October 1986

Suicide is forbidden by Islam.[16] "Shaykh al-Sheikh, the grand *mufti* of Saudi Arabia, condemns suicide bombing as un-Islamic."[17] It's up to all mainstream Islamic leaders to end the militants' distortion of their faith. They must widely proclaim that martyrdom cannot be won by suicide. Just as God has endowed His people with free will—so must all religions and nations honor it. As long as that free will does not harm others, it will obey God's laws.

The Koran also strictly forbids the murder of noncombatants for any reason. Islamic leaders across the world must make this perfectly clear to their followers. That is what a heroic Iranian reformer just did.

Islam is the religion of peace, of rights, of justice, not tyranny, violence and prisons—let alone terrorism and killing people and torture in prisons. . . .
All of these things are against Islam. . . . In one word: What you would like for yourself, you must do for others. These are all the human rights and freedoms, which the Prophet [Mohammed] calls justice.[18]
—Grand Ayatollah Saanei, 11 February 2004

America Must Not Respond in Kind to Evil

The end does not justify the means. That is the misguided reasoning of the Islamic militant.[19] America cannot stoop to his level. History's longest democratic experiment must not accept the killing of noncombatants as an unavoidable consequence of war. While freedom is a noble cause, it cannot be exported by force. As the most powerful nation on earth, the U.S. must show the greatest restraint.

Mainly responsible for America's tactical stagnation has been its arms manufacturers. Death from afar is less moral than death from close range because of its greater difficulty with target verification. Machines don't have consciences, people do; and the most logical candidate for doing the right thing in combat is the frontline fighter. Here's what a lifelong enemy of Communism has to say about the dangers of unchecked industrial influence.

> Capitalism, [when] undisciplined by morality, will self-destruct.[20]
> — Pope John Paul II

America offers its citizens tremendous freedom. When irresponsibly practiced, that freedom breeds excess. When that excess gets media attention, America appears far more decadent than it really is. But this individual freedom is worth the cost. When responsibly practiced, it generates widespread solvency and heroic philanthropy. Individual Americans are among the world's most generous contributors to foreign aid. The United States should more widely publicize this fact.

America has come to a juncture in her history. At a time when legality has become synonymous with morality, its citizens must find a way to put "God" back into their way of life. While halting abortion may be their first priority, regulating the manufacture/sale of arms should not be far behind. How can a nation that readily removes urban opposition through standoff barrage tell its undersupported opponent not to use car bombs? Noncombatants die either way.

Not Every Resistance Fighter Is a Terrorist

Of all the wars on which the U.S. has embarked, the "War on Terrorism" is perhaps the most dangerous. It is the most dangerous because of its name. While fewer than a thousand misguided souls may have been blowing things up since 1980, whole national, religious, and ethnic groups have been blamed for their actions. The very word "terrorist" connotes someone who is subhuman. To combat a terrorist, one is often tempted to do less-than-human things.

Anyone interested in pursuing this line of thought should read *Devil's Guard* by George Robert Elford.[21] It chronicles the exploits of a German *SS* Battalion that joined the French Foreign Legion during the Indochinese War. The members of that battalion also called their opponents "terrorists." Whenever a Viet Minh was rumored to have committed an atrocity, the *SS* men felt fully justified in doing the same thing to every "sympathizer" they encountered. From a tactical standpoint, their forays into North Vietnam look impressive. From a religious standpoint, they show the battalion's gradual and unmistakable descent into group evil.[22] Near the end of the war, the *SS* men routinely poisoned wells and killed witnesses. While they may have disrupted enemy supply lines, they did so at great cost to their overall cause. By losing their moral compass, they had inspired their opponents to persevere.

After the McCarthy witch hunts of the "War on Communism," one wonders what will now happen to tactical reformers in the United States. Will their constructive criticism be construed as providing comfort to the enemy? Without admitting to an occasional battlefield loss, the U.S. military would have no reason to take corrective action. Its "top-down" bureaucracy prevents it from rapidly adjusting to guerrilla initiatives. That was proven 30 years ago. If it additionally loses its moral compass (as did the Soviets in Afghanistan), it may have great trouble winning the peace.

Nation Building Is More Difficult in the Middle East

When Germany and Japan were rebuilt after WWII, their occupations were uncontested. If anything has been learned from this study, it is that there are no clear-cut political or religious delineations between warring factions of the Middle East. Theirs is a power struggle—pure and simple—among all those who want to rule next. Any simplistic attempt to categorize combatants is fruitless. In the Iran-Iraq War for instance, the Baathist Syrian regime sided with Iran against the Baathist Iraqi regime. Concurrently in Lebanon, Iran-backed (Shiite) *Hezbollah* often fought with Syria-backed (Shiite) *Amal*.[23]

What is certain is that people expect security from whoever is in charge locally.

Democracy Takes Hold More Slowly in a Tribal Setting

According to Istanbul's Museum of Archeology, people have been living between the Tigris and Euphrates Rivers for 60,000 years. Around 2500 B.C., their Sumerian descendants invented numbers and multiplication tables. Abraham was born in Ur. This is not an area devoid of culture or wisdom, just one in which people assume more of a tribal than a national identity.

Whether or not America should now be exporting democracy to the region can be debated somewhere else. What matters here is that the Muslim insurgents—for whatever reason—are resisting a representative form of government. By undermining security, they have managed to delay the elections that were originally scheduled for the summer of 2004 in both Iraq and Afghanistan.[24] For this reason alone, the fledging democracies should be given every chance to succeed. They may check Muslim expansionism.

Counterinsurgency Lessons from the Region

The all-too-convenient response to terrorism is to inflict equal or greater pain on its perpetrators and all who support them. Inherent to this approach is never bowing to the terrorists' demands. How well it works should be implicitly obvious from the ongoing events in Israel and Chechnya. The Turkish government made the same mistake during the first attempt to quell its Kurdish insurrection.

Human rights groups here [in Iraq] say Turkish security forces destroyed as many as 4000 villages and displaced hundreds of thousands of Kurds. . . . More than 30,000 people died. . . .

The climate between the Turks and Kurds has changed sharply in recent months as the country's leaders have eagerly pushed for entry into the European Union. At the insistence of the Union, the Turkish government has enacted measures to expand the rights of its 14 million Kurds, who have long been denied the legal and cultural freedoms enjoyed by other Turkish citizens.[25]

— *New York Times International,* 24 October 2003

The Turkish government has shifted from a scorched-earth policy to one of discontent abatement. Its new strategy shows much greater promise than the one being pursued by the Russians in Chechnya.

The [Russian] army has destroyed Chechnya as both

an economic and political entity. And over time, the Chechen rebellion has become more desperate, more extreme and more Islamist. . . .

. . . [O]ne has to ask, was there any other way? Turkey's experience with the Kurds suggests that there might have been.

In the mid-1990's, Turkey was racked by suicide bombings. . . . Today suicide bombings have largely disappeared from Turkish life. Why? . . .

. . . [T]he army directed its fire at the rebels and not the surrounding population. In fact, the Turks worked very hard to win over the Kurds, creating stable government structures for them, befriending them, and putting forward social-welfare programs.[26]
— *Newsweek,* 25 August 2003

Bombardment Only Makes Things Worse

For more than a month before truck bombs demolished both the Marine barracks and the French compound in Beirut on 23 October 1983, American ships and French planes had been bombarding Muslim positions above the city.[27] The Western way of war had become self-prophesying. Its distant impacts had evoked some that were much closer. Associated with every bombardment is unexploded ordnance. Those shells and bombs can be easily boobytrapped or otherwise returned to sender. Over the years, America's adversaries have never suffered from a shortage of explosives.

The conventional response in Lebanon was not simply inappropriate or ineffectual but assured escalating disaster.[28]

Just before the 2003 invasion of Iraq, the U.S. attempted 50 "decapitation" airstrikes against Iraqi leaders. While no Iraqi leaders were confirmed killed, the strikes were launched against heavily populated areas and contributed to the estimated 10,000 civilians killed in the invasion.[29] The "shock and awe" of it all apparently did little to dissuade the Iraqis from mounting a guerrilla-type defense. One wonders then about the advisability of the ensuing airstrikes against any location remotely linked to al-Zarqawi. At what point

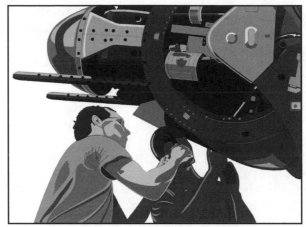

Figure 11.1: It's Harder to Avoid Errors with Standoff Weaponry
(Source: *Corel Gallery Clipart*—People, One Mile Up, #34H005)

does the cost in human suffering to Fallujah's women and children outweigh the benefit of removing a few thugs from their midst? Al-Zarqawi is not a military mastermind, he is a deranged killer. That he has recently been credited with every crime in northern Iraq removes attention from real culprits.

The Underlying Problem

During the occupations of Afghanistan and Iraq, poor intelligence and standoff weaponry have led to similar mistakes. The following happened in the first location. (See Figure 11.1.)

> In December 2001, a tip from a warlord, Badshah Khan-Zadran, sent American AC-130 gunships and Navy fighters to attack a convoy of vehicles full of Afghan tribal elders on their way to show allegiance to the post-Taliban government: 65 civilians were reportedly killed.
> In July 2002, at least 48 people were killed and 117 wounded when U.S. warplanes attacked a wedding party in the town of Deh Rawud in Central Afghanistan. The U.S. military said a gunship had come under fire in the area.[30]
> — *Christian Science Monitor,* 18 March 2004

In May of 2004, another wedding was hit near the Syrian border in Iraq. While the U.S. military maintained the target was a suspected safe house for foreign fighters, Iraqi officials said a helicopter killed 40 adults and children at a wedding. Later, Associated Press Television News (APTN) produced videotape of the wedding party before and after the strike.[31] In a place where vengeance is everyone's sacred duty, mistakes like these can do irreparable damage.

Some Wars Cannot Be Won By Force of Arms

When war is fought across the full political, media, and moral spectrum, it cannot be won by firepower. In fact, the paradoxical advice of Christ may be the only way to win a 4th generation war. That means strictly complying with the Catholic prerequisites for a "just" war and then killing as few enemy soldiers as possible.[32] To do so safely, U.S. troops will need vastly more short-range skill.

In this new kind of "4th-generation" conflict, civilian casualties must be avoided at all costs. The United States can no longer depend on its edge in technology and firepower. A guerrilla-infested area cannot be adequately pacified by overflying it with remotely piloted vehicles (RPVs) that fire "Hellfire" missiles on command. With standoff weaponry, the margin for error is too great. All supporting-arms targets must be confirmed from close range by skilled infantrymen with Christian ideals. That won't happen until America's leaders become more concerned over collateral damage.

> The Pentagon says it "monitors" civilian casualties but doesn't keep such figures [those of the people accidentally killed]. . . .
> . . . Between 8,789 and 10,638 civilians have died since war began March 19, 2003, according to one group of British and American researchers that surveys media reports and eyewitness accounts.[33]
> — *Christian Science Monitor,* 31 March 2004

The "eye-for-an-eye" foreign policy hasn't worked for the Israelis, and it won't work for the United States. That is the advice of the Torah and Koran, not of the New Testament.

Religion Cannot Be Ignored

Americans should not make the mistake of assuming that the Sunnis and Shiites are always at odds. Where they share common danger or goals, they have demonstrated a remarkable ability to come together quickly. Just before the U.S. invaded Iraq, avowed Sunni Saddam Hussein had a long conference with his former mortal enemies—the Shiite leaders of Iran.

This religious schism between Shiites and Sunnis is not, however, mutually antagonistic in the manner of Catholics and Protestants in Northern Ireland or Christians and Muslims in Beirut. "My mother is Sunni, my father Shia," says Baghdad native Fareer Yassin. . . . I have heard similar stories from many Iraqis, who also point out that direct clashes between the two communities are extremely rare and that discrimination against the Shiites has inevitably been orchestrated by rulers . . . for political, not religious reasons.[34]
— *Smithsonian,* December 2003

The United States, on the other hand, must find some way to return to its Christian roots. Nine out of ten Americans profess to believe in God,[35] and the rest are mostly agnostic. For the sake of one or two atheists, the U.S. Supreme Court has distorted the societal norm. How can America hold other nations accountable on human rights, when it won't save 43 million of its own children? The Supreme Court is not the final authority on morality. In the mid-1800's, it held that slaves were not human. Only God can determine what's moral, and any country that intentionally disassociates itself from God will pay the price. In a Godless world, there can be no peace.

The best way to prevent another world war is for the believers of every faith to now come together. They all worship the same God. Retribution is not His will.

Literally hundreds of U.S. units in Iraq and Afghanistan have conducted their own community service projects. By so doing, they have collectively asserted that humanitarian aid and simple kindness can make a far bigger difference in these types of wars than bullets and bombs.

More Than "Political" Truth Will Be Required

There is only one way to break the circle of violence. Someone in high office has to have the political fortitude to stick to a policy of minimal force. In Baghdad alone from 1 May to 29 December 2003, there were more than 2000 occupation-related deaths according to *Newsweek*.[36] Ominously, all official counting ceased on 11 December 2003.

> Iraqi Health Ministry officials ordered a halt to a count of civilian casualties from the war and told workers not to release figures already compiled. . . .
> Dr. Nagham Mohsen, the head of the ministry's statistics department, said the order came from the ministry's director of planning, Dr. Nazar Shabandar, who told her it was on behalf of Abbas [the Health Minister]. She said the U.S.-led Coalition Provisional Authority, which oversees the ministry, didn't like the idea of the count either.[37]
> — Associated Press, 11 December 2003

As with the Russians in Afghanistan, there is now tremendous political pressure on the U.S. military to avoid American casualties. The enemy knows this and has been using it to his advantage. If he succeeds in relegating U.S. forces to their protected compounds, he will have captured the initiative. To succeed against urban or rural guerrillas, American infantrymen must closely interact with local inhabitants. Only with more movement skills can they do so at minimal risk.

The Real Quagmire

There is ample evidence that both *Hezbollah* and *al-Qaeda* are conducting a "4th-generation" type of war.[38] They are attempting to erode their foe's popular support. In this endeavor, their principal tool is the media. Through it, they readily point out any excess, whether by force or exaggeration. A politically sensitive foe might come to see the media as his enemy and suppress any potentially embarrassing detail. Unfortunately, there is a price to be paid for this type of secrecy. An army that never admits to error has no reason to improve. While the term "4th-generation warfare" may be new, many of its components are not. Chinese and North Vietnamese armies have fought in much the same way for over 50 years.

To defeat a "4th-generation" opponent, one must search for "ultimate truth," quickly admit any setback, and then readily adapt to unforeseen circumstances. He must accomplish the latter without sacrificing his ideals.

Tactics and Morality Are Not Mutually Exclusive

American military leaders have been entrusted with not only the lives of their subordinates, but also with their souls. Those leaders who don't think they can protect both at once should look for a new line of work. For in their well-meaning quest for surgical warfare, they have jeopardized their ultimate mission—peace in the world.

Guerrilla wars cannot be won without first capturing the hearts and minds of the people. That's not done through a show of conventional force. Small units must track down and arrest the perpetrators of any civil disobedience, much as a policeman would. That takes more skill than U.S. line squads now possess. Those squads will need specially trained point men, mantrackers, and forward observers. All must be well versed in police protocol. That more senior military leaders don't say so has more to do with the political process than with ultimate truth.

Our policy, strategy, tactics, et cetera, are still screwed up [in Iraq].[39]
— Gen. A.C. Zinni USMC (Ret.), 18 January 2004

As the most powerful nation on earth, America must now reject the "eye-for-an-eye" approach to battlefield opposition. Christianity differs from other Abrahamic religions in that it requires its followers to love their adversaries. That means arresting suspected insurgents where possible and then putting them on trial by their own countrymen. It does not mean rocketing suspected hideouts every time they fill with people. While politically lucrative, the standoff approach to war harms too many noncombatants. This is a multidimensional struggle in which the side that uses the least force will win. Without infantry squads that can operate alone and tactically escape encirclement, the United States cannot hope to use less firepower in battle.

12 The Tactical Part of the Equation

- Must World War III be fought in a conventional manner?
- What must U.S. forces do to get ready for such a war?

U.S. MARINE CORPS CORPORAL, 1982

(Source: Courtesy of Orion Books from *Uniforms of the Elite Forces,* ©1982 by Blandford Press Ltd., Plate 5, No. 15, *FM 90-3* (1977), p. 4-2)

WWIII Need Not Be Waged by Conventional Means

To counter Western technology, Eastern armies have turned to tiny maneuver elements. Available to them are the tactically superior (surprise-oriented) infantry techniques described in previous publications.

Many U.S. military theorists now believe that "4th-generation warfare" will be the 21st-Century norm.[1] This new way of fighting is—at the same time—martial, electronic, and psychological. Thus, WWIII could resemble a worldwide Maoist guerrilla movement. As such, it might end as Vietnam did.

To keep the current conflagration from spreading to *Maggido,* the West must now combine apparent opposites—morality and tactics. While democracy and free enterprise may be the world's best hope, Eastern culture produces better light infantry. To match it, the U.S. military must follow the Oriental model—something it has long resisted, even in defeat. To achieve peace in the Middle East, it must hunt down, capture, and prosecute individual terrorists while concurrently removing the reasons for their discontent. In the process, it cannot inadvertently kill many noncombatants. For so doing will only expand the population base on which the guerrilla so badly depends.

This new "dual role" for the U.S. military cannot be accomplished through self-righteous resolve and greater firepower. It will require more respect for Eastern culture and non-American life in general. What makes the GI's life more valuable than the life he is liberating? If American policemen could so easily resort to bombs, no bystander would be safe. Some 60 years after Pearl Harbor, the events of 7 December 2003 should serve as a warning. On that date, a U.S. "Warthog" A-10 bomber mistakenly killed 9 Afghan children while targeting a "suspected terrorist."[2] When the Afghan government, United Nations, and Human Rights Watch complained of excess force, the U.S. military was quick to classify all details and claim that such things—while regrettable—are perfectly admissible in an active war zone.[3]

Noncombatants made little strategic difference in the conventional wars of the 20th Century, but they make a tremendous difference in the unconventional or 4th-generation wars of the 21st. These are wars that will be waged across the full political and spiritual spectrum. Whichever side gains the moral high ground will win. No amount of talk about "regrettable error," "collateral damage," "fog of war," or anything else will lessen the effect of civilian deaths on popular opinion. America's new adversaries will take full advantage of every targeting error and cultural indiscretion.

> The Afghan will never turn the other cheek, a killing must be avenged by a killing, and so it goes on from generation to generation.[4]
> — Brigadier Yousaf, Afghan Service Bureau Chief

With the "obscure-movement" techniques of a *ninja,* two American special operators could have spirited away the above-mentioned suspect for questioning, and the children would still be alive. Assassination by laser-guided munition is little better than that by suicide car bomb. For the third time in 50 years, the U.S. military will need more tactical skill. While the official chronicles may not admit it, those forces suffered a tactical tie in Korea and a tactical loss in Vietnam. Their equipment may have changed, but their short-range maneuvers haven't. U.S. squads can still only advance after massive barrages and as part of their company. In essence, they have been overprotected. In a cruel paradox of war, light infantry must be allowed to sustain a few casualties to gain proficiency. U.S. forces are fighting for Iraq in much the same way the Soviets did for Chechnya. Most often credited for the Soviet loss in Afghanistan was their lack of light infantry.[5]

The U.S. Has No Light Infantry Either

Several divisions within the U.S. Army and Marine Corps claim to be light infantry, but they really aren't. (See Figure 12.1.) True

Figure 12.1: The U.S. Has No Truly Light Infantry
(Source: Corel Gallery Clipart—Weapons, One Mile Up, #45A111)

light infantrymen relish close combat. They thrive on being out-numbered, getting surrounded, and having too little firepower to break out. Their limited indirect-fire assets are generally reserved for diversionary missions. The ten Chinese divisions that sneaked into the Chosin Reservoir in November 1950 to blunt the U.S. offensive were light infantry.[6] So too was the North Vietnamese division that held Hue City for most of February 1968 and then mysteriously disappeared.[7]

> Light infantry is a surprise and terrain-dependent force. These protect it from tanks and artillery, compartmentalize its opponents, and mask its movements. . . .
> The characteristic of light-infantry tactics everywhere is infiltration in the attack and ambush and counterstroke in the defense.[8]
> — U.S. Defense Agency Study

By comparison, U.S. infantry forces have become too dependent on their technology and firepower. Without it, they would have fared much less well since 1917. For whether guerrilla or line infantry, their Eastern opponent has been forced by his lack of wherewithal to evolve tactically. To become light infantry, one has minimally to want to.

Question: As the Chief of the Infantry, you and the Chief of the Artillery have joined to send the message through the Army "Indirect fires first is the American way of war." What does that mean?

Answer: "Never send a Soldier, when a bullet (of some caliber) will do. The intent is for the infantry to engage the enemy with somebody else's ordnance—indirect fire or close air support (CAS) or some other means—and we need to apply those effects to avoid having to commit Soldiers in the close fight.[9]
— U.S. Army's Chief of Infantry, 30 May 2004

It Takes More Troop Skill and Initiative to Beat Guerrillas

U.S. Marine sentries saw the offending yellow truck make a

trial run around their barracks parking lot at 5:00 A.M. on that awful morning in October 1983.[10] Then, they could not load their weapons in time to stop it at 6:22 A.M.[11] The enemy tactic should have come as no surprise because the U.S. embassy had been blown up the same way six months before.[12] While those barracks guards have probably blamed themselves for the tragedy, it was not their fault. Nor was it the fault of the "rules of engagement." It was the fault of a "top-down" control structure that effectively saps the initiative of its lowest ranks. Until the U.S. military joins most Eastern armies in shifting to the more productive "bottom-up" approach to training and operating, this type of tragedy will continue to occur. (See Figure 12.2.)

More is at stake now than in 1983. Without more short-range skill and on-the-spot decision making, U.S. troops cannot win a guerrilla, terrorist, or unconventionally fought world war.

Figure 12.2: Frontline Fighters Best Decide What's Feasible

(Source: *SoldF: Soldaten i falt*, © 2001 Forsvarsmakten, Stockholm, pp. 28-29)

America Must Shift Its Focus

The principal threat to world peace is not *al-Qaeda*. It is Lebanese *Hezbollah* and its Iranian sponsor.

Senior American officials have singled out Hezbollah as the "A team" of terrorism, more menacing than al-Qaeda. Senator Bob Graham, the Florida Democrat who was chairman of the Senate Intelligence Committee, has suggested that Hezbollah . . . is the most dangerous terrorist group on earth.[13]
— *New York Times,* 24 December 2002

For some reason, the U.S. media has understated *Hezbollah's* role in Iraq. Middle Eastern experts readily admit that most of the suicide car and belt bombings were *Hezbollah* inspired. So too was the Sadr Rebellion. American leaders may have intentionally downplayed *Hezbollah's* role to keep Israel in check.

As it [the American government] engaged in a cat-and-mouse game with Lebanese authorities over . . . individuals directly involved in terrorist acts, the U.S. government had maintained a hands-off policy toward Hezbollah itself. In fact, its involvement in the 1990's as a broker of the agreements between Israel and Hezbollah to avoid targeting civilians meant the U.S. had granted de facto diplomatic recognition to the organization. . . .
Reports in the Lebanese press in the immediate aftermath of September 11 spoke of an understanding between the U.S., Lebanon, and Syria: America would avoid targeting Hezbollah in the war on terror and, in turn, the others would ensure Hezbollah would not launch any major cross-border attacks on Israel.[14]
— Lawrence Pintak, well-traveled foreign correspondent

U.S. Forces Must Change Their Whole Way of Operating

To more safely occupy a nation, America can no longer ruin its infrastructure. Bosnian society has yet to rebound from the short aerial attack on its transportation network. Even when the priority is to rebuild that infrastructure (as in Iraq), the ensuing guerrilla effort may preclude it. The most precise of standoff weaponry still produces civilian casualties. It is therefore largely counterproductive in the Muslim world—where vengeance is a duty.

Everyone wants to minimize U.S. casualties, but there are better ways to do so than by allowing U.S. ground forces to eliminate everything in their path. Military historians assert that bombardment has yet to pave the way for infantry through a world-class defense.[15] For centuries, military leaders have tried unsuccessfully to limit the bloodshed through more violence. Why the Pentagon pays more attention to weaponry than tactics probably has more to do with political economics than with military strategy. Perennially at the top of the list are aircraft, missiles, and large-caliber guns. Many of the key billet holders within both the Army and Marine Corps are supporting-arms officers. Most aviators and artillerymen are "firepower" oriented. They don't realize that covert ground elements can do just as much strategic damage. They assume that firepower-deficient armies have been sacrificing their infantrymen at short range. They have difficulty envisioning a way of war that might require little, if any, control from above. They assume that U.S. ground forces have been tactically evolving as quickly as their Eastern counterparts and will always take fewer casualties with enough preliminary bombardment. Unfortunately, many of their assumptions are wrong. Firepower-deficient Eastern armies have been taking most of their losses at long range. Unlike Western armies, they haven't asked their frontline fighters to rush machineguns for 85 years. Historical exceptions are the result of unforeseen threat or intended feint.[16] All the while, U.S. preparatory fire has mostly hit dummy frontline positions and in the process compromised what little surprise the infantrymen could muster.

In essence, the firepower proponent has been doing too good a job. In the process, he has exceeded his prerogative. His stock in trade exists only to facilitate maneuver, not the other way around. In his zeal to protect every U.S. life in the short run, he has unwittingly jeopardized thousands of lives of every description in the long run. Until he realizes that tactical and technical innovation can coexist, he will continue to force equipment on U.S. ground forces that they neither want nor need. Every new contraption takes days, if not weeks, to master. A continual barrage of "gear updates" removes the opportunity for tactical technique practice, much less improvement. Several Eastern armies already train their soldiers in both conventional and unconventional warfare. Until U.S. forces follow suit, they may have trouble winning any terrorist, guerrilla, or 4th-generation conflict.

Through better tactics, U.S. forces could take fewer casualties at close range without alienating the local population and without sacrificing their long-range capabilities. More powerful than firepower in this new kind of war will be the preservation of infrastructure. For it is the lack of social services that gives the foe his recruiting base. In the 21st Century—as it was at the end of WWII—food, water, sewers, clinics, and jobs will do infinitely more to secure the ultimate victory than bombs. Better small-unit tactical technique costs nothing. It requires only a slower operational pace and the authority to experiment at the company or school level. America could usefully divert much of what it now spends on precision munitions to social services. Its national-security agencies must find some way to streamline their bureaucracies. Low-ranking infantrymen should be exempted from large-unit exercises, VIP demonstrations, and administrative duties. For it is only then that they will have the time to acquire world-class skill.

Squad-Level Infantry Training Must Be Experimental

Hezbollah and *al-Qaeda* trainers are not handcuffed by inane standardization and bureaucratic procedure. They can copy tactical technique from any source and then experiment with it under simulated combat conditions. As such, they will eventually become more effective at short range than U.S. forces.

The American enlistee primarily learns how to use his equipment and follow orders. He is not shown the state of the art for individual and small-unit maneuver. Instead, he is conditioned to follow—to the letter of the law—squad tactics manuals that haven't significantly changed in 50 years. He is at a considerable disadvantage in any one-on-one encounter with his woods-wise Eastern counterpart. Not trained as a guerrilla, he has a hard time thinking like one.

In other words, the U.S. infantryman lives in a doctrinally driven, "top-down" training environment. Such an environment cannot match the learning dynamics of its experimentally driven, "bottom-up" antithesis. Unfortunately, most Eastern armies,[17]

Hezbollah, and *al-Qaeda* all follow the latter. One produces standardized procedures that are situationally dismissive, painfully predictable, and technologically dated. The other produces current guidelines that are circumstantially unique, surprise oriented, and threat compensating. (See Figure 12.3.)

The Exception to Emulate

While Marine infantry units have struggled for years to improve their squads' tactical proficiency, a military police (MP) contingent actually succeeded. Its constant practice instilled teamwork. Its adding of aggressors to each training scenario produced progressively better technique. If the wars in Iraq and Afghanistan are to be won, all U.S. infantry units must be allowed to copy the method.

Figure 12.3: GIs Are the World's Best at Using Their Gear
(Source: Corel Gallery Clipart, Weapons, One Mile Up, #45A106)

"We're a S.W.A.T. [Special-Weapons Assault Team] for the Marine Corps," said Staff Sgt. Steven Rowe, commander, Special Reaction Team [SRT], Provost Marshal's Office, Marine Corps Base. "Our mission is to train, practice and rehearse for any situation, such as hostages, barricaded suspects and felony arrests." . . .

As the only military SRT on Okinawa, the unit constantly trains to hone the tightly knit team's skills, often training six or seven days a week.

"Today we're going over basic entry and room clearing," Rowe said. "These guys do this a thousand times and they know how to do it, but as a team you're not a really well-rounded until you do it a thousand times together."[18]

— *Camp Lejeune Globe,* 29 April 2004

Overwhelming Firepower Will No Longer Prevail

Any traveler to the Middle East knows how to elude unwanted interest: (1) announce a bogus destination, and then (2) take a random cab. Of course, counter-terrorism experts have a much longer list: e.g., (1) wear local garb, (2) vary departure times, and (3) don't take the same route back to the hotel. Yet in Iraq, foreign workers approach Coalition headquarters in white SUVs; U.S. troops cover the same patrol routes in HMMWVs; and American raiders approach their targets in helicopters. All the while, U.S. leaders wonder why things aren't going better.

To beat Muslim rebels, U.S. forces must become less predictable. They can no longer afford the patterns of Vietnam. While not as tactically proficient as the Viet Cong, militant Muslims still rehearse every attack *ad nauseum.* The best way to defend against such an attack is to continually vary one's routine and defensive disposition. Simply by regularly repositioning obstacles and sentries, one could foil the average Muslim attack.

While *Hezbollah's* community watch apparatus makes it hard to surprise, its Shiite fundamentalist viewpoints provide an opportunity. Simply by dressing diminutive American servicemen in black robes and *berkas* (women's scarves), a U.S. commander could infiltrate any number of raiders into a *Hezbollah* stronghold. The same holds true of the Sunni fundamentalist areas of Afghanistan. There, the women even cover their eyes with netting. Of course, local customs must first be checked. In many areas, women cannot wander alone.

America's Need to Adapt Tactically

Of utmost importance to winning the peace in the Middle East will be the early detection of enemy pre-mission activity. Every U.S. soldier and Marine must come to realize that Eastern tactics are not "asymmetric" per se, just intentionally different from their own. Each must contribute to "battlefield intelligence" and look for ways to do his/her job with less force. Then, and only then, will U.S. small-units develop sufficient tactical ruses and technique variations to quell the violence without concurrently alienating the population.

As difficult as it may be to accept, the Germans, Russians, Japanese, Chinese, North Vietnamese, Turks, Iraqis, Iranians, Palestinians, Afghans, and Chechens all know how to fight a different way at short range.[19] They also know how to fight the Western (U.S., British, and French) way. When confronted by superior firepower, they retreat from what looks like a succession of Western-style defensive positions. As soon as their adversary gets tired or outruns his support, they reappear at short range. So doing makes his supporting arms useless. Without commensurate tactical skill, that adversary will soon suffer more casualties than he thought necessary.

Real-Time Intelligence

As every military excess proves doubly counterproductive in a Muslim country, U.S. forces must use their supporting arms much more sparingly in an urban environment. Only deserving of demolition is the building that is expertly defended, free of noncombatants, and unavoidable. Few, if any, of the buildings already targeted in Iraq have fit this description. Like the Iranian Revolutionary Guards, U.S. forces will need Vietnam vintage CAPs (Combined Action Platoons) embedded in every neighborhood. Only then will they acquire enough real-time intelligence to counter another insurgency.

While no Muslim sect is any more culpable than any other, *Hezbollah* still feels more comfortable in Shiite surroundings. In Lebanon, the Shiites were the peasant farmers in the Bekaa Valley and southern portions of the country.[20] In Iraq, *Hezbollah* has just

Figure 12.4: Bunkered Occupiers Will Be Vulnerable
(Source: *FM 5-13* (1969), p. 12)

opened an office in Basra. However, it sometimes has a presence in Sunni areas as well. In Iraq, it has worked hard to keep its resupply route to Syria open and to let Sunni separatists take the blame.

Defense

That the foe rehearses each attack in a life-size mockup for up to a year makes him formidable, but not invincible. He has a weakness. He will not expect what has recently been changed. Simply by randomly altering lines, illumination, patrols, and outposts, U.S. forces should be able to catch him off balance. Against such a foe, one must not be too obvious or predictable. (See Figure 12.4.)

One becomes a suicide bomber though a misguided idea. Thus, he can be combatted through ideas. Radio broadcasts should continually stress that for a Muslim, suicide is neither glorious nor holy.

238

Observation Posts

On 18 April 2004,[21] a U.S. Marine leader in Fallujah indicated that a fire team had been cut off from the main body. In all probability, that fire team had been manning an outpost. In mid-June, four other Marines were killed in Ramadi.[22] While the incident was officially reported as an "ambush," the close proximity of the bodies atop a flat-roofed house suggests that the Marines had been surprised while manning an observation post. To preclude this type of problem in the future, sentry post personnel should be secretly inserted by patrol (i.e., 14 go out and 10 return). They should also have a way to sneak back to friendly lines (like through a drainage ditch or sewer).

Patrolling

In a country as large and hot as Iraq, a "high-tech" army is tempted to patrol by vehicle. Unfortunately, the insurgents have made the killing of armored vehicles one of their top priorities. At present, they are content to use the Afghan/Chechen method—a barrage of IEDs and RPGs from every side. (Refer back to Figures 5.1 and 11.4.) Soon, they will turn to the *Hezbollah* method—massive explosion from below. When buried in the road and remotely detonated, as little as 100 pounds of explosive can blow off the turret of a main battle tank. Other than varying one's route or schedule, there is no defense for this type of attack. Foot patrolling is more safe and productive. However, it takes special movement skills in a built-up area. Every infantryman must learn through repetitive, simulated combat how best to avoid the first bullet.

In response to an "ambush" in Fallujah in April 2004, Marines called in "Cobra" gunships, engaged in a running gunfight, and then dropped two 500-pound laser-guided bombs.[23] In urban terrain (where collateral damage must be avoided at all costs), those in the kill zone should enter an undefended building to act as decoy, while the rest (or reinforcements) secretly outflank the enemy. Supporting arms should be reserved for reinforced strongpoints in a defensive matrix. Seldom does someone's living quarters qualify.

On 26 April 2004, ABC carried images of a Marine unit that had taken fire while patrolling the "occupied" portion of *Fallujah*.[24] At a building's center, a dozen or so Marines were being told which

Figure 12.5: Motorized Occupiers Can Be Easily Targeted
(Source: *Corel Gallery Clipart*—Weapons, One Mile Up, #45A020)

floor or window to defend. In an urban environment where the foe may have fuel-air-explosive tipped RPG rounds and shoulder-fired thermobaric weapons, bunching up in the same room can be a bad idea. For quicker dispersion and return fire from within a building, every fire team should be preassigned a cover sector. Such a sector might be described as follows: "From the right corner of the structure across the street to the end of the street."

Countering IEDs

The new foe relies heavily on command-detonated explosives. They can do no harm if spotted early. To spot IEDs in time, every U.S. soldier or Marine must become expert observers. Two *ninjutsu* eye exercises would help: (1) defocusing on something close to increase peripheral vision, and (2) looking at things progressively closer to better distinguish ground detail.

Approach March for an Attack

One cannot sneak up on a guerrilla in an armored personnnel carrier or helicopter. Instead of moving all the way to the objective by vehicle, the assault force must cover the final distance on foot. (See Figure 12.5.) While this may be difficult in a *Hezbollah* controlled area, it is not impossible. People can drop out of a patrol at a rest stop. They can disembark a commodity convoy at a dip in the road. They can dress up like women and then move in twos and threes to a rendezvous point.

In Iraq, armored personnel carriers are about to become too dangerous for passengers. They will be subjected to remotely detonated, below-ground explosives. Helicopters are not a good idea either. Both Lebanese and Chechen militants succeeded in downing choppers full of troops. The Iraqi insurgents may be just waiting for the chance.

Overcoming the Community Watch Network

As of 4 August 2004, al-Sadr had a gunman on every street corner in the holy cities and East Baghdad.[25] As the Iranian Revolutionary Guard and *Hezbollah* deploy sentries the same way,[26] this should come as no surprise. Very probably *al-Sadr* uses his mentors' other intelligence methods as well—e.g., binocular reconnaissance from minarets, religious requirements for citizens, payment for telephone tips, warnings during daily prayer, and tailing intruders. This early warning network has too many checks and balances to permit its penetration by force. More productive would be camouflage, stealth, and deception.

The Attack Itself

To successfully assault a guerrilla base, one must have almost total surprise. In a built-up area, preparatory fire not only compromises that surprise, but also alienates residents. An assault force can often use local guides to wend its way through enemy ambushes, outposts, and obstacles. Some guides will know an unopposed way into the objective itself.

Prepared enemy positions require "deliberate" attacks. To be deliberate, an attack must entail some sort of reconnaissance and rehearsal. In decreasing order of safety, the principal categories of deliberate attack are short-range infiltration, night, and daylight.[27] For every possible compromise to surprise, a feint is planned. If the attackers cannot enter the objective silently, they use concussion grenades in possible combination with a nearby, delay-fuzed, precision mortar barrage. Unsilenced small arms telegraph intentions and should be used only as a last resort.

In urban terrain, one must attack more quickly than the enemy believes possible. This is done by withholding noise. It is far better to "pie off" a room than to "frag" it. The objective, after all, is to preserve the lives of ordinary citizens while taking their oppressors hostage.

Resupply

No number of gun trucks, tanks, or helicopter gunships can protect an American convoy from RPG gunners who are positioned right next to a road at intervals equaling the doctrinal distance between trucks. There is only one way to defend against this type of attack. The fuel and ammunition trucks must be somehow camouflaged. Every truck must also have a rifleman at each corner with a 90° field of fire. Upon ambush, a small reaction force moves outboard to take the instigators under machinegun fire from an unprotected flank.

Shutting Down Enemy Supply Lines

The supply lines into Iraq and Afghanistan very probably operate the same way as those into Vietnam. Instead of jungle cover, they rely on deep defiles and tunnels. To find them, one has only to plot all firefights, enemy sightings, and recovered caches. By connecting the dots in the suspected direction of travel, one can readily determine the approximate route. Then, with trained trackers, he can discover its exact trace, underground waystations, and source. The main conduits into Afghanistan are probably the same as in 1987. (Relook at Map 6.2.)

To shut down the Iraqi insurgent's source of supply, the U.S. military first must drop less heavy ordnance. Every 500 pound dud produces enough explosive for five car bombs. It must also start searching for explosives that look like other things. In Lebanon, they were disguised as rocks. More obvious ordnance was transported in false-bottomed trucks.

Indigenous-Defense-Force Training

To win in Afghanistan and Iraq, the opposition need not decisively beat U.S. forces. It has only to bottle them up, subvert or overpower local-police or national-guard units, and then wait. That's how it got rid of the Russians and Israelis.

There is a way to disrupt the militants' so-far-successful formula. Indigenous law-enforcement and defense-force detachments will not have precision supporting arms at their disposal. To survive, they will depend almost entirely on short-range-combat skill. With better small-unit techniques than are currently available within the U.S. military, they could routinely weather a surprise encounter with a larger opponent. While the best techniques now come from East Asia, Posterity Enterprises of Emerald Isle, NC, could also provide the training.

The Muslim Militant Can Be Beaten

Middle Eastern fighters are not as good at working together as the East Asian Viet Cong. Their heritage is one of independent bands harassing a larger foe, stretching his formation and supply lines, and then swarming in on his detached elements. Their two- or three-man hunter-killer teams seem to do all right on their own, but they may have trouble mounting a squad-sized or larger attack of any complexity. With little or no fire support, they often assign missions in the same attack to separate bands. While doing so may encourage initiative, it jeopardizes last-minute or emergency coordination. Once U.S. forces recognize their tactical patterns, they should be able to disrupt them.

The Muslim guerrilla is highly motivated and eager for close combat, but he generally lacks the discipline of a U.S. infantryman.

As with the Japanese soldier who too easily accepted death, he is no match for a properly trained American. Therein lies the secondary purpose of this book. Previous Posterity Press publications have described how to more effectively train that American at the company level. He must know more than just how to use his equipment and follow orders. He must be able to outthink and outmaneuver his Muslim counterpart in a one-on-one encounter.

Hezbollah still depends on money.[28] Without foreign funding and African diamond proceeds, it would hold much less sway over the local populace.

An Unpleasant Prospect

Sudan has been the meeting place of *Hezbollah* and *al-Qaeda* leaders. It has also been frequented by the Muslim Brotherhood and Chinese. Around 1995, a Western traveler saw a white-haired man on Chinese TV say that he expected all of Southeast Asia to fall under the Chinese sphere of influence within ten years.[29] As of 4 January 2004, there has been foreign subversion in Myanmar and a Muslim uprising in pro-Western Thailand.[30] What if China needed oil or a diversion to take back Taiwan? Through the Muslim Brotherhood, it could influence the activities of the PLO, *Hezbollah,* Iranian Revolutionary Guard, Taliban, and *al-Qaeda.* While these Muslim factions may still be tactically challenged, the North Koreans have one of the best light infantry forces in the world.[31] What if the Iranian Revolutionary Guard and its Lebanese creation were to hire North Korean advisors? Recently appearing in the *Tehran Times* was a full page article about Kim Jong Il and North Korea's "unprecedented success." Of particular concern was the amount of credit given to the North Korean military.

> He *[Kim Il Sung's* son and successor] has given top national priority to military affairs. . . . In this course, a modern and independent defense industry has been developed, and all the people have been put under arms while the whole country has been fortified.
>
> In the latter half of the 1990's he, through his dynamic *Songun* revolutionary leadership, . . . made it possible to put up the high goal of building a great prosperous powerful socialist nation. . . .

Songun means giving top national priority to military affairs and making the Korean People's Army the main force of revolution.[32]
— *Tehran Times,* 5 June 2004

Would China's problems with its Muslim Uighurs in Xinjiang province preclude such a strategy?[33] For the Chinese, opposites hold great promise. China and Iran both, after all, do have revolutionary governments. From the ranks of the "Muslim Brotherhood" have come two founders of *al-Qaeda*—Azzam and al-Zawahiri. Azzam wanted to retrieve all lands previously Muslim, to include Burma and the Philippines.[34] At that time, India and Vietnam were also partially Islamic. The Muslim Brotherhood has been in operation throughout the Middle East since 1938. It must have had something to do with the first Palestinian training camps. Their graduates have since gone on to lead the region's largest militant organizations (to include the Iranian *Sepah*).

If such an alliance exists, it would encompass one third of the world's population. In an unconventional conflict, that many people could be hard to beat.

There Is Great Risk in Ignoring the Lessons of History

America has once again become embroiled in a guerrilla war—not one this time, but two so far (and potentially others). It has tried for 30 years to rise above the vestige of a similar affair in which the foe had no tanks or planes. Yet, the U.S. military has done nothing to preclude its recurrence. Its Vietnam-era forces were not defeated in Congress; they were defeated on the ground through a relative deficit in short-range-combat skill. Since that time, its small-unit tactics haven't changed, and its enlisted field skills have deteriorated. What happened in Vietnam (and more recently in Mogadishu) is about to happen again unless those two problems are corrected immediately. There has been some progress of late, but not nearly enough. Force-fed "simu-nitions" training (like paintball) does help the individual rifleman to take cover. Unfortunately, it does not provide his squad with advanced maneuver technique. Until that squad learns how to secretly approach an opponent, its members will unnecessarily get hurt.

While not as brutal as the Russians, American forces have been fighting the same way—avoiding casualties through the liberal use of supporting arms. The Russians also tried—through overwhelming bombardment—to keep any serious opposition at least 300 yards away in Chechnya.[35] They did so to avoid the casualties of close combat. Of course, noncombatants got killed in the process. In a guerrilla war, harming civilians does little more than fuel the opposition.

At least, the Russians were honest enough to admit the greater talent—at close range—of their Muslim adversaries.[36] They faulted their conscript policy—claiming that recent draftees would always be less motivated and able than seasoned freedom fighters. As the U.S. military is an all-volunteer force, it doesn't have that excuse. It doesn't do well at short range simply because it has failed to adopt the "bottom-up" way of training and operating that has served East Asian armies so well for 85 years. What is most disturbing is that U.S. leaders have been unwilling to admit to, or apprise their subordinates of, any tactical deficiency. One division withholds (from the press) details of each death in Afghanistan; it doesn't "want enemy forces to know any areas where U.S. troops might be vulnerable."[37] The enemy can plainly see where U.S. troops are vulnerable; the only ones to suffer from this type of secrecy are the troops' replacements. In 1917, the decision to ignore tactical innovation was made at the highest echelons of the French army.[38] Look how well it has served that country.

That U.S. battle chronicles don't mention any tactical shortfall is easy to explain. To the victor goes the interpretation of history. Still, in America's hour of need, it may be useful to admit that its 20th Century battles were not won by frontline maneuver. They were won by overwhelming mass. In a politically charged environment, military bureaucracies will sometimes work harder to look good than to be good. If they have prepared for all-out war, they may not consider a low-level conflict to be a war at all. For it, they might only need "containment operations." What results is every guerrilla's dream.

Armies need not have—as their highest priority—error avoidance. Anyone familiar with the senseless slaughter of early WWI and the recent trends within the U.S. military should closely consider this quote from the British Infantry Training Manual of the period.

Any enunciation by officers responsible for training of principles other than those contained in this manual, or any practice of methods not based on those principles is forbidden.[39]

> — *Company and Platoon Drill*
> War Office, 10 August 1914

Epilogue

This book has alluded to a tactical shortfall within the U.S. military so that its correction might speed up the Middle Eastern peace process. Muslim militants should not draw too much comfort from this problem. It has existed in America since before WWII. Thousands of young U.S. soldiers and Marines have already died because of it. Yet, in that great war, their more fortunate brethren still prevailed against two of the world's best light infantry forces—the Germans and Japanese. It was not only through overwhelming firepower that they did so. From the bottom up, they managed to slightly improve upon some of their standard maneuvers. Through trial and error, riflemen and fire teams learned how to sneak up on their immediate adversary. Then, by word of mouth, they shared this knowledge with each other. Any nonrates lucky enough to survive their first taste of combat became the "corporate knowledge" of their units. Always following the spirit of their orders, they tried hard to accomplish their commander's intent. In boot camp, their "fierce individualism" had been replaced with a "group mentality." Then, in extended combat, their collective effort temporarily overcame various training deficiencies. It was only then that what they had learned the hard way failed to enter the U..S. military's organizational memory.

With better tactical technique, U.S. infantrymen would suffer fewer casualties at short range. Those, who readily admit that, can now win a guerrilla war. They will not allow the organized ignorance of the Vietnam era to be repeated. Yes, those riflemen and small-unit leaders who stick to outmoded procedures, blindly follow orders, or forget each other's welfare may quickly fall by the wayside. But those who remain will become a force to be reckoned with. They will work diligently—in their spare time if need be—to acquire state-of-the-art, light-infantry skills (as fully documented by Posterity Press). Remembering their Heavenly Father's love for all of His children throughout the world, they will use minimal force and dispense mercy whenever possible. They will not allow themselves to hate. Instead, they will follow the paradoxical advice of Christ—to love adversary and sympathizer alike. Some may make the ultimate sacrifice for their beliefs, but none will allow their souls to be tarnished. Light infantrymen like these cannot be denied the ultimate victory.

Notes

SOURCE NOTES

Illustrations

Picture on page 3 reproduced after written assurance from Orion Books, London, that the copyright holders for *ARMY UNIFORMS OF WORLD WAR I,* text by Andrew Mollo, color plates by Pierre Turner, could no longer be contacted. It is from Plate 106 of the Orion publication. Copyright © 1977 by Blandford Books Ltd. All rights reserved.

Map on page 7 reproduced after being unable to contact The Empire Press, Jarrold & Sons, Ltd., Norwich, UK, on *THE HISTORY OF THE NORFOLK REGIMENT: 1685-1918,* Vol. II. Copyright © n.d. by F. Loraine Petre. All rights reserved.

Map on page 13 reproduced after asking the permission of Simon & Schuster Ltd., London, UK, from *ALL THE KINGS MEN* by Nigel McCrery. Copyright © 1992 by Nigel McCrery. All rights reserved.

Pictures on pages 19, 49, 50, 51, 67, 129, and 173 reproduced after written assurance from Orion Books, London, that the copyright holders for *WORLD ARMY UNIFORMS SINCE 1939,* text by Andrew Mollo and Digby Smith, color plates by Malcolm McGregor and Michael Chappell, could no longer be contacted. They are from Part II (Plates 122, 119, 107, 114, 8, 115, 54 respectively) of the Orion publication. Copyright © 1975, 1980, 1981, 1983 by Blandford Books Ltd. All rights reserved.

Pictures on pages 29, 183, and 227 reproduced after written assurance from Orion Books, UK, that the copyright holders for *UNIFORMS OF THE ELITE FORCES,* text by Leroy Thompson, color plates by Michael Chappell, could no longer be contacted. They are from Plate 24 (No. 70), Plate 26 (No. 77), and Plate 5 (No. 15) of the Orion publication respectively. Copyright © 1982 by Blandford Books Ltd. All rights reserved.

Map on page 97 with permission of Pen & Sword Books Ltd., South Yorkshire, UK, and Brigadier Yousaf, from *BEAR TRAP: AFGHANISTAN'S UNTOLD STORY* by Brigadier Mohammad Yousaf and Major Mark Adkin. It is from Map 9 of the Pen & Sword publication. Copyright © n.d. by Leo Cooper. All rights reserved.

Photo on page 121 reprinted after written assurance from *THE ASSOCIATED PRESS* that it was from a Pakistani handout of unclear origin. Copyright © 2004. All rights reserved.

Picture on page 231 reproduced after asking the permission of the Swedish Army, from *SOLDF: SOLDATEN I FALT,* as published by Forsvarsmakten. It appears on pages 28 and 29 of the Swedish publication. Copyright © 2001 by Forsvarsmakten, Stockholm. All rights reserved.

Maps on pages 4, 20, 30, 57, 68,74, 88, and 132 reprinted after written assurance from *GENERAL LIBRARIES OF THE UNIVERSITY OF TEXAS AT AUSTIN* that they are in the public domain.

Text

Reprinted with permission of *DEBKAFILE,* Israel, from "New Warfront Opens in Iraq Three Months before Handover," by Art Theyson, 5 April 2004, and "Shiite Radicals Join with Sunni Insurgents in Ramadi," 7 April 2004. Copyright © 2004 by DEBKAfile. All rights reserved.

Reprinted with permission of the *MARINE CORPS GAZETTE,* from the following articles: "Counterguerrilla Warfare in South Lebanon," by Lt.Col. David Eshel (IDF Ret.), July 1997; "A Tale of Two Cities—Hue and Khorramshahr," by Lt.Col. Robert W. Lamont, April 1999; "Russian Lessons Learned from the Battles for Grozny," by Lt.Col. Timothy L. Thomas and Lester W. Grau, April 2000; "Russia's 1994-96 Campaign for Chechnya: A Failure in Shaping the Battlespace," by Maj. Norman L. Cooling, October 2001; and "The Hezbollah Model: Using Terror and Creating a Quasi-State in Lebanon," by Lt.Cmdr. Youssef H. Aboul-Enein, June 2003. Copyrights © 1997, 1999, 2000, 2001, and 2003 by the Marine Corps Association. All rights reserved.

Reprinted with permission of the *NEW YORK TIMES,* from "Hezbollah Becomes Potent Anti-U.S. Force," by Neil MacFarquahar, 24 December 2002, and "Kurds Are Finally Heard: Turkey Burned Our Villages," by Dexter Filkins, 24 October 2003. Copyrights © 2002 and 2003 by New York Times. All rights reserved.

ENDNOTES

Preface

1. John L. Esposito, *Unholy War: Terror in the Name of Islam* (London: Oxford Univ. Press, 2002), pp. 26, 38.
2. Ibid., p. 28.
3. Ibid., p. 158.
4. Ibid.
5. *Catholic Almanac,* comp. and ed. Felician A. Foy O.F.M. and Rose M. Avato (Huntington, IN: Our Sunday Visitor Publishing, 1998), pp. 290-296.
6. Esposito, *Unholy War,* p. xi.
7. *The Jerusalem Bible,* ed. Alexander Jones et al (Garden City, NY: Doubleday, 1966), Romans 12 (19-21), p. 286.

Introduction

1. *Warfare in Lebanon,* ed. Kenneth J. Alnwick and Thomas A. Fabyanic (Washington, D.C.: Nat. Defense Univ., 1988), p. 15; Martin van Creveld, *The Sword and the Olive: A Critical History of the Israeli Defense Force* (New York: PublicAffairs, 1998), pp. 307, 341, 360.
2. Matt Kelley, AP, "Rumsfeld Trip Highlights Accomplishments in Iraq," *Jacksonville (NC) Daily News,* 5 September 2003, p. 1A.
3. *Random House Encyclopedia,* electronic ed., s.v. "Mohammed."
4. *Islam Empire of Faith,* PBS Home Video (Garner Films in conjunction with PBS and Devillier Donegan Enterprises), videocassette #B8511; *Random House Encyclopedia,* electronic ed., s.v. "Islam."
5. *Random House Encyclopedia,* electronic ed., s.v. "Ali."
6. Dan Murphy, "Sadr The Agitator: Like Father, Like Son," *Christian Science Monitor,* 27 April 2004, p. 6.
7. *Islam Empire of Faith.*
8. Andrew Cockburn, "Iraq's Oppressed Majority," *Smithsonian,* December 2003, p. 100; *Random House Encyclopedia,* electronic ed., s.v. "Shi'a."
9. "CIA—The World Factbook," from its website, www.cia.gov.
10. "Afghanistan Country Study," *DA PAM 550-65,* Area Handbook Series (Washington, D.C.: Hdqts. Dept. of the Army, n.d.); Cockburn, "Iraq's Oppressed Majority," December 2003, p. 100.
11. *Random House Encyclopedia,* electronic ed., s.v. "Shi'a," "Imamis," and "Isma'ilis."
12. Edward Burman, *The Assassins — Holy Killers of Islam* (New York: HarperCollins, 1988); Farhad Daftary, *The Ismaili: Their History and Doctrines* (Cambridge, UK: Cambridge Univ. Press, 1990), pp. 1-7.

13. Ibid.; *World Religions: From Ancient History to the Present,* ed. Geoffrey Parrinder (New York: Facts on File Publications, 1971), p. 498.

14. "Sacrifices of the Fidais," from www.ismaili.net.

15. Ibid.; Burman, *The Assassins.*

16. Arkon Daraul, *Secret Societies* (n.p.: Fine Communications, 1999).

17. Burman, *The Assassins.*

18. *The Travels of Marco Polo, The Venetian,* trans. and ed. William Marsden and re-ed. Thomas Wright (n.p.: publisher not provided, n.d.).

19. Ibid.

20. Bernard Lewis, *The Crisis of Islam: Holy War and Unholy Terror* (isbn 0739302191), Random House Audio Books, #RHCD251.

21. "Assassins," from www.geocities.com; "Sacrifices of the Fidai."

22. Dr. Haha Lung, *Knights of Darkness: Secrets of the World's Deadliest Night Fighters* (Boulder, CO: Paladin Press, 1998), pp. 14, 15.

23. Pico Iyer, "Grim Reminders of the Ancient Assassins," *Smithsonian,* October 1986, pp. 145-162.

24. Burman, *The Assassins.*

25. Ibid.

26. Dr. Masaaki Hatsumi, *Ninjutsu: History and Tradition* (Burbank, CA: Unique Publications, 1981), author's preface.

27. Wes Moore, "Hasan bin Sabbah and the Secret Order of Hashishins," from www.disinfo.com; Iyer, "Grim Reminders of the Ancient Assassins."

28. Farhad Daftary, *The Ismaili: Their History and Doctrines* (Cambridge, UK: Cambridge Univ. Press, 1990), pp. 1-7; "Hasan bin Sabbah and the Nizari Ismaili State in Alamut," from www.ismaili.net.

29. *Random House Encyclopedia,* electronic ed., s.v. "Jerusalem."

30. *Random House Encyclopedia,* electronic ed., s.v. "Crusades."

31. Lawrence Pintak, *Seeds of Hate: How America's Flawed Middle East Policy Ignited the Jihad* (London: Pluto Press, 2003), p. 173; *Islam Empire of Faith.*

32. Christopher Hollis and Ronald Brownrigg, *Holy Places: Jewish, Christian, and Moslem Monuments in the Holy Land* (New York: Praeger Publishers, 1969), p. 172; *Random House Encyclopedia,* electronic ed., s.v. "Saladin."

33. Iyer, "Grim Reminders of the Ancient Assassins."

34. Ibid.

35. *Random House Encyclopedia,* electronic ed., s.v. "Crusades."

36. *Random House Encyclopedia,* electronic ed., s.v. "Genghis Khan" and "Kublai Khan."

37. "The Mongol Empire," World of Wonder, *Jacksonville (NC) Daily News,* n.d.

38. *Random House Encyclopedia,* electronic ed., s.v. "Tatars."

39. *The Travels of Marco Polo.*

40. Daftary, *The Ismaili,* pp. 1-7; *Websters New Twentieth Century Dictionary,* 2d ed., s.v. "Levant."

41. "History of the Ismaili Imams Tarikh-e Imamat," from www.amaana.org and www.alamut.com; Burman, *The Assassins.*

42. "Iran Country Study," *DA PAM 550-68,* Area Handbook Series (Washington, D.C.: Hdqts. Dept. of the Army, 1989), p. 14.

43. Daftary, *The Ismaili,* pp. 1-7.

44. Lung, *Knights of Darkness,* p. 13.

45. "Ugarit: Archeological Background," from the Quartz Hill School of Theology website, www.theology.edu.

46. Extracted from the Ismaili Heritage Society's website, www.ismaili.net.

47. Ali tahir bin Sa ibn Qalanisi, "Tarikhi Dimashq" and "Ismaili Mission in Syria," from www.ismaili.net.

48. "A Day with the Assassins," from www.bootsnall.com.

49. Lewis, *The Crisis of Islam.*

50. Lung, *Knights of Darkness,* p. 14.

51. H. John Poole, *The Tiger's Way: A U.S. Private's Best Chance for Survival* (Emerald Isle, NC: Posterity Press, 2003), pp. 27-32.

52. Robert D. Kaplan, *Soldiers of God: With Islamic Warriors in Afghanistan and Pakistan,* revised ed. (New York: Vintage Books, 2001), pp. 20, 82.

53. *The Bear Went over the Mountain: Soviet Combat Tactics in Afghanistan,* trans. and ed. Lester W. Grau, Foreign Mil. Studies Office, U.S. Dept. of Defense, Ft. Leavenworth, KS (Washington, D.C.: Nat. Defense Univ. Press, 1996), originally published under its Russian title (Soviet Union: Frunze Mil. Acad., n.d.), p. 16.

54. Ali Jalali and Lester W. Grau, *Afghan Guerrilla Warfare: In the Words of the Mujahideen Fighters* (St. Paul, MN: MBI Publishing, 2001), first published as *The Other Side of the Mountain* (Quantico, VA: Marine Corps Combat Development Cmd., 1995), p. xviii.

55. Quintan Wiktorowicz, *Global Jihad: Understanding September 11,* Unabridged Audio Books (Falls Church, VA), compact disk #isbn 158472269x.

56. *Random House Encyclopedia,* electronic ed., s.v. "Jordan."

57. Sepehr Zabih, *The Iranian Military in Revolution and War* (London: Routledge, 1988), p. 14.

58. Ibid., p. 37.

59. Ibid., p. 184.

60. *Warfare in Lebanon,* ed. Alnwick and Fabyanic, pp. 74, 75.

61. Sun Tzu, *The Art of War,* trans. and intro. Samuel B. Griffith, foreword by B.H. Liddell Hart (New York: Oxford Univ. Press, 1963), p. 84.

Chapter 1: *Gallipoli's Underreported Tactics*

1. *The Concise Encyclopedia of Ancient Civilizations,* ed. Janet Serlin Garber (New York: Franklin Watts, 1978), pp. 30, 31.

2. Robert B. Asprey, *War in the Shadows* (Garden City, NY: Doubleday & Co., 1975), p. 49.

3. Ibid., p. 61.

4. Ibid., p. 51.

5. Paul Begg, "Into Thin Air," in no. 31, vol. 3, *The Unexplained: Mysteries of Mind Space & Time,* from Mysteries of the Unexplained Series (Pleasantville, NY: Readers Digest Assn., 1992), p. 125.

6. Nigel McCrery, *All the King's Men* (New York: Simon & Schuster, 1999), previously titled *The Vanished Battalion;* "All the Kings Men," *Exxon Masterpiece Theater*, BBC in conjunction with WGBH Boston, NC Public TV, 26 November 2000.

7. Petre, F. Loraine, "The 1/4th and 1/5th Battalions (Territorial)," chapter 4 of volume II of *The History of the Norfolk Regiment: 1685-1918* (Norwich, UK: Empire Press, n.d.).

8. McCrery, *All the King's Men,* pp. 63-67.

9. Loraine, "The 1/4th and 1/5th Battalions."

10. McCrery, *All the King's Men,* pp. 65-67.

11. Ibid.

12. Ibid.

13. Ibid., p. 67.

14. Ibid.

15. Ibid.

16. Ibid., pp. 70, 71.

17. Ibid.

18. Ibid., p. 72.

19. Loraine, "The 1/4th and 1/5th Battalions."

20. McCrery, *All the King's Men,* p. 71.

21. Ibid.

22. Ibid., p. 72.

23. Ibid., pp. 72, 81; Capt. Evelyn Beck, as quoted in *All the King's Men,* by McCrery, p. 87.

24. McCrery, *All the King's Men,* p. 72.

25. Lt.Col. Villiers Stuart, as quoted in *All the King's Men,* by McCrery, pp. 72, 73.

26. Loraine, "The 1/4th and 1/5th Battalions."

27. H. John Poole, *Phantom Soldier: The Enemy's Answer to U.S. Firepower* (Emerald Isle, NC: Posterity Press, 2001), pp. 125-138.

28. Poole, *Tiger's Way,* pp. 143-176.

29. Capt. Montgomerie, as quoted "The 1/4th and 1/5th Battalions," by Loraine.

31. McCrery, *All the King's Men,* p. 77.

32. Ibid., p. 79.

33. Capt. Evelyn Beck, as quoted in *All the King's Men,* by McCrery, p. 87.

34. Ibid., p. 73.

35. Ibid., p. 77.

36. Pvt. Tom Williamson, as quoted in *All the King's Men,* by McCrery, p. 88.

37. Poole, *Phantom Soldier,* p. 37.

38. McCrery, *All the King's Men,* pp. 83-86.

39. Ibid., pp. 80, 81.

40. Poole, *Phantom Soldier,* pp. 125-138.

41. Lt. Mehmed Fasih, *Gallipoli 1915: Bloody Ridge (Lone Pine) Diary* (Istanbul: Denizler Kitabevi, 1997), p. 7.

42. Ibid., pp. 18-20.

43. Ibid., pp. 36, 67.

44. Ibid., p. 114.

45. Ibid., p. 117.

46. Ibid., p. 139.

47. Poole, *Tiger's Way,* pp. 143-146.

48. Fasih, *Gallipoli 1915,* p. 10.

49. Ibid., p. 155.

50. Ibid., p. 128.

51. Ibid., p. 81.

52. Ibid., pp. 81, 93, 134, 166.

53. Ibid., pp. 93, 94, 183.

54. Ibid., p. 188.

55. Ibid., p. 64.

56. Ibid., p. 90.

57. Ibid., p. 153.

58. Ibid., p. 74.

59. Ibid., p. 78.

60. Ibid., p. 3.

61. Ibid., p. 188.

62. Ibid., p. 111.

63. Ibid., p. 176.

64. Ibid., pp. 7, 103.

65. "Turkey Country Study," *DA PAM 550-80,* Area Handbook Series (Washington, D.C.: Hdqts. Dept. of the Army, 1995), p. 30.

Chapter 2: *Lessons from the Iran-Iraq War*

1. Dilip Hiro, *The Longest War: The Iran-Iraq Military Conflict* (New York: Routledge, 1991), p. xxv.

2. "Iran Country Study," p. 267.

3. Zabih, *The Iranian Military,* p. 14.
4. Ibid., pp. 210-212.
5. Ibid., p. 211.
6. Ibid., p. 14.
7. Ibid., p. 143.
8. Ibid., p. 160.
9. Ibid., p. 152.
10. Robin Wright, "A Reporter at Large—Tehran Summer," *The New Yorker,* 5 September 1988, p. 40, as quoted in *Warriors of Islam: Iran's Revolutionary Guard,* by Kenneth Katzman (Boulder, CO: Westview Press, 1993), p. 63.
11. Kenneth Katzman, *Warriors of Islam: Iran's Revolutionary Guard* (Boulder, CO: Westview Press, 1993), pp. 82-84.
12. Ibid., pp. 84, 85.
13. Memo for the record by H.J. Poole.
14. Ibid.
15. Zabih, *The Iranian Military,* p. 213.
16. "Iran Country Study," pp. 272, 273.
17. Ibid., pp. 273, 274.
18. Zabih, *The Iranian Military,* p. 240.
19. "Iran Country Study," p. 275.
20. Zabih, *The Iranian Military,* p. 252.
21. Ibid.
22. Ibid., p. 14.
23. Memo for the record from H.J. Poole.
24. H.J. Poole, *The Last Hundred Yards. The NCO's Contribution to Warfare* (Emerald Isle, NC: Posterity Press, 1997), pp. 32, 33.
25. Wright, *Sacred Rage: The Wrath of Militant Islam* (New York: Simon & Schuster, 1985), pp. 33-35, as quoted in *Warriors of Islam,* by Katzman, p. 12.
26. "Iran Country Study," p. 272.
27. Lt.Col. Robert W. Lamont, "A Tale of Two Cities—Hue and Khorramshahr," *Marine Corps Gazette,* April 1999, pp. 32-35.
28. Katzman, *Warriors of Islam,* p. 64.
29. Memo for the record by H.J. Poole.

Chapter 3: *Israel's Expulsion from Southern Lebanon*

1. J. Bowyer Bell, *Dragonwars: Armed Struggle & the Conventions of Modern War* (New Brunswick, NJ: Transaction Publishers, 1999), p. 18.
2. Zabih, *The Iranian Military,* pp. 160, 217.
3. Ibid.

4. Ibid., pp. 152-153, 160; Edgar O'Balance, "The Iranian Armed Forces," *Marine Corps Gazette,* August 1980, p. 50.

5. Lt.Cmdr. Youssef H. Aboul-Enein, "The Hezbollah Model: Using Terror and Creating a Quasi-State in Lebanon," *Marine Corps Gazette,* June 2003, p. 34; "Iran Country Study," p. 227; Pintak, *Seeds of Hate,* p. 226.

6. Wright, *Sacred Rage,* pp. 33-35, as quoted in *Warriors of Islam,* by Katzman, p. 71.

7. *Warfare in Lebanon,* ed. Alnwick and Fabyanic, p. 25.

8. "Ugarit."

9. Lung, *Knights of Darkness:,* p. 15.

10. Aboul-Enein, "The Hezbollah Model," p. 35.

11. *Warfare in Lebanon,* ed. Alnwick and Fabyanic, pp. 71, 72.

12. Ibid., p. 71.

13. Ibid., p. 54.

14. Zabih, *The Iranian Military,* pp. 210-212.

15. Aboul-Enein, "The Hezbollah Model," p. 34.

16. Ibid., pp. 34, 35.

17. Ibid., p. 34.

18. *Warfare in Lebanon,* ed. Alnwick and Fabyanic, p. 21.

19. David Gardner, "'Israel': Hizbollah Sharpens Up Its Tactics," *London Financial Times,* 1997.

20. Martin van Creveld, *The Sword and the Olive: A Critical History of the Israeli Defense Force* (New York: PublicAffairs, Perseus Books, 1998), p. 341.

21. Ibid., p. 361.

22. Ibid.

23. Ibid., pp. 342, 343.

24. Ibid., p. 351.

25. Ibid, pp. 348, 349.

26. Lt.Col. (Ret., IDF) David Eshel, "Counterguerrilla Warfare in South Lebanon," *Marine Corps Gazette,* July 1997, p. 43.

27. Ibid.

28. Aboul-Enein, "The Hezbollah Model," p. 35.

29. Gardner, "Israel."

30. Eshel, "Counterguerrilla Warfare in South Lebanon," p. 42.

31. Yossi Melman, "Ambush of Naval Squad 'No Accident'," *Ha'aretz* (Tel Aviv), 13 August 1998.

32. Ibid.

33. Scott Peterson, "In a War It Cannot Win, Israel Tries New Tactics," *Christian Science Monitor,* 9/20 October 1997.

34. Van Creveld, *The Sword and the Olive,* p. 304.

35. Melman, "Ambush of Naval Squad 'No Accident'," *Ha'aretz* (Tel Aviv), 13 August 1998.

36. "The Battle That Helped Change the Course of the 'Israeli' Occupation," *Daily Star* (Lebanon), 6 September 2000.

37. Naomi Segal, Jewish Telegraphic Agency, "IDF Absolved of Blame in Deaths of Naval Commandos in Lebanon," *San Francisco Jewish Community Publication,* 31 October 1997.

38. Van Creveld, *The Sword and the Olive,* pp. 341, 342.

39. Peterson, "In a War It Cannot Win."

40. Eshel, "Counterguerrilla Warfare in South Lebanon," p. 42.

41. Ibid., p. 43.

42. Ibid., p. 42.

43. Joseph C. Goulden, *Korea: The Untold Story of the War* (New York: Times Books, 1982), p. 295.

44. Eshel, "Counterguerrilla Warfare in South Lebanon," p. 42.

45. Harel Amos, "Probe into IDF Kidnappings Critical of Army's Conduct," *Ha'aretz* (Tel Aviv), 10 October 2000.

46. Lee Hockstader, "Israeli Army Suffers Pair of Sharp Blows," *International Herald Tribune,* 16 February 2002, reprinted from *Washington Post,* n.d.

47. Eshel, "Counterguerrilla Warfare in South Lebanon," p. 42.

48. Aboul-Enein, "The Hezbollah Model," p. 35.

49. Eshel, "Counterguerrilla Warfare in South Lebanon," pp. 42, 43.

50. Peterson, "In a War It Cannot Win."

51. Ibid.

52. "Fighter Strolls around Sojod Base, Raises Flag, Punches Soldier and Gets Away . . . ," *Daily Star* (Lebanon), 12 August 1998; David Rudge, "IDF Probes Hizbullah Infiltration 2 Soldiers Wounded in South Lebanon," *Jerusalem Post* (Israel), 12 August 1998, daily ed., p. 3.

53. "Fighter Strolls around Sojod Base . . . ."

54. Eshel, "Counterguerrilla Warfare in South Lebanon," p. 42.

55. James F. Dunnigan and Albert A. Nofi, *Dirty Little Secrets of the Vietnam War* (New York: Thomas Dunne Books, 1999), pp. 265, 266.

56. Eshel, "Counterguerrilla Warfare in South Lebanon," p. 42.

57. Van Creveld, *The Sword and the Olive,* p. 288.

58. Nguyen Khac Can and Pham Viet Thuc, *The War 1858 - 1975 in Vietnam* (Hanoi: Nha Xuat Ban Van Hoa Dan Toc, n.d.), figure 754; Andrew Mollo and Digby Smith, *World Army Uniforms Since 1939,* part 2 (Poole, UK: Blandford Press, 1981), pp. 18, 19.

59. Grant Evans and Kelvin Rowley, *Red Brotherhood at War: Indochina since the Fall of Saigon* (London: Verso, 1984), p. 161.

60. Nyan Chanda, *Brother Enemy: The War after the War* (New York: Collier Books, 1986), p. 361.

61. Gardner, "Israel."

62. Van Creveld, *The Sword and the Olive,* pp. 341, 342.

63. Pintak, *Seeds of Hate,* p. 292.

64. Ibid., p. 295.
65. *Warfare in Lebanon,* ed. Alnwick and Fabyanic, p. 15.
66. Van Creveld, *The Sword and the Olive,* pp. 307, 341, 360.
67. "Hezbollah," *Encyclopedia,* www.nationmaster.com, 5 July 2004.

Chapter 4: *Palestinian Fighters*

1. Desmond McForan, *The World Held Hostage: The War Waged by International Terrorism* (New York: St. Martin's Press, 1986), p. 5.
2. Ibid.
3. Ibid., p. 10.
4. Ibid., p. 94.
5. Bell, *Dragonwars,* p. 18.
6. Pintak, *Seeds of Hate,* pp. 68, 69; Eric Hammel, *The Root: The Marines in Beirut, August 1982 - February 1984* (Pacifica, CA: Pacifica Press, 1985), pp. 16-20.
7. Ibid., pp. 29-34; "Terrorism," *Frontline,* PBS, NC Public TV, n.d.; Pintak, *Seeds of Hate,* pp. 69-72.
8. Pintak, pp. 18, 19.
9. *"Hezbollah* Reference Page," from www.military.com, 17 June 2004.
10. Esposito, *Unholy War,* p. 96.
11. "Hamas (Islamic Resistance Movement)," *Patterns of Global Terrorism, 2002* (Washington, D.C.: U.S. Dept. of State, April 2003), from its website.
12. Aboul-Enein, "The Hezbollah Model," p. 35.
13. Ramit Plushnick-Masti, AP, "Militant Groups Join Forces, Get Hezbollah Help," *Jacksonville (NC) Daily News,* 28 October 2003, p. 1A.
14. Esposito, *Unholy War,* p. 98.
15. Ibid., p. 99; "Hamas," *Patterns of Global Terrorism.*
16. Ben Lynfield, "Hamas Seeks Primacy in Gaza," *Christian Science Monitor,* 3 March 2004, p. 1.
17. ABC's Nightly News, 6 March 2004.
18. "Hamas and the Al Aqsa Martyrs Brigade Claimed Responsibility," News in Brief, *Christian Science Monitor,* 15 March 2004, p. 20.
19. Jason Keyser, AP, "Israel Bombs Syria," *Jacksonville (NC) Daily News,* 6 October 2003; "Popular Front for the Liberation of Palestine–General Command (PFLP-GC)," *Patterns of Global Terrorism, 2002* (Washington, D.C.: U.S. Dept. of State, April 2003), from its website.
20. Dr. David H. Reinke (expert on parapsychology and Eastern religions), in e-mails to the author, October 2003 - August 2004.
21. Fr. Patrick Gaffney (recognized authority on the Middle East), in a letter to the author, 29 August 2004.

22. "Israeli: Palestinians Get Bonus for Killings," World Briefs Wire Reports (AP), *Jacksonville (NC) Daily News,* 25 February 2004, p. 5A.

23. Mark Clayton, "Reading into the Mind of a Terrorist," *Christian Science Monitor,* 30 October 2003, p. 11.

24. Ilene Prusher, "As Life Looks Bleaker, Suicide Bombers Get Younger," *Christian Science Monitor,* 5 March 2004, pp. 1, 5.

25. Ali Daraghmen, AP, "Israelis Stop Teen Wearing Bomb Vest," AOL News, 25 March 2004.

26. ABC's Nightly News, 26 March 2004.

27. Ibid.

28. Julie Stahl, "'Paradise Camps' Teach Palestinian Children to Be Suicide Bombers," Cybercast News Service, 23 July 2001.

29. "Double Bombing Kills 11 Israelis, Wounds At Least 18," World Briefs Wire Reports (AP), *Jacksonville (NC) Daily News,* 15 March 2004, p. 6A.

30. "Hamas Militants Killed in Air Strike," World Briefs Wire Reports (AP), *Jacksonville (NC) Daily News,* 4 March 2004, p. 5A.

31. Cameron W. Barr, "Gaza Bomb Attack: Strategy Shift?", *Christian Science Monitor,* 16 October 2003, p. 1; Ibrahim Barzak, AP, "Bomb Tagets Diplomatic Convoy," *Jacksonville (NC) Daily News,* 16 October 2003, p. 6A.

32. Margot Dudkevitch, "3 Soldiers Killed as Tank Hits Mine: Gaza Roadside Attack Is Second in a Month," *Jerusalem Post* (Israel), 15 March 2002.

33. Arieh O'Sullivan, "A Much More Worrisome Ambush," *Jerusalem Post* (Israel), 15 March 2002.

34. Nidal al-Mughrabi, Reuters, "Israeli Soldiers Feared Dead in Second Ambush in Gaza," AOL News, 12 May 2004; NPR's "Morning Edition," 13 May 2004.

35. ABC's Morning News, 11 May 2004.

36. O'Sullivan, "A Much More Worrisome Ambush."

37. Harvey Morris and Avi Machlis, "Palestinian Checkpoint Sniper Kills 10 Israelis," *London Financial Times,* 4 March 2002.

38. Scott Peterson, "Tough U.S. Tactics Quell Fallujah Unrest, But at What Cost," *Christian Science Monitor,* 20 April 2004, p. 5.

39. Poole, *Tiger's Way,* pp. 280-290.

40. Poole, *Phantom Soldier,* pp. 163-198.

41. Lynfield, "Hamas Seeks Primacy in Gaza," p. 6.

42. "Israeli Troops Enter Camp on Gaza-Egyptian Border," News Digest Wire Reports (AP), *Jacksonville (NC) Daily News,* 10 October 2003, p. 2A.

43. Poole, *Tiger's Way,* pp. 167, 255.

44. Joshua Hammer, "Guns over Gaza," *Newsweek,* 5 April 2004, pp. 40, 41.

45. Cameron W. Barr, "A Smaller Intifada Resumes," *Christian Science Monitor,* 11 January 2004, p. 7.

46. Gaffney letter.

47. "Fatalities in the al-Aqsa Intifada," B'Tselem, the Israeli Info. Center for Human Rights in the Occupied Territories, from its website, www.btslem.org.

48. "Hamas Boss Says No Truce with Israel," World Briefs Wire Reports (AP), *Jacksonville (NC) Daily News,* 25 September 2003, p. 5A.

49. Lara Sukhtian, AP, "Palestinians Bury Leader Killed by Israel," *Jacksonville (NC) Daily News,* 23 March 2004, p. 4A.

50. "U.S. Vetoes Resolution to Hamas' Leader Death," News Digest Wire Reports (AP), *Jacksonville (NC) Daily News,* 26 March 2004, p. 2A.

51. "At Least 10 Palestinians Die in Israeli Tank Attack," from AP, *Jacksonville (NC) Daily News,* 20 May 2004, p. 5A.

52. Ilene R. Prusher and Ben Lynfield, "Killing of Yassin a Turning Point," *Christian Science Monitor,* 23 March 2004, pp. 1, 10.

53. NPR's "Morning Edition," 13 May 2004.

54. Poole, *Tiger's Way,* pp. 261-265.

55. "Militants Target Israeli Army Outpost," from AP, *USA Today,* 27 June 2004.

56. Ibid.

57. Nicholas Blanford, "Gauge of Mideast Tensions on Lebanon's Border with Israel," *Christian Science Monitor,* 11 August 2004, p. 7.

58. Nicholas Blanford, "Hizbullah Reelects Its Leader," *Christian Science Monitor,* 19 August 2004, p. 6.

Chapter 5: *Chechen Rebels*

1. Maj. Norman L. Cooling, "Russia's 1994-96 Campaign for Chechnya: A Failure in Shaping the Battlespace," *Marine Corps Gazette,* October 2001, p. 62.

2. Ibid., pp. 62-66.

3. Lt.Col. Lester W. Grau, *Russian-Manufactured Armored Vehicle Vulnerability in Urban Combat: The Chechnya Experience,* as quoted in "Kings of the Road: Heavy and Light Forces in MOUT," by Capt. John W. Karagosian and Capt. Christopher M. Coglianese, Training Notes, *Infantry Magazine,* January-February 2004, pp. 41-42.

4. Cooling, "Russia's 1994-96 Campaign for Chechnya," pp. 62-66.

5. Ibid.

6. Ibid.

7. Lt.Col. Timothy L. Thomas and Lester W. Grau, "Russian Lessons Learned from the Battles for Grozny," *Marine Corps Gazette,* April 2000, p. 46.

8. Cooling, "Russia's 1994-96 Campaign," p. 68.

9. "The Second Chechen War," *P31,* ed. Mrs. A.C. Aldis (Sandhurst, UK: Conflict Studies Research Centre, June 2000).

10. C.W. Blandy, "Moscow's Failure to Understand," chapt. 3 of "The Second Chechen War," p. 12.

11. Dr. M.A. Smith, "The Second Chechen War: The All Russian Context," chapt. 2 of "The Second Chechen War," p. 4.

12. Blandy, "Moscow's Failure to Understand," p. 15.

13. M.J. Orr, "Better or Not So Bad? An Evaluation of Russian Combat Effectiveness in the Second Chechen War," chapt. 7 of "The Second Chechen War," p. 94.

14. L.W. Grau (FSMO), "Technology and the Second Chechen Campaign: Not All New and Not That Much," chapt. 8 of "The Second Chechen War," p. 105.

15. Blandy, "Moscow's Failure to Understand," p. 15.

16. Thomas and Grau, "Russian Lessons Learned," *Marine Corps Gazette,* p. 47.

17. Grau, "Technology and the Second Chechen Campaign," p. 106.

18. Pavel Felgenhauer, "Defense Dossier: Guerrilla War Can't Be Won," *Moscow Times,* 9 March 2000.

19. Poole, *Tiger's Way,* p. 121.

20. Thomas and Grau, "Russian Lessons Learned from the Battles for Grozny," p. 48.

21. Orr, "Better or Not So Bad?", pp. 96, 97.

22. Grau, "Technology and the Second Chechen Campaign," p. 107; Blandy, "Moscow's Failure to Understand," p. 17.

23. Sophie Lambroschini, "Russia: Self-Deception Underlie Recent Chechen Debacles," *Center for Defense Info. (CDI) Weekly,* no. 4, 10 March 2000.

24. "Blair Meets with Putin As Battle Continues in Chechnya," CNN News, 11 March 2000.

25. "Rebel Ambush Leaves 37 Russians Dead in Chechnya," CNN News, 3 March 2000.

26. Andrew Harding, "Grozny Is a City of Rubble," BBC News, 10 March 2000.

27. "Blair Meets with Putin As Battle Continues in Chechnya."

28. "Rebel Ambush Leaves 37 Russians Dead in Chechnya."

29. Sergeant Michael D. Wilmoth and Lt.Col. Peter G. Tsouras, "Ulus-Kert: An Airborne Company's Last Stand," *Military Review* (U.S. Army Cmd. and Gen. Staff College, Ft. Leavenworth, KS), July - August 2001.

30. "Grozny Is a City of Rubble."

31. "Rebel Ambush Leaves 37 Russians Dead in Chechnya."

32. Blandy, "Moscow's Failure to Understand," p. 17.

33. Jeffery Taylor, "Georgia at a Crossroads," *Smithsonian,* April 2004, p. 107.

34. Blandy, "Moscow's Failure to Understand," p. 17.

35. Grau, "Technology and the Second Chechen Campaign," p. 108.

36. Ibid., p. 102.

37. "Scores Feared Dead in Chechnya Crash," BBC News, 19 August 2002.

38. Grau, "Technology and the Second Chechen Campaign," p. 107.

39. Poole, *Phantom Soldier,* pp. 33-46.

40. Dr. S.J. Main, "'Counter-Terrorist Operation' in Chechnya: On the Legality of the Current Conflict," chapt. 4 of "The Second Chechen War," p. 24.

41. Vladimir Putin, as quoted in "'Counter-Terrorist Operation' in Chechnya," by Dr. S.J. Main, p. 24.

42. Andrei Pilipchuk, trans. A. Ignatkin, "Colonel General Vladimir Moltenshoy: We Grab the Criminals by the Short and Curlies," *Krasnaya Zvezda* (Russia), 28 September 2002.

43. Rache Harvey, "Tension Rising in Chechen Conflict," BBC News, 19 August 2002.

44. ABC's Nightly News, 13 March 2004; NBC's Nightly News, 9 May 2004.

45. Faye Bowers, "Al Qaeda's New Young Guard: A Shift in Tactics," *Christian Science Monitor,* 13 February 2004, pp. 1, 4.

46. Pilipchuk, trans. A. Ignatkin, "Colonel General Vladimir Moltenshoy: We Grab."

47. Andrei Pilipchuk, trans. A. Ignatkin, "Colonel General Vladimir Moltenshoy: The People of Chechnya Are Not Silent," *Krasnaya Zvezda* (Russia), 11 June 2002.

48. Lester W. Grau and Charles Cutshaw, "Russian Snipers: In the Mountains and Cities of Chechnya," *Infantry Magazine,* summer 2002, p. 10.

49. Orr, "Better or Not So Bad?", p. 100.

50. Fred Weir, "Chechnya's Troubled Election," *Christian Science Monitor,* 17 September 2003, p. 6.

51. Jim Krane, AP, "Iraqi Insurgents Use Tactics They Learned from Chechens, Taliban, Al-Qaida," *Herald Sun* (Australia), 6 January 2004.

52. Simon Ostrovsky, "A Soldier's Tale of Fear and Loathing," *Moscow Times,* 17 March 2004, p. 1.

53. *The Bear Went over the Mountain,* p. 205.

54. Orr, "Better or Not So Bad?", p. 92.

55. "11 Soldiers Killed in Chechnya," World Briefs Wire Reports (AP), *Jacksonville (NC) Daily News,* 13 April 2004, p. 5A .

56. "Russian Team Promises Renewed Effort to Rebuild Chechnya," Reuters, *Christian Science Monitor,* 17 May 2004, p. 7.

57. Fred Weir, "Russia Loses Key Chechen Ally," *Christian Science Monitor,* 10 May 2004, p. 6.

58. "Attacks Raise Specter of New Chechen War," World Briefs Wire Reports (AP), *Jacksonville (NC) Daily News,* 24 June 2004.

59. Scott Peterson, "Chechen Rebels' Deadly Return," *Christian Science Monitor,* 23 June 2004, p. 6.

60. "Dysfunctional Chechnya Votes for President Today," from AP, *Jacksonville (NC) Daily News,* 29 August 2004.

Chapter 6: *Afghan Mujahideen*

1. Kaplan, *Soldiers of God,* p. 81.
2. "Afghanistan Country Study," p. 7.
3. Kaplan, *Soldiers of God,* p. 80.
4. "Afghanistan Country Study," p. 29.
5. Kaplan, *Soldiers of God,* p. 82.
6. Jalali and Grau, *Afghan Guerrilla,* pp. xiii-xxii.
7. "CIA — The World Factbook."
8. "Afghanistan Country Study."
9. Ibid.
10. Farhad Daftary, *The Assassin Legends: Myths of the Isma'ilis* (London: I. B. Tauris, 1994; reprinted 2001).
11. Jalali and Grau, *Afghan Guerrilla,* p. xvi.
12. Kaplan, *Soldiers of God,* p. 17.
13. Ibid., p. 235.
14. C.J. Dick, "Mujahideen Tactics in the Soviet-Afghan War" (Sandhurst, UK: Conflict Studies Research Centre, Royal Mil. Acad., n.d.).
15. Topkhana, as quoted in *Afghan Guerrilla,* by Jalali and Grau, p. 301.
16. Ibid.
17. Akhtarjhan, as quoted in *Afghan Guerrilla,* by Jalali and Grau, p. 312.
18. Shahabuddin, as quoted in "Night Stalkers and Mean Streets," by Ali A. Jalali and Lester W. Grau (Ft. Leavenworth, KS: Foreign Mil. Studies Office, 1998), *Infantry Magazine,* January-April 1999.
19. Brigadier Mohammad Yousaf and Maj. Mark Adkin, *Bear Trap: Afghanistan's Untold Story* (South Yorkshire, UK: Leo Cooper, n.d.).
20. Jalali and Grau, *Afghan Guerrilla,* p. 404.
21. Ibid., p. 401.
22. Yousaf and Adkin, *Bear Trap.*
23. Jalali and Grau, *Afghan Guerrilla,* p. 409.
24. Ibrahim, as quoted in *Afghan Guerrilla,* by Jalali and Grau, pp. 286-289.
25. Ibid., p. 295.

26. Jalali and Grau, *Afghan Guerrilla,* p. 409; Topkhana, as quoted in *Afghan Guerrilla,* id., p. 301.

27. Ibid., p. 401.

28. Wiktorowicz, *Global Jihad.*

29. Akhtarjhan, as quoted in *Afghan Guerrilla,* by Jalali and Grau, p. 316.

30. Yousaf and Adkin, *Bear Trap.*

31. Brigadier Mohammad Yousaf, *The Silent Soldier: The Man behind the Afghan Jehad* (South Yorkshire, UK: Leo Cooper, n.d.).

32. Kaplan, *Soldiers of God,* p. 162.

33. Yousaf and Adkin, *Bear Trap.*

34. Kaplan, *Soldiers of God,* p. 132.

35. Dick, "Mujahideen Tactics," p. 6.

36. Farouq, as quoted in *Afghan Guerrilla,* by Jalali and Grau, p. 391.

37. Yakub, as quoted in *Afghan Guerrilla,* by Jalali and Grau, p. 368.

38. Shabuddin, as quoted in *Afghan Guerrilla,* by Jalali and Grau, p. 385.

39. Kaplan, *Soldiers of God,* p. 44.

40. Ibid.

41. Ibid., p. 163.

42. Ibid., pp. 161, 162.

43. Dick, "Mujahideen Tactics," pp. 9, 10.

44. Yousaf and Adkin, *Bear Trap.*

45. Ibid.

46. Kaplan, *Soldiers of God,* pp. 12, 13.

47. Grau, "Technology and the Second Chechen Campaign," p. 104.

48. Yousaf and Adkin, *Bear Trap.*

49. Grau, "Technology and the Second Chechen Campaign," p. 108.

50. Dick, "Mujahideen Tactics," p. 7.

51. Ibid.

52. Malang and Seddiq, as quoted in *Afghan Guerrilla,* by Jalali and Grau, pp. 35, 39, 44.

53. Ibid., p. 63.

54. Jalali and Grau, *Afghan Guerrilla,* editor's commentary, p. 65.

55. Rahim and Gul, as quoted in *Afghan Guerrilla,* by Jalali and Grau, pp. 21, 23.

56. Malang, as quoted in *Afghan Guerrilla,* by Jalali and Grau, p. 44.

57. Jalali and Grau, *Afghan Guerrilla,* editor's commentary, p. 67.

58. Ibid., p. 12.

59. Akbar, as quoted in *Afghan Guerrilla,* by Jalali and Grau, p. 5.

60. Kochay, as quoted in *Afghan Guerrilla,* by Jalali and Grau, pp. 59-61.

61. Rahim, as quoted in *Afghan Guerrilla,* by Jalali and Grau, p. 21; Poole, *Phantom Soldier,* p. 138.

62. Qader and Qasab, as quoted in *Afghan Guerrilla,* by Jalali and Grau, p. 31.

63. Hemat and Seddiq, as quoted in *Afghan Guerrilla,* by Jalali and Grau, pp. 30, 40.

64. Khan, Wakil, and Kochay, as quoted in *Afghan Guerrilla,* by Jalali and Grau, pp. 49, 53, 65.

65. Sadeq, as quoted in *Afghan Guerrilla,* by Jalali and Grau, p. 17.

66. Hemat, as quoted in *Afghan Guerrilla,* by Jalali and Grau, p. 30.

67. Ibid., p. 27.

68. Hemat, as quoted in *Afghan Guerrilla,* by Jalali and Grau, p. 66; id., *Afghan Guerrilla,* editor's commentary, p. 66.

69. Jalali and Grau, *Afghan Guerrilla,* editor's commentary, p. 19; Hemat, as quoted in *Afghan Guerrilla,* id., p. 28.

70. Hemat, as quoted in *Afghan Guerrilla,* by Jalali and Grau, p. 11.

71. Akbar, as quoted in *Afghan Guerrilla,* by Jalali and Grau, p. 5.

72. Qader and Qasab, as quoted in *Afghan Guerrilla,* by Jalali and Grau, p. 32.

73. Ibid., p. 31.

74. Jalali and Grau, *Afghan Guerrilla,* editor's commentary, p. 41.

75. Tayeb, as quoted in *Afghan Guerrilla,* by Jalali and Grau, p. 55.

76. Kaplan, *Soldiers of God,* p. 159.

77. Akbar and Hemat, as quoted in *Afghan Guerrilla,* by Jalali and Grau, pp. 6, 9.

78. Jalali and Grau, *Afghan Guerrilla,* editor's commentary, p. 41.

79. Dick, "Mujahideen Tactics," p. 4.

80. Shahin, as quoted in *Afghan Guerrilla,* by Jalali and Grau, pp. 379, 380.

81. Jalali and Grau, *Afghan Guerrilla,* p. 70.

82. Shahabuddin, Rahim and Kochay, as quoted in *Afghan Guerrilla,* by Jalali and Grau, pp. 76, 77, 82, 83.

83. Ibid.

84. Jalali and Grau, *Afghan Guerrilla,* editor's commentary, p. 72.

85. Gul, as quoted in *Afghan Guerrilla,* by Jalali and Grau, p. 97.

86. Habib, as quoted in *Afghan Guerrilla,* by Jalali and Grau, p. 73.

87. Gul, as quoted in *Afghan Guerrilla,* by Jalali and Grau, pp. 89, 93.

88. Jalali and Grau, *Afghan Guerrilla,* editor's commentary, p. 103.

89. Khan et al, as quoted in *Afghan Guerrilla,* by Jalali and Grau, p. 119.

90. Dick, "Mujahideen Tactics," p. 8.

91. Sarshar, as quoted in *Afghan Guerrilla,* by Jalali and Grau, p. 387.

92. Dick, "Mujahideen Tactics," p. 7.

93. Ibid., p. 13.

94. Kaplan, *Soldiers of God,* p. 159.

95. Kochay, as quoted in *Afghan Guerrilla,* by Jalali and Grau, p. 83.

96. Ibid.

97. Kaplan, *Soldiers of God,* p. 162.

98. Malang, as quoted in *Afghan Guerrilla,* by Jalali and Grau, p. 123.

99. Jalali and Grau, *Afghan Guerrilla,* editor's commentary, p. 125.

100. Lt.Col. Robert W Lamont, "'Urban Warrior'—A View from North Vietnam," *Marine Corps Gazette,* April 1999, p. 33.

101. Wakil, as quoted in *Afghan Guerrilla,* by Jalali and Grau, p. 135.

102. Sadeq, as quoted in *Afghan Guerrilla,* by Jalali and Grau, p. 127.

103. Shahabuddin, as quoted in "Night Stalkers," by Jalali and Grau.

104. Dick, "Mujahideen Tactics," p. 9.

105. Kaplan, *Soldiers of God,* p. 158.

106. Ibid., p. 62.

107. Ibid. pp. 176, 177.

108. Kaplan, *Soldiers of God,* p. 18.

109. Wiktorowicz, *Global Jihad.*

110. Kaplan, *Soldiers of God,* p. 36.

111. Ibid., p. 76.

112. Farouq, as quoted in *Afghan Guerrilla,* by Jalali and Grau, p. 391.

113. Akhtarjhan, as quoted in *Afghan Guerrilla,* by Jalali and Grau, p. 396.

114. Ibid.

115. Farouq, as quoted in *Afghan Guerrilla,* by Jalali and Grau, p. 389.

116. Attributed to Jalali and Grau.

117. Akhtarjhan, as quoted in "Night Stalkers," by Jalali and Grau.

118. Shahabuddin, as quoted in "Night Stalkers," by Jalali and Grau.

119. Kaplan, *Soldiers of God,* p. 176.

120. Yousaf, *Silent Soldier.*

121. Dick, "Mujahideen Tactics," pp. 10, 11.

122. Ibid.

123. Jalali and Grau, *Afghan Guerrilla,* editor's commentary, p. 262.

124. Ibid., p. 300.
125. Ibid., p. 405.
126. Yousaf and Adkin, *Bear Trap.*
127. Kaplan, *Soldiers of God,* p. 16.
128. Farouq, as quoted in *Afghan Guerrilla,* by Jalali and Grau, p. 391.
129. Ibid., pp. 379, 380.
130. Kaplan, *Soldiers of God,* pp. 39, 83.
131. Yousaf, *Silent Soldier.*
132. Ibrahim, as quoted in *Afghan Guerrilla,* by Jalali and Grau, p. 289.
133. Jalali and Grau, *Afghan Guerrilla,* p. 267.
134. Tayeb and Qader, as quoted in *Afghan Guerrilla,* by Jalali and Grau, pp. 244, 257.
135. Jalali and Grau, *Afghan Guerrilla,* editor's commentary, p. 261.
136. Kako and Ghani, as quoted in *Afghan Guerrilla,* by Jalali and Grau, p. 307.
137. Ibid., p. 308.
138. Jalali and Grau, *Afghan Guerrilla,* p. 268.
139. Akhtarjhan, as quoted in *Afghan Guerrilla,* by Jalali and Grau, p. 314.
140. Baloch, as quoted in *Afghan Guerrilla,* by Jalali and Grau, pp. 298-300.
141. Kako and Ghani, as quoted in *Afghan Guerrilla,* by Jalali and Grau, p. 308.
142. Tayeb, as quoted in *Afghan Guerrilla,* by Jalali and Grau, p. 244; id., *Afghan Guerrilla,* editor's commentary, p. 261.
143. Ibid.
144. Padshah, as quoted in *Afghan Guerrilla,* by Jalali and Grau, p. 281.
145. Jalali and Grau, *Afghan Guerrilla,* editor's commentary, p. 256.
146. Habib, as quoted in *Afghan Guerrilla,* by Jalali and Grau, p. 257.
147. Rahman, as quoted in *Afghan Guerrilla,* by Jalali and Grau, p. 324.
148. Jalali and Grau, *Afghan Guerrilla,* editor's commentary, p. 239.
149. Ibrahim, as quoted in *Afghan Guerrilla,* by Jalali and Grau, p. 286.
150. Ibid., p. 287.
151. Omar and Haqani, as quoted in *Afghan Guerrilla,* by Jalali and Grau, p. 320.
152. Omar et all, p. 325.

153. *Mao Tse-tung: An Anthology of His Writings,* ed. Anne Fremantle (New York: Mentor, 1962), pp. 126, 127.
154. Ibid., pp. 128, 129.
155. Poole, *Tiger's Way,* pp. 111-130.
156. Akhtarjhan, as quoted in *Afghan Guerrilla,* by Jalali and Grau, p. 311.
157. Ibid., p. 396.
158. Jalali and Grau, *Afghan Guerrilla,* p. 267.
159. Yousaf and Adkin, *Bear Trap.*
160. Omar and Haqani, as quoted in *Afghan Guerrilla,* by Jalali and Grau, pp. 317-321.
161. Ibid., p. 317.
162. Qader, as quoted in *Afghan Guerrilla,* by Jalali and Grau, p. 261.
163. Jalali and Grau, *Afghan Guerrilla,* p. 267.
164. Ibid., p. 402.
165. Ibid., p. 404.
166. Yousaf and Adkin, *Bear Trap.*

Chapter 7: *More Recent Afghan Resistance*

1. "Backgrounder on Afghanistan: History of the War," as extracted from www.geocities.com on 29 July 2004.
2. "Son of al-Qaeda," *Frontline,* PBS, NC Public TV, 22 April 2004.
3. Scott Baldauf, "Afghans Yet to Lay Down Arms," *Christian Science Monitor,* 14 October 2003, p. 7.
4. Scott Baldauf, "New Thrust in Hunt for Bin Laden," *Christian Science Monitor,* 4 March 2004, p. 1.
5. Yousaf and Adkin, *Bear Trap.*
6. Jalali and Grau, *Afghan Guerrilla,* editor's commentary, p. 339.
7. Yousaf, *Silent Soldier.*
8. Yousaf and Adkin, *Bear Trap.*
9. Jason Burke, "Waiting for a Last Battle with the Taliban," *The Observer* (UK), 27 June 1999.
10. "Taliban Blamed for Deadly Afghan Resistance," World Briefs Wire Reports (AP), *Jacksonville (NC) Daily News,* 24 September 2003.
11. *"Harakat ul-Mujahidin* Reference Page," from www.military.com, 5 July 2004.
12. "Harakat ul-Mujahidin," *Patterns of Global Terrorism, 2002* (Washington, D.C.: U.S. Dept. of State, April 2003), from its website.
13. Sami Yousafzai and Ron Moreau, "Rumors of bin Laden's Lair," *Newsweek,* 8 September 2003, pp. 24-27.

14. Patrick McDowell, AP, "Pakistan Goes After Terrorists on Border," *Jacksonville (NC) Daily News,* 9 January 2004, p. 6A; Owais Tohid, "Tribes Inflamed by Qaeda Hunt," *Christian Science Monitor,* 20 October 2003, p. 6.

15. Gretchen Peters, "Bin Laden's Hideout in Wilds of Pakistan," *Christian Science Monitor,* 15 September 2003, p. 1.

16. McDowell, "Pakistan Goes After Terrorists," p. 6A.

17. Poole, *Tiger's Way,* pp. 168-171.

18. Matthew Pennington, AP, "Pakistan Unsure If Target Is al-Zawahri," *Jacksonville (NC) Daily News,* 21 March 2004, p. 5A.

19. Tohid, Owais and Faye Bowers, "U.S. Pakistan Tighten Net on Al Qaeda," *Christian Science Monitor,* 22 March 2004, pp. 1, 10.

20. Ibid.

21. Ibid.

22. Owais Tohid, "Pakistan Marks Pro-Al Qaeda Clan," *Christian Science Monitor,* 23 March 2004, p. 6.

23. Ibid.

24. Ansnullah Wazir, AP, "Terror Suspects May Have Escaped through Tunnel," *Jacksonville (NC) Daily News,* 23 March 2004, p. 1A.

25. Paul Haven, AP, "Elders Deny Terrorist Ties," *Jacksonville (NC) Daily News,* 13 April 2004, p. 5A.

26. Sami Yousafzai and Michael Hirsh, "The Harder Hunt for bin Laden," *Newsweek,* 29 December 2003 - 5 January 2004, pp. 58, 59.

27. Paul Haven, AP, "Pakistan Traps al-Qaida Target," *Jacksonville (NC) Daily News,* 19 March 2004, pp. 1A, 7A.

28. Poole, *Tiger's Way,* p. 162.

29. Paul Haven, AP, "Pakistani Troops May Have al-Zawahri Cornered," AOL News, 18 March 2004.

30. ABC's Nightly News, 25 April 2004.

31. Owais Tohid, "Al Qaeda Supporters Strike Back in Pakistan," *Christian Science Monitor,* 25 March 2004, p. 4.

32. ABC's Nightly News, 25 April 2004.

33. Gretchen Peters, "Foreign Fighters Snub Pakistan's Olive Branch," *Christian Science Monitor,* 3 May 2004, 7; Stephen Graham, AP, "U.S. Slams Pakistan in War on Militants," *Jacksonville (NC) Daily News,* 4 May 2004, p. 5A.

34. Faye Bowers, "Averting 9/11: How Close We Came," *Christian Science Monitor,* 25 March 2004, p. 1.

35. Dr. Robert Perry Bosshart (longtime resident of SE Asia and recent contract employee in Afghanistan), in letter to the author of 10 September 2004.

36. Ansnullah Wazir, AP, "Fight Wanes between Troops, Suspected al-Qaida," *Jacksonville (NC) Daily News,* 22 March 2004, p. 4A.

37. Pennington, "Pakistan Unsure If Target Is al-Zawahri," p. 5A.

38. Owais Tohid, "Pakistan Tries Amnesty to Stem Support for Al Qaeda," *Christian Science Monitor,* 26 April 2004, p. 7.

39. Peters, "Foreign Fighters Snub," p. 7.

40. Stephen Graham, AP, "U.S. Slams Pakistan in War on Militants," *Jacksonville (NC) Daily News,* 4 May 2004, p. 5A.

41. Ann Scott Tyson, "Going in Small in Afghanistan," *Christian Science Monitor,* 14 January 2004, pp. 11-13.

42. McDowell, "Pakistan Goes After Terrorists," p. 6A.

43. Tim McGirk, "Battle in 'the Evilest Place'," *Time Magazine,* 3 November 2003, East Asia edition, pp. 32-35.

44. Peters, "Bin Laden's Hideout," p. 1.

45. Tyson, "Going in Small," pp. 11-13.

46. Halima Kasem, "Brewing Power Struggle in Kabul," *Christian Science Monitor,* 17 October 2003, p. 6.

47. "Battle Plan under Fire," *Nova*, PBS in conjunction with WGBH Boston, NC Public TV, 4 May and 7 July 2004.

48. McGirk, "Battle in 'the Evilest Place'," pp. 32-35.

49. Ron Moreau and Sami Yousafzai and Zahid Hussain, "Holy War 101," *Newsweek,* 1 December 2003, pp. 28, 29.

50. Noor Khan, AP, "Police Swarm Village after Attack on Copter," *Jacksonville (NC) Daily News,* 24 February 2004, p. 5A.

51. Pauline Jelinek, AP, "U.S. Plans Spring Offensive in Afghanistan," AOL News, 30 January 2004.

52. "U.S. Forces in Afghanistan Were Alerted to Prepare for a New 'Spring Offensive'," News in Brief, *Christian Science Monitor*, 29 January 2004.

53. Stephen Graham, AP, "Factional Fighting Spills Afghan Blood," *Jacksonville (NC) Daily News,* 8 February 2004, p. 5A.

54. L.Cpl. Samuel (casualty from 2d Battalion, 8th Marines), in conversation with author, 12 March 2004.

55. Stephen Graham, AP, "U.S. Defends Raid That Killed Afghan Children," *Jacksonville (NC) Daily News,* 11 March 2004, p. 7A.

56. "Attacks Leave Five Dead in Afghanistan," World Briefs Wire Reports (AP), *Jacksonville (NC) Daily News,* 15 March 2004, p. 6A.

57. Scott Baldauf, "U.S. Hunts Bin Laden; Locals Seek Security," *Christian Science Monitor,* 15 March 2004, pp. 1, 7.

58. Ibid.

59. "Suicide Bomber Kills Peacekeeper, Civilian in Afghan Capital," World Briefs Wire Reports (AP), *Jacksonville (NC) Daily News,* 28 January 2004.

60. Jelinek, "U.S. Plans Spring Offensive."

61. Stephen Graham, AP, "Blast Deadly for U.S.," *Jacksonville (NC) Daily News,* 31 January 2004, p. 1A.

62. "Iran Report," Radio Free Europe/Radio Liberty, vol. 5, no. 3, 28 January 2002, from its website www.rferl.org via www.globalsecurity.org.

63. Stephen Graham, AP, "Latest Assault Leaves 2 Brits, Afghan Interpreter Dead," *Jacksonville (NC) Daily News,* 6 May 2004, p. 8A.

64. Stephen Graham, AP, "U.S. Urges Afghan Defense Chief to Keep the Peace," *USA Today,* 28 July 2004, p. 13A.

65. "United Nations Refugee Worker from France Is Shot to Death in Afghanistan," News Digest Wire Reports (AP), *Jacksonville (NC) Daily News,* 17 November 2003, p. 2A.

66. McDowell, "Pakistan Goes After Terrorists," p. 6A.

67. Noor Khan, AP, "U.S. Company's Copter Hit in Afghanistan," *Jacksonville (NC) Daily News,* 23 February 2004, p. 3A.

68. Capt. Nelson G. Kraft, "Lessons Learned from a Light Infantry Company during Operation Anaconda," *Infantry Magazine,* summer 2002, p. 30.

69. Wazir, "Fight Wanes between Troops," p. 4A.

70. Tohid, "Al Qaeda Supporters," p. 4.

71. Poole, *Tiger's Way,* pp. 280-283.

72. Owais Tohid and Scott Baldauf, "Pakistani Army Must Go through the Pashtuns," *Christian Science Monitor,* 25 June 2004, p. 7.

73. ABC's Nightly News, 27 June 2004.

74. Stephen Graham, AP, "U.S. Commander Pledges Restraint in Afghan Sweeps," *Jacksonville (NC) Daily News,* 10 August 2004, p. 2A.

75. Amir Shah, AP, "U.S.-Brokered Cease-Fire Halts Deadly Afghan Infighting," *Jacksonville (NC) Daily News,* 18 August 2004. p. 7A.

76. ABC's Nightly News, 17 September 2004.

Chapter 8: *The Iraqi Opposition*

1. John J. Lumpkin, AP, "U.S. Identifies Sources of Much Iraqi Violence," *Jacksonville (NC) Daily News,* 14 November 2003, p. 5A.

2. Scott Ritter, "Defining the Resistance in Iraq—It's Not Foreign and It's Well Prepared," *Christian Science Monitor,* 10 November 2003, p. 9.

3. Peter Grier and Faye Bowers, "Iraqi Militants Raise Pitch of Attacks," *Christian Science Monitor,* 22 April 2004, p. 10.

4. Paul Wolfowitz, Deputy Secretary of Defense, on ABC's Nightly News, 29 April 2004.

5. Memo for the record by H.J. Poole.

6. Moore, "Hasan bin Sabbah."

7. Cockburn, "Iraq's Oppressed Majority," p. 102.

8. "Assassins"; "Sacrifices of the Fidai."

9. "Truth, War, and Consequences," *Frontline.* NC Public TV, 9 October 2003.

10. "Americans Die in Convoy Attack" photograph, AOL News of 2 May 2004, and *Jacksonville (NC) Daily News* of 3 May 2004, p. 1A.

11. Ibid., caption.

12. Scott Peterson, "The Rise and Fall of Ansar al-Islam," *Christian Science Monitor,* 16 October 2003, p. 12; Cameron W. Barr, "In Iraq, U.S. Sees Influence of Al-Qaeda," *Christian Science Monitor,* 11 August 2003, p. 11; Lumpkin, "U.S. Identifies Sources," p. 5A.

13. Peterson, "The Rise and Fall of Ansar al-Islam," p. 12.

14. Ken Dilanian and Drew Brown, Knight Ridder, "Postwar Iraq Has Become a Magnet for Terrorists," *Jacksonville (NC) Daily News,* 24 August 2003, p. 4A; NPR's "Morning Edition," 9 October 2003.

15. Tarek Al-Issawi, AP, "19 Held in Najaf Bombing," *Jacksonville (NC) Daily News,* 31 August 2003, p. 6A.

16. James Hider, "Iraq's Leaky Border with Iran," *Christian Science Monitor,* 27 August 2003, p. 17.

17. Lumpkin, "U.S. Identifies Sources," p. 4A.

18. "Hundreds Have Entered Iraq from Saudi Arabia Disguised As Shi'ite Pilgrims," *Geostrategy-Direct,* 16 March 2004.

19. Nicholas Blanford and Dan Murphy, "For Al Qaeda, Iraq May Be the Next Battlefield," *Christian Science Monitor,* 25 August 2003, p. 12.

20. Peter Grier and Faye Bowers, "Iraq Blast Fits Pattern of Sabotage," *Christian Science Monitor,* 20 August 2003, p. 11.

21. Blanford and Murphy, "For Al Qaeda, Iraq," p. 12.

22. Lumpkin, "U.S. Identifies Sources," p. 5A.

23. Charles J. Hanley, AP Special Correspondent, "Attackers Burn, Loot Army Supply Train in Iraq," *Jacksonville (NC) Daily News,* 1 November 2003, p. 7A.

24. Juan Cole, "The United States and Shi'ite Religious Factions in Post-Ba'thist Iraq," *Middle East Journal,* vol. 57, no. 4, autumn 2003, p. 548.

25. Charles J. Hanley, AP Special Correspondent, "Americans Hunt for Missiles, Clues," *Jacksonville (NC) Daily News,* 4 November 2003, p. 1A.

26. Hanley, "Attackers Burn, Loot," p. 7A.

27. David Ignatius, "Hezbollah's Success," *Washington Post,* 23 September 2003, p. A27.

28. Ibid.

29. Joshua Hammer, "Holding the Line," *Newsweek,* 16 February 2004, p. 32.

30. Ibid., p. 33.

31. "Suicide Bomber Kills Peacekeeper."

32. Esposito, *Unholy War,* p. 69.

33. Charles J. Hanley, AP Special Correspondent, "Dozens Killed in Wave of Blasts," *Jacksonville (NC) Daily News,* 28 October 2003, p. 1A; ABC's Nightly News, 27 October 2004, p. 1A.

34. Nicholas Blanford, "Insurgent and Soldier: Two Views on Iraq Fight," *Christian Science Monitor,* 25 February 2004, p. 4.

35. Tarek Al-Issawi, AP, "Suicide Bombers Strike Almost at Will in Iraq," *Jacksonville (NC) Daily News,* 19 March 2004, p. 4A.

36. Nicholas Blanford, "As U.S. Draws Down, Doubt over Iraqis," *Christian Science Monitor,* 17 February 2004, p. 4.

37. Mariam Fam, AP, "Rebel Assault Routs Iraqi Cops," *Jacksonville (NC) Daily News,* 15 February 2004, pp. 1A, 6A.

38. Eric Hammel, *The Root: The Marines in Beirut, August 1982 - February 1984* (Pacifica, CA: Pacifica Press, 1985), p. 78; Van Creveld, *Sword and the Olive,* p. 303; *Warfare in Lebanon,* ed. Alnwick and Fabyanic, p. 21.

39. Cole, "The United States and Shi'ite Religious Factions," p. 544.

40. Ibid., p. 543.

41. Ibid., p. 546.

42. Dan Murphy, "Second Front in Iraq: Shiite Revolt," *Christian Science Monitor,* 6 April 2004, p. 10.

43. Art Theyson, "New Warfront Opens in Iraq Three Months before Handover," *DEBKAfile,* 5 April 2004.

44. Scott Peterson, "Shadows of Tehran over Iraq," *Christian Science Monitor,* 19 April 2004, pp. 1, 10.

45. Babak Dehghanpisheh, "The Shiite Hit List," *Newsweek,* 15 December 2003, p. 1.

46. Babak Dehghanpisheh and Melinda Liu and Rod Nordland, "We Are Your Martyrs," *Newsweek,* 19 April 2004, pp. 39-41.

47. Ibid., p. 39.

48. Katzman, *Warriors of Islam,* p. 99.

49. Cole, "The United States and Shi'ite Religious Factions," p. 554.

50. Murphy, "Second Front in Iraq," p. 10.

51. Dan Murphy, "No Wide Shiite Rally to Sadr's Forces," *Christian Science Monitor,* 7 April 2004, p. 4.

52. Cole, "The United States and Shi'ite Religious Factions," p. 550.

53. Terence Hunt, AP, "Annan Says U.S. Will Back U.N. Plan for Iraqi Vote," *Jacksonville (NC) Daily News,* 4 February 2004, p. 5A.

54. Bassem Mroue and Abdul-Qader Saadi, AP, "Fighting Spreads in Iraq," *Jacksonville (NC) Daily News,* 8 April 2004, p. 6A.

55. Peterson, "Shadows of Tehran over Iraq," p. 10.

56. Denis D. Gray and Scheherezade Faramarzi, AP, "U.S. Balks at Going after Cleric," *Jacksonville (NC) Daily News,* 4 May 2004, p. 1A.

57. Cole, "The United States and Shi'ite Religious Factions," p. 550.

58. Ali Akbar Dareini, AP, "Iran Ends Talks with U.S. on Restoring Order to Iraq," *Jacksonville (NC) Daily News,* 15 April 2004, p. 6A.

59. Sami Yousafzai and Ron Moreau and Michael Hirsh, "Bin Laden's Iraqi Plans," *Newsweek,* 15 December 2003, p. 27.

60. Vijay Joshi, AP, "U.S. Commander Says al-Qaida Working in Iraq," AOL News, 30 January 2004.

61. Dan Murphy, "Iraq Bombs Hit Kurdish Leaders," *Christian Science Monitor,* 2 February 2004, p. 11.

62. Peter Ford, "A Suspect Emerges As Key Link in Terror Chain," *Christian Science Monitor,* 23 January 2004, p. 7.

63. ABC's Nightly News, 9 February 2004.

64. Hamza Hendawi and Tarek al-Issawi, AP, "Suicide Attacks Kill More Than 140 at Iraqi Shiite Shrines," *Jacksonville (NC) Daily News,* 3 March 2004, p. 7A.

65. Ibid.; "Will We Get Him in '04," Periscope, *Newsweek,* 9 February 2004, p. 6.

66. Ibid.

67. Hamza Hendawi, AP, "Sunni Clerics Join Iraqi Shiites in Show of Unity," *Jacksonville (NC) Daily News,* 4 March 2004, p. 5A.

68. Jim Krane, AP, "U.S. Split on Foreign Involvement in Iraq," *Jacksonville (NC) Daily News,* 5 March 2004, p. 4A.

69. Christopher Dickey and Rod Nordland, "Shiites Unbound," *Newsweek,* 1 March 2004, p. 37.

70. Katarina Kratovac, AP, "Attacks Kill 3 American Soldiers," *Jacksonville (NC) Daily News,* 14 October 2003, p. 1A.

71. Bremer Meets, "Iraqi Fears Aiding Terror," *Jacksonville (NC) Daily News,* 12 November 2003, p. 1A; ABC's Nightly News, 11 November 2004.

72. "U.S. Casualties Mount in Iraq Despite Talk of 'Turning the Corner,'" News Digest Wire Reports (AP), *Jacksonville (NC) Daily News,* 4 February 2004.

73. Rod Nordland and Melinda Liu and Scott Johnson, "The Dark Road Ahead," *Newsweek,* 12 April 2004, pp. 28-32; ABC's Nightly News, 8 April 2004.

74. ABC's Nightly News, 1 May 2004.

75. Brad Knickerbocker, "Guerrilla Tactics vs. U.S. War Plan," *Christian Science Monitor,* 25 March 2003, p. 1.

76. ABC's Nightly News, 27 March 2003.

77. ABC's Morning News, 28 March 2003.

78. ABC's Nightly News, 30 March 2003.

79. NPR's "Morning Edition," 3 April 2003.

80. Christopher Torchia, AP, "Attacks on Foreign Civilians Suggest Tactics Change by Rebels," *Jacksonville (NC) Daily News,* 17 March 2004, p. 7A; Evan Thomas, "Groping in the Dark," *Newsweek,* 1 September 2003, p. 31.

81. Christopher Torchia, AP, "Marine among the Dead," *Jacksonville (NC) Daily News,* 27 March 2004, p. 6A; ABC's Nightly News, 25 November 2004 and 25 February 2005; D'arcy Doran, AP, "Saboteurs Hit Major Iraqi Oil Pipeline," *Jacksonville (NC) Daily News,* 17 August 2003, p. 6A; NPR's "Morning Edition," 21 December 2003; Lee Keath, AP, "Mediation Continues on Iraqi Constitution," *Jacksonville (NC) Daily News,* 1 March 2004, p. 6A.

82. "Official Insists U.S. Still Has Initiative in Iraq; Two Paratroopers Killed," News Digest Wire Reports (AP), *Jacksonville (NC) Daily News,* 9 November 2003, p. 2A; Hanley, "Attackers Burn, Loot," p. 1A.

83. Jim Krane and Hamza Hendawi, AP, "Blast Destroys Baghdad Hotel," *Jacksonville (NC) Daily News,* 18 March 2004, p. 6A; Robert H. Reid, AP, "5 Americans Die in Iraq," *Jacksonville Daily News,* 25 January 2004, p. 1A; Peter Glibbery (former British and South African soldier and DoD contractor in Iraq), in e-mails to the author, 5-16 October 2003.

84. Dilanian and Brown, "Postwar Iraq Has Become a Magnet for Terrorists," p. 4A.

85. ABC's Nightly News, 24 April 2004.

86. Torchia, "Attacks on Foreign Civilians," p. 7A.

87. Krane and Hendawi, "Blast Destroys Baghdad Hotel," pp. 1A, 6A.

88. Scheherezade Faramarzi, AP, "U.S. Steps Up the Pressure on Iraq Rebels," *Jacksonville (NC) Daily News,* 10 May 2004, pp. 1A, 6A.

89. ABC's Nightly News, 15-20 April 2004.

90. Dan Murphy, "As Violence Rises, Rebuilding Stalls," *Christian Science Monitor,* 16 April 2004, p. 1.

91. Scheherezade Faramarzi, AP, "Rebels Strike Kurds," *Jacksonville (NC) Daily News,* 2 February 2004, p. 1A.

92. ABC's Morning News, 3 February 2004.

93. Dan Murphy, "In the New Iraq, Local Officials Put Lives on the Line," *Christian Science Monitor,* 7 November 2003, p. 1.

94. Hanley, "Dozens Killed in Wave of Blasts," p. 1A; ABC's Nightly News, 27 October 2003.

95. Hamza Hendawi, AP, "Police Chief Reinstated after Weekend Clashes," *Jacksonville (NC) Daily News,* 7 October 2003, p. 4A.

96. Blanford, "Insurgent and Soldier," p. 4.

97. ABC's Nightly News, 27 December 2003.

98. Vijay Joshi, AP, "U.S. Apache Helicopter Shot Down over Iraq," *Jacksonville (NC) Daily News,* 14 January 2004, p. 5A.

99. Faramarzi, "Rebels Strike Kurds," p. 1A.

100. Mariam Fam, AP, "Suicide Bombing Kills Dozens outside Iraq Police Station," *Jacksonville (NC) Daily News,* 11 February 2004, p. 4A.

101. Tarek Al-Issawi, AP, "Suicide Bomber Attacks Iraqi Police Station in Kirkuk," *Jacksonville (NC) Daily News,* 24 February 2004, p. 4A.

102. Christopher Torchia, AP, "More Policemen Shot Dead in Iraq," *Jacksonville (NC) Daily News,* 24 March 2004, p. 4A.

103. Abbas Fayadh, "Suicide Attacks Kill At Least 68," *Jacksonville (NC) Daily News,* 22 April 2004, pp. 1A, 10A.

104. Todd Pitman, AP, "Being an Iraqi Cop No Longer a Cushy Job," *Jacksonville (NC) Daily News,* 1 August 2004, p. 5A; Scott Peterson, "Iraqi Police Walk Perilous Beat," *Christian Science Monitor,* 23 January 2004, p. 6.

105. Christopher Torchia, AP, "Gunmen Kill 3 Iraqi Women Working for Coalition," *Jacksonville (NC) Daily News,* 17 May 2004, 5A; Vijay Joshi, AP, "Nine Killed in Iraqi Violence," *Jacksonville (NC) Daily News,* 23 January 2004, p. 4A.

106. Vijay Joshi, "U.S. Commander Says al-Qaida Working in Iraq."

107. Hanley, "Dozens Killed in Wave of Blasts," p. 1A.

108. Dilanian and Brown, "Postwar Iraq Has Become a Magnet for Terrorists," p. 4A.

109. Ilene Prusher, "Turkish Conscripts Likely to Be Least Willing of the Coalition," *Christian Science Monitor,* 16 October 2003, p. 7.

110. Robert H Reid, AP, "Netherlands Embassy Attacked in Baghdad," *Jacksonville (NC) Daily News,* 31 January 2004, p. 5A.

111. Nadia About El-Magd, AP, "Blood Flows in Baghdad," *Jacksonville (NC) Daily News,* 19 January 2004, p. 2A.

112. NBC's Nightly News, 29 November 2003.

113. ABC'S Nightly News, 27 December 2003.

114. Slobodan Lekic, AP, "Truck Bomb Hits Italians at Iraq Base," *Jacksonville (NC) Daily News,* 13 November 2003, p. 1A.

115. Sameer N. Yacoub, AP, "Suicide Truck Bombing Kills 10 in Iraq," *Jacksonville (NC) Daily News,* 19 February 2004.

116. Ed Johnson, AP, "U.S. Allies in Iraq Refuse to Waiver, " *Jacksonville (NC) Daily News,* 16 March 2004, p. 6A.

117. Connie Cass, AP, "Iraqi Troops Failing," *Jacksonville (NC) Daily News,* 22 April 2004, p. 10A.

118. ABC's Morning News, 9 April 2004.

119. Vijay Joshi, "U.S. Commander Says al-Qaida Working in Iraq"; ABC's Morning News, 28 January 2004.

120. Howard Lafranchi and Nick Blanford, "Iraq Bombings Designed to Divide," *Christian Science Monitor,* 12 February 2004, p. 1; Mariam Fam, "Rebels Target Iraqis," *Jacksonville (NC) Daily News,* 12 February 2004, pp. 1A, 10A.

121. Lee Keath, AP, "Shiites Retreat in Najaf," *Jacksonville (NC) Daily News,* 13 April 2004, p. 2A.

122. Cass, "Iraqi Troops Failing," p. 1A.

123. Howard Lafranchi, "Why Anti-U.S. Fighting Grows in Iraq," *Christian Science Monitor,* 6 November 2003., p. 7; Hamza Hendawi, AP, "Insurgents Fire Rockets at U.S. Coalition Headquarters," *Jacksonville (NC) Daily News,* 8 March 2004, p. 4A.

124. Hanley, "Dozens Killed in Wave of Blasts," p. 1A.

125. El-Magd, "Blood Flows in Baghdad," p. 1A.

126. Ron Jensen, "No Cushy Ride for Supply Troops in Iraq," *Stars & Stripes,* 22 October 2003, Mideast edition, p. 8.

127. Mariam Fam, AP, "Attacks Intensify in Mosul; Iraqis Seeking Reconciliation with Turkey," *Jacksonville (NC) Daily News,* 6 November 2003, p. 4A.

128. Robert H. Reid, AP, "5 Americans Die in Iraq," *Jacksonville Daily News,* 25 January 2004, p. 1A.

129. ABC's Morning News, 9 April 2004.

130. Hamza Hendawi, AP, "Roadside Bombings Kill 6 American Soldiers," *Jacksonville (NC) Daily News,* 28 January 2004, p. 4A.

131. Lourdes Navarro, AP, "More Marines Join the Fight," *Jacksonville (NC) Daily News,* 11 April 2004, p. 6A.

132. ABC's Nightly News, 12 April 2004.

133. Gy.Sgt. Mark Oliva, "Marines Suspend Fallujah Offensive, Increase Humanitarian Efforts," *Camp Lejeune (NC) Globe,* 15 April 2004, p. 7A.

134. Sameer N. Yacoub, AP, "9 Americans Die in a Crash of Black Hawk," *Jacksonville (NC) Daily News,* 9 January 2004, p. 7A; Faramarzi, "Rebels Strike Kurds," p. 1A.

135. Evan Thomas and Babak Dehghanpisheh, "Inside Red Dawn: Saddam Up Close," *Newsweek,* 29 December 2003, p. 48.

136. Peter Glibbery (former British and South African soldier and DoD contractor in Iraq), in e-mails to the author, 5-16 October 2003.

139. Ritter, "Defining the Resistance in Iraq," p. 9.

138. Krane, "Iraqi Insurgents Use Tactics They Learned from Chechens, Taliban, Al-Qaida," *Herald Sun* (Australia), 6 January 2004.

139. Guilherme "Bill" Pereira (DoD contract employee in Iraq), in telephone conversation with the author, 28 June 2004.

140. "Two U.S. Soldiers Killed in Iraqi Roadside Blast," World Briefs Wire Reports (AP), *Jacksonville (NC) Daily News,* 13 March 2004, p. 7A.

141. *Iraq: New Fears of Suicide Blasts,* access@g2-forward.org, 12 April 2004.

142. Lekic, "Truck Bomb Hits Italians at Iraq Base," p. 1A.

143. Hanley, "Dozens Killed in Wave of Blasts," p. 1A .

144. Hanley, "Attackers Burn, Loot," p. 7A.

145. Charles J. Hanley, AP Special Correspondent, "Attack Dispels Hopes to a Quick End of Fighting in Iraq," *Jacksonville (NC) Daily News,* 3 November 2003, p. 4A.

146. Paul Garwood, AP, "U.S. Toll in Iraq Hits 500 Dead," *Jacksonville (NC) Daily News,* 18 January 2004, p. 1A; CBS's Nightly News, 17 January 2004.

147. Sameer Yacoub, "Five U.S. Soldiers Killed in Iraq Attack," AOL News, 31 March 2004.

148. Sameer N. Yacoub, AP, "Four Dead Americans Dragged through Town," *Jacksonville (NC) Daily News,* 1 April 2004, p. 1A.

149. Jason Keyser and Lourdes Navarro, AP, "Marines in Heavy Night Fighting," *Jacksonville (NC) Daily News,* 15 April 2004, pp. 1A, 7A.

150. Ann Scott Tyson, "Inside One Day's Fierce Battle in Iraq," *Christian Science Monitor,* 21 July 2004, pp. 1, 10.

151. Dan Murphy, "Iraqi Shiite Split Widens," *Christian Science Monitor,* 15 October 2003, p. 4.

152. Poole, *Phantom Soldier,* pp. 125-138.

153. Niko Price, AP, "Rebel Attack Turns into a Big Firefight," *Jacksonville (NC) Daily News,* 1 December 2003, p. 3A.

154. Sabah Jerges, AP, "Iraqi Insurgency's New Lethal Phase," *Jacksonville (NC) Daily News,* 2 December 2003, p. 1A; Jim Krane, AP, "U.S. Gets Closer Look at Killer Opposition in Iraq," *Jacksonville (NC) Daily News,* 2 December 2003, p. 6A.

155. Capt. John B. Nalls, "A Company Commander's Thoughts on Iraq," *Armor Magazine,* February 2004.

156. Christopher Torchia, AP, "Terror Mounts in Iraq," *Jacksonville (NC) Daily News,* 19 March 2004, pp. 1A, 7A.

157. Eshel, "Counterguerrilla Warfare in South Lebanon," pp. 42, 43.

158. "U.S. Soldier Killed in Grenade Attack," News Digest Wire Reports, *Jacksonville (NC) Daily News,* 27 September 2003, p. 5A.

159. Rod Nordland, "Corkscrew over Baghdad," *Newsweek International,* 27 October 2003, Southeast Asia edition, p. 29.

160. Joshi, "U.S. Apache Helicopter Shot Down over Iraq," p. 5A; Yacoub, "9 Americans Die in a Crash of Black Hawk," pp. 1A, 7A.

161. Ibid.

162. Lee Keath, AP, "Two Crew Members Killed As U.S. Copter Crashes in Euphrates," *Jacksonville (NC) Daily News,* 26 February 2004, p. 4A.

163. "Copter Shooters Wising Up," access@g2-forward.org, 17 January 2004.

164. Grau, "Technology and the Second Chechen Campaign," pp. 102-108.

165. Arkady Shipunov and Gennady Filimonov, "Field Artillery to Be Replaced with Shmel Infantry Flamethrower," *Military Parade Magazine,* no. 29, September 1998.

166. Grau and Cutshaw, "Russian Snipers," p. 10.

167. Christopher Torchia, AP, "Violence Unsettles Iraqi Life," *Jacksonville (NC) Daily News,* 21 March 2004, p. 7A; ABC's Nightly News, 7 April 2004.

168. Abdul-Qader Saadi and Lourdnes Navarro, AP, "Uneasy Truce Holds in Fallujah," *Jacksonville (NC) Daily News,* 12 April 2004, p. 1A .

169. ABC's Nightly News, 12 April 2004.

170. ABC's Nightly News, 15 April 2004.

171. ABC's Morning News, 24 June 2004.

172. Hamza Hendawi, AP, "Shiite Leader Says U.N. Plan Unacceptable," *Jacksonville (NC) Daily News,* 24 January 2004, p. 5A; Yacoub, "9 Americans Die in a Crash of Black Hawk," p. 1A; Joshi, "U.S. Apache Helicopter Shot Down over Iraq," p. 5A.

173. Todd Pitman, AP, "Marines Seal Off Holy City," *Jacksonville (NC) Daily News,* 13 August 2004. ABC's Nightly News, 30 July 2004; ABC's Morning News, 5 August 2004; Abdul Hussein al-Obeidi, AP, "Iraqi Leader Calls for End to Violence," *Jacksonville (NC) Daily News,* 9 August 2004, p. 6A; Yehia Barzanji, AP, "Suicide Bombing at Iraqi Police Academy Kills 20," *Jacksonville (NC) Daily News,* 5 September 2004, p. 9A; Danica Kirka, AP, "U.S. Bombs Insurgent-Held Iraqi Cities," AOL News, 9 September 2004.

174. Dan Murphy, "In Tough Iraq Conflict, Civilians Pay High Price," *Christian Science Monitor,* 21 January 2004, p. 4.

175. "The Army Will Temporarily Boost Its Forces by 30,000 over the Next Four Years," News in Brief, *Christian Science Monitor,* 30 January 2004, p. 24.

176. "Marines Tackle Rebellion in Fallujah," from Knight Ridder, *Jacksonville (NC) Daily News,* 28 March 2004, p. 6A.

177. Jim Krane, AP, "Private Army Grows Up around U.S. Military," *Jacksonville (NC) Daily News,* 30 October 2003, p. 4A.

178. Clayton Collins, "War-Zone Security Is a Job for . . . Private Contractors," *Christian Science Monitor,* 3 May 2004, p. 2.

179. John Walcott, Knight Ridder, "Guerrilla Strikes a Part of Larger Strategy among Iraqi Insurgents," *Jacksonville (NC) Daily News,* 1 December 2003, p. 6A; Yacoub, "Four Dead Americans Dragged," p. 1A.

180. ABC's Nightly News, 1 April 2004.

181. Lee Keath, AP, "Two U.S. Officials Killed by Gunmen," *Jacksonville (NC) Daily News,* 11 March 2004, p. 7A.

182. Anthony Shadid, "Heavy Fighting, U.S. Casualties in Ramadi," *Washington Post,* 6 April 2004.

183. "Shiite Radicals Join with Sunni Insurgents in Ramadi," *DEBKAfile,* 7 April 2004.

184. Theyson, "New Warfront Opens in Iraq."

185. Daniel Cooney, AP, "Gunmen Kill 4 Iraqis in Attacks on Police Officers," *Jacksonville (NC) Daily News,* 4 April 2004, p. 9A.

186. Khalid Mohammed, AP, "Deadly Day inside Iraq," *Jacksonville (NC) Daily News,* 5 April 2004, pp. 1A, 2A.

187. "Shiite Radicals Join with Sunni Insurgents."

188. Shadid, "Heavy Fighting, U.S. Casualties in Ramadi."

189. Lee Keath, AP, "Chaos Grips Iraq," *Jacksonville (NC) Daily News,* 10 April 2004, p. 1A; Mroue and Saadi, "Fighting Spreads in Iraq," p. 6A.

190. Dan Murphy, "Shiites Taxing U.S. Forces," *Christian Science Monitor,* 8 April 2004, p. 10.

191. Navarro Lourdes, AP, "More Marines Join the Fight," *Jacksonville (NC) Daily News,* 11 April 2004, p. 1A.

192. Evan Thomas, "The Vietnam Question," *Newsweek,* 19 April 2004, p. 33.

193. Lee Keath, AP, "Shiite Militias Control Three Iraqi Cities," *Jacksonville (NC) Daily News,* 9 April 2004, p. 10A; ABC's Nightly News, 8 April 2004.

194. Ibid.

195. Hamza Hendawi, AP, "Deadly Day for U.S. in Iraq," *Jacksonville (NC) Daily News,* 7 April 2004, p. 9A.

196. Keath, "Chaos Grips Iraq," p. 5A.

197. Mroue and Saadi, "Fighting Spreads in Iraq," p. 6A.

198. Oliva, "Marines Suspend Fallujah Offensive," p. 1A.

199. Mroue and Saadi, "Fighting Spreads in Iraq," p. 6A.

200. Jim Krane, AP, "American Disappeared a Week Ago," *Jacksonville (NC) Daily News,* 17 April 2004, pp. 1A, 5A; Saadi and Navarro, "Uneasy Truce Holds in Fallujah," p. 4A.

201. Navarro, "More Marines Join the Fight," p. 6A.

202. Krane, "American Disappeared a Week Ago," pp. 1A, 5A; ABC'S Morning News, 13 April 2004.

203. Keyser and Navarro, "Marines in Heavy Night Fighting," pp. 1A, 7A.

204. Keath, "Shiites Retreat in Najaf," p. 1A.

205. Keyser and Navarro, "Marines in Heavy Night Fighting," pp. 1A, 7A.

206. Dan Murphy, "Moderate Shiites Gaining New Clout," *Christian Science Monitor,* 12 April 2004, p. 7.

207. Denis Gray and Scheherezade Faramarzi, AP, "U.S. Seizes Office from Militiamen," *Jacksonville (NC) Daily News,* 7 May 2004, p. 1A.

208. Faramarzi, "U.S. Steps Up the Pressure," pp. 1A, 6A.

209. NBC's Nightly News, 9 May 2004.

210. NPR's "Morning Edition," 11 May 2004.

211. Scott Peterson, "U.S. Pressure on Cleric Pushes Militants South," *Christian Science Monitor,* 10 May 2004, p. 4.

212. Ibid.

213. Saadi and Navarro, "Uneasy Truce Holds in Fallujah," p. 4A; Keath, "Shiites Retreat in Najaf," p. 1A.

214. Jason Keyser, AP, "Rock and Roll and Killer Flies on Front Line," *Jacksonville (NC) Daily News,* 17 April 2004, p. 5A.

215. ABC's Nightly News, 29 April 2004.

216. "Bush Administration Is under Increasing Fire for Iraq Policy," from Knight Ridder, *Jacksonville (NC) Daily News,* 30 April 2004, pp. 1A, 7A.

217. ABC's Morning News, 30 April and 1 May 2004.

218. Jim Krane, AP, "Rebels among the Force," *Jacksonville (NC) Daily News,* 30 April 2004, pp. 1A, 7A.

219. Warren P. Strobel, Knight Ridder, "Bush Abandons Initial Blueprint," *Jacksonville (NC) Daily News,* 1 May 2004, pp. 1A, 5A.

220. Poole, *The Tiger's Way,* pp. 267-278.

221. ABC's Noon News, 8 April 2004.

222. ABC's Nightly News, 7 April 2004.

223. Poole, *Tiger's Way,* pp. 280-296.

224. Oliva, "Marines Suspend Fallujah Offensive," p. 1A.

225. Pamela Constable, "Marines Battle Enemy Fighters in Fallujah," *Washington Post,* 6 April 2004.

226. Willis Witter, "Iraqi Snipers Work in Teams to Hit Marines," *Washington Times,* 12 April 2004.

227. Keyser and Navarro, "Marines in Heavy Night Fighting," p. 7A.

228. Ibid.

229. Scott Peterson, "Fallujah Firefight Rekindles," *Christian Science Monitor,* 27 April 2004, p. 7.

230. Ron Harris, St. Louis Post-Dispatch, "Marines Return to Violent City," *Jacksonville (NC) Daily News,* 19 April 2004, p. 5A.

231. Ron Harris, St. Louis Post-Dispatch, "5 Marines, Scores of Iraqis Die in Battle," *Jacksonville (NC) Daily News,* 18 April 2004, p. 4A.

232. Poole, *The Last Hundred Yards,* pp. 310, 311.

233. Harris, "Marines Return to Violent City," p. 5A.

234. Bassem Mroue, AP, "Fallujah Fight Rages," *Jacksonville (NC) Daily News,* 27 April 2004, p. 1A.

235. Keath, "Chaos Grips Iraq," p. 5A.

236. Evan Thomas and John Barry, "A Plan under Attack," *Newsweek,* 7 April 2003, p. 29.

237. Nordland et al, "The Dark Road Ahead," pp. 28-32.

238. ABC's Nightly News, 17 May 2004.

239. Robert H. Reid, AP, "U.S. Says It Never Had Custody of Beheaded American," *AOL News,* 12 May 2004.

240. Hamza Hendawi, AP, "Big Blasts Rock City near Shrine," *Jacksonville (NC) Daily News,* 14 May 2004, p. 6A.

241. Ibid.

242. Hamza Hendawi, AP, "Najaf Battle Grows," *Jacksonville (NC) Daily News,* 15 May 2004, p. 7A.

243. Ibid.

244. Ibid.

245. Torchia, "Gunmen Kill 3 Iraqi Women," p. 5A.

246. Orly Halpern, "U.S. Closes In on Deal with Iraqi Cleric," *Christian Science Monitor,* 25 May 2004, pp. 1, 10.

247. Ibid.

248. G.I. Wilson, "Iraq: Fourth Generation Warfare (4GW) Swamp."

249. "Encyclopedia: Hezbollah," www.nationmaster.com, 5 July 2004.

250. "Group Says Thousands Ready for Suicide Raids," Across the Region, *Daily Star* (Lebanon), 7 June 2004, p. 2.

251. "Nearly 40 People Stopped at Border," Across the Region, *Daily Star* (Lebanon), 8 June 2004, p. 2.

252. Memo for the record by H.J. Poole.

253. "Despite Having Agreed to a Truce," World News in Brief, *Christian Science Monitor,* 11 June 2004.

254. Chris Tomlinson, AP, "Bomb Blast Kills 2 Iraqi Soldiers," *Jacksonville (NC) Daily News,* 21 June 2004, p. 4A; "Iraq Blasts Damage Oil Pipeline, Hit Exports," Reuters, *Turkish Daily News* (Istanbul), 16 June 2004, p. 6.

255. Robert H. Reid, AP, "Car Bombs, Armed Attacks Take a Heavy Toll," *Jacksonville Daily News,* 25 June 2004, pp. 1A, 5A.

256. ABC's Nightly News, 24 June 2004.

257. Robert H. Reid, AP, "Insurgents Gun Down 4 Marines," *Jacksonville Daily News,* 22 June 2004, p. 1A.

258. Reid, "Car Bombs, Armed Attacks Take a Heavy Toll," pp. 1A, 5A.

259. ABC's Morning News, 25 June 2004.

260. Reid, "Car Bombs, Armed Attacks Take a Heavy Toll," p. 1A.

261. Nicholas Blanford, "Iraqi Kidnappings Hard to Stop," *Christian Science Monitor,* 9 June 2004, p. 6.

262. Tomlinson, "Bomb Blast Kills 2 Iraqi Soldiers," p. 4A.

263. Chris Tomlinson, AP, "Militants Threaten to Behead Hostages," *Jacksonville (NC) Daily News,* 28 June 2004, pp. 1A, 2A.

264. Pereira telephone conversation.

265. Blanford, "Iraqi Kidnappings Hard to Stop," p. 6.

266. Dan Murphy, "Can Self-Rule Bring Security?", *Christian Science Monitor,* 25 June 2004, pp. 1, 4.

267. Todd Pitman, AP, "Strike Targets Terrorist," *Jacksonville (NC) Daily News,* 26 June 2004, pp. 1A, 6A; Reid, "Car Bombs, Armed Attacks Take a Heavy Toll," pp. 1A, 5A; Hamza Hendawi, AP, "Insurgents Strike Iraqi Cities, Killing Dozens," AOL News, 24 June 2004.

268. Tomlinson, "Bomb Blast Kills 2 Iraqi Soldiers," p. 4A.

269. Todd Pitman, AP, "U.S. Warplanes Bomb Suspected Terror Den," *Jacksonville (NC) Daily News,* 2 July 2004, pp. 1A, 4A; ABC's Nightly News, 5 July 2004.

270. Todd Pitman, AP, "Jets Target Rebels," *Jacksonville (NC) Daily News,* 1 July 2004, p. 6A; Robert H. Reid, AP, "Militants Behead South Korean Hostage," *Jacksonville (NC) Daily News,* 23 June 2004, pp. 1A, 6A; Tomlinson, "Bomb Blast Kills 2 Iraqi Soldiers," p. 4A; Pitman, "Strike Targets Terrorist," pp. 1A, 6A; ABC's Morning News, 1 July 2004; ABC's Nightly News, 5 July 2004.

271. Ravi Nessman, AP, "U.S. Launches Airstrike in Fallujah," *Jacksonville (NC) Daily News,* 6 July 2004, pp. 1A, 2A.

272. ABC's Nightly News, 18 July 2004.

273. Pitman, "Jets Target Rebels," p. 6A.

274. Pitman, "U.S. Warplanes Bomb Suspected Terror Den," p. 4A.

275. Fisnik Abrashi, AP, "Militant Cleric Vows to Keep Fighting in Iraq," AOL News, 5 July 2004.

276. Ann Scott Tyson, "Sadr's Militia Regrouping, Rearming," *Christian Science Monitor,* 15 July 2004, pp. 1, 7; Jamie Tarabay, AP, "U.S. Chopper Downed amid Fierce Fighting in Iraq," AOL News, 5 August 2004.

277. Danica Kirka, AP, "Philippines Pulls More Troops from Iraq," *Jacksonville (NC) Daily News,* 17 July 2004, p. 5A; "Iraq's Coalition of the Willing," Reuters News Service, *Christian Science Monitor,* 27 July 2004, p. 4.

278. CBS's Morning News, 4 July 2004.

279. ABC's Nightly News, 15 July 2004.

280. Todd Pitman, AP, "3 Marines Die in Convoy Blast," *Jacksonville (NC) Daily News,* 30 June 2004, pp. 1A, 6A.

281. Ann Scott Tyson, "At Sprawling U.S. Airbase in Iraq, a Crescendo in Attacks," *Christian Science Monitor,* 1 July 2004, p. 7.

282. Brad Knickerbocker, "How Iraq Will Change U.S. Military Doctrine," *Christian Science Monitor,* 2 July 2004.

283. Abdul Hussein al-Obeidi, AP, "Holy City Najaf Fighting Worst Since Saddam Fell," *Jacksonville (NC) Daily News,* 7 August 2004, pp. 1A, 4A.

284. Ibid.

285. Babak Dehganpisheh, "A War's Hidden Hands," *Newsweek,* 6 September 2004, pp. 52-53.

286. Scott Baldauf, "Sadr Loyalty Grows, Even as Sistani Returns," *Christian Science Monitor,* 26 August 2004, p. 6.

287. Pintak, *Seeds of Hate,* pp. 19, 111.

288. Ibid., p. 185.

289. Tarek El-Tablawy, AP, "Iraq a Fertile Ground for Militants," *Jacksonville (NC) Daily News,* 11 July 2004, p. 5A.

290. *"Hezbollah* Ideology," from www.military.com, 18 June 2004.

291. FOX News, 28 August 2004.

292. Scott Baldauf, "Sadr Forces Push Terror Offensive," *Christian Science Monitor,* 11 August 2004, pp. 1, 10.

293. Scott Baldauf, "Najaf Battle a Crucial Test for Allawi," *Christian Science Monitor,* 11 August 2004, pp. 1, 5; Pitman, AP, "Marines Seal Off Holy City," p. 4A.

294. Charles Crain, "U.S. Troops Battle al-Sadr Supporters in Najaf," *USA Today,* 13 August 2004, p. 6A.

295. ABC's Nightly News, 12 August 2004.

296. ABC's Nightly News, 18 August 2004.

297. "Iraq Militant OKs Peace Plan," from AP, *Jacksonville (NC) Daily News,* 19 August 2004, p. 10A.

298. Abdul Hussein al-Obeidi, AP, "Mosque Turnover Disputed," *Jacksonville (NC) Daily News,* 21 August 2004, p. 6A; ABC's Nightly News, 22 August 2004.

299. ABC's Nightly News, 26 August 2004.

300. Scott Peterson, "Economic Fallout of $50 a Barrel," *Christian Science Monitor,* 27 August 2004, p. 6.

301. Scott Baldauf, "Standoff Bolstered Sadr's Support," *Christian Science Monitor,* 30 August 2004, p. 4.

302. Jim Krane, AP, "Iraq Insurgent Force May Number 20,000," AOL News, 9 July 2004.

302. "Violence Surge Threatens Vote Exit Strategy," by Knight Ridder, *Jacksonville (NC) Daily News,* 15 September 2004, p. 10A.

304. Abdul Hussein al-Obeidi, AP, "U.S. Increases Pressure on Najaf," *Jacksonville (NC) Daily News,* 24 August 2004, p. 3A.

305. Kim Housego, AP, "I MEF Loses 7 in Blast," *Jacksonville (NC) Daily News,* 7 September 2004, p. 1A.

306. Kirka, "U.S. Bombs Insurgent-Held Iraqi Cities"; Scott Johnson and Babak Dehghanpisheh, "It's Worse Than You Think," *Newsweek,* 20 September 2004, p. 33.

307. ABC's Morning News, 8 September 2004.

308. ABC's Nightly News, 14 September 2004.

Chapter 9: *How Islamic Guerrillas Are Trained*

1. T.P. Schwartz, "The Qur'an as a Guide to Conduct of and in War, Including Treatment of Prisoners of War," *Marine Corps Gazette,* February 2002, p. 43; T.P. Schwartz, "Waging War against Hostile Combat Units That Fight According to *Al Qur'an,*" *Marine Corps Gazette,* September 2002, p. 75.

2. McForan, *The World Held Hostage,* p. 94.

3. Katzman, *Warriors of Islam,* p. 32.

4. Zabih, *The Iranian Military,* p. 17.

5. Ibid., p. 217.
6. Katzman, *Warriors of Islam,* p. 92.
7. Ibid., pp. 49, 86.
8. Pintak, *Seeds of Hate,* pp. 113, 184.
9. Katzman, *Warriors of Islam,* p. 67.
10. Zabih, *The Iranian Military,* p. 219.
11. Ibid., p. 176.
12. Ibid., p. 184.
13. Ibid., p. 243.
14. Ibid., p. 176.
15. Eshel, "Counterguerrilla Warfare in South Lebanon," p. 41.
16. Ibid.
17. Katzman, *Warriors of Islam,* p. 15.
18. Keyser, AP, "Israel Bombs Syria."
19. "The Ayn Tzahab Training Camp in Syria," Israel News Agency, 5 October 2003.
20. "Sudan: Militant Training Camps," U.S. State Dept. Daily Press Briefing Answers, 23 April 2002.
21. Yousaf and Adkin, *Bear Trap.*
22. "Pakistan's Double Standards," *Pravda* (Russia), 18 September 2001.
23. Wiktorowicz, *Global Jihad.*
24. "*Al-Qaeda* Training Tape Assessment," given to author by Marine sergeant during an instructional visit to 1st Battalion, 5th Marines in October 2003.
25. Peterson, "The Rise and Fall of Ansar al-Islam," p. 13.
26. Memo for the record by H.J. Poole.
27. "*Al-Qaeda* Training Tape Assessment."
28. Stephen K. Hayes, *The Mystic Arts of the Ninja: Hypnotism, Invisibility, and Weaponry* (Chicago: Contemporary Books, 1985, p. 134.
29. "Hypnosis," chapt. in *The Complete Manual of Fitness and Well-Being* (Pleasantville, NY: The Reader's Digest Assn., 1984), p. 330.
30. Stephen K. Hayes, *Legacy of the Night Warrior* (Santa Clarita, CA: Ohara Publications, 1985), p. 26.
31. Stephen K. Hayes, *Ninjutsu: The Art of the Invisible Warrior* (Chicago: Contemporary Books, 1984), p. 153.
32. Ibid., p. 154; Hatsumi, *Ninjutsu: History and Tradition,* p. 13.
33. Hayes, *The Mystic Arts of the Ninja,* p. 136.
34. Hatsumi, *Ninjutsu: History and Tradition,* p. 12.
35. Hayes, *The Mystic Arts of the Ninja,* pp. 132-138.
36. Ashida Kim, *Secrets of the Ninja* (New York: Citadel Press, 1981), pp. 5-31.
37. Hatsumi, *Ninjutsu: History and Tradition,* author's preface.
38. Hayes, *Ninjutsu: The Art of the Invisible Warrior,* p. 154.
39. Hayes, *The Mystic Arts of the Ninja,* p. 137.

40. Hayes, *Ninjutsu: The Art of the Invisible Warrior,* p. 157.
41. Ibid.
42. Ibid.
43. Ibid.
44. Hayes, *The Mystic Arts of the Ninja,* p. 139.
45. "Hypnosis," chapt. in *The Complete Manual of Fitness and Well-Being,* p. 330.
46. Stephen K Hayes, *The Ninja and Their Secret Fighting Art* (Rutland, VT: Charles E. Tuttle Co., 1981), p. 18.
47. Mar Roman, AP, "Terror Suspects Kill Selves As Spanish Police Close In," *Jacksonville (NC) Daily News,* 4 April 2004, p. 8A.
48. Clayton, "Reading into the Mind of a Terrorist," p. 11.
49. Reinke e-mails.

Chapter 10: *The Muslim Militants' Pattern*

1. Hammel, *Root,* p. 78.
2. Ibid., pp. 284, 306, 421, 422.
3. Bell, *Dragonwars,* p. 47; Hiro, *The Longest War,* p. 83.
4. Katzman, *Warriors of Islam,* p. 135.
5. Ibid., pp. 1-50.
6. "Killings in Austria, Emirates Laid to Iran," *Washington Post,* 3 August 1989, p. A1, in *Warriors of Islam,* by Katzman, p. 100.
7. Katzman, *Warriors of Islam,* p. 135; Pintak, *Seeds of Hate,* p. 233.
8. Mohammed Shirazi, *Psychological Warfare and Propaganda Concepts and Applications,* second edition (Tehran: Secretariat of the First Conference on the Role of Propaganda in War, 2001; prepared in the Public Relations and Publications Directorial of the Office of the Representative of the Supreme Leader [Vali-e Faghih] in the Faculty of Command and Control of the Islamic Revolutionary Guards Corps [of Iran]), publisher credits; Khamenei, as quoted from Reuters, 2 November 1985, in *Seeds of Hate,* by Pintak, p. 235.
9. Katzman, *Warriors of Islam,* p. 177.
10. Ibid., p. 70.
11. Poole, *Tiger's Way,* p. 287.
12. Katzman, *Warriors of Islam,* p. 60.
13. Zabih, *The Iranian Military,* pp. 184, 252.
14. Poole, *Phantom Soldier,* pp. 83-105.
15. Zabih, *The Iranian Military,* p. 240.
16. Ibid., p. 252.
17. Ibid.
18. Katzman, *Warriors of Islam,* p. 2.
19. Shirazi, *Psychological Warfare.*
20. Hiro, *The Longest War,* p. 51.

21. Katzman, *Warriors of Islam,* p. 11.
22. "Oldest Iranian Qanat Found in Bam," *Tehran Times* (Iran), 5 June 2004, p. 3.
23. Wright, *Sacred Rage*, pp. 33-35, in *Warriors of Islam,* by Katzman, p. 12.
24. Shirazi, *Psychological Warfare,* pp. 19-23.
25. Ibid., p. 27.
26. Ibid., p. 28.
27. Ibid, pp. 32, 33.
28. Ibid.
29. Ibid., pp. 45, 46.
30. Ibid. pp. 103-115.
31. Ibid., p. 48.
32. *"Hezbollah* Ideology."
33. "Hizballah," *Patterns of Global Terrorism, 2002* (Washington, D.C.: U.S. Dept. of State, April 2003), from its website; "Hezbollah," *Encyclopedia,* www.nationmaster.com, 5 July 2004.
34. Allan Topol, "Why Turkey?", from www.military.com, 26 November 2003.
35. "Hizballah," *Patterns of Global Terrorism, 2002; "Hezbollah* Reference Page."
36. "Hizballah," as extracted from an article by the Info. Div., Israel Foreign Ministry in Jerusalem, and posted at the Internat. Policy Inst. for Counter-Terrorism (ICT) website.
37. Aboul-Enein, "The Hezbollah Model," p. 34.
38. Ibid., p. 35; "Hezbollah," *Encyclopedia,* www.nationmaster.com, 5 July 2004.
39. Pintak, *Seeds of Hate,* pp. 112, 141.
40. Adnan El-Ghoul and Khalil Fleihan, "Border Situation Tense after Israeli Airstrike," *Daily Star* (Lebanon), 9 June 2004, pp. 1, 2; Blanford, "Hizballah Reelects Its Leader," p. 6.
41. Ibid.
42. El-Ghoul and Fleihan, "Border Situation Tense after Israeli Airstrike," pp. 1, 2.
43. Neil MacFarquahar, "Hezbollah Becomes Potent Anti-U.S. Force," *New York Times,* 24 December 2002.
44. *"Hezbollah* Reference Page"; memo for the record by H.J. Poole.
45. MacFarquahar, "Hezbollah Becomes Potent Anti-U.S. Force."
46. Ibid.
47. Ben Venzke and Aimee Ibrahim, *The al-Qaeda Threat: An Analytical Guide to al-Qaeda's Tactics and Targets* (Alexandria, VA: Tempest Publishing, 2003), p. 40.
48. "Al-Qaida," *Patterns of Global Terrorism, 2002* (Washington, D.C.: U.S. Dept. of State, April 2003), from its website; attributed to Esposito.

49. Ibid.

50. Scott Peterson, "Revenge Fuels Chechen Flames," *Christian Science Monitor*, 8 October 2003, p. 6; Venzke and Ibrahim, *The al-Qaeda Threat*, p. 39.

51. Abu-Ubayd al-Qurashi, "The Fourth Generation of Wars," Strategic Studies, initially in Arabic at al-Ansar website (linked to *al-Qaeda)*, then FBIS (Foreign Broadcasting Information Service) translation at www.geocities.com, 28 February 2002, pp. 15-21.

52. Chris Suellentrop, "Abdullah Azzam - The Godfather of Jihad," slate.msn.com.

53. Venzke and Ibrahim, *The al-Qaeda Threat*, p. 7.

54. Ibid., p. 39.

55. Al-Qurashi, "The Fourth Generation of Wars," pp. 15-21.

56. *"Al-Qaeda* Training Tape Assessment."

57. Ibid.

58. Grau, "Technology and the Second Chechen Campaign," pp. 102, 107.

59. Ibid., p. 104.

60. Grau and Cutshaw, "Russian Snipers," p. 10.

61. Shipunov and Filimonov, "Field Artillery to Be Replaced with Shmel Infantry Flamethrower."

62. Pereira telephone conversation.

63. Photograph, *Newsweek*, 1 September 2003, p. 38.

64. Scott Johnson, "Inside an Enemy Cell," *Newsweek*, 18 August 2003.

65. Evan Thomas and Rod Nordland, "How We Got Saddam," *Newsweek*, 22 December 2003, p. 27.

66. "Afghanistan Country Study."

67. "China Puts 700,000 Troops on Alert in Sudan," newsmax.com, 27 August 2000.

68. Bill Gertz, "Notes from the Pentagon," *Washington Times*, 5 March 2004.

69. "Iran Signs $20-Billion Gas Deal with China," UPI, 20 March 2004.

70. Zabih, *The Iranian Military*, p. 183.

71. Edgar O'Balance, "The Iranian Armed Forces," *Marine Corps Gazette*, August 1980, p. 49.

72. *"Terrorist Group Profiles,"* from Dudley Knox Library, Naval Postgraduate School website.

73. Dick, "Mujahideen Tactics"; "Hamas," *Patterns of Global Terrorism*.

74. "Hamas," Internat. Policy Inst. for Counter-Terrorism (ICT) website.

75. Pintak, *Seeds of Hate*, p. 315.

76. Lumpkin, "U.S. Identifies Sources," p. 5A; Dehganpisheh, "A War's Hidden Hands," pp. 52-53.

77. Esposito, *Unholy War,* p. 139.

78. Theyson, "New Warfront Opens in Iraq."

79. Col. (Res.) Jonathan Fighel, "Sheikh Abdullah Azzam," Internat. Policy Inst. for Counter-Terrorism (ICT) website.

80. Suellentrop, "Abdullah Azzam"; Esposito, *Unholy War,* p. 7.

81. Ibid.

82. "The Striving Sheik: Abdullah Azzam," *Nida'ul Islam Magazine,* no. 14, July-September 1996.

83. Topkhana, as quoted in *Afghan Guerrilla,* by Jalali and Grau, p. 301.

84. Esposito, *Unholy War,* pp. 50, 51, 84.

85. Yousaf and Adkin, *Bear Trap.*

86. Ibid.

87. Ibid.

88. Jalali and Grau, *Afghan Guerrilla,* p. xix.

89. Yousaf and Adkin, *Bear Trap.*

90. Kaplan, *Soldiers of God,* p. 217.

91. Wiktorowicz, *Global Jihad.*

92. Yousaf, *Silent Soldier.*

93. Dick, "Mujahideen Tactics."

94. Katzman, *Warriors of Islam,* p. 126.

95. "Iran Country Study," p. 269.

96. Ibid., pp. 231, 232.

97. Yousaf and Adkin, *Bear Trap.*

98. Scott Peterson, "Hostile in Public, Iran Seeks Quiet Discourse with U.S.," *Christian Science Monitor,* 25 September 2003, p. 7.

99. Faye Bowers, "Iran Shows New Willingness to Deal with U.S.," *Christian Science Monitor,* 24 October 2003, p. 3.

100. Ford, "A Suspect Emerges," pp. 1, 7.

101. CBS's "20/20," 21 March 2004.

102. Esposito, *Unholy War,* pp. 18, 19.

103. CBS's "20/20," 22 March 2004.

104. Esposito, *Unholy War,* pp. 18, 19.

105. *Britannica.com,* s.v. "Muslim Brotherhood."

106. *Encyclopedia.com,* s.v. "Muslim Brotherhood"; Esposito, *Unholy War,* pp. 94, 95.

107. Pintak, *Seeds of Hate,* p. 326.

108. McForan, *The World Held Hostage,* p. 94.

109. Katzman, *Warriors of Islam,* p. 32.

110. Dan Murphy, "In Iraq, a 'Perfect Storm'," *Christian Science Monitor,* 9 April 2004, p. 5.

111. Gaffney letter; Yousaf, *Silent Soldier.*

112. Esposito, *Unholy War,* pp. 15-17.

113. Jalali and Grau, *Afghan Guerrilla,* p. 410.

114. Burke, "Waiting for a Last Battle with the Taliban."

115. Yousaf and Adkin, *Bear Trap.*

116. Topkhana, as quoted in *Afghan Guerrilla,* by Jalali and Grau, p. 301.

117. Ansnullah Wazir, AP, "Pakistani Troops Kill 11 on Border," *Jacksonville (NC) Daily News,* 29 February 2004, p. 4A.

118. Yoni Fighel and Yael Shahar, "The Al-Qaida-Hizballah Connection," as posted on 26 February 2002 at the Internat. Policy Inst. for Counter-Terrorism (ICT) website.

119. Howard Lafranchi, "Anti-Iran Sentiment Hardening Fast," *Christian Science Monitor,* 22 July 2004, pp. 1, 10.

120. "Who Did It? Foreign Report Presents an Alternative View," *Jane's Foreign Report 19, 2001,* at www.janes.com, in *Seeds of Hate,* by Pintak, p. 307.

121. Blanford, "Hizbullah Reelects Its Leader," p. 6.

122. "The 9/11 Commission Report: The Terrorist Plot," *Los Angeles Times,* 23 July 2004, pp. A1, A15.

123. *Random House Encyclopedia,* electronic ed., s.v. "Crusades."

124. Esposito, *Unholy War,* p. 10.

125. Ibid., p. 7.

126. Azzam, as quoted in *Unholy War,* by Esposito, p. 7.

Chapter 11: *The Response Must Be Unconventional*

1. Faramarzi, "Rebels Strike Kurds," p. 1A.

2. Murphy, "Iraq Bombs Hit Kurdish Leaders," p. 11.

3. "Suicide Bomber Kills Peacekeeper."

4. Mariam Fam, AP, "Bomber Targets Leading Sheiks, Blows Himself Up," *Jacksonville (NC) Daily News,* 10 February 2004, p. 6A.

5. "Shiites March throughout Middle East," from AP, *Jacksonville (NC) Daily News,* 22 May 2004, p. 10A.

6. Major network newscast, 2002.

7. Clayton, "Reading into the Mind of a Terrorist," p. 11.

8. Lewis, *The Crisis of Islam.*

9. ABC's Nightly News, 14 January 2004.

10. Reinke e-mails.

11. Matthew Barakat, AP, "Psychiatrist: Sniper Suspect Could Not Tell Right from Wrong ," *Jacksonville (NC) Daily News,* 11 December 2003, p. 4A.

12. Ibid., p. 5A.

13. Attributed to Daftary.

14. Ibid.

15. Iyer, "Grim Reminders of the Ancient Assassins."

16. Esposito, *Unholy War,* p. 99.

17. Ibid., p. 100.

18. Grand Ayatollah Saanei, as quoted "Iran's Revolution at 25: Out of Gas," by Scott Peterson, *Christian Science Monitor,* 11 February 2004, p. 7.

19. Esposito, *Unholy War,* p. 42.

20. Pope John Paul II, as quoted in "Witness to Hope: The Life of Karol Wojtyka, Pope John Paul II," PBS TV, n.d.

21. George Robert Elford, *Devil's Guard* (New York: Dell, 1985), pp. 1-329.

22. Thomas S. Green, S.J., Weeds among the Wheat (Notre Dame, IN: Ave Maria Press, 1984), pp. 7-204.

23. "Iran's Besharati, RafiqDust in Syria for Talks," *Paris Magasino,* 12 May 1988, in *Warriors of Islam,* by Katzman, p. 97.

24. "For Security Reasons, the Long-Awaited National Election in Postwar Afghanistan," News in Brief, *Christian Science Monitor,* 29 March 2004, p. 20.

25. Dexter Filkins, "Kurds Are Finally Heard: Turkey Burned Our Villages," *The New York Times International,* 24 October 2003, p. A3.

26. Fareed Zakaria, "Suicide Bombers Can Be Stopped," *Newsweek,* 25 August 2003, p. 57.

27. Bell, *Dragonwars,* pp. 39, 43, 44.

28. Ibid., p. 48.

29. "Battle Plan under Fire."

30. Scott Baldauf and Faye Bowers, "Why Catching bin Laden Is Difficult," *Christian Science Monitor,* 18 March 2004, pp. 1, 10.

31. Scheherezade Faramarzi, AP, "Iraqis, U.S. at Odds on Attack," *Jacksonville (NC) Daily News,* 20 May 2004, p. 1A; "Military Says Attack Target Was Safehouse," from AP, *Jacksonville (NC) Daily News,* 21 May 2004, p. 9A; Anthony Deutsh, AP, "Military Says No Evidence of Wedding at Attack Site," *Jacksonville (NC) Daily News,* 23 May 2004, p. 4A; ABC's Morning News, 24 May 2004.

32. Pope John Paul II, *Crossing the Threshold of Hope* (New York: Alfred A. Knopf, 1995), pp. 205, 206.

33. Brad Knickerbocker, "Who Counts Civilian Casualties," *Christian Science Monitor,* 31 March 2004, p. 15.

34. Cockburn, "Iraq's Oppressed Majority," pp. 99-101.

35. NBC's "Dateline," 27 February 2004.

36. "In a Time of War," photograph caption, *Newsweek,* 29 December 2003.

37. Niko Price, AP, "Official: Ministry Ordered a Halt to Civilian Toll Count," *Jacksonville (NC) Daily News,* 11 December 2003, p. 8A.

38. Al-Qurashi, "The Fourth Generation of Wars," pp. 15-21.

39. Gen. Anthony C. Zinni USMC (Ret.), as quoted in "For Zinni, a War That Ignores the Facts," by Thomas E. Ricks, *Washington Post,* 12-18 January 2004, nat. weekly ed., p. 9.

Chapter 12: *The Tactical Part of the Equation*

1. William S. Lind, "Fourth Generation Warfare's First Blow: A Quick Look," *Marine Corps Gazette,* November 2001; William S. Lind, Maj. John F. Schmitt, and Col. Gary I. Wilson, "Fourth Generation Warfare: Another Look," *Marine Corps Gazette,* December 1994 (reprint November 2001); William S. Lind, Col. Keith Nightengale, Capt. John F. Schmitt, Col. Joseph W. Sutton, and Lt.Col. Gary I. Wilson, "The Changing Face of War: Into the Fourth Generation," *Marine Corps Gazette,* October 1989 (reprint November 2001).
2. Aijaz Rahi, AP, "Anger and Confusion," *Jacksonville (NC) Daily News,* 8 December 2003, p. 6A.
3. Graham, "U.S. Defends Raid That Killed Afghan Children," p. 7A.
4. Yousaf and Adkin, *Bear Trap.*
5. *The Bear Went over the Mountain,* ed. Grau, p. 205.
6. Poole, *Phantom Soldier,* p. 89.
7. Jack Schulimson, Lt.Col. Leonard A. Blaisol, Charles R. Smith, and Capt. David A. Dawson, *U.S. Marines in Vietnam: The Defining Year, 1968* (Washington, D.C.: Hist. & Museums Div., HQMC, 1997, p. 29: Poole, *Phantom Soldier,* pp. 163-198.
8. Steven L. Canby, "Classic Light Infantry and New Technology," Defense Advanced Research Project Agency (Potomac, MD: C&L Associates, 1983), p. iv.
9. Maj.Gen. Paul D. Eaton (U.S. Army's Chief of Infantry), "Indirect Fires First: The American Way of War," interview by Patrecia Slayden Hollis, *Infantry Magazine,* fall 2003, p. 39.
10. Hammel, *Root,* p. 293.
11. Ibid., pp. 293-295; Bell, *Dragonwars,* pp. 17-58.
12. Pintak, *Seeds of Hate,* p. 91.
13. MacFarquahar, "Hezbollah Becomes Potent Anti-U.S. Force."
14. Pintak, *Seeds of Hate,* p. 318.
15. Poole, *Last Hundred Yards,* pp. 52-54.
16. Poole, *Phantom Soldier,* pp. 57-82.
17. Poole, *Tiger's Way,* pp. 37-44, 349-353.
18. Cpl. Ryan Walker, "SRT Trains to Go beyond Call of Duty," *Camp Lejeune Globe,* 29 April 2004.
19. Poole, *Tiger's Way,* pp. 143-296.
20. Pintak, *Seeds of Hate,* p. 18.
21. ABC's Nightly News, 18 April 2004.
22. Reid, "Insurgents Gun Down 4 Marines," p. 1A.

23. Fayadh, "Suicide Attacks Kill At Least 68," p. 10A.

24. ABC's Nightly News, 26 April 2004.

25. Dan Murphy, "Sadr Army Owns City Streets," *Christian Science Monitor,* 4 August 2004, pp. 1, 7, 10.

26. Memo for the record by H.J. Poole.

27. Poole, *Last Hundred Yards,* pp. 177-250.

28. Pintak, *Seeds of Hate,* p. 226.

29. Memo for the record by H.J. Poole.

30. "Terrorism by Muslim Radicals," News in Brief, *Christian Science Monitor,* 31 March 2004, p. 20.

31. Poole, *Tiger's Way,* pp. 9-18.

32. "Forty Years of Prominent Statesman," Special Report, *Tehran Times* (Iran), 5 June 2004, p. 6.

33. Pennington, "Pakistan Unsure If Target Is al-Zawahri," p. 5A.

34. Esposito, *Unholy War,* p. 7.

35. "The Second Chechen War," ed. Aldis.

36. Felgenhauer, "Defense Dossier."

37. "DoD Identifies Lejeune Marines Killed in Afghanistan," Staff and Wire Reports (AP), *Jacksonville (NC) Daily News,* 28 June 2004, p. 1A.

38. Bruce I. Gudmundsson, *Stormtroop Tactics: Innovation in the German Army 1914-1918* (Westport, CT: Praeger Pubs., 1989), p. 173.

39. *Company and Platoon Drill,* ed. R. Meade (n.p.: British War Office, 1914), p. 2.

Glossary

A-10	Aircraft designator	U.S. "Warthog" tank-killer aircraft
ABC	American Broadcasting Company	U.S. TV network
AC-130	Aircraft designator	U.S. propeller-driven plane with 105mm howitzer, 40mm cannon, gatling guns
AH-64	Aircraft designator	U.S. "Apache" attack helicopter
AK-47	Weapon designator	Eastern assault rifle
ANA	Afghan National Army	Afghan security force during U.S. occupation
AP	Associated Press	U.S. news agency
APTN	Associated Press Television News	U.S. TV network
BBC	British Broadcasting Corporation	British TV network
BMP	Military-equipment designator	Soviet armored personnel carrier
CAP	Combined-Action Platoon	U.S. Marine Corps contingent that was stationed inside a Vietnamese village
CAS	Close Air Support	Bombing near ground troops

CBS	Columbia Broadcasting System	U.S. TV network
CH-53	Aircraft designator	U.S. cargo helicopter
CIA	Central Intelligence Agency	U.S. spy organization
CNN	Cable News Network	U.S. TV network
CPA	Coalition Provisional Authority	Interim government in Iraq
DRA	Democratic Republic of Afghanistan	Soviet puppet regime
FAE	Fuel Air Explosive	Flame device that sucks up all oxygen
FSB	Russian acronym	Russian security service now running the war in Chechnya
GI	Government Issue	U.S. enlisted soldier
HI	Harakat-i-Islami	Movement of Ayatollah Muhsini in Afghanistan
HIH	Afghan acronym	Party of Gulbuddin Hekmatyar in Afghanistan
HIK	Afghan acronym	Party of Mawlawi Yunus Khalis in Afghanistan
HIND	Military-equipment designator	Soviet attack helicopter
HMMWV	American acronym	Modern equivalent of U.S. jeep
HQ	Headquarters	Unit commander's location
HUM	*Harakat ul-Mujahidin*	*Al-Qaeda*-linked group previously active in Kashmir

ICDC	Iraq Civil Defense Corps	Iraqi security troops for U.S. occupation
IDF	Israeli Defense Forces	Israel's military
IED	Improvised Explosive Device	Name allocated to roadside bombs in Iraq and Afghanistan
IRGC	Iranian Revolutionary Guard Corps	Iranian defense force
IRMA	(Islamic Revolutionary Movement)	Afghan party of Mohammad Nabi Mohammadi
IRNA	Iranian acronym	Iranian news service
ISI	Inter-Services Intelligence	Pakistani intelligence agency
JUI	*Jamiat-i-Ulema-i-Islam*	Fundamentalist Pakistani political party
JUI-F	*Jamiat-i-Ulema-i-Islam* (Fazlur Rehman faction)	A military branch of *JUI*
KGB	Russian acronym	Soviet spy agency
KHAD	Afghan acronym	Secret police under Soviet puppet regime
LoC	British acronym	Soviet zone of operations in Afghanistan
LZ	Landing Zone	Area suitable for landing helicopters
M-113	Vehicle designator	U.S. armored personnel carrier
M-14	Iraqi agency designator	Part of former Iraqi intelligence service

M-16	Rifle designator	U.S. assault rifle
MK	Military-equipment category	As applied to Israeli reconnaissance drone
MK III	Military-equipment designator	Israeli "Merkava" heavy tank
MoD	Ministry of Defense	Soviet headquarters in Afghanistan
MP	Military Police	Service branch law enforcement
NATO	North Atlantic Treaty Organization	European alliance
NBC	National Broadcasting Company	U.S. TV network
NCF	Noncompliant Forces	Enemy in Iraq
NCO	Noncommissioned Officer	Enlisted military leader
NPR	National Public Radio	Nonprofit radio network
NVA	North Vietnamese Army	North Vietnam forces
NWFP	Northwest Frontier Province	Pakistani region next to Afghanistan
OMON	Russian acronym	Russian Interior Ministry troops in Chechnya
PA	Palestinian Authority	Palestinian agency governing Gaza Strip and West Bank
PBS	Public Broadcasting Service	U.S. educational television network
PFLP	Popular Front for Liberation of Palestine	Palestinian group
PLA	People's Liberation Army	Red Chinese forces

PLO	Palestine Liberation Organization	Coalition of Palestinian groups
POW	Prisoner of War	Captured soldier
RL	Rocket Launcher	Device for firing parabolic rocket
RPG	Rocket Propelled Grenade (Launcher)	Shoulder-fired antitank weapon used throughout the Eastern world
RPO-A	Military-equipment designator	Russian thermobaric weapon
RPV	Remotely Piloted Vehicle	Robot reconnaissance aircraft
SA-7	Surface-to-air missile designator	Soviet antiaircraft weapon
SA-16	Surface-to-air missile designator	Soviet antiaircraft weapon
SCIRI	Supreme Council for Islamic Revolution in Iraq	Iraqi organization of exiles in Iran
SLA	South Lebanese Army	Border defense force during Israeli presence in Lebanon
SOP	Standard Operating Procedure	Established methods for a military unit
SPETSNAZ Russian acronym		Soviet commandos
SRT	Special Reaction Team	Hostage rescue unit
SS	*Schutzstaffel*	Elite guard of the German Nazi Party
SUV	Sports Utility Vehicle	U.S. all-terrain truck
SWAT	Special-Weapons Assault Team	Paramilitary police

307

TOS-1	Military-equipment designator	Russian thermobaric-missile launcher
TOW	American acronym	Wire-guided antitank missile
TV	Television	Electronic device for viewing pictures
UN	United Nations	International body
US	United States	America
USSR	Union of Soviet Socialist Republics	Former Soviet Union
VC	Viet Cong	Guerrillas in Vietnam
VIP	Very Important Person	Dignitary
WWI	World War One	Global conflict from 1914-1918
WWII	World War Two	Global conflict from 1939-1945
WWIII	World War Three	Next global conflict

Bibliography

U.S. Government Publications

"Afghanistan Country Study." *DA PAM 550-65*. Area Handbook Series. Washington, D.C.: Hdqts. Dept. of the Army, n.d. From the Illinois Inst. of Technology website, www.gl.iit.edu.

The Bear Went over the Mountain: Soviet Combat Tactics in Afghanistan. Translated and edited by Lester W. Grau, Foreign Mil. Studies Office, U.S. Dept. of Defense, Ft. Leavenworth, KS. Washington, D.C.: Nat. Defense Univ. Press, 1996. Originally published under its Russian title. Soviet Union: Frunze Mil. Acad., n.d.

Canby, Steven L. "Classic Light Infantry and New Technology." Produced under contract MDA 903-81-C-0207 for the Defense Advanced Research Project Agency. Potomac, MD: C&L Associates, 1983.

"CIA — The World Factbook." From its website, www.cia.gov.

Eaton, Maj.Gen. Paul D. (U.S. Army's Chief of Infantry). "Indirect Fires First: The American Way of War." Interview by Patrecia Slayden Hollis, *Infantry Magazine,* fall 2003.

Grau, Lt.Col. Lester W. *Russian-Manufactured Armored Vehicle Vulnerability in Urban Combat: The Chechnya Experience.* N.p.: publisher unknown, n.d. As quoted in "Kings of the Road: Heavy and Light Forces in MOUT," by Capt. John W. Karagosian and Capt. Christopher M. Coglianese. Training Notes. *Infantry Magazine,* January-February 2004.

Grau, Lester W. and Charles Cutshaw. "Russian Snipers: In the Mountains and Cities of Chechnya." *Infantry Magazine,* summer 2002.

"Iran Country Study." *DA PAM 550-68*. Area Handbook Series. Washington, D.C.: Hdqts. Dept. of the Army, 1989.

"Iraq Country Study." *DA PAM 550-31*. Area Handbook Series. Washington, D.C.: Hdqts. Dept. of the Army, n.d.

Jalali, Ali A. and Lester W. Grau. *Afghan Guerrilla Warfare: In the Words of the Mujahideen Fighters.* St. Paul, MN: MBI Publishing, 2001. Originally published as *The Other Side of the Mountain.* Quantico, VA: Marine Corps Combat Development Cmd., 1995.

Jalali, Ali A. and Lester W. Grau. "Night Stalkers and Mean Streets: Afghan Urban Guerrillas." Ft. Leavenworth, KS: Foreign Mil. Studies Office, 1998. From its website, fmso.leavenworth.army.mil, and *Infantry Magazine,* January-April 1999.

Kraft, Capt. Nelson G. "Lessons Learned from a Light Infantry Company during Operation Anaconda." *Infantry Magazine,* summer 2002.

"Lebanon Country Study." *DA PAM 550-24.* Area Handbook Series. Washington, D.C.: Hdqts. Dept. of the Army, n.d.

Oliva, Gy.Sgt. Mark. "Marines Suspend Fallujah Offensive, Increase Humanitarian Efforts." *Camp Lejeune (NC) Globe,* 15 April 2004.

"Pakistan Country Study." *DA PAM 550-48.* Area Handbook Series. Washington, D.C.: Hdqts. Dept. of the Army, 1994.

Patterns of Global Terrorism, 2002. Washington, D.C.: U.S. Dept. of State, April 2003. From its website.

Schulimson, Jack, Lt.Col. Leonard A. Blaisol, Charles R. Smith, and Capt. David A. Dawson. *U.S. Marines in Vietnam: The Defining Year, 1968.* Washington, D.C.: Hist. & Museums Div., HQMC, 1997.

"Sudan: Militant Training Camps." Answers from U.S. State Dept. Daily Press Briefing, 23 April 2002.

"Terrorist Group Profiles." From Dudley Knox Library, Naval Postgraduate School website, web.nps.navy.mil.

"Turkey Country Study." *DA PAM 550-80.* Area Handbook Series. Washington, D.C.: Hdqts. Dept. of the Army, 1995.

Warfare in Lebanon. Edited by Kenneth J. Alnwick and Thomas A. Fabyanic. Washington, D.C.: Nat. Defense Univ., 1988.

Wilmoth, Sergeant Michael D. and Lt.Col. Peter G. Tsouras. "Ulus-Kert: An Airborne Company's Last Stand." *Military Review* (U.S. Army Cmd. and Gen. Staff College, Ft. Leavenworth, KS), July-August 2001. From its website, www-cgsc.army.mil.

Civilian Books, Magazine Articles, and Videotape Presentations

Aboul-Enein, Lt.Cmdr. Youssef H. "The Hezbollah Model: Using Terror and Creating a Quasi-State in Lebanon." *Marine Corps Gazette,* June 2003.

Abrashi, Fisnik. Associated Press. "Militant Cleric Vows to Keep Fighting in Iraq," AOL News, 5 July 2004. From its website.

Abu-Ubayd al-Qurashi. "The Fourth Generation of Wars," Strategic Studies. Initially in Arabic at al-Ansar website (jihadist linked to *al-Qaeda).* Then FBIS translation at www.geocities.com, 28 February 2002.

Al-Issawi, Tarek. Associated Press. "19 Held in Najaf Bombing." *Jacksonville (NC) Daily News,* 31 August 2003.

Al-Issawi, Tarek. Associated Press. "Suicide Bomber Attacks Iraqi Police Station in Kirkuk." *Jacksonville (NC) Daily News,* 24 February 2004.

Al-Issawi, Tarek. Associated Press. "Suicide Bombers Strike Almost At Will in Iraq." *Jacksonville (NC) Daily News,* 19 March 2004.

Al-Mughrabi, Nidal. Reuters. "Israeli Soldiers Feared Dead in Second Ambush in Gaza." AOL News, 12 May 2004. From its website, www.aol.com.

Al-Obeidi, Abdul Hussein. Associated Press. "Holy City Najaf Fighting Worst Since Saddam Fell." *Jacksonville (NC) Daily News,* 7 August 2004.

Al-Obeidi, Abdul Hussein. Associated Press. "Iraqi Leader Calls for End to Violence." *Jacksonville (NC) Daily News,* 9 August 2004.

Al-Obeidi, Abdul Hussein. Associated Press. "Mosque Turnover Disputed." *Jacksonville (NC) Daily News,* 21 August 2004.

Al-Obeidi, Abdul Hussein. Associated Press. "U.S. Increases Pressure on Najaf." *Jacksonville (NC) Daily News,* 24 August 2004.

Ali tahir bin Sa ibn Qalanisi. "Tarikhi Dimashq." From the Ismaili Heritage Society's website, www.ismaili.net.

"All the Kings Men." *Exxon Masterpiece Theater.* BBC in conjunction with WGBH Boston. NC Public TV, 26 November 2000. Text from the PBS website, www.pbs.org.

"*Al-Qaeda* Training Tape Assessment." Given to author by Marine sergeant during an instructional visit to 1st Battalion, 5th Marines in October 2003.

Amos, Harel. "Probe into IDF Kidnappings Critical of Army's Conduct." *Ha'aretz* (Tel Aviv), 10 October 2000. In 16 August 2003 e-mail from pglibbery@hotmail.com and previously from www.moqawama.tv, a website for the Islamic Resistance Support Organization.

"The Army Will Temporarily Boost Its Forces by 30,000 over the Next Four Years." News in Brief. *Christian Science Monitor,* 30 January 2004.

Asprey, Robert B. *War in the Shadows.* Garden City, NY: Doubleday & Co., 1975.

"Assassins." From www.geocities.com.

"At Least 10 Palestinians Die in Israeli Tank Attack." Associated Press. *Jacksonville (NC) Daily News,* 20 May 2004.

"Attacks Leave Five Dead in Afghanistan." World Briefs Wire Reports (AP). *Jacksonville (NC) Daily News,* 15 March 2004.

"Attacks Raise Specter of New Chechen War." World Briefs Wire Reports (AP). *Jacksonville (NC) Daily News,* 24 June 2004.

The Ayn Tzahab Training Camp in Syria." Israel News Agency, 5 October 2003. From its website, www.israelnewsagency.com.

Baldauf, Scott. "Afghans Yet to Lay Down Arms." *Christian Science Monitor,* 14 October 2003.

Baldauf, Scott. "Najaf Battle a Crucial Test for Allawi." *Christian Science Monitor,* 11 August 2004.

Baldauf, Scott. "New Thrust in Hunt for Bin Laden." *Christian Science Monitor,* 4 March 2004.

Baldauf, Scott. "Sadr Forces Push Terror Offensive." *Christian Science Monitor,* 11 August 2004.

Baldauf, Scott. "Sadr Loyalty Grows, Even as Sistani Returns." *Christian Science Monitor,* 26 August 2004.

Baldauf, Scott. "Standoff Bolstered Sadr's Support." *Christian Science Monitor,* 30 August 2004.

Baldauf, Scott. "U.S. Hunts Bin Laden; Locals Seek Security." *Christian Science Monitor,* 15 March 2004.

Baldauf, Scott and Faye Bowers. "Why Catching bin Laden is Difficult." *Christian Science Monitor,* 18 March 2004.

Barakat, Matthew. Associated Press. "Psychiatrist: Sniper Suspect Could Not Tell Right from Wrong." *Jacksonville (NC) Daily News,* 11 December 2003.

Barakat, Matthew. Associated Press. "Sniper Malvo Guilty of Murder." *Jacksonville (NC) Daily News,* 19 December 2003.

Barr, Cameron W. "Gaza Bomb Attack: Strategy Shift?" *Christian Science Monitor,* 16 October 2003.

Barr, Cameron W. "In Iraq, U.S. Sees Influence of Al-Qaeda." *Christian Science Monitor,* 11 August 2003.

Barr, Cameron W. "A Smaller Intifada Resumes." *Christian Science Monitor,* 11 January 2004.

Barzak, Ibrahim. Associated Press. "Bomb Tagets Diplomatic Convoy." *Jacksonville (NC) Daily News,* 16 October 2003.

Barzanzi, Yehia. Associated Press. "Suicide Bombing at Iraqi Police Academy Kills 20." *Jacksonville (NC) Daily News,* 5 September 2004.

"The Battle That Helped Change the Course of the 'Israeli' Occupation." *The Daily Star* (Lebanon), 6 September 2000. In 16 August 2003 e-mail from pglibbery@hotmail.com and previously from www.moqawama.tv, a website for the Islamic Resistance Support Organization.

"Battle Plan under Fire." *Nova.* PBS in conjunction with WGBH Boston. NC Public TV, 4 May and 7 July 2004.

Begg, Paul. "Into Thin Air." In no. 31, vol. 3, *The Unexplained: Mysteries of Mind Space & Time.* Mysteries of the Unexplained Series. Pleasantville, NY: Readers Digest Assn., 1992.

Bell, J. Bowyer. *Dragonwars: Armed Struggle & the Conventions of Modern War.* New Brunswick, NJ: Transaction Publishers, 1999.

"Blair Meets with Putin As Battle Continues in Chechnya." CNN News, 11 March 2000. From its website, www.cnn.com.

Blanford, Nicholas. "As U.S. Draws Down, Doubt over Iraqis." *Christian Science Monitor,* 17 February 2004.

Blanford, Nicholas. "Gauge of Mideast Tensions on Lebanon's Border with Israel." *Christian Science Monitor,* 11 August 2004.

Blanford, Nicholas. "Hizbullah Reelects Its Leader." *Christian Science Monitor,* 19 August 2004.

Blanford, Nicholas. "Insurgent and Soldier: Two Views on Iraq Fight." *Christian Science Monitor,* 25 February 2004.

Blanford, Nicholas. "Iraqi Kidnappings Hard to Stop." *Christian Science Monitor,* 9 June 2004.

Blanford, Nicholas and Dan Murphy. "For Al Qaeda, Iraq May Be the Next Battlefield." *Christian Science Monitor,* 25 August 2003.

Bosshart, Dr. Robert Perry (longtime resident of SE Asia and recent contract employee in Afghanistan). In letter to the author of 10 September 2004.

Bowers, Faye. "Al Qaeda's New Young Guard: A Shift in Tactics." *Christian Science Monitor,* 13 February 2004.

Bowers, Faye. "Averting 9/11: How Close We Came." *Christian Science Monitor,* 25 March 2004.

Bowers, Faye. "Iran Shows New Willingness to Deal with U.S." *Christian Science Monitor,* 24 October 2003.

Burke, Jason. "Waiting for a Last Battle with the Taliban."
    The Observer (UK), 27 June 1999. From its website,
    observer.guardian.co.uk.
Burman, Edward. *The Assassins — Holy Killers of Islam.* New
    York: HarperCollins, 1988. In "Origins of the Nizari
    Isma'ilis," from the Ismaili Heritage Society's website,
    www.ismaili.net.
"Bush Administration Is under Increasing Fire for Iraq Policy."
    From Knight Ridder. *Jacksonville (NC) Daily News,* 30 April
    2004.
Can, Nguyen Khac and Pham Viet Thuc. *The War 1858 - 1975
    in Vietnam.* Hanoi: Nha Xuat Ban Van Hoa Dan Toc,
    n.d.
Cass, Connie. Associated Press. "Iraqi Troops Failing."
    Jacksonville (NC) Daily News, 22 April 2004.
Chanda, Nayan. *Brother Enemy: The War after the War.*
    New York: Collier Books, 1986.
"China Puts 700,000 Troops on Alert in Sudan." At newsmax.com,
    27 August 2000.
Clayton, Mark. "Reading into the Mind of a Terrorist." *Christian
    Science Monitor,* 30 October 2003.
Cockburn, Andrew. "Iraq's Oppressed Majority." *Smithsonian,*
    December 2003.
Cole, Juan. "The United States and Shi'ite Religious Factions in
    Post-Ba'thist Iraq." *Middle East Journal,* vol. 57, no. 4,
    autumn 2003.
Collins, Clayton. "War-Zone Security Is a Job for . . . Private
    Contractors." *Christian Science Monitor,* 3 May 2004.
Company and Platoon Drill. Edited by R. Meade. N.p.: British
    War Office, 1914.
The Concise Encyclopedia of Ancient Civilizations. Edited by
    Janet Serlin Garber. New York: Franklin Watts,
    1978.
Constable, Pamela. "Marines Battle Enemy Fighters in Fallujah."
    Washington Post, 6 April 2004. From its website,
    www.washingtonpost.com.
Cooling, Maj. Norman L. "Russia's 1994-96 Campaign for
    Chechnya: A Failure in Shaping the Battlespace." *Marine
    Corps Gazette,* October 2001.
Cooney, Daniel. Associated Press. "Gunmen Kill 4 Iraqis in Attacks
    on Police Officers." *Jacksonville (NC) Daily News,* 4 April 2004.
"Copter Shooters Wising Up." Through access@g2-forward.org on
    17 January 2004.
Crain, Charles. "U.S. Troops Battle al-Sadr Supporters in Najaf."
    USA Today, 13 August 2004.

Daftary, Farhad. *The Assassin Legends: Myths of the Isma'ilis.*
London: I. B. Tauris, 1994; reprinted 2001. In a "Life-Long
Learning" article from the Inst. of Ismaeli Studies website,
www.iis.ac.uk.

Daftary, Farhad. *The Ismaili: Their History and Doctrines.*
Cambridge, UK: Cambridge Univ. Press, 1990. From
the Aga Khan Development website,
www.akdn.org.

Daraghmen, Ali. Associated Press. "Israelis Stop Teen Wearing
Bomb Vest." AOL News, 25 March 2004. From its website,
www.aol.com.

Daraul, Arkon. *Secret Societies.* N.p.: Fine Communications,
1999. From the Ismaili Heritage Society's website,
www.ismaili.net.

Dareini, Ali Akbar. Associated Press. "Iran Ends Talks with U.S.
on Restoring Order to Iraq." *Jacksonville (NC) Daily News,*
15 April 2004.

"A Day with the Assassins." From www.bootsnall.com.

Dehganpisheh, Babak. "A War's Hidden Hands." *Newsweek,*
6 September 2004.

Dehghanpisheh, Babak. "The Shiite Hit List." *Newsweek,*
15 December 2003.

Dehghanpisheh, Babak and Melinda Liu and Rod Nordland. "We
Are Your Martyrs." *Newsweek,* 19 April 2004.

"Despite Having Agreed to a Truce." World News in Brief.
Christian Science Monitor, 11 June 2004.

Deutsch, Antony. Associated Press. "Military Says No Evidence of
Wedding at Attack Site." *Jacksonville (NC) Daily News,*
23 May 2004.

Dick, C.J. "Mujahideen Tactics in the Soviet-Afghan War."
Sandhurst, UK: Conflict Studies Research Centre. From its
website, www.csrc.ac.uk.

Dickey, Christopher and Rod Nordland. "Shiites Unbound."
Newsweek, 1 March 2004.

Dilanian, Ken and Drew Brown. Knight Ridder. "Postwar Iraq Has
Become a Magnet for Terrorists." *Jacksonville (NC) Daily
News,* 24 August 2003.

"DoD Identifies Lejeune Marines Killed in Afghanistan." Staff and
Wire Reports (AP). *Jacksonville (NC) Daily News,* 28 June
2004.

Doran, D'arcy. Associated Press. "Saboteurs Hit Major Iraqi
Oil Pipeline." *Jacksonville (NC) Daily News,* 17 August 2003.

"Double Bombing Kills 11 Israelis, Wounds At Least 18." World
Briefs Wire Reports (AP). *Jacksonville (NC) Daily News,*
15 March 2004.

Dudkevitch, Margot. "3 Soldiers Killed as Tank Hits Mine: Gaza Roadside Attack Is Second in a Month." *Jerusalem Post* (Israel), 15 March 2002. In 20 August 2003 e-mail from pglibbery@hotmail.com and previously from *London Financial Times* website.

Dunnigan, James F. and Albert A. Nofi. *Dirty Little Secrets of the Vietnam War.* New York: Thomas Dunne Books, 1999.

"Dysfunctional Chechnya Votes for President Today." From Associated Press. *Jacksonville (NC) Daily News,* 29 August 2004.

"11 Soldiers Killed in Chechnya." World Briefs Wire Reports (AP). *Jacksonville (NC) Daily News,* 13 April 2004.

Elford, George Robert. *Devil's Guard.* New York: Dell, 1985.

El-Ghoul, Adnan and Khalil Fleihan. "Border Situation Tense after Israeli Airstrike." *Daily Star* (Lebanon), 9 June 2004.

El-Magd, Nadia Abou. Associated Press. "Blood Flows in Baghdad." *Jacksonville (NC) Daily News,* 19 January 2004.

El-Tablawy, Tarek. Associated Press. "Iraq a Fertile Ground for Militants." *Jacksonville (NC) Daily News,* 11 July 2004.

Eshel, Lt.Col. (Ret., IDF) David. "Counterguerrilla Warfare in South Lebanon." *Marine Corps Gazette,* July 1997.

Esposito, John L. *Unholy War: Terror in the Name of Islam.* London: Oxford Univ. Press, 2002.

Evans, Grant and Kelvin Rowley. *Red Brotherhood at War: Indochina Since the Fall of Saigon.* London: Verso, 1984.

Fam, Mariam. Associated Press. "Attacks Intensify in Mosul; Iraqis Seeking Reconciliation with Turkey." *Jacksonville (NC) Daily News,* 6 November 2003.

Fam, Mariam. Associated Press. "Bomber Targets Leading Sheiks, Blows Himself Up." *Jacksonville (NC) Daily News,* 10 February 2004.

Fam, Mariam. Associated Press. "Rebel Assault Routs Iraqi Cops." *Jacksonville (NC) Daily News,* 15 February 2004.

Fam, Mariam. Associated Press. "Rebels Target Iraqis." *Jacksonville (NC) Daily News,* 12 February 2004.

Fam, Mariam. Associated Press. "Suicide Bombing Kills Dozens outside Iraq Police Station." *Jacksonville (NC) Daily News,* 11 February 2004.

Faramarzi, Scheherezade. Associated Press. "Iraqis, U.S. at Odds on Attack." *Jacksonville (NC) Daily News,* 20 May 2004.

Faramarzi, Scheherezade. Associated Press. "Rebels Strike Kurds." *Jacksonville (NC) Daily News,* 2 February 2004.

Faramarzi, Scheherezade. Associated Press. "U.S. Steps Up the Pressure on Iraq Rebels." *Jacksonville (NC) Daily News,* 10 May 2004.

Fasih, Lt. Mehmed. *Gallipoli 1915: Bloody Ridge (Lone Pine) Diary.* Istanbul: Denizler Kitabevi, 1997.

"Fatalities in the al-Aqsa Intifada: 29 September 2000 to 12 July 2004." B'Tselem, the Israeli Info. Center for Human Rights in the Occupied Territories. From its website, www.btslem.org.

Fayadh, Abbas. "Suicide Attacks Kill At Least 68." *Jacksonville (NC) Daily News,* 22 April 2004.

Felgenhauer, Pavel. "Defense Dossier: Guerrilla War Can't Be Won." *Moscow Times,* 9 March 2000. As reprinted in *Center for Defense Info. (CDI) Weekly,* no. 5, 10 March 2000. From its website, www.cdi.org.

Fighel, Col. (Res.) Jonathan. "Sheikh Abdullah Azzam." From the Internat. Policy Inst. for Counter-Terrorism (ICT) website, www.ict.org.

Fighel, Yoni and Yael Shahar. "The Al-Qaida-Hizballah Connection." As posted on 26 February 2002 at the Internat. Policy Inst. for Counter-Terrorism (ICT) website, www.ict.org.

"Fighter Strolls around Sojod Base, Raises Flag, Punches Soldier and Gets Away . . ." *The Daily Star* (Lebanon), 12 August 1998. In 16 August 2003 e-mail from pglibbery@hotmail.com and previously from www.moqawama.tv, a website for the Islamic Resistance Support Organization.

Filkins, Dexter. "Kurds Are Finally Heard: Turkey Burned Our Villages." *The New York Times International,* 24 October 2003.

"For Security Reasons, the Long-Awaited National Election in Postwar Afghanistan." News in Brief. *Christian Science Monitor,* 29 March 2004.

Ford, Peter. "A Suspect Emerges As Key Link in Terror Chain." *Christian Science Monitor,* 23 January 2004.

Gaffney, Fr. Patrick (recognized authority on the Middle East). In a letter to the author, 29 August 2004.

Gardner, David. "Israel: Hizbollah Sharpens Up Its Tactics." *London Financial Times,* 1997. In 11 August 2003 e-mail from pglibbery@hotmail.com and previously from www.moqawama.tv, a website for the Islamic Resistance Support Organization.

Garwood, Paul. Associated Press. "U.S. Toll in Iraq Hits 500 Dead." *Jacksonville (NC) Daily News,* 18 January 2004.

Gavin, Patrick W. "The Martin Luther King Jr. America Has Ignored." *Christian Science Monitor,* 16 January 2004.

"Genesis of the word 'Assassin'." From the Ismaili Heritage Society's website, www.ismaili.net.

Gertz, Bill. "Notes from the Pentagon." *Washington Times,* 5 March 2004. From its website, www.washingtontimes.com.

317

Glibbery, Peter (former British and South African soldier and DoD contractor in Iraq). In e-mails from pglibbery@hotmail.com to the author, 5-16 October 2003.

Goulden, Joseph C. *Korea: The Untold Story of the War.* New York: Times Books, 1982.

Graham, Stephen. Associated Press. "Blast Deadly for U.S." *Jacksonville (NC) Daily News,* 31 January 2004.

Graham, Stephen. Associated Press. "Factional Fighting Spills Afghan Blood." *Jacksonville (NC) Daily News,* 8 February 2004.

Graham, Stephen. Associated Press. "Latest Assault Leaves 2 Brits, Afghan Interpreter Dead." *Jacksonville (NC) Daily News,* 6 May 2004.

Graham, Stephen. Associated Press. "U.S. Commander Pledges Restraint in Afghan Sweeps." *Jacksonville (NC) Daily News,* 10 August 2004.

Graham, Stephen. Associated Press. "U.S. Defends Raid That Killed Afghan Children." *Jacksonville (NC) Daily News,* 11 March 2004.

Graham, Stephen. Associated Press. "U.S. Slams Pakistan in War on Militants." *Jacksonville (NC) Daily News,* 4 May 2004.

Graham, Stephen. Associated Press. "U.S. Urges Afghan Defense Chief to Keep the Peace." *USA Today,* 28 July 2004.

Gray, Denis D. and Scheherezade Faramarzi. Associated Press. "U.S. Balks at Going after Cleric." *Jacksonville (NC) Daily News,* 4 May 2004.

Gray, Denis D. and Scheherezade Faramarzi. Associated Press. "U.S. Seizes Office from Militiamen." *Jacksonville (NC) Daily News,* 7 May 2004.

Green, Thomas S. Green, S.J. *Weeds among the Wheat.* Notre Dame, IN: Ave Maria Press, 1984.

Grier, Peter and Faye Bowers. "Iraq Blast Fits Pattern of Sabotage." *Christian Science Monitor,* 20 August 2003.

Grier, Peter and Faye Bowers. "Iraqi Militants Raise Pitch of Attacks." *Christian Science Monitor,* 22 April 2004.

"Group Says Thousands Ready for Suicide Raids." Across the Region. *Daily Star* (Lebanon), 7 June 2004.

Gudmundsson, Bruce I. *Stormtroop Tactics: Innovation in the German Army 1914-1918.* Westport, CT: Praeger Pubs., 1989.

Halpern, Orly. "U.S. Closes In on Deal with Iraqi Cleric." *Christian Science Monitor,* 25 May 2004.

"Hamas." From the Internat. Policy Inst. for Counter-Terrorism (ICT) website, www.ict.org.

"Hamas and the Al Aqsa Martyrs Brigade Claimed Responsibility for Two Terrorist Explosions." News in Brief. *Christian Science Monitor,* 15 March 2004.

"Hamas Boss Says No Truce with Israel." World Briefs Wire Reports (AP). *Jacksonville (NC) Daily News,* 25 September 2003.

"Hamas Militants Killed in Air Strike." World Briefs Wire Reports (AP). *Jacksonville (NC) Daily News,* 4 March 2004.

Hammel, Eric. *The Root: The Marines in Beirut, August 1982 - February 1984.* Pacifica, CA: Pacifica Press, 1985.

Hammer, Joshua. "Guns over Gaza." *Newsweek,* 5 April 2004.

Hammer, Joshua. "Holding the Line." *Newsweek,* 16 February 2004.

Hanley, Charles J. AP Special Correspondent. "Americans Hunt for Missiles, Clues." *Jacksonville (NC) Daily News,* 4 November 2003.

Hanley, Charles J. AP Special Correspondent. "Attack Dispels Hopes to a Quick End of Fighting in Iraq." *Jacksonville (NC) Daily News,* 3 November 2003.

Hanley, Charles J. AP Special Correspondent. "Attackers Burn, Loot Army Supply Train in Iraq." *Jacksonville (NC) Daily News,* 1 November 2003.

Hanley, Charles J. AP Special Correspondent. "Dozens Killed in Wave of Blasts." *Jacksonville (NC) Daily News,* 28 October 2003.

Hanley, Charles J. AP Special Correspondent. "Rockets Rake Coalition HQ." *Jacksonville (NC) Daily News,* 27 October 2003.

"Harakat ul-Mujahidin Reference Page." From www.military.com, 5 July 2004.

Harding, Andrew. "Grozny Is a City of Rubble." BBC News, 10 March 2000. From its website, news.bbc.co.uk.

Harris, Ron. St. Louis Post-Dispatch. "5 Marines, Scores of Iraqis Die in Battle." *Jacksonville (NC) Daily News,* 18 April 2004.

Harris, Ron. St. Louis Post-Dispatch. "Marines Return to Violent City." *Jacksonville (NC) Daily News,* 19 April 2004.

Harvey, Rache. "Tension Rising in Chechen Conflict." BBC News, 19 August 2002. From its website, www.news.bbc.co.uk.

"Hasan bin Sabbah and the Nizari Ismaili State in Alamut." From the Ismaili Heritage Society's website, www.ismaili.net.

Hatsumi, Dr. Masaaki. *Ninjutsu: History and Tradition.* Burbank, CA: Unique Publications, 1981.

Haven, Paul. Associated Press. "Elders Deny Terrorist Ties." *Jacksonville (NC) Daily News,* 13 April 2004.

Haven, Paul. Associated Press. "Pakistan Traps al-Qaida Target." *Jacksonville (NC) Daily News,* 19 March 2004.

Haven, Paul. Associated Press. "Pakistani Troops May Have al-Zawahri Cornered." AOL News, 18 March 2004. From its website, www.aol.com.

Hayes, Stephen K. *Legacy of the Night Warrior.* Santa Clarita, CA: Ohara Publications, 1985.

Hayes, Stephen K. *The Mystic Arts of the Ninja: Hypnotism, Invisibility, and Weaponry.* Chicago: Contemporary Books, 1985.

Hayes, Stephen K. *The Ninja and Their Secret Fighting Art.* Rutland, VT: Charles E. Tuttle Co., 1981.

Hayes, Stephen K. *Ninjutsu: The Art of the Invisible Warrior.* Chicago: Contemporary Books, 1984.

Hebbar, Harish. "Islam in Modern India." From www.boloji.com, an Indian website.

Hendawi, Hamza, Associated Press. "Big Blasts Rock City near Shrine." *Jacksonville (NC) Daily News,* 14 May 2004.

Hendawi, Hamza. Associated Press. "Deadly Day for U.S. in Iraq." *Jacksonville (NC) Daily News,* 7 April 2004.

Hendawi, Hamza. Associated Press. "Insurgents Fire Rockets at U.S. Coalition Headquarters." *Jacksonville (NC) Daily News,* 8 March 2004.

Hendawi, Hamza. Associated Press. "Insurgents Strike Iraqi Cities, Killing Dozens." AOL News, 24 June 2004. From its website, www.aol.com.

Hendawi, Hamza. Associated Press. "Najaf Battle Grows." *Jacksonville (NC) Daily News,* 15 May 2004.

Hendawi, Hamza. Associated Press. "Police Chief Reinstated after Weekend Clashes." *Jacksonville (NC) Daily News,* 7 October 2003.

Hendawi, Hamza. Associated Press. "Roadside Bombings Kill 6 American Soldiers." *Jacksonville (NC) Daily News,* 28 January 2004.

Hendawi, Hamza. Associated Press. "Shiite Leader Says U.N. Plan Unacceptable." *Jacksonville (NC) Daily News,* 24 January 2004.

Hendawi, Hamza. Associated Press. "Sunni Clerics Join Iraqi Shiites in Show of Unity." *Jacksonville (NC) Daily News,* 4 March 2004.

Hendawi, Hamza and Tarek al-Issawi. Associated Press. "Suicide Attacks Kill More Than 140 at Iraqi Shiite Shrines." *Jacksonville (NC) Daily News,* 3 March 2004.

"Hezbollah." *Encyclopedia.* At www.nationmaster.com, 5 July 2004.

"Hezbollah Ideology." From www.military.com, 18 June 2004.

"Hezbollah Reference Page." From www.military.com, 17 June 2004.

Hider, James. "Iraq's Leaky Border with Iran." *Christian Science Monitor,* 27 August 2003.

Hiro, Dilip. *The Longest War: The Iran-Iraq Military Conflict.*
New York: Routledge, 1991.

"Hizballah." As extracted from an article by the Info. Div, Israel
Foreign Ministry in Jerusalem. And posted on the Internat.
Policy Inst. for Counter-Terrorism (ICT) website,
www.ict.org.

Hockstader, Lee. "Israeli Army Suffers Pair of Sharp Blows."
International Herald Tribune, 16 February 2002. Reprinted
from *Washington Post,* n.d.

Hollis, Christopher and Ronald Brownrigg. *Holy Places: Jewish,
Christian, and Moslem Monuments in the Holy Land.*
New York: Praeger Publishers, 1969.

Housego, Kim. Associated Press. "I MEF Loses 7 in Blast."
Jacksonville (NC) Daily News, 7 September 2004.

"Hundreds Have Entered Iraq from Saudi Arabia Disguised
As Shi'ite Pilgrims." *Geostrategy-Direct,* 16 March 2004.
From seth.axelrod@ngc.com through
access@g2-forward.org.

Hunt, Terence. Associated Press. "Annan Says U.S. Will Back U.N.
Plan for Iraqi Vote." *Jacksonville (NC) Daily News,* 4 February
2004.

"Hypnosis." Chapt. in *The Complete Manual of Fitness and
Well-Being.* Pleasantville, NY: The Reader's Digest Assn.,
1984.

Ignatius, David. "Hezbollah's Success." *Washington Post,*
23 September 2003. From its website,
www.washingtonpost.com.

"In a Time of War." Photograph caption. *Newsweek,* 29 December
2003.

"Iran's Besharati, RafiqDust in Syria for Talks." *Paris* (Agence
France-Press [AFP]), 12 May 1988, English edition. In *The
Warriors of Islam,* by Kenneth Katzman. Boulder, CO:
Westview Press, 1993.

"Iran Report." Radio Free Europe/Radio Liberty, vol. 5, no. 3,
28 January 2002. From its website www.rferl.org via
www.globalsecurity.org.

"Iran Signs $20-Billion Gas Deal with China." United Press
International, 20 March 2004. From bdillon@pacbell.net
through access@g2-forward.org.

"Iraq: New Fears of Suicide Blasts." From bdillon@pacbell.net
through access@g2-forward.org on 12 April 2004.

"Iraq Blasts Damage Oil Pipeline, Hit Exports." Reuters. *Turkish
Daily News* (Istanbul), 16 June 2004.

"Iraq Militant OKs Peace Plan." From Associated Press. *Jacksonville
(NC) Daily News,* 19 August 2004.

"Iraq's Coalition of the Willing." Reuters News Service. *Christian Science Monitor,* 27 July 2004.

Islam Empire of Faith. PBS Home Video (Garner Films in conjunction with PBS and Devillier Donegan Enterprises), videocassette #B8511.

"Ismaili Mission in Syria." From the Ismaili Heritage Society's website, www.ismaili.net.

"Israeli: Palestinians Get Bonus for Killings." World Briefs Wire Reports (AP). *Jacksonville (NC) Daily News,* 25 February 2004.

"Israeli Troops Enter Camp on Gaza-Egyptian Border." News Digest Wire Reports (AP). *Jacksonville (NC) Daily News,* 10 October 2003.

Iyer, Pico. "Grim Reminders of the Ancient Assassins." *Smithsonian,* October 1986.

Jelinek, Pauline. Associated Press. "U.S. Plans Spring Offensive in Afghanistan." AOL News, 30 January 2004. From its website.

Jensen, Ron. "No Cushy Ride for Supply Troops in Iraq." *Stars & Stripes,* 22 October 2003, Mideast edition.

Jerges, Sabah. Associated Press. "Iraqi Insurgency's New Lethal Phase." *Jacksonville (NC) Daily News,* 2 December 2003.

The Jerusalem Bible. Edited by Alexander Jones et al. Garden City, NY: Doubleday, 1966. Romans 12 (19-21).

Johnson, Ed. Associated Press. "U.S. Allies in Iraq Refuse to Waiver." *Jacksonville (NC) Daily News,* 16 March 2004.

Johnson, Scott. "Inside an Enemy Cell." *Newsweek,* 18 August 2003.

Johnson, Scott and Babak Dehghanpisheh. "It's Worse Than You Think." *Newsweek,* 20 September 2004.

Joshi, Vijay. Associated Press. "Nine Killed in Iraqi Violence." *Jacksonville (NC) Daily News,* 23 January 2004.

Joshi, Vijay. Associated Press. "U.S. Apache Helicopter Shot Down over Iraq." *Jacksonville (NC) Daily News,* 14 January 2004.

Joshi, Vijay. Associated Press. "U.S. Commander Says al-Qaida Working in Iraq." AOL News, 30 January 2004. From its website, www.aol.com.

Kaplan, Robert D. *Soldiers of God: With Islamic Warriors in Afghanistan and Pakistan.* Revised edition. New York: Vintage Books, 2001.

Kasem, Halima. "Brewing Power Struggle in Kabul." *Christian Science Monitor,* 17 October 2003.

Katzman, Kenneth. *Warriors of Islam: Iran's Revolutionary Guard.* Boulder, CO: Westview Press, 1993.

Keath, Lee. Associated Press. "Chaos Grips Iraq." *Jacksonville (NC) Daily News,* 10 April 2004.

Keath, Lee. Associated Press. "Mediation Continues on Iraqi Constitution." *Jacksonville (NC) Daily News,* 1 March 2004.

Keath, Lee. Associated Press. "Shiite Militias Control Three Iraqi Cities." *Jacksonville (NC) Daily News,* 9 April 2004.

Keath, Lee. Associated Press. "Shiites Retreat in Najaf." *Jacksonville (NC) Daily News,* 13 April 2004.

Keath, Lee. Associated Press. "Two Crew Members Killed As U.S. Copter Crashes in Euphrates." *Jacksonville (NC) Daily News,* 26 February 2004.

Keath, Lee. Associated Press. "Two U.S. Officials Killed by Gunmen." *Jacksonville (NC) Daily News,* 11 March 2004.

Kelley, Matt. Associated Press. "Rumsfeld Trip Highlights Accomplishments in Iraq." *Jacksonville (NC) Daily News,* 5 September 2003.

Keyser, Jason. Associated Press. "Israel Bombs Syria." *Jacksonville (NC) Daily News,* 6 October 2003.

Keyser, Jason. Associated Press. "Rock and Roll and Killer Flies on Front Line." *Jacksonville (NC) Daily News,* 17 April 2004.

Keyser, Jason and Lourdes Navarro. Associated Press. "Marines in Heavy Night Fighting." *Jacksonville (NC) Daily News,* 15 April 2004.

Khan, Noor. Associated Press. "Afghan Officials Report U.S. Air Raid Kills 11 Civilians." *Jacksonville (NC) Daily News,* 20 January 2004.

Khan, Noor. Associated Press. "Police Swarm Village after Attack on Copter." *Jacksonville (NC) Daily News,* 24 February 2004.

Khan, Riaz. Associated Press. "U.S. Assists Pakistan in Battle." *Jacksonville (NC) Daily News,* 20 March 2004.

Khan, Noor. Associated Press. "U.S. Company's Copter Hit in Afghanistan." *Jacksonville (NC) Daily News,* 23 February 2004.

Kim, Ashida. *Secrets of the Ninja.* New York: Citadel Press, 1981.

Kirka, Danica. Associated Press. "Philippines Pulls More Troops from Iraq." *Jacksonville (NC) Daily News,* 17 July 2004.

Kirka, Danica. Associated Press. "U.S. Bombs Insurgent-Held Iraqi Cities." AOL News, 9 September 2004. From its website, www.aol.com.

Knickerbocker, Brad. "Guerrilla Tactics vs. U.S. War Plan." *Christian Science Monitor,* 25 March 2003.

Knickerbocker, Brad. "How Iraq Will Change U.S. Military Doctrine." *Christian Science Monitor,* 2 July 2004.

Knickerbocker, Brad. "Who Counts Civilian Casualties." *Christian Science Monitor,* 31 March 2004.

Krane, Jim. Associated Press. "American Disappeared a Week Ago." *Jacksonville (NC) Daily News,* 17 April 2004.

Krane, Jim and Hamza Hendawi. Associated Press. "Blast Destroys Baghdad Hotel." *Jacksonville (NC) Daily News,* 18 March 2004.

Krane, Jim. Associated Press. "Iraq Insurgent Force May Number 20,000." AOL News, 9 July 2004. From its website, www.aol.com.

Krane, Jim. Associated Press. "Iraqi Insurgents Use Tactics They Learned from Chechens, Taliban, Al-Qaida." *Herald Sun* (Australia), 6 January 2004. From access@g-2forward.org.

Krane, Jim. Associated Press. "Private Army Grows Up around U.S. Military." *Jacksonville (NC) Daily News,* 30 October 2003.

Krane, Jim. Associated Press. "Rebels among the Force." *Jacksonville (NC) Daily News,* 30 April 2004.

Krane, Jim. Associated Press. "Strike Kills 16 in Iraq." *Jacksonville (NC) Daily News,* 20 June 2004.

Krane, Jim. Associated Press. "U.S. Gets Closer Look at Killer Opposition in Iraq." *Jacksonville (NC) Daily News,* 2 December 2003.

Krane, Jim. Associated Press. "U.S. Split on Foreign Involvement in Iraq." *Jacksonville (NC) Daily News,* 5 March 2004.

Kratovac, Katarina. Associated Press. "Attacks Kill 3 American Soldiers." *Jacksonville (NC) Daily News,* 14 October 2003.

Lafranchi, Howard. "Anti-Iran Sentiment Hardening Fast." *Christian Science Monitor,* 22 July 2004.

Lafranchi, Howard. "Why Anti-U.S. Fighting Grows in Iraq." *Christian Science Monitor,* 6 November 2003.

Lafranchi, Howard and Nick Blanford. "Iraq Bombings Designed to Divide." *Christian Science Monitor,* 12 February 2004.

Lambroschini, Sophie. "Russia: Self-Deception Underlie Recent Chechen Debacles." *Center for Defense Info. (CDI) Weekly,* no. 4,10 March 2000. From their website, www.cdi.org.

Lamont, Lt.Col. Robert W. "A Tale of Two Cities—Hue and Khorramshahr." *Marine Corps Gazette,* April 1999.

Lamont, Lt.Col. Robert W. "'Urban Warrior'—A View from North Vietnam." *Marine Corps Gazette,* April 1999.

Lekic, Slobodan. Associated Press. "Truck Bomb Hits Italians at Iraq Base." *Jacksonville (NC) Daily News,* 13 November 2003.

Lewis, Bernard. *The Crisis of Islam: Holy War and Unholy Terror* (isbn 0739302191). Random House Audio Books, #RHCD251.

Lind, William S. (author of *Maneuver Warfare Handbook).* In telephone conversation with the author, February 2001.

Lind, William S. "Fourth Generation Warfare's First Blow: A Quick Look." *Marine Corps Gazette,* November 2001.

Lind, William S. *The Maneuver Warfare Handbook.* Boulder, CO: Westview Press, 1985.

Lind, William S., Maj. John F. Schmitt, and Col. Gary I. Wilson. "Fourth Generation Warfare: Another Look." *Marine Corps Gazette,* December 1994; reprint November 2001.

Lind, William S., Col. Keith Nightengale, Capt. John F. Schmitt, Col. Joseph W. Sutton, and Lt.Col. Gary I. Wilson. "The Changing Face of War: Into the Fourth Generation." *Marine Corps Gazette,* October 1989; reprint November 2001.

Lumpkin, John J. Associated Press. "U.S. Identifies Sources of Much Iraqi Violence." *Jacksonville (NC) Daily News,* 14 November 2003.

Lumpkin, John J. Associated Press. "U.S. Says Al-Qaeda Sympathizers Are Eyeing Iraq." *Jacksonville (NC) Daily News,* 15 October 2003.

Lung, Dr. Haha. *Knights of Darkness: Secrets of the World's Deadliest Night Fighters.* Boulder, CO: Paladin Press, 1998.

Lynfield, Ben. "Hamas Seeks Primacy in Gaza." *Christian Science Monitor,* 3 March 2004.

Lynfield, Ben. "Palestinian Security Feud Heats Up." *The Christian Science Monitor,* 26 August 2003.

MacFarquahar, Neil. "Hezbollah Becomes Potent Anti-U.S. Force." *New York Times,* 24 December 2002. As reproduced at www.free-lebanon.com.

Mao Tse-tung: An Anthology of His Writings. Edited by Anne Fremantle. New York: Mentor, 1962.

"Marines Tackle Rebellion in Fallujah." From Knight Ridder. *Jacksonville (NC) Daily News,* 28 March 2004.

McCrery, Nigel. *All the King's Men.* New York: Simon & Schuster, 1999. Previously titled *The Vanished Battalion.*

McDowell, Patrick. Associated Press. "Pakistan Goes After Terrorists on Border." *Jacksonville (NC) Daily News,* 9 January 2004.

McForan, Desmond. *The World Held Hostage: The War Waged by International Terrorism.* New York: St. Martin's Press, 1986.

McGirk, Tim. "Battle in 'the Evilest Place'." *Time Magazine,* 3 November 2003, East Asia edition.

Meets, Bremer. "Iraqi Fears Aiding Terror." *Jacksonville (NC) Daily News,* 12 November 2003.

Melman, Yossi. "Ambush of Naval Squad 'No Accident'." *Ha'aretz* (Tel Aviv), 13 August 1998. In 13 August 2003 e-mail from pglibbery@hotmail.com and first from www.moqawama.tv, a website for the Islamic Resistance Support Organization.

"Militants Target Israeli Army Outpost." Associated Press. *USA Today,* 27 June 2004. From its website, www.usatoday.com.

"Military Says Attack Target Was Safehouse." Associated Press. *Jacksonville (NC) Daily News,* 21 May 2004.

Mohammed, Khalid. Associated Press. "Deadly Day inside Iraq."
    Jacksonville (NC) Daily News, 5 April 2004.
Mollo, Andrew and Digby Smith. *World Army Uniforms Since 1939.*
    Part 2. Poole, UK: Blandford Press, 1981.
"The Mongol Empire." World of Wonder. *Jacksonville (NC) Daily
    News,* n.d.
Moore, Wes. "Hasan bin Sabbah and the Secret Order of
    Hashishins." From alephegeis@disinfo.net of 22 March 2001,
    as posted on www.disinfo.com.
Moreau, Ron and Sami Yousafzai and Zahid Hussain. "Holy War
    101." *Newsweek,* 1 December 2003.
Morris, Harvey and Avi Machlis. "Palestinian Checkpoint Sniper
    Kills 10 Israelis." *London Financial Times,* 4 March
    2002.
Mroue, Bassem. Associated Press. "Army Shifts Helicopter Flight
    Routes." *Jacksonville (NC) Daily News,* 18 November 2003.
Mroue, Bassem. Associated Press. "Fallujah Fight Rages."
    Jacksonville (NC) Daily News, 27 April 2004.
Mroue, Bassem and Abdul-Qader Saadi. Associated Press.
    "Fighting Spreads in Iraq." *Jacksonville (NC) Daily News,*
    8 April 2004.
Murphy, Dan. "As Violence Rises, Rebuilding Stalls." *Christian
    Science Monitor,* 16 April 2004.
Murphy, Dan. "Can Self-Rule Bring Security?" *Christian Science
    Monitor,* 25 June 2004.
Murphy, Dan. "In Iraq, a 'Perfect Storm'." *Christian Science
    Monitor,* 9 April 2004.
Murphy, Dan. "In the New Iraq, Local Officials Put Lives
    on the Line." *Christian Science Monitor,* 7 November 2003.
Murphy, Dan. "In Tough Iraq Conflict, Civilians Pay High Price."
    Christian Science Monitor, 21 January 2004.
Murphy, Dan. "Iraq Bombs Hit Kurdish Leaders." *Christian
    Science Monitor,* 2 February 2004.
Murphy, Dan. "Iraqi Shiite Split Widens." *Christian Science
    Monitor,* 15 October 2003.
Murphy, Dan. "Moderate Shiites Gaining New Clout." *Christian
    Science Monitor,* 12 April 2004.
Murphy, Dan. "No Wide Shiite Rally to Sadr's Forces." *Christian
    Science Monitor,* 7 April 2004.
Murphy, Dan. "Sadr Army Owns City Streets." *Christian Science
    Monitor,* 4 August 2004.
Murphy, Dan. "Sadr the Agitator: Like Father, Like Son."
    Christian Science Monitor, 27 April 2004.
Murphy, Dan. "Second Front in Iraq: Shiite Revolt." *Christian
    Science Monitor,* 6 April 2004.

Murphy, Dan. "Shiites Taxing U.S. Forces." *Christian Science Monitor,* 8 April 2004.

Nalls, Capt. John B. "A Company Commander's Thoughts on Iraq." *Armor Magazine,* February 2004.

Navarro, Lourdes. Associated Press. "More Marines Join the Fight." *Jacksonville (NC) Daily News,* 11 April 2004.

"Nearly 40 People Stopped at Border." Across the Region. *Daily Star* (Lebanon), 8 June 2004.

Nessman, Ravi. Associated Press. "U.S. Launches Airstrike in Fallujah." *Jacksonville (NC) Daily News,* 6 July 2004.

"Nights of Fear in Chechnya's Mountains." *Irish Examiner,* 21 March 2000. From its website, archives.tcm.ie.

"The 9/11 Commission Report: The Terrorist Plot." *Los Angeles Times,* 23 July 2004.

Nordland, Rod. "Corkscrew over Baghdad." *Newsweek International,* 27 October 2003, Southeast Asia edition.

Nordland, Rod and Melinda Liu and Scott Johnson. "The Dark Road Ahead." *Newsweek,* 12 April 2004.

O'Balance, Edgar. "The Iranian Armed Forces." *Marine Corps Gazette,* August 1980.

"Official Insists U.S. Still Has Initiative in Iraq; Two Paratroopers Killed." News Digest Wire Reports (AP). *Jacksonville (NC) Daily News,* 9 November 2003.

"Oldest Iranian Qanat Found in Bam." *Tehran Times* (Iran), 5 June 2004.

Ostrovsky, Simon. "A Soldier's Tale of Fear and Loathing." *Moscow Times,* 17 March 2004. In seth.axelrod@ngc.com from access@g2-forward.org.

O'Sullivan, Arieh. "A Much More Worrisome Ambush." *Jerusalem Post* (Israel), 15 March 2002. In 20 August 2003 e-mail from pglibbery@hotmail.com and previously from *London Financial Times* website.

"Pakistan's Double Standards." *Pravda* (Russia), 18 September 2001.

Pennington, Matthew. Associated Press. "Pakistan Unsure If Target Is al-Zawahri." *Jacksonville (NC) Daily News,* 21 March 2004.

Pereira, Guilherme (DoD contract employee in Iraq). In telephone conversation with author, 28 June 2004.

Peters, Gretchen. "Bin Laden's Hideout in Wilds of Pakistan." *Christian Science Monitor,* 15 September 2003.

Peters, Gretchen. "Foreign Fighters Snub Pakistan's Olive Branch." *Christian Science Monitor,* 3 May 2004.

Peterson, Scott. "Chechen Rebels' Deadly Return." *Christian Science Monitor,* 23 June 2004.

Peterson, Scott. "Economic Fallout of $50 a Barrel." *Christian Science Monitor,* 27 August 2004.

Peterson, Scott. "Fallujah Firefight Rekindles." *Christian Science Monitor,* 27 April 2004.

Peterson, Scott. "Hostile in Public, Iran Seeks Quiet Discourse with U.S." *Christian Science Monitor,* 25 September 2003.

Peterson, Scott. "In a War It Cannot Win, Israel Tries New Tactics." *Christian Science Monitor,* 9/20 October 1997. In 16 August 2003 e-mail from pglibbery@hotmail.com and previously from www.moqawama.tv, a website for the Islamic Resistance Support Organization.

Peterson, Scott. "Iran's Revolution at 25: Out of Gas." *The Christian Science Monitor,* 11 February 2004.

Peterson, Scott. "Iraqi Police Walk Perilous Beat." *Christian Science Monitor,* 23 January 2004.

Peterson, Scott. "Revenge Fuels Chechen Flames." *Christian Science Monitor,* 8 October 2003.

Peterson, Scott. "The Rise and Fall of Ansar al-Islam." *Christian Science Monitor,* 16 October 2003.

Peterson, Scott. "Shadows of Tehran over Iraq." *Christian Science Monitor,* 19 April 2004.

Peterson, Scott. "Tough U.S. Tactics Quell Fallujah Unrest, But at What Cost." *Christian Science Monitor,* 20 April 2004.

Peterson, Scott. "U.S. Pressure on Cleric Pushes Militants South." *Christian Science Monitor,* 10 May 2004.

Petre, F. Loraine. "The 1/4th and 1/5th Battalions (Territorial)." Chapt. 4 of vol. II (4th August 1914 to 31st December 1918) in *The History of the Norfolk Regiment: 1685-1918.* Norwich, UK: Jarrold & Sons Ltd., the Empire Press, n.d. From user.glo.be/~snelders/sand.htm.

Pilipchuk, Andrei. Translated by A. Ignatkin. "Colonel General Vladimir Moltenshoy: We Grab the Criminals by the Short and Curlies." *Krasnaya Zvezda* (Russia), 28 September 2002.

Pilipchuk, Andrei. Translated by A. Ignatkin. "Colonel General Vladimir Moltenshoy: The People of Chechnya Are Not Silent." *Krasnaya Zvezda* (Russia), 11 June 2002.

Pintak, Lawrence. *Seeds of Hate: How America's Flawed Middle East Policy Ignited the Jihad.* London: Pluto Press, 2003.

Pitman, Todd. Associated Press. "Being an Iraqi Cop No Longer a Cushy Job." *Jacksonville (NC) Daily News,* 1 August 2004.

Pitman, Todd. Associated Press. "Jets Target Rebels," *Jacksonville (NC) Daily News,* 1 July 2004.

Pitman, Todd. Associated Press. "Marines Seal Off Holy City." *Jacksonville (NC) Daily News,* 13 August 2004.

Pitman, Todd. Associated Press. "Strike Targets Terrorist."
   Jacksonville (NC) Daily News, 26 June 2004.
Pitman, Todd. Associated Press. "3 Marines Die in Convoy Blast,"
   Jacksonville (NC) Daily News, 30 June 2004.
Pitman, Todd. Associated Press. "U.S. Warplanes Bomb Suspected
   Terror Den." *Jacksonville (NC) Daily News,* 2 July 2004.
Plushnick-Masti, Ramit. Associated Press. "Militant Groups Join
   Forces, Get Hezbollah Help." *Jacksonville (NC) Daily News,*
   28 October 2003.
Pope John Paul II. As quoted in "Witness to Hope: The Life of Karol
   Wojtyka, Pope John Paul II." PBS TV, n.d.
Pope John Paul II. *Crossing the Threshold of Hope.* New York:
   Alfred A. Knopf, 1995.
Price, Niko. Associated Press. "Official: Ministry Ordered a Halt to
   Civilian Toll Count." *Jacksonville (NC) Daily News,*
   11 December 2003.
Price, Niko. Associated Press. "Rebel Attack Turns into a Big
   Firefight." *Jacksonville (NC) Daily News,* 1 December
   2003.
Prusher, Ilene. "As Life Looks Bleaker, Suicide Bombers Get
   Younger." *Christian Science Monitor,* 5 March 2004.
Prusher, Ilene. "Turkist Conscripts Likely to Be Least Willing
   of the Coalition." *Christian Science Monitor,* 16 October 2003.
Prusher, Ilene R. and Ben Lynfield. "Killing of Yassin a Turning
   Point." *Christian Science Monitor,* 23 March 2004.
Rahi, Aijaz. Associated Press. "Anger and Confusion." *Jacksonville
   (NC) Daily News,* 8 December 2003.
"Rebel Ambush Leaves 37 Russians Dead in Chechnya." CNN
   News, 3 March 2000. From its website,
   www.cnn.com.
Reid, Robert H. Associated Press. "Car Bombs, Armed Attacks Take
   a Heavy Toll." *Jacksonville Daily News,* 25 June 2004.
Reid, Robert H. Associated Press. "5 Americans Die in Iraq."
   Jacksonville Daily News, 25 January 2004.
Reid, Robert H. Associated Press. "Insurgents Gun Down 4
   Marines." *Jacksonville Daily News,* 22 June 2004.
Reid, Robert H. Associated Press. "Militants Behead South Korean
   Hostage." *Jacksonville (NC) Daily News,* 23 June
   2004.
Reid, Robert H. Associated Press. "Netherlands Embassy
   Attacked in Baghdad." *Jacksonville (NC) Daily News,*
   31 January 2004.
Reid, Robert H. Associated Press. "U.S. Says It Never Had Custody
   of Beheaded American." AOL News, 12 May 2004. From its
   website, www.aol.com.

Reinke, Dr. David H. (expert on parapsychology and Eastern religions). In e-mails from drdavidhreinke to the author, October 2003 - August 2004.

Ricks, Thomas. E. "For Zinni, a War That Ignores the Facts." *Washington Post,* 12-18 January 2004, nat. weekly edition.

Ritter, Scott. "Defining the Resistance in Iraq—It's Not Foreign and It's Well Prepared." *Christian Science Monitor,* 10 November 2003.

Roman, Mar. Associated Press. "Terror Suspects Kill Selves As Spanish Police Close In." *Jacksonville (NC) Daily News,* 4 April 2004.

Rudge, David. "IDF Probes Hizbullah Infiltration 2 Soldiers Wounded in South Lebanon." *Jerusalem Post* (Israel), 12 August 1998, daily edition. In 20 August 2003 e-mail from pglibbery@hotmail.com and previously from *Jerusalem Post* website archives.

"Russian Team Promises Renewed Effort to Rebuild Chechnya." Reuters. *Christian Science Monitor,* 17 May 2004.

Saadi, Abdul-Qader and Lourdnes Navarro. Associated Press. "Uneasy Truce Holds in Fallujah." *Jacksonville (NC) Daily News,* 12 April 2004.

"Sacrifices of the Fidais." From the Ismaili Heritage Society's website, www.ismaili.net.

Samuel, L.Cpl. (casualty from 2d Battalion, 8th Marines). In conversation with author, 12 March 2004.

Schwartz, T.P. "The Qur'an as a Guide to Conduct of and in War, Including Treatment of Prisoners of War." *Marine Corps Gazette,* February 2002.

Schwartz, T.P. "Waging War against Hostile Combat Units That Fight According to *Al Qur'an.*" *Marine Corps Gazette,* September 2002.

"Scores Feared Dead in Chechnya Crash." BBC News, 19 August 2002. From its website, www.news.bbc.co.uk.

"The Second Chechen War." *P31.* Edited by Mrs. A.C. Aldis. Sandhurst, UK: Conflict Studies Research Centre, June 2000. From its website, www.da.mod.uk.

Segal, Naomi. Jewish Telegraphic Agency. "IDF Absolved of Blame in Deaths of Naval Commandos in Lebanon." *San Francisco Jewish Community Publication,* 31 October 1997. In 19 August 2003 e-mail from pglibbery@hotmail.com.

Shadid, Anthony. "Heavy Fighting, U.S. Casualties in Ramadi." *Washington Post,* 6 April 2004. Through access@g2-forward.org.

Shah, Amir. Associated Press. "U.S.-Brokered Cease-Fire Halts Deadly Afghan Infighting." *Jacksonville (NC) Daily News,* 18 August 2004.

"Shiite Radicals Join with Sunni Insurgents in Ramadi." *DEBKAfile* (Israeli Political Analysis, Espionage, Terrorism Security Bulletin), 7 April 2004. Through access@g2-forward.org.

"Shiites March throughout the Middle East." From Associated Press. *Jacksonville (NC) Daily News,* 22 May 2004.

Shipunov, Arkady and Gennady Filimonov. "Field Artillery to Be Replaced with Shmel Infantry Flamethrower." *Military Parade Magazine,* no. 29, September 1998. From its website, www.milparade.com.

Shirazi, Mohammad. *Psychological Warfare and Propaganda Concepts and Applications.* Second edition. Tehran: Secretariat of the First Conference on the Role of Propaganda in War, 2001; prepared in the Public Relations and Publications Directorial of the Office of the Representative of the Supreme Leader [Vali-e Faghih] in the Faculty of Command and Control of the Islamic Revolutionary Guards Corps [of Iran].

"Son of *al-Qaeda.*" *Frontline.* NC Public TV, 22 April 2004. From pbs.org.

Stahl, Julie. "'Paradise Camps' Teach Palestinian Children to Be Suicide Bombers." *Cybercast News Service,* 23 July 2001. From its website, www.cnsnews.com.

"The Striving Sheik: Abdullah Azzam." *Nida'ul Islam Magazine,* no. 14, July-September 1996. From www.islam.org.au.

Strobel, Warren P. Knight Ridder. "Bush Abandons Initial Blueprint." *Jacksonville (NC) Daily News,* 1 May 2004.

Suellentrop, Chris. "Abdullah Azzam - The Godfather of Jihad." From slate.msn.com.

"Suicide Bomber Kills Peacekeeper, Civilian in Afghan Capital." World Briefs Wire Reports (AP). *Jacksonville (NC) Daily News,* 28 January 2004.

Sukhtian, Lara. Associated Press. "Palestinians Bury Leader Killed by Israel." *Jacksonville (NC) Daily News,* 23 March 2004.

Sun Tzu. *The Art of War.* Translated and with introduction by Samuel B. Griffith, foreword by B.H. Liddell Hart. New York: Oxford Univ. Press, 1963.

"Taliban Blamed for Deadly Afghan Resistance." World Briefs Wire Reports (AP). *Jacksonville (NC) Daily News,* 24 September 2003.

Tarabay, Jamie. Associated Press. "U.S. Chopper Downed amid Fierce Fighting in Iraq." AOL News, 5 August 2004. From its website, www.aol.com.

Taylor, Jeffrey. "Georgia at a Crossroads." *Smithsonian,* April 2004.

"Terrorism by Muslim Radicals." News in Brief. *Christian Science Monitor,* 31 March 2004.

Theyson, Art. "New Warfront Opens in Iraq Three Months before Handover." *DEBKAfile* (Israeli Political Analysis, Espionage, Terrorism Security Bulletin), 5 April 2004. Through access@g2-forward.org.

Thomas, Evan. "Groping in the Dark." *Newsweek,* 1 September 2003.

Thomas, Evan. "The Vietnam Question." *Newsweek,* 19 April 2004.

Thomas, Evan and Babak Dehghanpisheh. "Inside Red Dawn: Saddam Up Close." *Newsweek,* 29 December 2003.

Thomas, Evan and John Barry. "A Plan under Attack." *Newsweek,* 7 April 2003.

Thomas, Evan and Rod Nordland. "How We Got Saddam." *Newsweek,* 22 December 2003.

Thomas, Lt.Col. Timothy L. and Lester W. Grau. "Russian Lessons Learned from the Battles for Grozny." *Marine Corps Gazette,* April 2000.

Tohid, Owais. "Al Qaeda Supporters Strike Back in Pakistan." *Christian Science Monitor,* 25 March 2004.

Tohid, Owais. "Pakistan Marks Pro-Al Qaeda Clan." *Christian Science Monitor,* 23 March 2004.

Tohid, Owais. "Pakistan Tries Amnesty to Stem Support for Al Qaeda." *Christian Science Monitor,* 26 April 2004.

Tohid, Owais. "Tribes Inflamed by Qaeda Hunt." *Christian Science Monitor,* 20 October 2003.

Tohid, Owais and Faye Bowers. "U.S. Pakistan Tighten Net on Al Qaeda." *Christian Science Monitor,* 22 March 2004.

Tohid, Owais and Scott Baldauf. "Pakistani Army Must Go through the Pashtuns." *Christian Science Monitor,* 25 June 2004.

Tomlinson, Chris. Associated Press. "Bomb Blast Kills 2 Iraqi Soldiers." *Jacksonville (NC) Daily News,* 21 June 2004.

Tomlinson, Chris. Associated Press. "Militants Threaten to Behead Hostages." *Jacksonville (NC) Daily News,* 28 June 2004.

Topol, Allan. "Why Turkey?" From www.military.com, 26 November 2003.

Torchia, Christopher. Associated Press. "Attacks on Foreign Civilians Suggest Tactics Change by Rebels." *Jacksonville (NC) Daily News,* 17 March 2004.

Torchia, Christopher. Associated Press. "Gunmen Kill 3 Iraqi Women Working for Coalition." *Jacksonville (NC) Daily News,* 17 May 2004.

Torchia, Christopher. Associated Press. "Marine among the Dead." *Jacksonville (NC) Daily News,* 27 March 2004.

Torchia, Christopher. Associated Press. "More Policemen Shot Dead in Iraq." *Jacksonville (NC) Daily News,* 24 March 2004.

Torchia, Christopher. Associated Press. "Terror Mounts in Iraq." *Jacksonville (NC) Daily News,* 19 March 2004.

Torchia, Christopher. Associated Press. "Violence Unsettles Iraqi Life." *Jacksonville (NC) Daily News,* 21 March 2004.

The Travels of Marco Polo, The Venetian. Translated and edited by William Marsden and re-edited by Thomas Wright. N.p.: publisher not provided, n.d. From the China Inst. website, www.china-institut.org, and the Ismaili Heritage Society's website, www.ismaili.net.

"Truth, War, and Consequences." *Frontline.* NC Public TV, 9 October 2003.

"Two U.S. Soldiers Killed in Iraqi Roadside Blast." World Briefs Wire Reports (AP). *Jacksonville (NC) Daily News,* 13 March 2004.

Tyson, Ann Scott. "At Sprawling U.S. Airbase in Iraq, a Crescendo in Attacks." *Christian Science Monitor,* 1 July 2004.

Tyson, Ann Scott. "Going in Small in Afghanistan." *Christian Science Monitor,* 14 January 2004.

Tyson, Ann Scott. "Inside One Day's Fierce Battle in Iraq." *Christian Science Monitor,* 21 July 2004.

Tyson, Ann Scott. "Sadr's Militia Regrouping, Rearming," *Christian Science Monitor,* 15 July 2004.

"Ugarit: Archeological Background." From the Quartz Hill School of Theology website, www.theology.edu.

"United Nations Refugee Worker from France Is Shot to Death in Afghanistan." News Digest Wire Reports (AP). *Jacksonville (NC) Daily News,* 17 November 2003.

"U.S. Casualties Mount in Iraq Despite Talk of 'Turning the Corner'." News Digest Wire Reports (AP). *Jacksonville (NC) Daily News,* 4 February 2004.

"U.S. Forces in Afghanistan Were Alerted to Prepare for a New 'Spring Offensive'." News in Brief. *Christian Science Monitor,* 29 January 2004.

"U.S. Soldier Killed in Grenade Attack." News Digest Wire Reports (AP). *Jacksonville (NC) Daily News,* 27 September 2003.

"U.S. Vetoes Resolution to Hamas' Leader Death." News Digest Wire Reports (AP). *Jacksonville (NC) Daily News,* 26 March 2004.

Van Creveld, Martin. *The Sword and the Olive: A Critical History of the Israeli Defense Force.* New York: PublicAffairs, Perseus Books, 1998.

Venzke, Ben and Aimee Ibrahim. *The al-Qaeda Threat: An Analytical Guide to al-Qaeda's Tactics and Targets.* Alexandria, VA: Tempest Publishing, 2003.

"Violence Surge Threatens Vote Exit Strategy." By Knight Ridder. *Jacksonville (NC) Daily News,* 15 September 2004.

Walcott, John. Knight Ridder. "Guerrilla Strikes a Part of Larger Strategy among Iraqi Insurgents." *Jacksonville (NC) Daily News,* 1 December 2003.

Walker, Cpl. Ryan. "SRT Trains to Go beyond Call of Duty." *Camp Lejeune Globe,* 29 April 2004.

Wazir, Ansnullah. Associated Press. "Fight Wanes between Troops, Suspected al-Qaida." *Jacksonville (NC) Daily News,* 22 March 2004.

Wazir, Ansnullah. Associated Press. "Pakistani Troops Kill 11 on Border." *Jacksonville (NC) Daily News,* 29 February 2004.

Wazir, Ansnullah. Associated Press. "Terror Suspects May Have Escaped through Tunnel." *Jacksonville (NC) Daily News,* 23 March 2004.

Weir, Fred. "Chechnya's Troubled Election." *Christian Science Monitor,* 17 September 2003.

Weir, Fred. "Russia Loses Key Chechen Ally." *Christian Science Monitor,* 10 May 2004.

Wiktorowicz, Quintan. *Global Jihad: Understanding September 11.* Unabridged Audio Books (Falls Church, VA), compact disk, isbn #158472269x.

"Will We Get Him in '04'." Periscope. *Newsweek,* 9 February 2004.

Wilson, G.I. "Iraq: Fourth Generation Warfare (4GW) Swamp." From www.military.com, 18 June 2004.

Witter, Willis. "Iraqi Snipers Work in Teams to Hit Marines." *Washington Times,* 12 April 2004. At its website, www.washingtontimes.com.

World Religions: From Ancient History to the Present. Edited by Geoffrey Parrinder. New York: Facts on File Publications, 1971.

Wright, Robin. "A Reporter at Large—Tehran Summer." *The New Yorker,* 5 September 1988. In *Warriors of Islam,* by Kenneth Katzman. Boulder, CO: Westview Press, 1993.

Wright, Robin. *Sacred Rage: The Wrath of Militant Islam.* New York: Simon & Schuster, 1985. In *Warriors of Islam: Iran's Revolutionary Guard,* by Kenneth Katzman. Boulder, CO: Westview Press, 1993.

Yacoub, Sameer. Reuters. "Five U.S. Soldiers Killed in Iraq Attack." AOL News, 31 March 2004. From its website, www.aol.com.

Yacoub, Sameer N. Associated Press. "Four Dead Americans
Dragged through Town." *Jacksonville (NC) Daily News,*
1 April 2004.

Yacoub, Sameer N. Associated Press. "9 Americans Die in a Crash of
Black Hawk." *Jacksonville (NC) Daily News,* 9 January 2004.

Yacoub, Sameer N. Associated Press. "Suicide Truck Bombing Kills
10 in Iraq." *Jacksonville (NC) Daily News,* 19 February 2004.

Yousaf, Brigadier Mohammad. *The Silent Soldier: The Man behind
the Afghan Jehad.* South Yorkshire, UK: Leo Cooper, n.d.
From www.afghanbooks.com.

Yousaf, Brigadier Mohammad and Maj. Mark Adkin. *Bear Trap:
Afghanistan's Untold Story.* South Yorkshire, UK: Leo
Cooper, n.d. From www.afghanbooks.com.

Yousafzai, Sami and Michael Hirsh. "The Harder Hunt for bin
Laden." *Newsweek,* 29 December 2003 - 5 January 2004.

Yousafzai, Sami and Ron Moreau. "Rumors of bin Laden's Lair."
Newsweek, 8 September 2003.

Yousafzai, Sami and Ron Moreau and Michael Hirsh. "Bin Laden's
Iraqi Plans." *Newsweek,* 15 December 2003.

Zabih, Sepehr. *The Iranian Military in Revolution and War.*
London: Routledge, 1988.

Zakaria, Fareed. "Suicide Bombers Can Be Stopped." *Newsweek,*
25 August 2003.

About the Author

After almost 28 years as a commissioned and noncommissioned infantry officer, John Poole retired from the United States Marine Corps in April 1993. While on active duty, he studied small-unit tactics for nine years: (1) six months at the Basic School in Quantico (1966), (2) seven months as a rifle platoon commander in Vietnam (1966-67), (3) three months as a rifle company commander at Camp Pendleton (1967), (4) five months as a regimental headquarters company (and camp) commander in Vietnam (1968), (5) eight months as a rifle company commander in Vietnam (1968-69), (6) five and a half years as an instructor with the Advanced Infantry Training Company (AITC) at Camp Lejeune (1986-92), and (7) one year as the SNCOIC of the 3rd Marine Division Combat Squad Leaders Course (CSLC) on Okinawa (1992-93).

While at AITC, he developed, taught, and refined courses on maneuver warfare, land navigation, fire support coordination, call for fire, adjust fire, close air support, M203 grenade launcher, movement to contact, daylight attack, night attack, infiltration, defense, offensive Military Operations in Urban Terrain (MOUT), defensive MOUT, Nuclear/Biological/Chemical (NBC) defense, and leadership. While at CSLC, he further refined the same periods of instruction and developed others on patrolling.

He has completed all of the correspondence school requirements for the Marine Corps Command and Staff College, Naval War College (1000-hour curriculum), and Marine Corps Warfighting Skills Program. He is a graduate of the Camp Lejeune Instructional Management Course, the 2nd Marine Division Skill Leaders in Advanced Marksmanship (SLAM) Course, and the East-Coast School of Infantry Platoon Sergeants' Course.

In the 12 years since retirement, John Poole has heavily researched the small-unit tactics of other nations and written four previous books: (1) *The Last Hundred Yards: The NCO's Contribution to Warfare,* a squad combat study based on the consensus opinions of 1200 NCOs and casualty statistics of AITC and CSLC field trials; (2) *One More Bridge to Cross: Lowering the Cost of War*, a treatise on enemy proficiency at short range and how to match it; (3) *Phantom Soldier: The Enemy's Answer to U.S. Firepower,* an in-depth look at the highly deceptive Asian style of war; and (4) *The Tiger's Way: A U.S. Private's Best Chance of Survival,* a study of how Eastern fire teams and individual soldiers fight.

As of January 2005, John Poole had conducted multiday training sessions for 36 Marine battalions, one Navy special warfare group, and eight Marine schools on how to acquire maneuver (common-sense) warfare capabilities at the small-unit level. He has been stationed twice each in South Vietnam and Okinawa. He has visited Japan, Taiwan, the Philippines, Indonesia, South Korea, Mainland China, Hong Kong, Macao, North Vietnam, Myanmar (Burma), Thailand, Cambodia, Malaysia, Singapore, Tibet, Nepal, Bangladesh, India, Pakistan, Russia, East Germany, West Germany, Morocco, Israel (including the West Bank), Turkey, Iran, and Lebanon.

Name Index